A SYSTEMS THEORY OF RELIGION

Cultural Memory
in
the
Present

Mieke Bal and Hent de Vries, Editors

A SYSTEMS THEORY OF RELIGION ·

Niklas Luhmann

Edited by André Kieserling

*Translated by David A. Brenner
with Adrian Hermann*

STANFORD UNIVERSITY PRESS

STANFORD, CALIFORNIA

Stanford University Press

Stanford, California

English translation ©2013 by the Board of Trustees of the Leland Stanford Junior University. All rights reserved.

A Systems Theory of Religion was originally published in German under the title *Die Religion der Gesellschaft*. © Suhrkamp Verlag Frankfurt am Main 2000.

The translation of this work was funded by Geisteswissenschaften International-Translation Funding for Humanities and Social Sciences from Germany, a joint initiative of the Fritz Thyssen Foundation, the German Federal Foreign Office, the collecting society VG WORT and the German Publishers & Booksellers Association.

Printed in the United States of America on acid-free, archival-quality paper

Library of Congress Cataloging-in-Publication Data

Luhmann, Niklas, 1927-1998, author.
 [Religion der Gesellschaft. English]
 A systems theory of religion / Niklas Luhmann ; Edited by André Kieserling ; Translated by David A. Brenner with Adrian Hermann.
     pages cm.--(Cultural memory in the present)
 "Originally published in German under the title Die Religion der Gesellschaft."
 Includes bibliographical references and index.
 ISBN 978-0-8047-4328-0 (cloth : alk. paper)--ISBN 978-0-8047-4329-7 (pbk. : alk. paper)
  1. Religion and sociology. 2. Social systems. 3. System theory. I. Kieserling, André, editor. II. Title. III. Series: Cultural memory in the present.
 BL60.L83513 2013
 306.6--dc23   2012031152

Typeset by Bruce Lundquist in 11/13.5 Adobe Garamond

Contents

Editor's Note

Niklas Luhmann's work on this book, which he began in the early 1990s, was interrupted by illness and finally by his death. By that point, the forthcoming publication of his social theory already overshadowed all other projects to be published.[1] The time remaining to him did not suffice to put the text presented here into a form that would he would have found compelling. Attached to the manuscript were references to more recent literature he wanted to follow up on, as well as brief notes on additional aspects of the topic, letting us know that the text was supposed to be longer. There is no indication that Luhmann thought the book was in a publishable form as it stood, but what we have here doubtless comes close. The text is much more than a mere fragment, and a bit more time would presumably have sufficed for Luhmann to complete work on it.

The book presented here is based on a computer printout made in February 1997.[2] Luhmann had apparently looked over this copy, and he attached typed additions to it at different points. In editing the text, I have limited myself to integrating these additions into the main manuscript, correcting typographical errors and filling in gaps in the reference material. In addition, I have updated notes in which the author cites himself to make it easier for the reader to find the most current version of his theory. In accordance with Luhmann's usual practice, an index has been supplied.

· · ·

Bernd Stiegler at Suhrkamp Verlag and Veronika Luhmann-Schröder, who owned the rights, cooperated with each other and with the editor in the most productive way imaginable in preparing the manuscript for publication. I hereby express my gratitude to them both.

André Kieserling
Munich, May 2000

1

Religion as a Form of Meaning

I

How does one identify certain social appearances as religion? That is the question one has to start with.

For a person of faith, this question may be meaningless. Such a person can say what he believes and abide by that. He may dispute whether calling it "religion" benefits him at all. He may even reject the designation, seeing it as classifying phenomena in a way that places him in a category with things he would reject as not worth believing. The idea of religion thus seems to be a cultural one, an idea that calls for a certain tolerance.

However, for those who do not believe what they might like to signify with the term "religion," the notion has its problems and limitations. And then there are those who might wish to communicate about religion without having to commit to a faith of their own. And those who wish to problematize the notion, or at least distinguish it from other ideas. Neither "ontological" nor "analytical" solutions are of any help these days. In the ontological tradition, no one should have a problem with this, for what that tradition holds to be religion emerges out of the essence of religion. If any mistakes were made, one would merely have to recognize them and clean them up—an attitude that itself approximates faith. By contrast, the analytical thinker claims he is free to determine the scope of his own thought. For him, only propositions can be true, not ideas. However, he is confronted with having to limit arbitrariness (a methodological concession), a problem that cannot be resolved (least of all "empirically"). If the ontologist is too close to religion, the analytic thinker is too far away from it. The worst thing to do would be to look for a (practical) solution somewhere in "the middle." These two solutions are unusable by us, leaving us without a principle to convey.

If looking for more concrete answers, one can differentiate between sociological (Emile Durkheim) and phenomenological ones (Rudolf Otto).[1] At present, however, we are not interested in their content but in how they are derived.

Durkheim views religion as a moral—and thus a social—fact.[2] Through morality and religion, society makes itself the transcendence that God, whose facticity is now disputed, can no longer offer.

As a moral fact, religion is defined in two ways: by a moment of desire (*désir*), which appraises values, and by a moment of sanction that limits what is permitted (*sacré*). We can see that morality—and along with it, religion—emerges in a twofold process of expansion and contraction. It is based on a type of self-dissolution also linked to forms that operate as a unit, as a stabilized tension. These forms command our attention in the face of the unbearable possibility that their unity might again be dissolved into distinction.* On this basis as well, religious forms are developed by further distinguishing between sacred and profane. While morality is defined by a distinction in which both sides claim one another, religion is characterized by a relationship of exclusion. In each of these cases, the aim is to understand society as a comprehensive system. This is also true of religion if one does not stop at the sacred as such but instead proceeds with the distinction between sacred and profane. Society thus distinguishes religion by marking off its domain as sacred against everything that cannot be signified the same way. Yet Durkheim does not see the form of religion in this distinction itself. Instead, he interrogates the domain of the sacred for specific religious forms (keep this in mind, because this is the point where we part ways with Durkheim).

---

* *Differenz* in Luhmann's work is in many respects equivalent to *Unterscheidung* (usually rendered as *distinction*), but *Unterscheidung* tends to highlight the operation, while *Differenz* signifies the separation (i.e., "difference") the operation establishes. Whereas *Differenz* connotes a dividing line (closely following George Spencer-Brown's usage), with overtones of Derrida's *différance*, *Unterscheidung* is closer to the sense of *form* in the distinction between *form* and *medium*.—Trans.

Something similar is at work in Max Weber's sociology of religion. Weber avoids defining the essence of religion, saying he is merely interested in "the conditions and effects of a certain type of communal action."[3] (Here he is only saying that one has to observe what people think religion is, rather than committing ourselves to an answer.) The problem for Weber was how human action could be given a cultural meaning. A related problem for him was how other orders of life, such as the economy or eroticism, might construct meaning in each of their respective domains. Religion itself assumes a distinction between everyday and extraordinary occurrences. It finds that the extraordinary ones need forms that give the world additional religious meanings, producing a need to rationalize these excesses.[4] Georg Simmel, too, starts with a distinction between *religious* and *religioid*—a distinction that makes it possible for religion to develop enhanced forms.[5] René Girard's theory of religion is also structured around expansion and contraction. It assumes desire itself is implicated in a conflict of imitation, hence activating religious prohibitions that appear to be religion because they are restrictive.[6] The conflict of imitation itself, the dangerous paradox that people fight over the same desires, has to be represented symbolically. The imitation takes place in the form of a sacrifice intended to redeem something else.

In formulating this list (which is certainly not comprehensive), I am not merely surveying a few well-known ideas in the sociology of religion. Rather, I am still trying to make progress in answering the question of what lets us recognize religion. And in the cases examined there appears to be a specific dynamic at work: there are expansions that call for limitation and limits that make possible expansion. Hence, it would not be absurd when looking at religion to think about money as well. And that mysterious symbolic identity setting culture off against the spread of "materialism" would be termed "society."

Both Durkheim and Simmel use a more circumscribed idea of religion in which not everything sacred and every "religioid" relation to social life can be viewed as religion. For Durkheim, religion only emerges when faith becomes systematized. For Simmel, it only emerges in a clear, objectified consciousness of form, capable of critical judgment (but also subject to possible doubts). This distinction is significant and remains so, particularly in research on the evolution of religion, on how more demanding forms arise that (at first) seem improbable. The distinction, however, has been rejected or even forgotten in the more recent sociological research on the idea of religion.[7] And more recent religious developments in this century cannot clearly be distinguished as religions. Nor can they be seen as establishing new forms of the sacred that are somehow free of religion.

While sociological approaches try hard to stay impartial about religious belief—and Durkheim explains this by examining primitive religions with no concept of divinity or mysteries—the phenomenological search for ideas uses the exact opposite approach. Phenomenology attempts to define religion by describing how meaningful content appears religious, that is, "holy."[8] It assumes it is possible to have direct access to the "thing itself," a type of access that cannot be relativized by social conditions.[9] The difficulty is how to get from there to the temporality and historicity of religion. (The way that Husserl analyzed the relationship of temporality to consciousness is simply not adequate in this case.)

Determining what is holy (or numinous) leads to a paradox if it becomes something binding for the observer. What is holy attracts us, leaving us awestruck. It exercises a horrifying fascination on us. At the same time, there are subtle differences one has to respect. Even if we are presupposing a god-oriented religion, the *intention* of the god is not to spread fear and terror but rather his holy essence. What is more, the deity is not the fear-arousing event itself; he is merely *within it*.[10] In each case, it has to be accepted that a unity is at work (even if it is a paradoxical one). Salvation lies in danger, redemption in sin. Since the eighteenth century, the term "sublime" has been used to avoid conflict with a religion domesticated by theologians and their "good god." Whatever the case, paradox appears in the form of the holy.

It is striking that the transcendental theory underlying Husserl's phenomenology is simply overlooked in Schütz's social phenomenology, which does not even ask what the costs of doing without it would be. What Schütz is giving up is the super-distinction of empirical versus transcendental, as well as the analysis of consciousness (declared transcendental), that intentional processing of consciousness by which Husserl pointed out the unity of self-reference (*noēsis*) and other-reference (*noēma*). It no longer lets us hear Heidegger's warnings about reductive analyses that are anthropological, psychological, or even biological.[11] Instead, the observer is merely being asked to stay "attuned."[12] But what it misses out on is the justification for universality found in the transcendentality of consciousness, that possibility of making statements that are valid for *every* empirical consciousness. Now there may be good reasons to do without such universality, (precisely) from the viewpoint of sociologists but also from that of a language-oriented philosopher such as Jürgen Habermas. But it should not by any means lead people to repress the theory problem in favor of scrutinizing phenomena. The paradox of the holy is both the beginning and end of analysis, leaving us with the same problem, of how an observer can distinguish religion in a way that is valid for other observers and that could be distinguished—which is our main aim here (!)—from simple attitudes of faith.

In every respect, the traditional idea of religion, an idea sociology also uses, maintains a reference to one's personal existence.[13] But if the scientific tradition does not wish be implausible or incomprehensible, it has to be linked to what otherwise (and elsewhere) is said about humanity. Or at least it has to retain some contact with it. This "humanistic" tradition is nonetheless endangered when it changes what it wishes to understand as "humanity," as well as when it has to deal with a number of very different exemplars of the category. And when forming such ideas, it is difficult to do justice to every single human being.

If, however, one questions this humanistic definition of *religion*, then one has to question the reduction of religion to a phenomenon of consciousness even more. Consciousness serves to externalize (hence the term "phenomenon") the results of neurobiological operations, thus introducing the distinction between other- and auto-reference to our understanding of human experience and activity. Yet even religion needs to ask about the meaning of this basic distinction or be able to grasp its unity as a source of its own production of meaning. Religion is not simply reflection performed by consciousness, because that would mean turning the "self" of consciousness into an "object" and treating it as a thing, with terms such as *soul*, *spirit*, and *person*. Religion cannot be adequately understood according to the schemas of consciousness (subject/object, observer/object) because it is located on both sides of the distinction between self- and other-reference.

The strong focus on humanity is likely why the classical sociology of religion does not deal with communication (or only in a very external sense). This deficit (assuming it is one) can provide a starting place for a new description of what newer sociological theories of religion should do.

Put differently, the goal is to replace the idea of humanity with that of communication, thus replacing the traditional theory of religion centered on anthropology with a theory of religion centered on society. Just how productive this approach is will be the subject of detailed discussion in the chapters that follow. For now, it suffices to indicate how radical this shift in metaphors, this new description, is.

In previous attempts to answer what the essence of religion is, there is a tendency for fissures or aporias to become apparent, making those attempts "deconstructable," one might say (taking a cue from Jacques Derrida or Paul de Man). These are texts that undermine their own declared objectives, especially when one considers the classical instruments of logic and epistemology. The sociology of religion treats religions as social facts or forms, claiming that it is able to provide a "non-religious" description of them. Yet what are the status and truth of such a description in a society that frees religion from the frameworks of logic and epistemology, enabling religion to get a look at the generation of forms per se? The phenomenology of religion has to accept premises of transcendental theory, so it does not simply confuse "phenomena" with "facts" or misunderstand the paradox of "intersubjectivity" as "inter*objectivity*." In the same society, however, there are also religions that speak of the "subject" and question its transcendental self-certainty, attempting to respond to the self-*un*certainty by offering something meaningful.

If religion in turn constitutes forms by means of limitation and exclusion, is not every explanation of religion religious, since it is falling back on a method of limitation and exclusion? Or, asking the question differently: can there be a scientific description of religion if religion claims that it can justify the exclusionary power of forms (as "this and not that")? Can we then still proceed according to the science of causation, or do we have to fall back on cybernetic theories, which have a preference for circular explanations (based on an operative self-limitation of the circle)? And if religion is a paradoxical mode of observation, how does one explain the generating of forms (= distinctions) to which further observations are connected? And aren't both these questions asking the same thing, how one might deal with circular, self-referential relationships?

As soon as someone thinks they can say what religion is and how the religious can be distinguished from the non-religious, another can come and negate this criterion by making reference (for example) to an existing

God, *precisely in that way making use of a religious quality.* For what else can it be (besides religious) whenever someone negates what someone else thinks is religion? The problem does not lie (as Wittgensteinians might think) in a gradual expansion of "family resemblances." Nor is the problem (as was Wittgenstein's point of departure) the impossibility of defining something adequately. Rather, even though we can only present it as an assumption at this point, it appears that religion is one of many things that signifies itself and is capable of giving itself a form. But that also means that religion determines itself and excludes everything that is incompatible. Yet how does it do so if there are (for instance) other religions, heathens, the *civitas terrena* [secular society, viz., Augustine's City of Man, as opposed to the City of God (*Civitas Dei*)], or evil? Religion can only be the subject of itself if it includes what is being excluded, if it is assisted by a negative correlate. The system is only autonomous if it is able to monitor what it is not. In this light, religion can only (externally) be defined in the mode of a second-order observation, as an observation of its own self-observation—and not by the dictates of some external essence.

II

The most general untranscendable medium for constructing every form that can be used by psychic and social systems we call "meaning." For more than a century, the term "meaning" has been used vaguely and for many things—*pollachōs legomenon,** we might say with Aristotle.[14] It seems clear that the idea of meaning cannot be applied to things. (It makes no sense to ask about the meaning of a frog.) Seen in historical perspective, the semantics of meaning suggest that the ontological description of the world has been subjected to a new description. But this still does not explain what might be meant by "meaning." We want to try to remedy this multivalence by resorting to a distinction, specifically the distinction between medium and form. Such a distinction might let us disregard the inadequately formulated question of "what meaning means."[15]

The notion of medium makes "meaning" something that cannot be observed—just as little as light can be.[16] In fact, observations assume distinguishable forms, forms that can only be formed in a medium and only

---

* "Things said in many senses."—Trans.

so that other possibilities of forming forms are excluded from consideration in that moment. Hence, the unobservability of meaning also gives us a first indication that this all might have something to do with religion.

All psychic and social systems determine and reproduce their operations exclusively in this medium of meaning. There may well be some "meaningless" disruptions, but even for them semantic forms can be sought and immediately found. Otherwise, such forms might be forgotten or used to link up with other operations. The universality of a medium that constitutes its own system is the other dimension of systems theory's insight that systems can only operate with their own operations (and not somehow in their environment). Or put another way, that the system is an operatively closed system. One can encounter the limits of the medium from within, but these limits do not take the form of a line that can be crossed; rather, they take the form of a *horizon* (to use Husserl's excellent metaphor).[17] And thus the world is accessible to systems that process meaning only as a horizon—clearly not as a distinct line somehow drawn but instead as the implication of every single operation's recursivity, of the operation's ability to be identified.

Meaning as a medium cannot, then, be negated. Indeed, if it is to be possible as an operation, every negation assumes that the negated is determined or assigned a meaning. The unity of meaning and non-meaning is in turn meaningful. And one need not have a "meaning criterion" for it, which would only lead to the question of whether the criterion itself is meaningful or not. In the medium of meaning, of course, one is able to think that there are entities such as stones (for instance), entities for which the world has no meaning. That may, incidentally, also be the case for brains. The medium of meaning thus contains evidence of its own boundaries. But in that case, one is are also saying that these boundaries cannot be exceeded by meaningful operations. One can only touch the boundary on its internal side, allowing the meaning of its form to show us that there has to be something outside it.[18]

In psychic experience and in communication, we can therefore deal with what is meaningless by giving it a form.[19] This form suggests that further operations are not applicable, or that it is necessary to look for other possible connections. It is traditionally referred to as "paradox." If our starting idea is right, that every determined meaning includes its own ability to be negated, then there cannot be any meaning of the world whose negation could not be conceivable. Or, if one formulates it according to the doctrine governing proofs for God's existence, there is no meaning for which existence is a necessary predicate. Meaning is only given when something can be formulated both positively and negatively. If one side of this distinction is eliminated, the other side would also lose its meaning. One has to conclude that every meaning (and thus every ultimate meaning too) can only maintain its own unity as a paradox, as a sameness of affirmation and negation, of true and untrue, of good and bad (or whatever positive or negative fixations one might choose). Consequently, there is no unity on which everything else can be grounded. Whatever is determined has to accept the form of unfolding a paradox—that is, replacing the unity of paradox by distinguishing among definable identities (in a way that is somehow plausible but also historically relative). This experience repeats itself for Hölderlin, for whom no more answers can be provided by a mandatory God. If, in moving toward a final unity, we wish to overcome the "divisions in which we think and exist" [Hölderlin, February 24, 1796, to Friedrich Niethammer][20] and to communicate this as poetry, only paradoxical formulations are available.

In the form of paradoxes, which are unsustainable and need to be resolved or supplemented, what we already know about meaning is demonstrated: that even the negative self-references solidify into a form that says something, symbolizes something, and that clarifies something to be an impossibility. In what follows, we shall return to this topic at length. For the time being, it suffices to note that even paradoxes achieve reality in the network of meaningful operations—albeit only there.

In a very formal way, then, meaning can be characterized if one excludes one thing: that one can exclude anything from it. In elaborating on this proposition, the existing literature goes in two directions, corresponding precisely to the two approaches, outlined in the previous section, to defining the idea of religion. In each case, one has to assume that meaningful operations appear as selections. Hence, one might say the world is complex (for an observer) and, therefore, that every combination of elements (= operations) can only be selectively carried out by neglecting or rejecting other possibilities. Those possibilities, however, can still be seen as performing the operation and thus reveal the contingency of its selection. The world can only be realized by setting limits and by making use of time.[21] Or, in keeping with phenomenological tradition, one can analyze the appearance of semantic forms and thus see how every actual intention is given in the form of a core of meaning. This core makes reference to countless other possibilities of actualizing meaning, and thus in part to what exists prior to it, in part to what it can be linked. The distinction between these two possibilities of representation is based on the distinction between subject and object. The complexity thesis represents an objective notion of the world (the opposing side saying it is objectivistic). Phenomenology understands itself as a subjective (thus, as a subjectivistic) way to analyze performances of consciousness that create meaning. If, however, both points of departure lead to the same result, the distinction between object and subject will fall apart without being sublated into spirit [*Geist*]. Or it will appear in the foreground, as a distinction that can be made depending on what one intends as an observer.

If we proceed using systems theory, applying the distinction between system and environment, then we have to derive the classical subject-object distinction from a distinction between systems. What is objective is what demonstrates itself in communication. What is subjective is what demonstrates itself in processes of consciousness. These processes in turn subjectively treat as objective what demonstrates itself in communication, while communication marginalizes as subjective what it cannot agree to. Such an argument does not make any claims that systems theory is superior. The point is that one has to observe observers with the help of the question (or distinction) of which distinctions they are using.

Let us now look at the notion of meaning. Leaving aside subjects, objects and references to systems, one might define this notion by a purely modal-theoretical distinction between reality (actuality) and possibility (potentiality), as the specific notion that represents the unity of this difference. For something (whatever it may be) has meaning whenever it makes reference to other possibilities in actual experience or communication (in what then emerges). In particular, without this reference actuality would not at all be possible as meaningful actuality. By that account, and for an observer who makes such distinctions, meaning is the unity of the difference between reality and possibility.

The modal-logical form of possibility is appropriate for defining more precisely what could be meant by "medium." Possibilities are only loosely associated with one another. If one of them is actualized, it does not simply follow that certain others will also be realized.[22] There may be conditions involved that make such connections more or less likely, all the way to excluding every other possibility—something that an observer might observe as a necessity. Without losing ourselves in the modal-logical problems this creates, let us simply confirm that we can proceed on this basis by distinguishing loose and fixed coupling. Taking up a suggestion by Fritz Heider (originally elaborated for perceptual media), one can describe a medium as the unity of the difference between loose and fixed coupling.[23] This requires further explanation.

Loosely coupled splinters of meaning (words, for example) are available en masse and serve as a medial substrate. In the process of semantic selection that assumes these splinters, they are coupled into fixed forms (perceivable things and comprehensible statements). The distinction can only be linked to on that side of the distinction between loose and fixed coupling. (In our examples, only things can be seen, and only comprehensible communications can be followed or responded to.) But since *every* connection has to choose a form or make a distinction, what is regenerated in all meaningful operations is the medium of other possibilities. And what is finally regenerated is the unmarkable condition of the world, which no longer excludes anything. There is always something held back so that everything defined also remains deconstructable.[24] Each distinction creates surroundings for itself where further distinctions can be introduced.[25] The term "intertextuality" articulates a similar thought in literary studies. It expresses the idea that, for all their insularity (such as their aesthetic closure), texts always make reference to other texts. As a result, every text can be conveyed by inconclusive references—something that would also be true when making a literary-critical analysis of holy texts (and which such texts in turn would have to disavow). Meaning is deferral, *différance* (Derrida), "unlimited semiosis" (Pierce). Yet we have to be able to believe that every actualization has a secure foothold somewhere, since we are certain that it will ultimately continue.

A parallel moment is when all ontic certainties dissolve into relationships of time. The connective capacity [*Anschlußfähigkeit*] also implies that every actualization has to accept the form of an event that, in being actualized, has already been extinguished again. Forms need to accept the form of a structure, which can be recognized again, even though that does not save them forever. The resulting iron law is then valid for the medium of meaning and all media (such as language) that derive from it: what is not utilized is stable and, by contrast, what is utilized is not stable. The great advantage of this solution is that it enables the systems (to which it is available) to adapt temporarily to temporary situations. Those systems are then able to be drawn into more complex, temporally unstable environments. Once directed toward environments, they do not stay attached to them—which is only a different way of formulating their differentiation and operative autonomy.

The unity of the medium (as a unity of loose and fixed coupling) therefore displays itself temporally. In addition, the actualization (including reactualization) of forms serves to reproduce a medial substrate. Words are always remembered when used often enough, thus signifying with sentences the same (and different) things time after time. The medium can only be reproduced as the unity of its difference. But equally clear is that it can only happen on one side, on the operatively functional side of the distinction.

Even if meaning can be actualized at the point where an operation is using meaning, the medium as such remains invisible. What is meant by the medium as such is the unity of the distinction between loose and fixed coupling and the unity of the distinction between reality and possibility. In its actual form-defining operation, the medium is reproduced, but its reproduction only takes place in the form of potentializing what has just been excluded, of remembering other possibilities of combining forms. Every determination, including the determinations of "only possible," "unlikely," or "impossible," emerges out of an "unmarked space" that is also reproduced in the process. Even if the medium is signified as "meaning" or the unmarked space is signified as "world," this semantic granting of form occurs in a domain (specifically) identified for such operations. A word, or even an idea, is being applied in distinction to multiple others. And this granting of form gets involved in this distinction, which it cannot signify in the same moment.

If meaning is signified as a medium, it is being signified as a category that cannot be negated. For a negation would be a signification that in turn would assume a medium—and assume meaning as the most general medium. To deny meaning would move in the direction of "performative self-contradiction." If one signifies something as "meaningless," one has to assume a different, opposing idea as "meaning." Yet language can assist us in addressing this problem. It makes it possible for us to distinguish between "meaningful" and "meaningless" by using the medium of meaning.

Yet that leaves us with the problem of what might possibly be meant by the term "meaningful."

Following up on a suggestion by Alois Hahn, the feeling of meaninglessness and the search for meaningful meaning can apply to the self-description of psychic and social systems.[26] Self-descriptions here are assumed to be referring to the identity of systems, to something inside the system that cannot be deemed interchangeable. In the structures brought into play, meaning and meaninglessness diverge. In the case of the religious system, then, one has to pay attention to the elements of faith being proposed if one wants to know what is meaningless in that system. That clearly does not keep this statement from actualizing meaning itself, or from being possible in another way. And perhaps we are now on the trail of a problem that gets at the roots of religious communication.

The transition from denotative to meaningful speech clearly has costs and risks, which have been bitterly experienced by religion. This transition exposes what is deemed meaningful to interpretation, re-description [*Wiederbeschreibung*], and new descriptions. In this way, topics that religion finds meaningful are exposed to trends of the time. On the one hand, interpretations and new descriptions are always producing both continuity and discontinuity—or, to be precise, continuity *through* discontinuity. On the other, the forms of faith still possible are changing, for example, becoming "texts" that can be interpreted or filled with new, timely meanings. A written version of this text can help us, but the distinction between written and oral is not particularly insightful. Instead, the text's value for those who are faithful depends on its ongoing "redescription."[27] Only in this sense can a text continue to be a living text—to put it metaphorically. But "redescriptions" are communications only possible in retrospect. They make the faithful uncertain, since they do not know what might be redescribed next. Attempts are made to help them out by distinguishing between essential and inessential [*nebensächlichen*] sections of the text. The thesis that the text only has symbolic meaning works in similar way. But the risk of a religious communication claiming it is meaningful cannot be effectively eliminated, because that risk lies in the temporal dimension, not the factual one. The stabilizing of religion in textual form opens up a domain of sensitivity that can also be used against religion.

After these initial considerations, it should no longer need to be explained that religion has to be sought in the forms of the medium of meaning. But this still does not explain which distinctions specify religion (compared to the rest of the world), and what will enable religion to reject what is "meaningless" and build bridges to a meaningful life. And when asking about distinctions, one is also asking about the person who makes them: the observer. The question then becomes: who is the observer of religion? Theologians might surprise us by answering: God. So as not have to be the observer themselves? (And is one supposed to believe that?)

III

In this next phase, we are going to have to pose the question of how the world generates distinctions. How and why does it produce such a strange, asymmetrical form, one side of which is available for operations that can be linked to other operations—while the other side makes itself necessary precisely in staying unmarked? And, moreover, what becomes of the world itself if, in the act of creation, it allows distinctions to be made? And why does it begin with "heaven and earth" and not another way? Why does it begin with a division, a distinction in this unreflective being? Is it only so that the one making the distinction can himself avoid entering the distinction?

At the start, we tried out the idea that an observer makes the distinction. And that we thus have to observe the observer if we want to know which distinctions he is making and how he decides how to construct meaning. We want to stick with this terminology, but we shall have to clarify it as it applies itself, since it is an autological concept. The distinction between observer and distinction is itself a distinction, causing us to ask: who is the observer here? Or more precisely: how must an observer be constituted so that he is in a position to distinguish between his distinctions and himself? Starting with the stipulation "draw a distinction," [the British mathematician] George Spencer-Brown attempts to develop a calculus that is able to handle problems in arithmetic and algebra with only one operator. In doing so, he is confronted with the same problem—resolving it with the notion of identity.[28] However, that result does not mean one has to stop asking questions since, in the framework of distinction theory, identity is a rather unsettling concept.

Let us continue with this approach by considering that operations in general and observations in particular are not possible as distinct events but instead presuppose recursive networks by which such events reproduce themselves and by which this reproductive context is marked off from an environment that contributes only resources and interruptions. These networks point to the formation of a system and, more precisely, the formation of operatively closed autopoietic systems. Under additional conditions, they are capable not only of differentiating themselves but also of distinguishing between themselves and their environment. The distinction between system and environment is thus doubled onto itself and, according to our premises, does so on the side of connective capacity—on the side of a system. In Spencer-Brown's terminology, there is a "re-entry" of form into the form, a puzzling process (which the end of the calculation shows was assumed from the outset).[29]

And in order to clarify what has been happening, I have inserted an additional distinction into the tautology of a distinction (that is distinguishing itself): the distinction between system and environment. In the process, the world remains the "wherein" of this event, the condition not marked by this or another distinction, the condition that forms the other side for every marking. Substituting a different distinction cannot be justified logically in this case. Yet whoever does not wish to proceed as proposed has to make a distinction in another way, if he does not want to get stuck in a paradox of tautology ("what is different is the same"). While the operation of substitution is not logical, it is compatible with the world. And it can be recognized by the fruit it bears.

The identity of the "marked" observer is thus the identity of a system. That should not, however, lead us to conclude prematurely that the system is only observing its environment. One would have to consider to what extent this is true for animals or for human perceptions. Yet the complex theoretical architecture we have become involved in also protects us from wrong conclusions. As a consciousness or as a social system, the observer can find orientation in a distinction between system and environment, of self- and other-reference, that has been copied into himself. And he has to proceed this way (even though he produces all references internally), since otherwise he would constantly be confusing his own conditions with those of the environment, and then be unable to learn from—or even be irritated by—the environment. Precisely if one is dealing with an operatively closed system that with its own operations cannot reach further into the environment (or even contact it), then survival (= a continuation of autopoiesis) in that instance will depend completely on the internally available distinction between self- and other-reference that guides learning. Whatever has been built up structurally remains an internal condensate, a construction.[30] And there are enough examples of constructions that cannot be sustained and of systems that are ruined by their construction of themselves. One timely example is how state and the economy are constructed in communist socialism. However, self-determination (or self-organization) using the distinction between self- and other-reference is an indispensable presupposition of evolutionary selection. All higher forms of consciousness and all social communication depend on it. Societies would never have gotten under way if people had not learned to distinguish between words (self-reference) and things (other-reference).

In contrast to distinction itself, which operates by taking hold of something signified coming out of the unmarked space of the world (and thus distinguishes it from the unmarked domain of the world), the distinction between self- and other-reference has the significant advantage of *being capable of connection on both sides.* The system can observe itself as observing.[31] It can relate observational sequences both to the environment and to itself. It can also constantly cross back and forth, traversing the boundary of self and other *without losing orientation.* Under this special condition, then, Spencer-Brown's "law of crossing" is *not* valid.[32] Instead, we can use externally calculated specifications to understand better our own conditions (and possibilities of movement, for instance). Seen conversely, we can consider modifying our own circumstances when we find that the environment is showing us different sides in response to such modifications. We should speak of information and information-processing only under this strongly limiting condition—understanding "information" in Gregory Bateson's sense as a difference that makes a difference.

We replaced the classical notion of the subject with that of the observer in order to make it clear that the operations producing (and reproducing) the medium of meaning take place in the real world and not in a transcendental sphere beyond reality. This substitution clearly influences how one conceives of reality, making reality a rhetorical construct in "conformity to orthodox practices of writing and reading."[33] This way, one can see communication as having the possibility of forming a counternotion to reality, whether it is an ideality or subjectivity.

Nonetheless, where does that leave the observer who uses this distinction between self- and other-reference to offset the "loss of reality" produced by operative closing? Having said all that, it would be a logical error to think that the "self" of self-reference is identical with the observer. Philosophy of the subject has had its disappointments with this assumption, and we do not need to repeat them.[34] The observer is the unity of the difference between self- and other-reference. Therefore, he cannot signify himself, remaining invisible to himself.

And the same goes for the world that, to the observer, would have to function for him as the unity of the difference between system and environment. The entire observational apparatus of a distinction that can be signified on both sides now finds itself built into the unmarked space of the world out of which an observer makes observations. Nothing then is changed by the evolutionary achievement of "meaning"—which in the first place makes possible consciousness, society, language, culture (and might one even say religion?). One may concede that it is still possible, and that it makes sense in the world of meaning, to retain the intention to observe the unity of the difference. But this sense takes on the form of a paradox, that fundamental paradox of the sameness of what is different.

IV

In observing how the world and the observer are unobservable, one has begun to observe religion. A few matters still have to be clarified, however. And some additional distinctions distinguished.

The distinction between observer and world is different from the distinction between observer and observed, for it moves in the direction of the distinction between the observable and unobservable with which the world observes itself (though we do not know how). An observer can observe that—and how—an observer is observing. There are thoroughly observable second-order observations. Yet no matter which order is involved, the operation of observing moves from the unobservable to the observable. Spencer-Brown's directive "Draw a distinction!" is telling us to cross *this* boundary.[35] There is no level of observing where we can get around making an initial distinction—not even if we are observing observers, and not if we are observing ourselves as observers. Put more simply: the operation of observing remains unobservable to itself. It makes use of a distinction, and the asymmetry of this distinction replaces and conceals the asymmetry of observing. Observing moves inside, not outside, of its distinction. In all observation, it is true that "[d]istinction is perfect continence."[36] Observation itself, however, is the excluded third figure, the unity of a distinction not distinguishable in the distinction itself. A "blind spot," one might say, is required. Or, to speak transcendentally, the unobservability of observation is the condition of making observation possible, the condition making it possible to access objects.

If we observe observers as observers (and not as things or "objects" but as "subjects"), then this has to be accounted for on both levels. The second-order observer can observe an observer of the first order as an *observer* (and not as a thing) only if he sees that the (first-order) observer does *not* see that he is not seeing what is not seeing. Here *formulating* (or observing) can only take place with the help of negations. But this description of what happens may not do justice to the facts. For the operation of observing *operates* free of negation (even when it is negating). It does what it does, and that is its reality.

We can formulate such conclusions traditionally, referring to them as the liberty of the other observer, or as a norm of respecting the way he makes decisions, or as an "internal infinity" of the subject. That puts us near the domain of morality. And near the necessity of setting some limits. But these formulations already make use of conventions of social attribution, appropriate only for psychic systems, not social ones (always included when one is talking about observers). If we start there, we might only obtain notions of religion that are culturally or historically specific. Whether they are correct is not the issue, but we should still keep our options open here.

It seems we have located the source of the problems treated as forms of religious meaning and exposed to evolution in this domain of unobservability where observation and the world (as a precondition of observation) cannot be distinguished (in the "unmarked state"). While this assumption cannot be made more specific, it is covered by our analysis of the medium of meaning. For this medium offers precisely the surplus capacity needed. Even what is unobservable can be built into operations as meaning because meaning is something that cannot possibly be excluded. We might give what stays inaccessible the form of negation or (in the case of logically higher claims) that of paradox. We might also signify what is unobservable, knowing full well that our description does not suit its intention. At that point, we can develop an understanding of symbols that specifically reflects this unsuitability. Formulated according to the old cybernetics, it is a problem of the "requisite variety,"[37] and the attempt to find a solution appears to consist in monitoring one mystery by means of another.

In such cases, there is no one certain or correct answer. Most of the options give us a rough notion of how to analyze the evolution of religion. Yet at present we can only say that the structural barrier inherent in observation itself can become an irritating factor in the cosmos of meaning, a demand for the production of meaning par excellence. Religion has to do this with the inclusion of the excluded, the presence of an absence that is first objectified then localized and universalized. But everything thought and said about these issues here and elsewhere, in religion and in its sociological analysis, can only be a *cipher* [Chiffre]* for what is intended.

V

Again, one of Spencer-Brown's terms can help at this point, and it is the limit term of his calculus: the term "re-entry." Reentry can be said to refer to some very different distinctions. We had mentioned above how it was possible for the distinction between system and environment to reenter the system.[38] In the case of religion, though, the distinction between observable and unobservable reenters the observable realm.

Simple observation only requires crossing a boundary that distinguishes what is to be signified from everything else. This boundary did not previously exist, but only emerges in being crossed. The distinction has to be a moment of operation (otherwise, nothing could be signified in distinction to something else), yet it does not have to be marked as a form. In the event of a reentry, something different is at work, because that operation can only be realized if a distinction is signified that reenters its self-created realm. In Spencer-Brown's terms, the "cross" (a directive to cross) has to be utilized as a "marker" (a signification of form).[39] And such operations can be carried out without using the marker for crossing.

At this point, we do not have to ask which conditions make reentry possible. These conditions, after all, are laden with mathematical preconditions (the operative prehistory of the calculus). What is more important

* A cipher [*Chiffre*] for Luhmann is not simply a symbol, nor does it simply refer to something else. It is instead a linguistic device whose function is more indexical than indicative (or iconic).—Trans.

is the form of the operation that has been made possible. Since it utilizes both distinctions as one, reentry is a paradoxical operation, rendering the distinction between cross and marker an ambivalent one. Yet at the same time, reentry is an operation that distinguishes itself from the imaginary space that it presupposes. That space is divided up by the distinction—and it thus cannot be observed as a unity. The distinction is marked as a form—a form with two sides—and then it is copied into the one side of the form. We therefore have to assume there is an imaginary space that concedes self-mobility (or the capacity to signify itself) to the divided space. Perhaps we ought to say that this imaginary space does not emerge until the reentry is completed. Whatever the case, however, the specificity of the operation is guaranteed by the specificity of the distinction with which it is performed—by this distinction and no other.

The depiction of reentry (in line with its name) gives the impression that the initial distinction has to be made first, after which reentry can be performed within it. The stage must first be constructed on which the play is supposed to be performed, and then it has to be separated from the space of the audience, making it clear where reality and simulated reality are situated. But after that, all kinds of things—deception, error, and unobservability—can be performed on the stage. In addition, the spectator sees and understands the performed distinction between truth and deception as a reality, as long as he ignores that the distinction, in truth, is deceptive. The theater can only symbolize the world by means of a reentry that is prevented from abolishing itself.[40] But if that is the case: can one not just as well proceed in the opposite direction, giving priority to the form *in* the form? Instead, could one assume that the starting distinction is being invented as the frame of the frame, if one is unable to deal with the world as it represents itself (as with the distinction between sacred and profane, for instance)? Can one not project a distinction outward in a kind of "framing up" so that it is enclosing itself?

These kinds of questions are of secondary importance. Constructing a mathematical calculus may have other priorities at this point than sociocultural evolution. Being able (indeed *having*) to keep such questions open is predetermined by the idea of observation as a distinguishing practice. After all, observing does not mean depicting pre-given structures of the world (which are then able to result in something true or false). Nor does it mean producing something corresponding to it (which is then able to succeed or fail depending on its model or purpose). Rather, observing is producing the capacity for connection by making distinctions. After that, how productive the beginning was is seen in the degree to which it can be continued and the complexity it can achieve. For our purposes, it is enough to recognize the problem and avoid deciding in advance for one or the other sequence.

But let us focus on the case at hand. We are assuming it involves the distinction between the observable and unobservable. Other distinctions can follow thereafter, depending how the observation field of religion develops. However, where we have to start is with the distinction between the observable and unobservable. That distinction does not permit a meaningful (productive) crossing of the boundaries. If a boundary is crossed, the "law of crossing" applies, along with the "form of cancellation." When we return, we stand there as if nothing had happened,[41] because observing can only take place on the side of the observable (even if that side only exists because the other side is there). It is not a matter of making the unobservable observable—of depicting it or representing it. Doing so would certainly be a categorical error or imply a transition to a different kind of distinction. What is finally at issue is the reentry of the form into the form, the reentry of the *distinction* into what is distinguished by it. Put differently, the *distinction* between the observable and unobservable has to be made observable in what is observable (*where* else?). The issue is not one or the other side of this distinction but its *form*, the distinction itself.

Since religion often does not provide enough information about itself, we need these complex preconsiderations to arrive at a conclusion. Forms of meaning are experienced as religious if their meaning refers back to the unity of the difference between observable and unobservable, if *for that* a form is found. Religion has nothing to do with a "crisis of meaning," which has only been a big topic for around a hundred years. Themes such as "loss of meaning," "loss of identity," and "loss of world" are only phantom pains[42] in the wake of large-scale historical amputations—such as the murder of a king or the relinquishing of home life for schools, factories, and offices. And if that description is accurate, it would be unreasonable to ask religion to be concerned with such things. Religion also does not understand meaning as a "need" to be satisfied. It does not exist in order to provide the "search for meaning" with a likelihood of success.

Those are still functional definitions from anthropology. It is also not the problem that Jacques Derrida is addressing: of how the use of a sign cannot be repeated and that the sign can therefore not have a referent that stays the same from one situation to the next. From this, Derrida concludes that the metaphysics of the presence of being has deceived us. It may instead be the case that time changes everything and constantly demands new inscriptions, or that all *différence* ultimately displaces difference (*différance*) and that, as a result, every resistance can be deconstructed. Yet all that only dissolves the ancient holy alliance between religion and cosmology or between theology and ontological metaphysics—*while we cannot dispute that all this has also been religion.* This outcome only compels us to ask why things are this way, why one has to make distinctions in the schema of being/non-being or of presence/absence or that of repetition/non-repetition. It is pretty much undeniable that this makes sense. It leaves us with the question of what cannot be unobserved if one is making distinctions this way or any other way. The problem of religion, what distinguishes it from all other endeavors, is how meaning is possible if it is the case that something always remains unobservable.

As we can now reconstruct it, unobservability is not something that refers to a practical type of inaccessibility but rather what it is that makes observation itself unobservable, which is always something twofold: observing per se and the unmarked state of the world itself, out of which it distinguishes what it signifies. Thus, religion does not compensate for defects, worries, or insecurities but rather for the necessary condition that each thing has to be defined (as one thing and not another)—whether by means of experience or action, by psychic or social systems.

Each distinction, once it has been marked, provides a new freedom to concern itself with additional distinctions. This very marking has such an effect because it makes a distinction distinguishable, in contrast to simply moving on to what it signifies. Using Gotthard Günther's terms, this operation is "transjunctional," an operation deciding whether a distinction is accepted or rejected.[43] At this level of abstraction, one may already see a relationship of religion to freedom, even if it is only the freedom to doubt.

In addition, this lets us see (and we can expand on this another time) that religion can only offer paradox as its final, concluding thought. And as its mode of operating with such paradox, religion can only offer what is commonly referred to as "faith." Religious meaning is also open to reference in this direction. It is still always possible to ask what the unity of the final distinction is and fail to get a reply. But that is precisely and inevitably why religious meaning also has a peculiar certainty about it, and one that is blameless: that is just how it is.

VI

In connection with language, which operates according to a yes/no code, and with ontological metaphysics, which assumes a distinction between being and nonbeing, theology has had its troubles with negations. It can afford to formulate its own statements as negative theology, but it cannot afford to negate the existence of God. Under the conditions given, however, negation is an elementary operation that cannot be analyzed further. Yet this is subject to revision if we accept the results of our previous considerations.

For world and meaning are now being presented as objects that cannot be negated. And distinguishing is such a constitutive moment in the operation of observing that we cannot negate away the one side of the distinction without destroying the possibility of observation itself. In the operative use of distinctions, we cannot assume that the other side of the distinction is insignificant because it is not at all there. Although that other side has to be excluded from the respectively chosen signification, it also has to be accessible for additional operations. The boundary between one and the other side of a distinction cannot be imagined at all unless we think that it could be crossed and the other side could be signified as well. That is why the "crossing" (Spencer-Brown) of the boundary cannot be understood as a negation. As a result, for Spencer-Brown, the "cross" is the signification of signification because signifying calls for a crossing (and thus a reproduction) of the boundary between unmarked and marked space. Buddhism expands the possibilities of negation, encompassing the foundation for existence in them. But we are then confronted with the question of whether we are describing the world justly. From the unmarked space of this world, everything that is determinate has to be distinguished—but the world cannot be negated.[44] The unmarked space is not observable, but it is not therefore a void.

In light of all that, negation is an operation that presupposes a great deal. Mainly, it presupposes a specification of the negated (since one cannot negate the world and the meaning of the negating operation). And it presupposes memory since what has to be negated has to remain identical with everything that could also be affirmed. Hence, only sufficiently complex systems have at their disposal the possibilities of negation.

Supposedly, we need negations only whenever the possibility of crossing a distinction presents itself *and we would like to reject it*. Negations are needed whenever we want to stay on one side of a distinction, such as treating a tomato as a tomato and not as an apple (as might appear possible at certain moments). Negation would thus be a rejection of crossing. As a result, when perceiving something, we do not normally need any negations; instead, we only need distinctions that are clear. Negation in that case is merely an operation for protecting against deception. By contrast, negation is a constitutive component in establishing binary codes (a point I shall elaborate on later), precisely because crossing is still possible and provided for. Negation is here—and only here—a reflection of crossing, of the permanent possibility of crossing or *not* crossing a boundary.

At the same time, this explains the linguistic difficulties we constantly deal with. Language is in no sense just a grammatically ordered mass of signs but rather primarily a binary-coded form of communication that makes available yes-versions and no-versions of everything to be communicated. Since we have to use language, it seems the world is an *un*marked space or an *un*ending thing—in contrast to marked space or the finitude of things. Yet that is merely a linguistic problem that ensues when we signify the world *in the form of language*, meaning when we make distinctions *in the form of language*. But every distinction (even this one) becomes real only by operating in the world, and even the distinction between marked and unmarked space produces in practice (what we might call) an unmarked space for taking up the distinction.

Sometimes, theories of this kind are described as theorizing the primacy of the positive. But that description is inadequate because one cannot speak of something being positive unless one assumes that it might also be negative. That, however, is precisely what should be called into question. We are speaking more of the peculiarity of meaning-processing systems and of what world, meaning, and (finally) religion might mean for them. We can therefore only speak of "primacy" with reference to a meaning-processing system if we choose to indicate "inside" and "outside" with regard to such a system, which in any event can only happen from the inside. The distinction between inside and outside, which demands we give it a systems reference, takes the place of the distinction between being and non-being in the onto-theological tradition.

VII

In discussing psychic systems as observers, the thoughts outlined above do not stray from the familiar territory of tradition. The notion that the eye cannot see its seeing has been a topos since Plato, at least until Fichte contradicted it. That is the very reason the eye requires a special part of the soul for being reflective.[45] Beyond that, it is not really surprising that the human capacity for knowledge is cognitively inadequate. Fire is, after all, not something that can burn (and therefore extinguish) itself. The following considerations, however, are about neither perception nor consciousness. Consciousness externalizes the (internally elaborated) results of neurophysiological operations, thus performing the constitution of an "external world" and operating with the distinction between self- and other-reference. It hence remains bound to the subject/object schema. In a reflective mind-set, it can only imagine itself in analogy to things, as a sub-object, as a soul, spirit, self, or ego. Yet this is the source of religion's problem, if only because religion can—and finally must—ask about the meaning of this subject/object distinction.

I do not wish to dispute that religious thematics makes reference to humanity. But that is something that involves themes and not the primary operations of religion. There are powerful myths, such as the myth of God becoming man or the myth of the ego's subjectivity, which are supposed to help an individual come to terms with being one among many. But these myths exist only as concentrations of communication. In the context of a sociological theory, then, religion can be exclusively conceived of as a communicative event. We are not in any way questioning whether processes of consciousness are also at work here. Without consciousness, there is no communication. Yet the realization of religion, just like the realization of social order per se, cannot be understood as an aggregate of operations of consciousness (each closed to itself). Approached that way, a theory of the emergence of social order would be seen as extremely unlikely. It would be as if a Michelangelo sculpture could emerge just from blasting a vein of marble. Not only the emergence but also the continual maintenance and reproduction of a social order can be explained only by an operation that works exactly this way, precisely on the basis of communication actually taking place and reproducing itself. It is exclusively an issue of religious communication, a religious meaning that becomes actualized in communication as a meaning of communication. In contrast to the statements religion makes about itself, one is not dealing with religious entities (with deities, for instance) that people assume to exist. It only interests us that such statements are made. (If they were not made, we would not have any reason to worry about whether they were adequate or not.) In addition, we are making abstractions of statements that are about states of consciousness (each of which has been individualized). At issue is not "humanization," that religion is being reduced to anthropology in the nineteenth-century fashion. In this sense, communication is the only systems reference that we are permitting. We clearly assume that communication is only possible in it when certain structural couplings of a psychic, organic, chemical, or physical type have been preserved.

Analyzing specific performances of consciousness would never make religion comprehensible and in particular would not explain the evolution of religion's major forms. The primary achievement of consciousness (in humans as well as more highly developed animals) is allowing the results of neurophysiological brain operations to appear as an "external world" and enabling a (consciously) living organism to be oriented by the distinction between self- and other-reference. This can take place by direct perception, but also by highly varied types of simulation. We also know that the human capacity to distinguish through consciousness is enhanced by language and is equipped with its own type of memory and learning ability. Human beings can also remember what they have perceived (or heard or read) in the form of language. In the area of genuine operations of consciousness, what is unobservable would always appear (if provided with an index of reality) as something concealed, "behind" or "in" something else already there. Religious communication, when offering something consciously imaginable, also uses metaphors such as "behind" and "in." But the signifying space that religion occupies and develops is not opened up until there is a linguistic coding of communication according to "yes" (acceptance) and "no" (rejection). Meanings that insist explicitly that what is intended, stated, or to be understood *is inaccessible to consciousness* cannot be realized unless there is communication. This way, forms of meaning such as being "behind" something, being "in" something, being invisible, and being unrepresentable are established as metaphors and brought into circulation. Moreover, consciousness has to get used to this kind of language. At the same time, however, the correlates in consciousness for what is being preached are still highly uncertain. Nor are they disposed toward communication. Communication generates its own forms of understanding as a condition of finishing and restarting its own operations, and it does not register conscious willfulness unless communication itself is disrupted by it. A particular sociocultural evolution based on communicative autopoiesis is conditioned on communication (to a large extent) being *indifferent* while also *sensitive* in a specific (but self-defined) way toward what simultaneously operates as consciousness.

Accordingly, communication is understood as a mode of operation that reproduces itself from its own products. Stated another way, it is the operational mode of an "autopoietic" system, and it demands that a synthesis of information, utterance [*Mitteilung*], and understanding be achieved to such a degree that communication can be continued. In every communicative operation, constative (informative) and performative (utterative) components of communication have to be balanced and understood in relation to one another. To that extent, religious *faith* is and remains something *professed*. But the *unity* of this event is produced as communication and not as an (unavoidably precarious) state of consciousness among its participants.

Communication is always an observational operation because it assumes at least (1) that information and utterance can be distinguished, and (2) that the understanding from which this distinction proceeds does not coincide with utterance but is distinguishable from it. Equally complex are the demands made on the participation of psychic systems, which then have a disruptive effect on communication. But if one starts with social systems (and not actual human beings), communication is the primary operation and remains so. In the case of such research, one can also overlook what is happening psychically. Whatever processes of psychic actualization want to become communicatively relevant have to make themselves discernible as communication. Otherwise, they remain an inconsequential alteration of the environment for the social system of a society.

Treating communication as a synthesis of three components—information, utterance, and understanding—does not allow a reifying or ontological prioritizing of one or the other component. Communication does not have an origin in either the objective meaning of information, the subjective agent uttering something, or (lastly) the societal [*gesellschaftlich*] context and its institutions that make understanding possible. Communication is its own product.[46] It is thus in a position to switch its focus of orientation repeatedly, depending on where the next communication is looking for a problem—whether in surprising information, intentions of utterance, or difficulties of understanding. This analysis leads us back to the indispensable presupposition of meaning. For meaning is the very medium that enables these components to exchange leadership status—and which reproduces itself in this process. In such a manner, objects, subjects, and conditions of understanding are not preexisting givens but "eigenvalues"* of communication that owe their stability to the recursivity of communication.

At this point, we have to presume this notion of communication without explaining it further.[47] Yet in what follows, it is important that everything said about observation will also be valid for communication. Hence, even social systems are observing systems—sui generis ones, with their own distinctions and with no inherent capacity for perception. The same thing applies to the critical premise that observation is unobservable. A communicative system, just like a system of consciousness, clearly has the ability to make reference to itself. And on the level of primary operations, communication can signify communications, about which we can communicate further. In addition, a communicative system can even thematize its own identity, using self-significations, making self-descriptions, and proposing (and discussing) theories about itself. Having said all that, these things always take place through operations that do not rule out but precisely assume (as in Wittgenstein's notion of the rule) that there are also other communicative operations within the system.

Here, too, reflection is always conditioned by and connected with a previous distinction, which is not thematized in observation itself but operates as its blind spot. And the same thing is applicable even at the primary level of communicative operations with respect to distinguishing information, utterance, and understanding. In the moment of actualizing

---

* The term "eigenvalue" (from German *eigen* "own, particular" + English "value") has many applications in both pure and applied mathematics; it derives ultimately from the German word *Eigenwert, "intrinsic value"*).—Trans.

the unity of what has been distinguished that way, communication is incapable of signifying itself; it can only perform operations. And if this unity is something important, additional communication has to be mobilized, which in turn can only be realized operatively. "Are we making ourselves clear?" one might ask.

The following chapters deal repeatedly with this problem, which (following its own logic) can variously be called the distinction between operation and observation; the unobservability of the world and of observation; the paradox of the sameness of the distinguished; and the reentry of the distinction into itself. To understand these things, it is critical that we also (indeed, that we *absolutely*) make reference to the observational operations of communication. One should not be misled in everyday communication by those who make "humanity"—and not communication—responsible for things that cannot be observed or by those who argue that weaknesses in seeing or expressing religious (e.g., mystically inclined) communication are basic human conditions. These are only some of the semantic forms concealing the deeper paradox of the communicatively produced unobservability of observation. And if I am correct here, sociology—and not psychology or anthropology—is the most appropriate science of religion.

VIII

We can repeat and elaborate the insights that follow by distinguishing operation from observation when asked how far cognitive capacities go. In religious traditions, it has always been obvious that humanity is presumed to be limited in its cognitive abilities. Attributes such as omniscience are reserved (as counternotions) for God. In today's cognitive sciences, similar problems arise, yet these are not formulated using the distinction between humanity and God (finite and infinite). Our starting thesis is rather that no system can guarantee cognitively that it has adapted to its environment.[48] Cognition is always only an additional procedure that is based in systems operations, and its primary function is to enable the temporary adaptation of the system to temporary environmental conditions. We thus always have to assume that the world (or, as seen by the system, the environment) is tolerating the self-reproduction of the system.

This is not only true for all living organisms and human consciousness but (in a modified form) for all kinds of communicative systems.

To be sure, every communication inescapably activates an "information" component (otherwise, it would not be communication). It has to refer to something determinate, giving the form of information to its point of reference. It has to understand what it indicates as a difference that makes a difference by being processed cognitively.[49] However, for communication to occur at all, an utterance of information is additionally required and ultimately an understanding that is sufficient for further communication, oriented on the difference between utterance and information. Communication is thus never just cognition that is reproducing itself or based on information. Its specific achievement is not copying ("representing") these environmental conditions into the system, but constantly negotiating between informative (constative) and utterative (performative) components of its *own* mode of operation. Communication, like the brain, operates subject to the environment but without having contact to it. After all, as an operation that reproduces the system of operations by recursively accessing other operations, communication also has to open itself to environmental presuppositions, ones that it cannot grasp or thematize in itself. Communication presupposes an environment that normally tolerates it—not only systems of consciousness but also an ecological environment that is discontinuous enough and filled with surprises. Stoppages and interruptions are thereby not ruled out, but they have to be able to disrupt communication, and they have to be events that can be defined as opposed to the normal state of the world.

None of this can be changed by structural formations specialized in the cognitive processing of information, such as a knowledge that can be applied repeatedly, or as a meaningful semantic featuring of signs, or as a proven method of acquiring and testing knowledge. On the one hand, these kinds of structures presuppose being activated by communication. Nor do they exist prior to operation. And further, their evolution is guided by the main interest of all cognition in enabling temporary adaptations to temporary situations. The issue is not (and never is) making an inventory of the world ("the way it is") that is better, more accurate, or more deeply focused—but rather only constructing something internally with which the system can keep helping itself. Extending cognitive capacities in the direction of digitalization, storage, refinement of distinctions, or learning speed (with a previously incorporated variability of all knowledge) is not then going to improve the system's global security but will at most serve to enhance its own capacity for disruption. The system can then characterize and process what is more surprising and still unknown, thus enlarging the sphere of communications that can be understood. But none of this provides a guarantee that the societal system [*Gesellschaftssystem*] will be able to adapt itself better. So, evolution also does not mean selecting knowledge that can improve the adaptation of the system to its environment. Rather, it is only testing forms with which the system's autopoiesis can be continued, in spite of a level of complexity nearing improbability (or, in the terminology of cybernetics, despite the "reinforcement of deviation").[50] Evolution's achievement is to produce a high probability of maintenance in the face of a slight probability of emergence. This means forming systems.

The autopoiesis of communicative operations projects a future that is still open and as yet unknown. It is a future—and this alone is certain—in which more and more operations will be possible. Uncertainty thus also means uncertainty without end, an uncertainty that reconstitutes itself with every determination. The possibility of making corrections is thereby guaranteed and sufficient. Neither transcendental guarantees nor a prioris are needed. And corrections may be sufficient in almost all function systems: in politics, the economy, science, and (nowadays) even in intimate relationships. If, however, more is called for, different kinds of semantic resources will have to be introduced.

Starting with these theoretical points has wide-ranging consequences both for the evolution of life and the evolution of the communicative system of society. We are breaking with the traditional assumption that the world is existentially given and can be comprehended with a bivalent yes/no logic. From such beginnings, religion had to ally itself with ontology, thus accepting a cosmology or even postulating a creator (with an attribute of being) who has made and sustains everything that exists. By contrast, shifting the point of departure to operative constructivism and emphasizing the operative presuppositions of each cognition lead us to a completely different problem. If the world and the (continuously presupposed) adaptation of systems are removing themselves from observation and, even more, from cognitive processing, then how can the system develop trust in something like meaning? One does not have to go far to see that religion is responsible for this.

IX

In concluding the present chapter, we ought to consider the meaning of death. In all religions and in all theories of religion, it is likely that death plays a significant role. Death is one of the fundamental experiences of human life, specifically as an experience affecting everyone, regardless of their destiny in life or social status. Temporally speaking, death has a certain peculiarity in that it can happen to us at any time, even when one is not expecting it at all. Seen in social terms, this applies to our experience of others' deaths as well as to the possibility (at any moment) of our own. These universalisms also indicate—and hardly need further explanation—that the meaning of death is a problem where religion has to prove itself. In other function systems and organizations, death plays a limited role. Medicine, for instance, ceases to make efforts when death sets in. In insurance companies, death is a value (that can be calculated with astonishing accuracy), and insurance statistics refer to their own paradox: the precision of making predictions in large numbers is *conditioned by* the unpredictability of the individual case. In organizations, death causes problems of succession. In political systems, it can even create moments of considerable insecurity. Law provides death with legal consequences. In none of these cases does its meaning seriously affect the functioning of the system.

In the case of religion, the situation appears to be different. No religion can avoid saying something about this problem, even religions that allow death just to happen without providing a ritual for those affected to shape their distress and assure themselves that others share in it.[51] A pervasive phenomenon is the belief in the spiritual survival of the dead, often as ominous ancestors who have to be appeased or unfortunate souls for whom we have to say masses. The semantics of bodily death contain features that signify something outlasting physical death, freed by it, or even only appearing in death (such as is the case with the body by means of conception and birth). Thus, a clear body/soul distinction, as Christian religion formulates it, cannot be presumed but is much more an accomplished evolution of a certain kind. Not least, this leads to a significant reduction of corporeal semantics that might then be recomplexified in the domains of natural science or medicine.

Christian cosmology reflects on death with two distinct images of time, *both* of which refer to *life*, being formulated as life. *Aeternitas* is the time of God's life, simultaneous with all times, the time of a simple (and thus indissoluble) life without becoming or expiring, and thus a time without succession. *Tempus*, on the other hand, is the time of human life as a life of a dissolvable *compositum* that does not partake of eternal life except through the soul. The distinction of times, even the distinction-maintaining time of *tempus*, only arises by means of creation; hence, the question of time before creation does not make sense.[52] The discrepancy in the two notions of time is simultaneously marked and resolved by not knowing the future. It not only means that one cannot know when one will die but also that the future beginning with our death is unknowable—a gap then filled by the professional knowledge of theologians, chiefly through the schema of heaven and hell. The care of others, either by an individual or a priest, requires that rules for living be constructed and observed, rules that assure us—or at least make it likely by means of divine mercy—that one will achieve redemption in heaven upon death and not be assigned eternally to hell. The cosmology of this double time is at once a "frame" that transfers the distinction between life and death onto another distinction, thus giving this distinction a meaning that older terminologies referring to living bodies (for instance, the Greek *aiōn*) can no longer offer.

In conventional theories of religion, the distinction is not made clearly between functions (for society) and performances (for other systems). On the basis of anthropological axioms, we presuppose that people are in need of comfort when next of kin die and in need of support when their own death is near. In death, our entire life is mirrored. Life is only comprehensible as a unity when viewed from its endpoint, which religious productions of meaning can then link up with. In modern, functionalistic interpretations, the corresponding rituals are then assigned a "latent" function of resolving tension and translating the demands of psychological strain into harmless activities. This may be quite accurate for the performance of religious methods of faith, religious consolation, or religious rituals. Seen also from the standpoint of evolution, one might assume that incentives are at work for developing and testing certain semantics and practices, which themselves are actualized in the event of a death along with paradigms that can be repeated. But all this tells us nothing about the societal function of religion or about the ways religions deal with death.

For now, we are not talking about biological death as such but about the *knowledge* of death. This knowledge is communicable. It is articulated in the medium of meaning—even if it is only made operative with the distinction between life and death. More typically, solutions of this problem take on the form of resuming death in life[53]—whether proceeding from the idea of life after death or from the distinction between eternal life for God and a finite one for humans. Since there are no operations that are essentially free of meaning, either for consciousness or communication, death can only be presented in the medium of meaning, or (more precisely) only as one of the forms of the medium of meaning. And here—not in the supposed "meaninglessness" of death—is precisely where the problem seems to lie.[54]

Meaning is a medium of autopoietic systems. That is why, on the level of (conscious and/or communicative) operations, there is no end to it. Every element produced is produced for and by the reproductive relationship of the elements. As a result, there cannot be a "final element," because no element could be a "final" one. The same structure can be found in the medium of meaning and especially in the temporal form of meaning. Each form of meaning forms itself by referencing other possibilities. From the standpoint of time, there is neither an absolute beginning nor an absolute end in which the question of a *before* or *after* would not be posed. The dismissing of this question, as in Augustine's doctrine of the eternal present of God's life (and the supporting quotations from Psalms),[55] operates with an unimaginable concept of time that is paradoxical and undifferentiated—demonstrating precisely that it is religious. In the medium of meaning, such assessments [*Festsetzungen*] cannot appear as anything other than positings [*Setzungen*] of faith. Undifferentiated time—without future or past, without year or day, and without succession—is itself a caesura, an act of "writing" (in Derrida's sense) which relies on distinguishing itself from the temporal understanding of living human beings.

On the level of autopoietic operations, as well as on the level of semantics that serve to observe them, there can be neither death nor an ending without an "afterwards." Consciousness cannot think a final thought and thus cannot imagine how a final thought would feel (so to speak). And it is even more obvious that one can still always communicate about any death and what happened can at least be understood to the degree it is still possible to communicate further. For psychic as well as for social systems (and for *both* because one is talking about meaning as the medium of observing their operations), death is both certain knowledge and certain ignorance. In comprehending it, the medium of meaning starts to contradict itself. It is a limit-experience contradicting the form of a limit, having to assume that there is another side. Each interpretation based on this can hardly deny that it is only an interpretation. It is able to locate its own non-knowledge ontologically in the world; it can, as it were, cosmologize it. It can interpret such non-knowledge according to the schema of immanence/transcendence. Apparently, however, death cannot be singled out as a unique problem to be presented with a solution (which would be immediately contestable). Such interpretations do not become plausible unless they are interpreted as religion, and that means as a system that can sufficiently mobilize knowledge and actualize redundancies so that death (as a case in which meaning itself is experienced as paradoxical) retreats, being absorbed into a world that can be dealt with as well-known and familiar.

2

Coding

Whatever religion might be, it depends on fashioning forms in the medium of meaning. Just the same way that meaning is treated in other contexts. This does not tell us for the present in what sense religion is specific, but to make the transition, we can fall back on the discussion of forms launched in chapter 1. It is no use asking what the "meaning of religion" is, as if religion were something preexisting, because any answer to this question is obliged to use a form, and thus to make a distinction indicating religion and excluding "everything else." But how could religion accept a production of meaning that excludes "everything else," using the inside of its form as an excuse for ignoring the unmarked state of the world—and thus the observer as well?

Regardless of how we draw the boundary between marked and unmarked, it is precisely this boundary that any valid assignment of meaning in the form of religion must identify as its problem.

This means that *every* use of form involves religion, because every use of form generates an unmarked state. (Without marking, of course, there would be nothing that is "*un*marked"; the world must always first be transformed into an imaginary space by distinguishing between marked and unmarked.) But nevertheless, with *universal competence*, religion envisages a *specific* distinction, just that of marked/unmarked (observable/unobservable). Yet how can this be called a distinction or a form if the other side, the outside of the distinction, eludes marking—and if that is precisely the *condition* of marking itself?

Let us take a second look at this problem by asking what the code of religion is. Coding presupposes that *both* sides of a distinction serving as a code can be indicated, if only by distinguishing between a positive value and a negative one. We'll come back to this. What is of interest here is only an earlier problem, namely, what happens when the code of religion takes the place originally (and universally) occupied by the distinction of marked/unmarked. We can assume that this is how religion makes itself distinguishable. That is, it becomes a system with this (and no other) code. Further, the observer can then be observed as someone who uses this form and who (with the help of this distinction) gives religious meaning to what he is signifying. And that, in fact, is how sin "enters the world."

Actually, *both* sides of the code should be distinguished in relation to their unmarked states. There cannot be two unmarked states, because that would presume digitalization,* or marking. Evidently, there is a third possibility (excluded for logical reasons): the chaos that is inadmissible in an orderly world. However, is it not the world itself that is being excluded from the world? How does this world *in* the world come into being, this inclusion of the excluded third possibility?

If we let this question guide us, we immediately see a range of helpful possibilities. Myths of the world's origins can then be told, gaining in plausibility by narration, the placing of distinctions coordinated with one another in a sequence. There are exclusions, taboos, and rules of purity and purification presenting an order by excluding something else.[1] Another solution is to see the world itself as distinguishable. We can signify it if we juxtapose it with something else—whether the one God or nothingness. We can then make the non-world side of this distinction symbolic so as to signal its incomprehensibility. That would appear to suffice for presupposing the world itself in the mode of the observable. As in the biblical paradise, prohibitions on knowledge can be introduced, or the idea that the observer is the "devil." In each of these ways, religion generates a semantics of its coding, which can communicate and absorb uncertainty in particular historical societies. Religion canonizes itself and marginalizes those who question it.

Nevertheless, we cannot completely exclude the possibility that questions will be posed about the unity of the code, the unity of positive

* For Luhmann, "digitalization" designates a binary system, in contrast to an analog system.—Trans.

(e.g., good) and negative (e.g., bad), the unity of marked and unmarked, and the unity of the distinction itself (which is necessary for form). Philosophers concede we have to tolerate skepticism (leading nowhere) as the "free side of every philosophy."[2] But that is only a different way of formulating our problem. Behind every indication marking something, there is always the unobservable unity of its difference. It's what is called a paradox.

II

If one thing is certain, it is that a paradox (even in the form of a tautology) can never be transformed into an identity without losing some of its meaning. The same would hold for the identity of a redeeming God, the identity of a redeeming nothingness, and the identity of a principle. For resolving a paradox into understandable identities, a distinction is needed. In place of the black hole of paradox, which does not release any information to the outside, we have to substitute distinguishable identities. These then limit what people can expect of them. Language may hide these distinctions by attributing characteristics or activities to a subject (of an utterance). But if we move away from this habit of attribution, we immediately see differences between God and redemption, nothingness and redemption, and principle and recognition. In such cases, we have to ask what distinctions are substituted for the distinction of observable/unobservable so that this paradox can be resolved [*entfalten*] into identities—that in turn can be enhanced—such as "God" and "redemption."

As soon as we come to deal with resolving paradoxes, we are also dealing with history. Transformations in that domain do not follow logically but creatively, and not in some necessary form but contingently.[3] Society can thus select appropriate ways to resolve paradoxes, depending on the significations it can most plausibly operate with.[4] In addition, certain figures have to be distinguishable, and they thus expose themselves to "critique." Surprise attacks or ambushes by the unmarked state (precisely because nothing is marked there) can never be ruled out entirely. Long-term (evolutionary) stability can only be achieved when modifications are made, when the same is constantly varied. Identity is constituted by repetition, but repetition occurs in different situations and activates different contexts—often even different *distinctions*—that indicate the same thing using different counterterms. What has proven itself identical in repetition

is simultaneously condensed and confirmed, reduced to a kernel of meaning (its essence, or *essentia*) and confirmed by extending its "meaning"
for some other thing. Ontological metaphysics accounted for this phenomenon by distinguishing between substantial and accidental certainties.
There are thus identities that outlive themselves, semantics worth preserving that represent communications worth preserving.[5]

But the referential excesses of all meaning always leave open the option of seeing certainties *as limitations* and asking questions about the other
side. As a result, the technique of the medieval *quaestiones disputatae* practically became a form of learned sport. When scholastic authority was no
longer sufficient to answer the questions being disputed, it became a legitimate form of communication to make paradoxes.[6] We regularly find paths
leading back to that beginning, to paradox as a form in which religion is
no longer recognizable as religion. Yet that is precisely why religion mo-
bilizes tendencies that preempt paradoxes (or at least leave them to small
realms of systemic self-observation). That way, religion does not fall victim
to the apathy of "anything goes," leaving us asking which forms of meaning succeed at resolving paradox, for how long, and in which societies.

Among the myriad distinctions possible in the context of religion, we
are looking for one that enables us to recognize religion as religion. Recognizing religion as religion is a process of attribution about which observers
can agree or disagree, for the classic question about the "essence" of religion
will be answered differently by different observers. If we ask the question
this way, from the *outside*, religion can be distinguished in various ways,
often directed toward those elements of meaning we would like to see qualify as religion. For one person, choosing the organic menu at the university
cafeteria is a religious choice; for another person, it is not. If we stick with
the question of essence (and thus an ontological treatment of the problem),
we cannot avoid religious pluralism (under current societal conditions)—
pluralism both in the sense of a plurality of religions with their respective
followers, and in the sense of disagreeing about which elements of meaning
qualify as religion in the first place.

Deferring this line of questioning, we therefore consult only a single
observer, religion itself. The question then becomes: how does religious
communication recognize it is dealing with religious communication? Or
put differently, how does religion distinguish *itself*? As external observers,
we rely on religion's self-observations. We do not prescribe but rather ac-

cept what describes itself as religion. Still, we are presupposing (and here we may be mistaken or contradicted by facts) that there is a guiding distinction for religion, one that reformulates the basic paradox of the reentry of form into form. We are presuming that religion has some grounds to begin with for differentiating itself and for copying this difference onto itself. We are thus presuming that religion can make a distinction between self- and other-reference and, in addition, that the "self" of this reference still cannot answer the question of *how* religion recognizes itself as religion.

III

To reconsider the issue, let us return to the thesis that the world of meaning (in other words, reality) has to be divided up if something is to be observed. But that would only mean that every observation depends on a distinction that has been operatively completed. In religious communication, we are dealing with a specific case we can call (all too generally) "reality doubling." Certain types of things or events are assigned a special meaning, taking them out of the regular world (where they are still accessible) and granting them a special "aura," a special circle of reference. Something similar is at work in the cases of play, art, and statistical analysis. These are perhaps surprising relatives of religion, if not quite on a par with it.[7] This kind of distinction appears to exist in all social systems.[8] The only thing that varies is how we attribute conditions and events to it. Such variation is the starting point for possible differentiations that ultimately distinguish and classify errors, norm violations, religious problems, special artistic achievements, and so on. Even the "transcendental reduction" of Husserlian phenomenology follows this schema: the ontological question and the "natural view" of the world are bracketed out (*epochē*), and the freedom thus gained for the variation of possibilities is used to discover stable eigenvalues (here still referred to as "essences").

For the world, as a result, the meaning of the term "reality" has to be restricted. Until it is qualified, reality (and with it, fate) does not come to be or signify and thus distinguish itself from something else. The world contains something that in this narrow sense is not real but nonetheless can serve (and be observed) in the position of an observer. Everything that exists is no longer real simply by existing as it does. Rather, a special (let us call it a *real*) reality is generated through the existence of something that is different/distinguished from it. Until now, the field of religious studies has been interested primarily (if not exclusively) in understanding the specific phenomenon of the holy or sacred. It assumes that "what is" questions bring us closer to the issue. If, however, we let ourselves be guided by an approach based in difference theory, we can ask what happens with the *other* side when the world is divided into sacred and other. To an observer, reality only starts to emerge when there is something (in the world) we can distinguish it from. Without that distinction, reality cannot at all be solidified in comparison to the rather fluid world of the imagination. And only then can we speculate on relationships, mirror relations, or intervening activities that connect the two parts of the world, the real reality and the imaginary one. It was therefore likely the primary activity of religion to constitute reality by preparing something for observation that did not fall under the category of "reality."

Such a revolutionary development, one with massive consequences, must always have been associated with the linguistic use of signs. On the one hand, cognition is thus equipped with a capacity to err, and communication with a capacity to lie. Realities can thereby be observed that are not— if we may formulate it this way—"referentially real." But there is more, for we can also double reality by artificial and consensual means: by reducing and expanding it. This doubling is precisely at work in the cases cited above of play, art, statistics, and religion. It is not meant to be switched off again, as when errors are made. Rather, it has a positive connotation and is reproduced as worthy of being preserved. At the same time, doubling projects onto the world the first commandment of all observation: "Draw distinctions!" As a result, we always have to indicate to which side of a distinction we are assigning other distinctions, indications, and observations.

This leads to a further question: how can we reproduce such a distinction between reality and imagination, one that is seriously intended (and should not be taken for an error)? There must be signs that keep us from getting confused, quasi-objects[9] such as prophets or footballs, letting us to recognize that sequences can be assigned to reality's double. Or there must be statistical or game rules guaranteeing that we stay in the realm of the probable/improbable and do not make the error of assuming that certain events are concrete (which in fact are not). Precisely in the case of religion, however, shouldn't there also be the possibility of *allowing* confusion, indeed of *producing* it intentionally in certain situations, as ecstatic cults do?

Perhaps the most notable (but certainly very early) form of designating an imaginary reality of the religious can be found in *limiting communication* through the form of the *mysterious* [*das Geheimnisvolle*]. It can thus be communicated but is only revealed in special circumstances or for those expressly initiated. By means of this form of the mysterious, the sacred distinguishes and protects itself against being trivialized. The problematic of the arbitrariness of possible claims about the other side of reality, intrinsic to reality doubling itself, is thus socially controlled: not just *anybody* can come and maintain just *anything*. This kind of social control is presupposed in classical sociology by what is termed "institutionalization."

Representing the sacred as a mystery has important advantages. It distances what we perceive but leaves it in a perceivable state. What is deemed sacred, for instance, may be bones,[10] statues, images, or certain natural objects like mountains, springs, or animals. They are, to use the terms of the previous chapter, visualizations of a reentry. Each of these is "something tangible" and is at the same time more than that. We are not really allowed to take hold of it, even if we could. The problem of doubling is transferred into an ambivalence protected by "modesty" (*aidōs*) and is thus neutralized by an ambiguity specific to the object.

As long as a mystery can be objectified in a perceivable state, it can be presupposed in communication. It remains a mystery, but one that exists (can be shown). We see it because others see it, too. Here we avoid a problem that arises as soon as the mysterious has to be communicated as a mystery, because mysteries in communication can be guessed at or given away. They cannot be constructed, only deconstructed. They cannot be represented as artifacts of communication without it causing a performative contradiction. In a communicative context, we help ourselves by making taboos. As a result, the breaking of taboos can no longer be ruled out, because even the taboo as a form has another side. It can be impaired, which under the right conditions (pointing also to the possibilities of evolution) enables taboo breaking ("unheard of" behavior) to emerge as the foundation of a new religion.

Another way of dealing with mysteries is to formulate them as functionally equivalent to a contradiction or paradox. A prohibition on observing them is replaced by a contradiction blocking itself or, in the case of paradox, by a claim claiming its opposite. God is thus to be feared and loved. He thus cannot accept his own death on the cross. He thus can only be visualized if we think beyond what cannot be thought of as larger or smaller. And, finally, paradox also leads us to fill morality with religious justifications and self-refutations. Precisely when we rely on our good works, it can be fateful. It is then recommended that we sin and repent.

As long as the mysterious stays in the realm of the perceivable, we can still imagine the distinction collapsing, with divinity itself appearing and being provoked into doing good or bad. Hence, there is not only symbolization and not only representation, but also something beyond the everyday that can still switch over from normal absence into presence. Then it is only an issue of recognizing this process—declared and prepared in the sacredness of objects, events, rituals, and cults—whenever it arrives and adapting it to our own interests through invocations, sacrifices, and the like. Alternatively, as in antiquity, mystery cults can be formed for making the mystery accessible, but only for those who are present and who have been initiated (all of which rules out being able to report on it to outsiders adequately and comprehensibly).

Although the mysterious is another form of reality, it is still a thing among things, a distinguishable event. Hence, it something toward which we behave in a conditioned and trained manner. As a form of societal religiosity, it is not invalidated or eliminated, but rather refashioned when a structural change takes place, for which I employ the concept of "coding." We can continue making the old distinction of real (or really *imagined*) things and events, but that too is reconfigured by a (very) much more radical distinction involving the world itself. For everything that exists, a two-part valuation has been made, and in the case of religion, it is the double valuation of everything as immanent and as transcendent. And everything that had previously been religious has to fit into this new context, being modified, regulated, or interpreted. At that point, the doubling of reality can be represented more abstractly as a transcendent meaning correlated to everything immanently observable. But the representation can only be realized if we can answer the question of which contents are capable of filling in such an abstract universal schema of meaning.

Among the most impressive evidence that religion begins in reality doubling is early Sumerian religion. Here all relevant appearances of the world, in nature and culture, are assigned gods, who are behind these appearances and responsible for them.[11] At that point, there is no order assumed in the relationship of the gods to one another, no special system to the religious cosmos. Such a point-by-point designation is not replaced by a system-to-system one until the Sumerian-Semitic religion of Mesopotamia develops further. In turn, the world of the gods becomes systematized according to a societal model of family structure and political authority. The analogy makes the order of this world and the other world plausible. The correspondence between those forms confirms that they are necessary, precisely because a this-worldly and an other-worldly reality had already been distinguished.

The basis for that distinction has archaic and primitive features. Revelations will come about in situations, ad hoc, in the form of inspiration and boundary crossings. These come about concretely and case by case. Until the rise of the major religions, no one talks about "holy scriptures" or canonizes revelation as the self-representation of a god. The European tradition is a rich one because Jewish tradition preserved a purely religious reality doubling fixed in textual form, thus partially influencing Christian doctrine, while Greek philosophy took a completely different path of linguistic-conceptual abstraction.[12] The theology of the rabbis preserves a communicatively binding relationship with God. As a result, the text cannot deceive but must be reinterpreted continually, however controversial the resulting interpretation may be. Controversy, as a form of resolving paradox, is thus a structure of tradition that must be maintained.[13] For Plato, by contrast, signification (naming) is vulnerable to deception,[14] and it has to be constantly reconfirmed with reality in the form of remembering prototypical ideas. In both cases, remembering is central. In one, a plan for creation must be preserved and actualized; in the other, forms are referred to that we can no longer experience purely but that account for the essence of things. Both versions articulate a distance between imaginary and real reality, but each provides a different semantics for the realization of the program. In both cases, the other side of remembering—forgetting—is to be forgotten. The dark side of producing and preserving religious forms remains the excluded other enclosed within them.[15]

IV

The notion of code should indicate a form that makes operational this problem of reality doubling and of establishing a real reality. Coding is by no means simply a way of recognizing something, a simple indication of reality doubling. A code projects *a different kind of distinction*, but one that only becomes possible given reality doubling. Through the distinction, it is led back into the unity of a divided worldview.

A code is a guiding distinction by which a system identifies itself and its own relationship to the world. Such a usage can be distinguished from the one common in linguistics and also (partly) in sociology.[16] Here, "code" is to be understood as a strictly binary schematism that knows only two positions or "values," excluding everything else in the sense of a *tertium non datur*.* Codes are generated in a process that duplicates what already exists, such as turning spoken language into writing, alleged truth into possible untruth, and so on.[17] We might also say that a reality first conceived (and simultaneously functioning) as "analog" is becoming "digitalized." It is thus reinterpreted as a binary schema, so that what is given only claims one side of the schema, and the other side is freed up for monitoring and reflection. In that case, one can already interpret the artificiality of all codings, making it possible to distinguish them as distinctions. We can therefore accept (or avoid) codes with the help of "transjunctional operations."[18] That is the only reason they are suitable for identifying what system the operations belong to.

Binary codes are distinctions of a special type. They are not merely significations that distinguish themselves by isolating something they have defined against the unmarked state. Nonetheless, they are not qualitative pairs—like heaven and earth, man and woman, or city and country—which hold out a prospect of equivalent possibilities of specification (= possibilities of connection) on both sides. They instead fix the system in an asymmetry that is commonly presented as a distinction between a positive and a negative value (such as good/bad, true/false, correct/incorrect, having/not having property).

Gotthard Günther indicates that the positive side of the distinction is a *designative* value and the negative side is a *reflective* one.[19] In that way, a (logical) functional distinction is already being expressed. The designation only serves to signify what in ontological terms is called "existence" or "being." The non-designative value thus remains free for other tasks that can generally be comprehended as reflecting what conditions the appearance of the designative value. If we transfer this distinction from logic into empirical systems research, the positive value acquires the sense of indicat-

* I.e., "excluding the third possibility."—Trans.

ing the adaptability of systems operations to systems operations. The system can only operate on this side. The negative value is once again freed up to make observable the meaning of such operations as information, with the proviso that even observation is only taking place in the form of a systems-internal operation.

Binary codes and those built asymmetrically onto themselves have a complicated relationship to other distinctions on which the operative closing of a system is based. It is especially important that they diverge from the distinction between system and environment, or between self- and other-reference. It would be a false application of the code if the system were to distinguish itself with the positive value and give the environment a negative one. In that case, the mobility introduced by the coding would only have been given up. In general, there is no correspondence in the environment of the system for its code. Codes instead serve to balance internally the consequences of operative closing. That is because a system (in and of itself), which cannot contact the environment with its own operations (being unable to operate across boundaries), would have to view each environmental condition as equally probable. The coding, however, put the system in a position to treat surprises as irritations, to digitalize them, to understand them as a problem of assigning the code values, or to develop corresponding programs for their repeated use—in short, to *learn*. In internally produced horizons of expectation, in assumptions about normality or in places of uncertainty, irritations are made visible as distinctions that can become distinctions and thus information. Everything developed in the practice of coded operations invariably remains a purely internal construction. But since irritations do not occur randomly (since the environment itself contains structures), an internal order can be built up with help of such coding. Although this order does not contain the environment and is not at all consistent with it, it is nonetheless sufficient for making it likely that the system's autopoiesis will continue as long as the environment does not change in decisive respects (with destructive consequences).

What is noteworthy about the special form of the distinction of the code is how reflexivity is built into it. Codes distinguish themselves from distinctions that only serve to indicate something, that only operate with a single value. They distinguish themselves from simple divisions ("heaven and earth") that leave what is divided up in nonreflexive being in the manner of types and genres. They also distinguish themselves from simple claims of copies (*imago Dei*) or mirrorings that have to assume an analogy of being (or *analogia entis*) in order to associate what has been distinguished. Ultimately, codes distinguish themselves from distinctions in which reflexivity is offered as a characteristic of distinguished objects, in the case of husband and wife or master and slave. Instead, codings use distinctions, the reflexivity of which *results from the distinction itself* and is built into the distinction, indeed making up its specific form and function. What is preexisting and thus directly observable is duplicated only for the sake of reflexivity. And that does not only mean that an addition is made with a specific capability. Rather, *both* sides of the distinction are set up for second-order observation and *thereby* linked. The positive value cannot be held without the negative one.[20] Hence, the forcing of a code always has positive as well as negative results.

But that is only the case for second-order observations and thus only for cases in which the system observes its own observations. In the direct operations of systems, a reference to code values appears to be dispensable. Courts do not use the distinction of law and non-law to ground their judgments; they assume it instead. Making reference to truth is not part of the language of research, just as an artist does not feel understood if we say to him that he made something beautiful. And there is also no consolation gained from referring to code values of religion. They should not be part of the sermon and are not an argument for conversion or for faith.

In second-order observation, nonetheless, one can see the complex structure of coding that has always been implicated. This coding changes the meaning of crossing a boundary. A positive value can only retain its positivity if the *countervalue is positively excluded*. We assume this value can be considered for the entire domain where the code is applicable (again, indicating a unity) but that it can be excluded by determinable operations. Truth, as Karl Popper said, is only possible in the case of statements that could also be untrue. Property, according to Bartolus,* is characterized as available by the possibility that it has been or could be nonproperty. The theories of property protection are suppressed by theories of acquiring property. "Original sin" is transformed by baptism into a status that makes it advantageous to sin and to be forgiven for it. The modal form of contingency is therefore valid for coded domains. That is precisely why there

---

* Refers to a renowned medieval Italian jurist.—Trans.

have to be additional arrangements (*suppléments* in Derrida's sense) for such provinces of meaning, for making decidable the state of something which is being signified.

Codes are a precise copy of the paradox that they serve to resolve. At first glance, there is no apparent benefit to them. As soon as we ask what comprises the sameness of the positive and negative value or what comprises the unity of the distinction, we again come across the fundamental paradox of the sameness of what is different. Here, too, a question cannot be asked and a return to unity cannot be completed. Yet the advantage in such cases (and this is crucial) is that there are several codings: good/bad, as well as true/untrue, property/non-property, superior power/inferior power. The codes, as a result, can be identified by *being distinguished from one another instead of our questioning their internal unity*. For instance: it is a matter of morality, not of law, and of property, not of power. The separation frees up the combinatrics, enabling an immoral application of the law, or an illegal acquisition of property, or an unwelcome ("welcome/ unwelcome"!) transfer of property into power. Such internal problems in the space for combining the codings will attract attention and communication and will make us forget that this is precisely how the paradox of the sameness of difference becomes invisible. It is particularly true in modern societies that are no longer ordered hierarchically (in strata). By contrast, hierarchical societies (and hence aristocratic ones) at their height had to rely on maintaining a concurrence of all positive values, agreeing on the "good life" or (ultimately) on God. Such was the culminating point of goodness (diligence, *virtus*), of having goods, power, and the competence to evaluate right and wrong (*iurisdictio*). Under these presuppositions, the doctrine of transcendentals could declare "the one, the true, and the good" to be all the same thing. Any distinction between them could be outsourced to the idea of nature, where there were successful and failed natures. Yet in a functionally differentiated society, in which systematic differentiation is based on a variety of codings, this form of integration has to be relinquished along with the enormous relevance of morality. Typical system codes are thus distinguished from moral coding, avoiding any congruence of positive/negative values with those of morality. Property and law, truth, and even political power have to be available for immoral applications. These fields are limited solely by their semantic apparatuses, which does not exclude but rather opens up the possibility of uninhibited evaluations, even moral ones. Correspondingly, a logic enabling descriptions that are "polycontextural" (Günther) is needed.[21]

In addition to relying on the distinguishing of different codes from each other, there is already an indication that the paradox is resolved in the functional asymmetry of the codes. If it is already the case that only the positive value is capable of operations (= of use, = of function), that value can be maintained as the dominant one. The argument would then be: one is correct to distinguish between right and wrong (since otherwise the courts would not operate), and it is good to distinguish between good and bad (since otherwise everything could be legitimated, even racism). Even in present-day discussions, this is an argument that cannot be taken apart easily (and I speak here on the basis of experience). Actually, the sole alternative is to return to the paradox of the nondifference of the different. That, however, confronts us with an almost compulsive fear of paradox, then leading to the circumstance that the logic of self-reference—meaning the application of the code to the code itself—is not accepted.

If logic wants to handle positive/negative distinctions *operatively* (meaning as a unity), it too has to revert to a distinction, and the classic one is conjunction/disjunction. No unity is *ever* self-evident. As Gotthard Günther has shown, there is still a need for structurally rich logics that are not fixed on the material dimension but might also include the social dimension (for Günther, meaning the majority of subjects, you-subjectivity), as well as the temporal dimension (for Günther, particularly that which is historically new).[22] Günther refers to the operation he now wishes to introduce as "transjunction." Its accomplishment is to select positive/negative distinctions. In other words, it is an operation providing a freedom (which is not implied by classic bivalent logic) to accept or reject distinctions. Quite apart from its consequences for logic, the result is that a transition is made from first-order to second-order observation.[23] It is clear that coded systems have to operate (observe) on the assumption of strict bivalence— and even if only because that is the fastest way to establish order. Hence, they cannot do without the *tertium non datur*. Yet at the same time, logical and social-theoretical reflection shows that coded systems presuppose indifference toward all other codings. As a result, a completely logical description has to take on a third value, one that is able to signify the acceptance of its own code while rejecting all others.[24] This code selection may be designated as a self-indication.[25] Yet that too would be an operation dependent on distinction, leading to the question of what is on the other side of the distinction. For observers there is no concluding operation, no resting or fixed point of calculations. Inevitably, we are confronted with a paradox in the search for unity, that is, with a demand to continue. For observers are autopoietic systems that can only produce their operations on the assumption that other operations will follow. Their world is therefore an endless world, a "horizon" always holding out the prospect of other possibilities.

The social-theoretical relevance of this (inevitably) abstract analysis derives from the insight that the distinction between accepting and rejecting a code takes place on the level of second-order observation. The issue is not to reject a system (or person) using a certain code. Nor is it the aim to provoke counterrejections, opposites, or conflicts. The logical structure of transjunctional operations has its societal correlate in a principle of tolerance (or, if you will, of irony). That in turn is a prerequisite of functional differentiation, assuming (on the one hand) the operative closing of partial systems and creating (on the other hand) the possibility of displacing problems onto the system of whichever code is most suited to defining and solving them.

In the end, we have to agree that the societal order of the codings and their rejection values dismantles not only the bivalent logic but also the meta-coding of the tradition, specifically the meta-coding by means of the distinction of being/non-being. Husserl's transcendental phenomenology had already introduced a rejection value to this end, which he called *Epoché*. There and especially in Heidegger's *Being and Time*, this led to an extension of temporal structure as a condition of the world's appearance.[26] In operative constructivism, consequently, the logical proposition of identity must be reformulated. It is no longer "A is A" but instead "if A, then A." Which is to say that identity can only be constituted in operative sequences, functioning as a structural condition enabling a sequence to be formed in the first place, one that is highly selective and self-demarcating (or self-distinguishing). Even this leads us back to a distinction. Each repetition has to identify what is repeated and in the process *condense* it into what has been adopted from the earlier context. And it has to *confirm* this identity, thus assuring that it also fits into a different context.[27] In this way, the preconditions are created for a further distinction, specifically for generalization and respecification, the evolutionary-theoretical relevance of which has been established chiefly by Talcott Parsons.[28]

V

For a theory of religion, claims to great precision in the understanding of binary codings only really pay off when religion is using a binary coding. It is thus not something self-evident but has to be demonstrated. Now, it is clear that religion can only be observed and described when it can be distinguished. We also assume that such a distinction can be made by religion itself and that this self-localization alone (on one and not the other side of the identity-granting distinction) can permit religion to become a system. But that does not in any way mean (in fact, it appears unlikely) that religion identifies itself with a distinction—instead of with holy meaning, with an idea, a founder, with God. We could therefore think that it fundamentally contradicts religion's self-production of meaning if we ask it to identify with a difference and distinguish itself by specifying its own code vis-à-vis the more mundane concerns of this world.

But such doubts evidently assume an inadequate understanding of the propositional world in operative constructivism, differentialist philosophy, the calculus of forms, and in second-order cybernetics. An adequate notion of code is not available and still has to be provided. The mere observation that sophisticated theological thinking (and even Buddhism could be included here) has always dealt with tautologies and paradoxes could encourage a new awareness in this case. For both forms, tautology and paradox, are built upon distinctions that sabotage themselves. The modern "deconstructive" theory of text, which today extends beyond its home field of literary criticism, arrives at the same result.[29] If a code of religion could be successfully identified, we might take up its latent suggestions, perhaps finding more than merely the admission that human comprehension is inadequate (which amounts to resolving the paradox/tautology with the help of an identity-stabilizing distinction of human/divine).

A second problem will cause us greater trouble. The differentiation of religion is also a historical process. For a sociologically informed observer, it is further linked to the evolution of the societal system [*Gesellschaftssystem*]—to the discovery of writing and the transition to more sophisticated forms of societal differentiation. One should definitely not assume that religion makes itself noticeable from the start in the strict form of binary coding. Whenever we talk about the distinction of religion, we have to account for what historically are very distinctive conditions making religious semantics seem plausible. For one, religious definitions (in Mesopotamia, for example)[30] are closely linked with the general societal distinction of familiar habitable land (on which the cults can also be sustained) and the surrounding, threatening wilderness. Only when societies become more complex do specifically religious pairs of oppositions appear and, along with them, specifically religious indications of code values with which these can be distinguished from other value pairs (for instance, rich/poor and powerful/ powerless). It only becomes reasonable to apply the idea of binary coding once the guiding religious distinctions can be distinguished from others.

As far as the historical semantics of religion are concerned, we cannot assume that there are identical designations. But that alone may not keep us from forming and applying a temporally abstract notion of coding. Because without such a notion or (put differently) without the historicist hypothesis that an epoch can only be described on its own terms, we could define incommensurabilities of historical "discourses," without once having asked whether connections could be identified between changes in societal structure and changes in historical semantics. We are applying the temporally abstract notion of code (just like a number of other systems-theoretical notions) on the level of second-order observation, and we thus have to respect the separation of levels. One has to grant historical religions rights to what they can see (and formulate) themselves and what eludes them. But that does not force us to do without more abstract analysis, using notions that prove to be reliable (or not reliable) for constructing theoretical complexity in scientific systems. To that extent, we also hold onto an operative constructivism and a theory of operatively closed systems. The strain of conceptualizing these takes place exclusively on the internal side of the form constituting science. It serves exclusively to improve scientific accomplishments.

The thesis of the considerations that follow is that the semantic elaboration of a code specific to religion is linked with the societal differentiation of a function system for religion. I shall avoid every causal determination according to which one of these is the cause of the other. It is more an issue of a relationship of mutual benefit or evolutionary fit. Yet more abstract versions of the code specific to religion can only make sense to the extent that religion differentiates itself with respect to situations, roles, cults, semantic formulas, social-critical distance, and doctrinal systematization. At the same time, what has to be explained here and now is any increase in autonomy or (even more) any critical distance from everyday "this-worldly" events, providing religion with an occasion for thinking that is directed toward distinctions. Differentiation benefits the code, and the code benefits differentiation. Evolution is consequently an evolution of this connection. Not until modern society do we need both an abstract and analytically complex notion of code to make comprehensible what religion means *for such a society*.

VI

In designating both values of religion's specific code, the distinction of *immanence* and *transcendence* is the most appropriate one. We can also say that a communication is always religious whenever it observes immanence from the standpoint of transcendence. At the same time, immanence stands for the positive value, for the value that provides the capacity to connect with psychic and communicative operations. Transcendence stands for the negative value from which what occurs can be viewed as contingent. In Günther's terminology, immanence is the code's *designative* value and transcendence is its *reflective* value. It should be noted that no preference is thereby expressed (even if there can clearly be preferential codes). The positive is not in some sense "better" than the negative. In the unity of the code, both values presuppose one other, reciprocally. Events in this world do not receive a religious meaning until they are seen from the perspective of transcendence. But producing meaning is also the specific function of transcendence, and it does not exist in and of itself. It is the ability of every boundary to be crossed in some direction. Still, a boundary is no place to live, and in a place that is always different, one cannot build a "mighty fortress."*[31] We are not disputing that there are religions, especially god-based ones, that judge this matter differently. But judgments about existence are the judgments of first-order observers. And in this case, a second-order observer might maintain, their function is to carry out and conceal the reentry of a code into the code, specifically allowing the difference of immanence and transcendence to be thought and said.

But we are getting ahead of ourselves. For now, it is important to clarify the prehistory of the differentiation of a specifically religious coding.

---

* Luhmann is referring directly to Martin Luther's hymn "A Mighty Fortress" ("Ein feste Burg").—Trans.

Many older religions are based on a notion of a space that connects transcendence with immanence. What is distant is unattainable, but at the same time something—if one were present—that could be observed as a familiar everyday world. If we could reach the summit of Mt. Olympus (though reverence might keep us from attempting it), we might be able to see the gods dining. Theologians may dispute that the issue here is one of transcendence (in the Jewish or Christian sense). Yet, from an evolutionary perspective, this image is an antecedent figure. It does not permit us to grant distinction to transcendence by giving it a unique (existence) predicate, but the transitions are fluid, leaving it to the religious imagination to bridge the distances that cannot be reached with entirely different objects. From the standpoints of comparative religion and evolutionary theory, we can hardly exclude this case of (mere) spatial transcendence, no matter how much one might concede to evolutionary innovations.

For the Western tradition, it is important to clarify the relationship of coded religion to ontological metaphysics. It is not enough to reconstruct the extent to which religious cosmology operates with basic assumptions of metaphysics. More significant is that both ontology and its logic are built on the distinction of being and nonbeing, and thus on the assumption of a logical bivalence that leaves the remaining problems untouched.[32] In its wake, all thinking and all efforts at knowledge conclude with being; conversely, there is no being that cannot be logically grasped. Put differently, we lack a structurally richer logic here that might regard this as a problem. Ontological metaphysics proceeds from a single guiding distinction. It describes the world "monocontexturally" (to borrow Günther's terminology).

In retrospect, one can thus ask what can (and cannot) be seen if an observer bases himself on ontology and bivalent logic as a primary distinction. Or one might ask what gets lost and remains invisible if one *starts* with the distinction of being and nonbeing and a correspondingly bivalent logical set of tools. Clearly, an ontological metaphysics can form ideas such as *nothingness*, *infinity*, or *time*. In the process, it may produce a certain overlapping of them in the direction of religion. The problem, however, lies in the exclusionary effect of logical-ontological bivalency or, put differently, in the invisibility of the observer who has accepted this schema "uncritically" and is unable to indicate himself. Here a world, a reality, remains unobserved. Due to its bivalent logic, metaphysics cannot even see (or formulate) that it does not see what it does not see. To that extent, no matter what theology clerics might formulate, the need for religion is dragged into modernity (as it were) on the back of metaphysics.

If we accept this as a problem of a highly developed semantics, there is still the question of how religion inserts its code (and thus itself) into a reality that is assumed and accepted by societal communication. We have to start with the thesis of a reality distinction separating the actual real from an imaginary one, thus constituting a "durable" reality in the world (as shown above).[33] This does not at first occur (and certainly not quickly) in the perfect form of coding, but as a division of the world (construed as close to perception) into a domain that is familiar, well-known, and operationally accessible—and another domain. Without immediately implying a coding, we can refer to this counterworld of reality as "transcendence," since if it is to be signified, we have to imagine that a boundary is being crossed.

This notion of transcendence presents itself as a standpoint from which to compare very different religious semantics, particularly those of primitive societies. This way, such religions may be taken more seriously as religions than they sometimes are in the quite folkloristic research of the relevant specialties.[34] Transcendence is for now the provision of a direction, and it refers to a crossing of boundaries. But from the outset, territorial boundaries are not what are meant (even when places are being "sacralized") but rather boundaries to the unattainable, boundaries not only outside but also within the society one is starting from. Transcendence, when it is specified, conceals the unfamiliar [*das Unheimliche*] but is unfamiliar itself and thus capable of destroying, dissolving, and passing through every meaning. That is why we interpret transcendence as a duplication that cannot be formulated (and that is concealed precisely by religion), duplicating what is present, attainable, and familiar into a different realm of meaning.

An operatively inaccessible realm, a second world, does not set any limits on fantasy. One would be able to maintain anything because nothing can be tested—just as people deal with negations in an unrestrained way. Transcending produces an excess of semantic possibilities and a corresponding need for limitations. It is no coincidence that the etymology of *religio* is based on the notion of "*rebinding*," and it is no coincidence that Durkheim, in his idea of *sacré*, highlights the sanction of a limitation. But to limit what as transcendence is supposed to be kept sacred invariably produces (as does every signifying operation) a new boundary that is capable of being crossed. Which would reveal that transcendence is still not (at all) *the* transcendence that flows into the limitless.

The pressures this problem generates make it more understandable why early religions take up countermeasures. They establish communicative constraints that in turn are sacralized, having absorbed all reflexivity. It is a mystery how the sacred gets determined. Otherwise, the ancestral bones stored in the tribal house [*Männerhaus*] as the reference point of all rituals seem to be merely bones and, moreover, bones that have to be restored if they are lost or deteriorate.[35] The problem is solved by the only operative mode available to the social system of society: communication, particularly the twofold process of expanding and inhibiting communicative possibilities. The sacred is depicted as a mystery, a prohibition, or an impossibility that communication can define something. And curious questioning (*curiositas*) is prohibited or discouraged by saying that only trivial results can be achieved, letting one know one is missing what is essential.

Conventionally, the immanence/transcendence distinction is presented in primitive religions as *dividing up* a world that unquestionably preexists. (Even that limits the possibility of thinking of the code as reality-doubling.) The code is explained by distinguishing between near and far, or heaven and earth.[36] The idea of eternal life after death, and thus a sublation of the fateful difference between immanence and transcendence, is often found associated with the religious locus heaven. In more elaborate versions of this idea (surely influenced by the major religions), we also find the idea that transcendence is a boundary crossing, itself without boundaries, even present in immanence.[37] People can then say plausibly that God is at the same time close and faraway, present everywhere. In so doing, they can count on the important, easily accessible semantic form of "existing in something": God is not a definite appearance but he exists *in one*.

A semantic and institutional reaction to the distinction between a this-worldly and an other-worldly world—a reaction that is typical and prevalent—is our need for interventions either by objects or actions. At the same time, the extensive (likely universal) dissemination of this type of intercession demonstrates that this rather foundational distinction is very ancient and is likely attributable to the genealogy of religions. The distinction itself can only be grasped by marking a boundary. One can be helped, for instance, by dividing up spaces or times—or by artificially making a part of the event unseen. The marking of the boundary itself has an ambivalent status: it belongs as much to one side as the other, and thus to both sides and none. It therefore symbolizes and realizes the unity of the distinction. Thus the marking itself is a *sacrum*, sacred and terror-inducing at the same time. From the start, the unity of the difference is a problem, even if it is not as such reflected upon but only allows itself to be approached with fear and trembling, or under the protection of certain blessings, or under technical measures such as those that guarantee shamans a favorable return from other-worldly excursions. To an extent, the sacred is concentrated on the boundary representing the unity of the distinction of transcendent and immanent.[38] Religion itself definitely does not take place in the world beyond.

Intercessors are necessary if the issue is not to mark the boundary but rather to pass through it, crossing it back and forth. They themselves are incarnations of paradox if we move away from their respective sensitivities and attempt to identify them. In his worldly life, Jesus of Nazareth is a human being (albeit one without sin). As Christ, he is the son of God. As part of the trinity, he is God, thus his own father, just as God the Father is his own son. Here the *mysterium* sabotages the distinction on which it is based. The differentiation of transcendence (God the Father) and immanence (the Son's earthly life) presumes that the problem is being explained—and denied—at same time. The renunciation of logic is not an error but the appropriate form of the problem. One might stop with that insight, but one can also attempt a new description of the problem.

Both markings and intercessions serve to permit the unfamiliar world (of transcendence) to appear in the familiar world. Restrictions can really only be institutionalized as forms, as semantic contents that can be signified and operatively connected. At issue is whether this or that object, this or that place, or this or that gesture or action is distinguished as holy in the immanence of the familiar world. If we take the constitutive distinction of religion in its original, concrete form as a distinction of familiar/unfamiliar, then religion only emerges when this form undergoes reentry into the form, when the distinction of familiar/unfamiliar reenters the familiar. This is the only way the religiously unfamiliar (here *transcendence*) can be distinguished from what is simply unknown or unusual. Nonetheless, this distinction too is the result of an evolution, which can be seen in just how long the unexpected or unusual, the surprising and monstrous, have been the occasion for religious interpretation.

In comparison to the classical sociology of religion that characterized religion by demarcating domains—making simple distinctions such as sacred/profane (Durkheim) or ordinary/extraordinary (Weber)—the figure of the reentry of a distinction offers us a place both to begin a more complex analysis and to have access to the paradox that is always concealed in religion. With respect to the evolution of religion, it still seems evident that in the imaginary realm of religious fantasy, there are no boundaries drawn for the hypertrophy of forms, and there are many impulses for variation.[39] Yet what also seems apparent is that resolving the fundamental paradox of reentry demands timely and convincing forms placing limits on what can ultimately be accepted. Put differently, in the this-worldly realm, one has to communicate with plausibility (if not with unquestionable evidence) when referring to the other-worldly realm. In addition, the difference between this- and other-worldly should be prevented from intruding into communication and deconstructing it as a "performative contradiction" (as in the failure of a magical performance).

An elaborate coding of religion assumes a reentry of the distinction into what it is distinguishing.[40] Only then can a code's distinction be construed as not limiting us to the option of one or the other side. For both sides can always be found on both sides. Here, the logical (or mathematical) consequence is that an incalculable intransparency is at work, one that can only be resolved by imagination. In the process, it becomes possible for us to participate on the side of immanence in the entirety of the code. On the other hand, it becomes possible for us to imagine that what happens immanently also matters transcendently. It is the only way that communication taking place in immanence can refer to the code. In any event, such a reentry results in structural uncertainty and must therefore depend on supplements (*parerga*) to guide the selections becoming necessary. In other words, communication has to rely on memory and ends up being ambivalent as far as the future is concerned. One might thus, for instance, regard one's own life as part of a narrative of sin and redemption, hoping one's sins may be forgiven, but not knowing for certain whether one's soul is among the saved.

If the reentry of the form into the form succeeds plausibly, something important has been accomplished: the social stabilization of religion. Its production of meaning is relocated to the primary distinction of its code, thus becoming independent of the coincidental appearance of unusual events, from solar eclipses to epileptic attacks. Religion can then be organized like a machine so that it includes the causes of the operations involved and is thus disconnected from the course the world is taking. This results in models of human behavior that are—not coincidentally—understood as circular. The repetition of rituals in Aztec religion is presented as parallel to the cyclical itinerary of the world and as maintaining it. Religious ceremonies can always be set in motion as necessary.[41] What needs to be done is known and can be repeated. Religion thus can function as a cybernetic feedback mechanism, although with the important distinction that it can make itself independent of triggering by environmental events (drought, plagues, and wars). There is the further distinction that it can also lead to overreaction and maladaptation if it trusts too much in the independent logic of its implementing apparatus.[42]

Religions are distinguished by the performance of reentry and the description of transcendence defined by it. Without assistance (or at least reassurance) by transcendent powers, nothing important can be accomplished. That is perhaps the most significant or at least oldest version of religion. Religion is said to motivate magical procedures—not in the sense (one might think) of needing additional empirical causes but rather inasmuch as possible resistances on the other side of the "Great Boundary" have to be eliminated. Magic relies on the simple distinction between visible and invisible things in the same world. It expresses the richness of nature, which extends beyond the visible. It is neither a meta-theory, then, nor a mode of second-order observation, with all the logical problems that would pose. Only the distinction itself, which divides the world into visible/invisible, remains unexplained. The effectual relation remains unknown—which is precisely why it is plausible. It permits no monitoring of errors, nor any cognitive development through learning. Remaining unknown contributes to respect for the holy and also confers authority on those who can credibly cite experience of it. To the extent that rituals are agreed upon, myths associated with them are gathered and recount why people do things they do. In retrospect, this may be taken for a form of naïveté. But naïveté is not the same as error. And there has never been a radical change, not even when a theology arose that by concealing the paradox lost its innocence, thus making the entire world sinful and in need of redemption.

Max Weber, as is well known, formulated the matter with his customary clarity: "The most elementary forms of behavior motivated by religious or magical factors are oriented to *this* world."[43] It is sensible to formulate it this way if one only needs to ward off theological prejudices and be able to describe early eras as also religiously motivated. In Weber's next paragraph, however, there is already a correction that introduces a difference.[44] For not even the everyday world of practical use, of interests, resistances, and dangers could really be experienced in this manner. Weber's characterization of "this-worldly" might also remain a modern reconstruction if the earliest religions had not already peered across the boundary. In his attempt better to understand Weber's understanding of religion, Hartmann Tyrell highlights the same exact distinction: "Social action can thus be called *religious* if there is also a *layer of meaning* in the orientations of the acting person(s) that refers to the 'extra-empirical,' to a meaningful other world—and can be called that if this action in some sense (symbolically at first) 'accounts for' the extra-empirical as it is occurring."[45] Only with this distinction is a reality constituted that needs expanding, and that is precisely where its religious form is found. But in the beginning, this naturally does not mean that the *purposes* of action also have to be directed toward the other-worldly, having to be redemptive purposes. It only means that the world can be experienced as religiously arranged.

In the early versions of religion, other-worldly powers are encountered as arbitrary, moody, vulnerable actors (but in that way also able to be influenced or appeased). They symbolize the way human life is exposed to an environment with uncontrollable effects, and they result from externalizing the problem of an endangered society. One cannot yet speak of a clear, well-formulated distinction of this-worldly and other-worldly. If that distinction is made available in the form of a fundamental exclusion, it is what makes it possible to discipline the world of the gods, mainly by copying onto it socially familiar structures such as family formation, political control, and writing. This development can primarily be seen in the foundations of the archaic-primitive Mesopotamian religion.[46] Even though the gods have writing and use it to determine fate each and every year, there are not yet "holy scriptures" and therefore no abstracting of the reentry that depends on them. Instead, relations to the divine world are regulated by a complex system of rules for divination. Only the later major religions use writing developed in the context of divination in order to fix sacred meaning in sacred form, thus assigning it to a primarily oral type of transmission.

For the moment, these suggestions may suffice to explain our thesis. Religion is characterized from its beginnings (what came before it would not yet be seen as "religion") by a distinction that identifies it and becomes tangible in the distinction's reentry into what is distinguished. The care taken in forming this idea is worth the time spent. Once the reentry takes place, an operation is carried out that (in and of itself) is paradoxical, a paradox that has to be made invisible. The ciphers [*Chiffrierungen*] used in these operations then appear as religion—and appear in all the major religions with the additional knowledge that they themselves are not the essence of what is intended.

We can additionally see that what is being copied into itself is a distinction and remains one. Simplifications take place time and again—and are combated as idolatry.[47] But we would misunderstand the specifics of ancient Egyptian piety, according to which the statues were gods, if we did not see that an incarnated difference was being worshipped. In addition, the theology of St. Augustine does not maintain that God is "the order" [*Ordnung*] and "the good," but that he has to accept the opposite as some kind of fatality in his creation; it maintains that he is specifically interested in the distinction.[48] It is never simply a matter of a (possibly conventional) sign of alterity. Even after the notion of the symbolic is available, it means more than just a sign. The issue is always the real presence of the difference—just as the size and ornamentation of a doorway indicate one is crossing the threshold into another room.

We can only make observations in the realm of the familiar, in a realm that (in contrast to transcendence) can be called immanence. Only here can something be signified, highlighted and—in distinction to everything else—be retained for additional operations. That also means that all the distinctions that can ever be made are immanent distinctions—even those of being and nonbeing, of sacred and profane, of divine and human. These achieve reality only by being communicated. That which all indications and distinctions are distinguished from is left behind as unmarked space. And in unmarked space, world and observer (as the blind spot of his observations) remain behind—unobservable because they are indistinguishable, as already explained.[49]

Religion can be seen as the attempt not simply to accept this inevitability. That is why the world that is observable through distinctions is duplicated and ultimately brought into the strict form of a code whose guiding difference is immanence/transcendence. Coding is nothing but a rewriting of the reality distinction into another form that is more strictly linked and more easily distinguished. It is then adapted to a new kind of experience of the world, making it more compatible with higher contingency. On the one hand, identities are also destabilized in this process. It is now no longer possible, at least in a more demanding form of religious observation, to sort things or events out as sacred/profane. Because now *everything* can be described from the standpoint of transcendence or immanence. And if we want to know how to classify things and events, that depends on the observer we have to observe. Religions are now required to provide criteria, rules, and programs. On the other hand, religion no longer gains a foothold by recognizing things or events, but by making a distinction that is self-contained and that interprets the world. It is thus able to cope with greater "worldly" uncertainties.

What is probably the most distinct caesura in this development is to be found in the religion of the Hebrews, specifically in the form of a resolute refusal to return the other-worldly to the this-worldly. Despite all the inconsistencies of the priestly religion that emerges, the god of the Hebrews has no name.[50] He eludes being known and dealt with by imagining himself as the future that he "will be."* He places himself in the world as a text. That text, which serves as a plan for constructing the world, is revealed to be a two-track tradition, a *written* specification for *oral* transmissions of interpretation that are open to the future. This text replaces all other forms of immanent reentry, especially following the destruction of the Second Temple [in Jerusalem by the Romans in 70 CE]. And the purpose of Talmudic tradition is to preserve the never-ending possibility of interpretation as *controversy*. In cases where decisions become necessary (mainly questions of law), there is a majority principle that cannot be sidetracked by interventions from the other world.[51] In a strict sense, the reentry of the distinction into itself can thus be shifted onto the other side, onto transcendence. A transcendent God is presented as an observer of the world, as a unity of observer and observation. All the sacred things of this world are, in comparison, merely a reflection.

A fully developed coding of religion does not emerge until then, a coding in which both sides of the form reappear (on both sides). The ques-

---

* Luhmann is evidently referring here to God's initial self-designation in Exodus 3:14.—Trans.

tion is no longer whether to divide the world up into realms of visible/invisible, familiar/unfamiliar, close/distant, only assuming that one side of the distinction is not the other. Instead, both values of the code perform a reciprocal production of meaning, thus concluding the religious signification against other codings. Sociologically, this process could be associated with the emergence of cultural elites outside (ascriptively given) social units of families or kin.[52] At the same time, religion becomes instituted both specifically and universally. In its specificity, it is based on the accentuated distinction between transcendent and mundane. In the process, a peculiarity emerges that distinguishes religious coding from other codings. The negative value of transcendence is posited as the basis and source of the coding itself. Transcendence, in producing its code, becomes the opposite of every other distinction. It has to be presumed as devoid of qualities. Even the distinction between distinction and nondistinction is alien to it, as noted by Nicholas of Cusa [1401-1464].[53] In comparison to other codings, this changes the way explanations are formed. In the case of religion, explanations are realized by *including* (not *excluding*) the opposite value—not as truth is realized by excluding untruth but by revaluing all distinctions in a transcendent production of meaning. But that which is set up as transcendence has to be capable of being discriminated, if only as indicating the right path to redemption. That too requires a reentry operation so that it can at least be observed.

There is no other coding that is concentrated this way. Religion's peculiarity consists in the radicality of distinguishing being directed against distinctions. It is the only way we can understand what is essential: *all* observing (all distinguishing, experiencing, acting, communicating) is *always* operating from the standpoint of unobservability, and that is why every return to that standpoint disavows its own specification. As a result, the appearance of religion in history is unavoidably linked to implementing a reentry, even if we can only see at the end that this was how it began.

VII

In religiously inspired communication, concrete objects, events, and actions that implement a religious reentry are not distinguished by this function or described as formally paradoxical. Such forms of observation freeing up contingency were not yet available in the earliest history of society. Instead, they appear somewhat ambivalently—using the threatening/helpful distinction in particular. It is a matter of fine-tunings, which in turn are able to be conditioned. As rituals or highly distinctive objects, they acquire a form that is unmistakable and invariant. We can know that crossing the internal boundary of the form ("either this or the other side") ought to be avoided by the strictness with which this invariance has to be observed (and is sensitive to mistakes). Crossing is not an operation that is possible; it congeals (one might say) into the identity of a sacred object. For now, one is saved from having to name the immanent/transcendent difference that is operating as a code. And in one respect, that will never change: a distinction can't be worshipped.

For now, nothing prevents us from being loyal to form, from repeating the same thing in endless variations. Contents (objects, buildings, rituals) may change, yet the formal typology of transferring ambivalence into identity remains the same. Or that is at least possible. But what can also happen is that questions are asked about the world, about the unity of the distinction that is determined to be identical in the sacred. Major religions only arise when this human tendency to contrive cosmologies prevails. The code appears as a dividing up of the world or also as a temporal dividing of the world making it possible to narrate a story and thus to have transcendence as an origin or meaning of dividing things up into before and after. The "dividing up" (and I am explicitly and deliberately selecting this term for the idea) takes place ontologically, which means in the form of statements about "what exists." It thus occurs in distinction to what does not exist. But this other side of the form of existence fades as long as we are unprepared to doubt the way the world appears to us. And if that happens, then this nothingness that negates the dividing up is transcendence that generates the dividing up of the world (into social classes, for example)—or tolerates it in order to differentiate itself from it.

In the context under discussion, we are not concerned with the history of religion or a theory of its morphogenesis or evolution, but only the phenomenology (if we can call it that) of religion's code. Problems of how to assign things emerge to the extent that the distinction between immanence and transcendence becomes visible as the form of religion. The same goes for every code. For its binary structure does not tell us which value—positive or negative—applies in an individual case. The meaning of coding, in fact, specifically consists in keeping this decision open. For the necessary instructions, each code thus requires a code-specific "supplement."[54] In the ancient world, there were already formulations for these, such as *kanōn, kritērion, regula*. Each term, stressing its own correctness, presumes reference to a binary structure.[55] In such a framework, I shall be speaking of programs (regulations). A mutually exclusive coding of right and wrong can be introduced only when there are legal norms with corresponding institutions (courts) for deciding in individual cases what is what is right and wrong (and not insisting on what is right, as in the case of Orestes or Kleist's Michael Kohlhaas). A teacher can give out good or bad grades only when there is an educational canon in which the requirements are outlined. The code of truth needs theories and methods. The property code, when it has to be translated into financial terms, needs rules of economic calculation (budgets and balances).[56] So if this is generally true, one should not expect anything different with the code of religion.

Yet here as well there is a problem of historical relativity, which cannot be ignored, but at this point cannot be elaborated. In older societies that have not yet completely adapted to functional differentiation, the programmatic level is used to integrate the more abstract extravagance of binary coding back into society. One finds plausibilities reintroduced that develop from the limitations imposed by the structure of society and, most of all, by its hierarchical (stratified) order. The codes themselves are interpreted hierarchically, provided with a natural and normative weighting of their good side. In the legal system, for instance, this happens by way of natural law. There the idea of nature not only refers to normative evidence but also to the fact that humans, as the result of their nature (= birth), belong to different strata. Natural law, even though it deals with purposes, could thus be viewed as participating in what medieval theologians called eternal law [*lex aeterna*].[57] Science has to come to terms with common sense and knowledge handed down. If science tries to break out of this frame, it appears in unscientific form: as paradox. The economy has to respect what in early modernity was still indicated as "domestic necessity," that which was necessary for maintaining the corporative distinction of "houses."[58] These constraints are only suspended in our functionally differentiated modern society. Function systems take over sole responsibility for their function and for the risks associated with abstract coding. Programs are released from the demands of social integration and specifically tailored to each of their codes. Law becomes positive law (which of course does not rule out making reference to moral criteria, practices, technical standards, etc.). Scientific theories are now exclusively scientific theories (which does not exclude them from dealing with theology, etc.). Programs compensate for the exclusion of third values by reincluding what was excluded, even if only on the level of those supplements, which assumes an accepted (not rejected) code. The only issue is how to assign the system's operations to the values of this code correctly.

Religion looks for and finds a possible solution for the evolutionary improbability of its coding by involving itself in an alliance with morality, albeit a precarious one. This alliance may have been facilitated by the fact that morality itself—especially in making negative judgments—was anchored in a cosmology, thus making judgments with unrestrained aversion. Evil (or the evil person) is found near what is ruined, impure, and (either intentionally or unintentionally) harmful—on the dark side of the world, against whose inexplicable power we try to protect ourselves.[59] The good side of morality then ties in with the currently accepted societal conventions. Morality starts to fall back on itself, so to speak, only with the decline of magical ideas in seventeenth- and eighteenth-century Europe.[60] As a consequence, religion itself is finally subordinated to moral judgment and called on to be tolerant and free of fanaticism.

Yet this is only one line of development, and one that triumphs rather late. For a long time, religion itself had trouble linking its code of transcendence with the code of morality. This may have to do with the emergence of significant major religions in the wake of social renewal movements. But even overlooking that history, every religion that makes arguments using transcendence has to ask what the *religious* meaning is of the (earthly) distinction between good and bad behavior—especially given that happiness and suffering do not appear to be distributed according to moral criteria.

In addition, morality has a tendency to direct our attention toward sin. For what is bad is easier to specify than what is good. Rhetoric from the pulpit can more readily articulate what is sinful than spell out what is good. A manual of confession will assemble a list of sins to be avoided. A list of good deeds will invariably have gaps, under circumstances leaving out those are the most important. An index of what is good can provide a pretext for not mentioning something that is crucial here and now. Life offers more chances to be good than can be recited in the form of a list, while the registry of what is bad can be closed but expanded if necessary.

The major religions understand transcendence as an option for the *good* side of human behavior. Those still "wild" religions of tribal societies already had to come to terms with societally accepted norms. They did not, for instance, explain norm violations as having been influenced by magic (which would have meant displacing the attribution of guilt), but accepted as guilty those who were evidently guilty. In the major religions, especially the monotheistic ones, something different is found: a kind of religious self-disciplining in the sense of moral values. The programs used to explain which actions imply transcendence (and which do not) are themselves formulated using the moral coding of "good" and "bad." The transcendent side of the code then takes on personal features so that we can understand that God (or the dominant god in the divine realm) wants what is good.[61] That does not have to lead to the religious acceptance of dominant moral notions, as evidenced by the prophets and their criticisms. But when moral ideas are being criticized, it is in accordance with a different morality that can be confirmed religiously. It might be the morality of covenantal loyalty to God or that of submission to a divine will, which manifests itself in authentic communication and may violate the prevailing familial and clan-oriented morality (such as Abraham's binding of Isaac, in clear contrast to Agamemnon's sacrifice of Iphigenia). Or it is a morality based on the law dictated by God or even a morality of love that respects the freedom of it being accepted or rejected. In tribal religions that receive stimuli from monotheistic major religions but mix them syncretically, the relationship of the high god to morality is for all these reasons still an ambivalent one. This relationship also gets redirected to the rules of dealing with intermediary religious powers or appearances that themselves can be influenced or dissuaded from negative intentions.[62] But there are also other instances where the major religions play moral politics as their institutions attempt to root out tribal and therefore particularistic moral patterns so as to replace them with universalistic ones that can be represented as expressing the divine will. The most impressive example can be found in the Middle Ages, when the politics of morality were facilitated not only by the sacrament of penance (or "confession") and the Church's well-developed legal standing but also by religious orders (such as the Franciscans) that preached directly to the people. The semantic innovations made by this program constituted an individualistic concept of morality directed at internal attitudes or internal agreement with one's own actions.[63] Such an idea is typical evidence that individualization was being used to undermine outmoded social classifications.

On its own, Christian theology might have recognized that morality, which is to say the distinction between good and evil, was something devilish. After all, human beings were not supposed to eat from the Tree of Knowledge. And blasphemy takes its revenge, inasmuch as each time one applies moral notions, one is brought back to the question of which interests and motives are being masked by morality. There is the well-known discussion of whether people would also behave morally "in the dark," or if they only act justly to maintain a good reputation. Alternatively, if theologians had to preach in a societal context permeated by morality, they could hardly avoid taking a position or calling for goodness in the name of God. Any attempt to refrain from judgment would be counterproductive. In that way, even theology becomes a victim of the Fall of Man, and it might comfort itself with the idea that the whole thing is ultimately staged by God, that the serpent was only a figure sent ahead to conceal the ambivalence of morality.

Accordingly, there are symptomatic autonomies in the relationship of religion to morality. These can be read as evidence that a code is being maintained whose values do not readily converge with the "good/bad" coding of conventional morality. First, there is the aforementioned possibility of critique. It has a social substratum in the differentiation of roles and systems (after these have been initiated) between royalty and priesthood, palace and temple. In addition, there is the possibility of prophetic or innovative religious critique within religion, a response to convergences within ruling circles. Second, a final moral valuation is explicitly left open—the paradigmatic figure being Judgment Day—as a sort of transcendental caveat to morality. And lastly, there is the putative problem of theodicy as a mysterious motive of both these distantiations. God apparently permits sin and innocent suffering to exist in the world as evidence that he has achieved self-realization beyond all distinctions. He offers the possibility of producing a reference to transcendence for everything that exists. Or, more concretely, he offers the opportunity to experience everything as a form of his closeness and love, witnessing that he is always accompanying and observing us. Yet that is supplemented by the idea (perhaps difficult to understand in such a light) that he himself opts to do good and not bad.

As an alternative—one repeatedly exposed to moralizing, of course—the Christian religion offers the theme of "sin." The marking of sin as "original sin" indicates that the issue is not guilt but destiny. Above all, however, sin is a temporal status that ends with death and cannot be continued either in heaven or in hell. It is a temporal status (temporal in the sense of *tempus*) to the extent that it is inflicted on people as long as they live, while also giving them an opportunity to take the path of redemption. By comparison, the norms of morality take on more the form of an error to be corrected, in particular making it possible to observe and judge others with respect to their moral violations. The problem thus lies in the social dimension, not the temporal one. This very distinction allows sinners to be observed from the standpoint of guilt. They are either praised or censured in their lifetimes, without knowing what the heavenly response will be. Yet moral judgment can in turn be a type of sin, perhaps even one of the worst cases of it (and this is something priests and theologians clearly don't like to admit).

Theology has had its troubles with this moral paradox. It has turned the reasons for it into divine intentions, in particular allowing freedom to be the culminating point of creation.[64] But it is not difficult to return to the other paradox: that the distinction between good and bad should itself be good and not bad.[65] Seen by an external second-order observer, this paradox can be alternatively resolved by substituting other distinctions in its place. Distinguishing between coding and programming is helpful here. The only reason there is a problem is because religion makes use of morality to assign to society those programs that are essential for interpreting the distinction between immanence and transcendence. Seen this way, religion's deployment of the code of morality (for its part, just a binary code fraught with paradox) is only an intermediate stage by which religion looks for a connection to societally acceptable distinctions. In a society where the code of morality is still uniformly practiced—but where programs of morality, their principles, rules, or solutions to value conflicts, can no longer achieve consensus—morality or religious ethics could therefore be seen as indispensable, even when their anchoring in society comes at the price of religious pluralism. But it might also be the case that the opposite, a move away from moral commitments, would be found more appropriate.

However, as a type of religiously grounded program, morality can fail or at least not be shielded from the (always possible) question of what justifies it and what its (often disastrous) consequences are. If so, what other possible programming of religious coding could there possibly be?

Or is this failure only an example of how religion's form of meaning defeats any determination of principles and criteria, thus allowing the distinction between coding and programming to fail? Another argument for this could be that other function systems are oriented toward continuous change in their programs (their theories, methods, educational criteria, legal regulations, budgets, etc.). Yet religion demands a type of faith that may be diversified as a pluralistic offering of different religions but that nonetheless cannot be put in the form of "today we'll do one thing, tomorrow another."

Such reservations do not mean one has to give up the idea of coding along with the idea of programming. Instead, we ought to ask about other possibilities for enriching the initially empty binary coding with content, thereby providing it with informational value in concrete situations. Here we might consider the possibility that schemas are selected for religious memory that then make it possible to distinguish *themes* and *symbolic contents* of communication—for instance, in understanding destiny as mercy.

VIII

It would surely be wrong to consider binary code simply as an effective cause or an independent variable for explaining the development of religion. As I have repeatedly stressed, evolutionary changes in the societal system (a topic needing separate study) are what determine which semantic provision of the code will enable religious communication to be recognized as such.[66] The dissolving of the coding relation between religion and ethics, for example, presupposes a functioning legal system. (Just as one might assume the opposite: that a renewed merger of religion and morality would mean trouble for a state founded on the rule of law.) In Europe, this medieval-era presupposition was fulfilled both in the domain of civil law and that of common law. It was extended by the "administrative law" originating in seventeenth-century territorial entities and could be used for assuring religious tolerance. By reflecting on societal structure this way, however, we still have not agreed how the code of religion itself might survive if detached from morality.

Giving up the productive difference of a specific code seems to be out of the question. In their closedness ("distinction is perfect continence") as well as their openness toward further determinations (supplements, programs), binary codes are an incentive for morphogenetic processes, which can then be connected. Using a metaphor introduced by Michel Serres, one might speak of "parasitically connected developments."[67] The generating of code-dependent programs dealt with in the previous section is but one example of these. In addition, we ought to consider what kind of decision burdens can be triggered by coding. There are questions searching for an answer (but also answers searching for their question) whenever binary coding becomes visible in the background of dogmatics. There are not only guidelines and texts for clarifying what can be said but also roles and addresses for competently interpreting or simply announcing religious inspiration.

Seen formally, the same problem is found in the code's bivalency, which provides for the exclusion of third values. But the issue here is an artificial (albeit functional) abstraction that does not suffice for societal communication. The code performs an extreme reduction of complexity with the sole function of enabling a more highly complex order to be constructed. Precisely on that account, it serves as an evolutionary "attractor," attracting parasites that are ready to submit to the code's demands and that do not attach themselves as third, fourth, and fifth values, but make use of a need for conditionings—regardless of opportunity or interest. In other words, these make use of the openness of the code's closedness, the need for additional determinations of meaning.

Doing so calls for decisions that can in turn attract parasites. The situation of decisions results from the distinction prestabilized by the code. But the decision itself is not a part of the alternative that has to be decided. If one is deciding whether a certain action corresponds to God's will, leads to salvation, or angers the ancestors, then the decision cannot apply itself as an additional variant to choose from. It remains a parasite—and now in the precise sense of an embedded, excluded third possibility. The question itself is structured for a decision, but the answer cannot simply consist in the self-signifying of the decision, in the decision saying: "I am deciding here for myself." The decision is not allowed to concede its paradox.[68] It must mystify itself, denying having been generated—and this is best done by attributing it to the person deciding. And that puts in motion a process of reinforcing divergences: the person individualizes her decisions, and the decisions individualize the person.

In establishing a binary code (however it is formulated for the present), this inclusion of the excluded third possibility, the assumption that what is absent is present, becomes a permanent problem. Repetitive situations come about, as well as rules that one can fall back on recursively. I referred to them previously as programs. Whenever decisions are being combined, uncertainty is absorbed, so that an earlier decision can be repeated only in the result communicatively transmitted but not in the decision's concrete situation or the considerations leading up to it.[69] The classic form of absorbing uncertainty bears the name of "authority." It allows something to grow—that is to say, complexity. It assumes that we assume it could provide solid reasons for its decisions. But at the same time, it assumes that this assumption does not have to be drawn on (or only in individual cases, and then only demonstratively or symbolically). It operates, in Hegel's appropriate formulation, "without excluding its *opposite*."[70] In this sense, the medieval technique of *quaestiones disputatae* is based on the assumption that authority is available for the *respondeo*. In the history of this form, one can see how the pretense of authority becomes uncertain (starting with William of Ockham), and how the paradox of opinion and counteropinion remains. The Middle Ages were also a time when organizational questions became important, because the absorption of uncertainty now had to be assumed by roles expressly organized for it—whether by Church councils or by the Roman *curia* in the name of the pope. However, that is when a problem typical of modernity arose: authority takes a risk every time it is utilized (something to which the French monarchy fell victim, for example).

Pierre Bourdieu is evidently thinking of similar derivations when he discusses symbolic violence, semantic detachment (*décollage sémantique*), and habitus.[71] His starting point, however, is not the form of the coding but the relationship of society to its economy, a relationship that cannot be disclosed. For that reason, Bourdieu does not reflect on the notion of symbolic violence, on how it is actually an autological concept. It applies to itself, only performed in the act of symbolic violence. Yet we shall have to accept this—which is why a more abstract version of the starting problem is recommended.

In any case, it has to be accepted on faith that a staging of symptoms is created by the parasitism of the code or in semantic detachment. The trace back to the paradox has to be erased (allowing us to open up the trace of that trace's erasure).[72] One can play that game and make do with the distinctions it permits, without seeing that these distinctions make a difference only because the game itself can be distinguished. The distinctions in the game represent the distinction of the game, which in turn can be expanded if reports are allowed to be made about paradox, mystery, the inscrutable will of God, or (directly) of the metaphor of the game.[73] One only has to know when such reports are appropriate, as in explaining death or even its circumstances—but not when the rope breaks with which the coffin is lowered into the grave.

In such cases, however, professional assistance is indispensable for each practitioner of religion. At least the layperson has to be informed by an expert when searching for the right path. Otherwise, he might make a mistake, "as if a man should think to find a way to *Heaven* as to *London*, by the greater track."[74]

IX

If we assume that the immanent/transcendent distinction functions as a binary code in religion, and that it lets us perceive what can (and cannot) be adapted as religious communication, we are struck by a significant discrepancy—perhaps corrupt, misguided, in any case secularized—namely, Kant's transcendental philosophy. In asking what the conditions are of the possibility of experience and in intending to avoid a logical circle in his answer (by not explaining experience in experiential terms), Kant then distinguishes between empirical and transcendental in relation to the operations of consciousness. In semi-ontological terms, a domain of causality can be distinguished from one of freedom. In that domain of freedom, there are sui generis facticities that are self-reflexively accessible to consciousness. In appealing to such facts, Kant attempts to explain conditions of the possibility of perception, of practical action, and of aesthetic judgment without having to resort to empirical contingencies.

Whether or to what extent his attempt succeeded is not the issue here. But it is striking that his undertaking is formulated in the same discourse of ontological metaphysics that he aims to break open. At least on the surface of things, it is not clear that we are talking about a secularization of the code of religion (and that is because for Kant, religion is about matters of faith and not about a primary distinction). However, the parallelism is striking if one defines religion not by the specifics of faith but by its code, the distinction by which it makes the world observable to itself.

The terminological proximity of transcendent/transcendental may not be a coincidence but rather evidence that the problem has been intentionally displaced—intentionally, perhaps, so that observers (like us) could understand it as secularization.

If one adopts this point of view, then some of what manifests itself subsequently is unsurprising. Most of all, there is the embarrassing tendency toward deifying the subject in the era around 1800. Or, looking past Kant and Fichte, one can see the Romantics searching for a new mythology that operates at a distance from reality, represented in part as irony and in part as reflection. The important thing now is written communication, specifically in the medium of print. It allows the problem to be concealed in inadequate formulations, letting us know that the Romantics cannot mean what they say and yet do not have to answer questions about it. That is why they put such a high value on "fragments." Their movement finds its provisional conclusion, its self-determined end, in Hegel's philosophy of the spirit. Or, more precisely, it formulates paradox as an "absolute spirit" that sublates all distinctions in itself—excluding only *exclusion*.

What this philosophy shares with religion and art is the plan of dismantling the world into reality and something besides it (just as later in Wittgenstein's *Tractatus* there is a language for describing the world and a language in which people can only be silent). This is a structure that might interest philosophers and logicians, or even mathematicians such as George Spencer-Brown.[75] A worldly discipline such as sociology is purportedly interested only in realities. But another displacement takes place if one has regrets about the lack of human beings (as bearers of transcendence) in sociological theories.[76] At the end of the secularization chain, there are supposedly deficits in theory, and the history of semantic deteriorations rules out seeing religion as utterly deficient in this point. Religion is clearly a different system, one that is not supposed intervene in academic debates. But if that is assumed, then we need to monitor its form within the system of science and thus be able to reject the distinction by which religion can be recognized as religion when necessary.

Man [*der Mensch*], having been transformed magically into a subject, is a particularly important object for social theorists. But why is that? Merely because we ourselves are the subjects? Or it is because man occupies the position of transcendence from which everything real can be described and explained? And if that is so, how can people in turn be perceived as real? Efforts to resolve this transcendental riddle have taken various paths—from a simple deconstruction of man (in the singular) to a language-analytical philosophy conditioned on linguistics, to a discourse theory that renders man anonymous (reducing him to a process-regulated use of reason), all the way to a theory of the observer as an unseen parasite of his observations. Yet one could, in parallel fashion, make sociology do something quite different. Instead of (or in addition to) deconstructing man by allowing religion—and only religion—to make original observations by means of immanent/transcendent coding, sociology could attempt to reconstruct a religion. One could thus avoid following a simply constructed asymmetry (such as Kant's): the thesis that the conditions of experience might lie in experience itself. One could make sense of the original paradox concealed by this distinction and see the miracles of imagination and creativity that religious communication can perform when attempting to resolve its paradox.

X

Let us now return to the question of just how the positions of the code of religion, the positions of transcendence and immanence, can be occupied. The obvious, most common answer is that the position of transcendence is reserved for God. It is the answer of the major religions to the extent that they allow at all for one God. The other side is occupied by man with all his inadequacies. It is characterized by sin, by the freedom to do evil, by a lack of insight. The difference can be bridged by relations of observation, which will be analyzed more carefully in a later chapter. No matter how inadequate or susceptible to sin he is, man is able to observe how God is observing him.

This schema of occupying positions comes with considerable subsequent costs that cannot be ignored when looking back on the tradition (if one takes the concept of code as a basis). This assignment of positions is burdened with the paradox of the moral code and the problem that God's observational criteria, which man is supposed to follow, cannot be perceived. The (now) classic theme of theodicy strains itself to reflect on this problem but does not go beyond posing it. In addition, God cannot be thought of as transcending every distinction if he is assigned to one and not the other side within the distinction (even if it is the code of religion).

But otherwise transcendence would become the value that includes immanence (as always had to be accepted if transcendence was understood as crossing every boundary, including its own). However, transcendence as the single value of the code cancels out the code in itself, and that is a form of mastering paradoxes also found when one hears that it is good to distinguish between bad and good. The code is operationalized through a reentry of form into form, of the distinction into itself.

The old notion still sustained by transcendental philosophy had been that what was immanently experienced could be explained from the standpoint of transcendence. God is said to have created the world, which would thereby correspond to his will. Putting it differently, the transcendental subject is said to accomplish the syntheses necessary for ordering the world he experiences. The reference to transcendence was able to explain things—and *reassure* us. By contrast, a systems-theoretical analysis makes us see how the world *overwhelms* consciousness and is (in *that* sense) transcendent. Thus understood, the reference to transcendence is not reassuring but *disturbing*. The recourse to elements of tradition, such as a need for redemption or for doubts in faith, can confirm precisely the inverse of this characterization. It clearly does not make much sense to resolve this interpretive conflict by wanting to restrict religion to one of the two viewpoints. Instead, the theory of binary coding encourages a new description of all the elements of tradition. If such a central system-defining, binary-coded distinction exists, the religious system is confronted by a question that cannot be answered: the question of the unity of the distinction. By committing to this (and no other) distinction, the system produces a corresponding unmarked space. And an external observer may still be able to see how a reentry of the distinction into what it distinguishes is clearly capable of producing a diversity of historical semantics of unstable plausibility and "believability." Yet being able to observe this would only be possible in the form of yet another resolution of a paradox. If we see transcendence as a justification, we wind up in an infinite regress when asking what justifies the justification. If we see transcendence as a notion contrary to the operative closedness of systems operating with meaning, it remains equally open what might correspond as a reality to this projection.

Sociology will not be able and will not want to answer these questions. Precisely as an empirical science and precisely in difficult questions of this sort, it relies on society to create the corresponding facts. In this instance, it relies on religion to decide on forms in which to communicate belief propositions. Nonetheless, sociology can present theoretically prepared questions to the reflective authority of the religious system, that is, to theology. It first produces an analysis of codings (which might be pursued with logic and mathematics more extensively than has been done here). Meaningful theological options are thus either restricted or otherwise burdened by having to relinquish their intelligibility. Moreover, studies of semantics and the social structure would be able to validate that an individual finds himself in a radically different situation in modern society than in the societies in which the major religions were developed.[77] The functional differentiation of modern society has left the regulation of societal inclusion to the function systems, thereby relinquishing inclusion that was closely based on stratification and morality. Religion responds here by intensifying our expectations of being convinced, while exempting us from participation. The individual finds himself needing an identity based on a self that has become obscure to itself. He might apply social resonance, love, or career in establishing his identity, but (each time) it will remain a construct grounded in uncertainty. Is it not closer to the truth to say that the individual is transcendent for *himself*? And don't we say this in the more Romantic sense of an ironic (because it is *reflective*) relationship to ourselves, instead of ultimately aiming to assure ourselves of some transcendental a prioris?

It is regarded as wisdom to claim that an individual cannot answer the question "Who am I?" Traditionally, this was a sign of weakness in his immanent existence—his orientation toward self-interest, his lack of insight, his sinfulness. This qualification was dictated by its counterpart of a self-completed transcendence. A different understanding would dictate that the individual himself is transcendence,[78] and he must then rely on committing himself to a continually unstable self-determination. We could understand that the individual experiences in himself the paradox of the unity of a distinction between immanence and transcendence. He may then tend to resolve it by means of externalization or reality-doubling, or by accepting nirvana or the unmediated existence of God. In the process, one loses the possibility of accepting faith based on authority. And one might even say that guilt and sorrow, exclusion and failures of all kinds, make this possibility more plausible than all the confirmations society can offer. Yet then, with or without God, religion would provide the possibility of communicating the unity of immanence and transcendence, a communication confirming for the individual that he might find himself in everything that happens.

In a society that discovers and accepts "subjective" individualism, a fundamental revolutionizing of religion's code appears to be necessary; it is registered on a semantic level as an insurrection (as nihilism, etc.). It is not that the code values of immanence/transcendence have been abandoned and that religion can then no longer be recognized. Rather, the occupying of these values, their connections to the world, becomes inverted. Transcendence is now no longer something far off (to which we can ultimately be indifferent), no longer "up in heaven."[79] It is now to be found in the inscrutability of one's own self, of the "I." This is a problem for Christian dogmatics, with its notion of a personal God. It may thus explain why Buddhism is so attractive at present, for it teaches that everything depends on our casting off daily habits of making distinctions and our returning in meditation to that void on which everything in existence, including one's own self, is ultimately based. (Buddhism thereby refuses the notion of the individual as "subject.") Despite all the problems involved in the persistence of various dogmatic religious positions, what is far away is a less convincing place for transcendence in our modern world. Instead, uncertainty is increasing among those who attempt to experience what they are or what constitutes their "identity."[80]

XI

Our analyses up to this point have stuck to the system reference "society" and disregarded processes of consciousness—in crass distinction to all attempts at explaining religion anthropologically or deriving it from the "needs" of individuals. Even the special coding of specifically religious communication is a social structure for which one cannot readily assume that there are psychic equivalencies. There is no doubting this if we stay within the theoretical framework of autopoietic, operatively closed systems. Yet this analysis can be extended if one asks what the conditions are of the possibility of religious experience, thus switching the system reference and proceeding from systems of consciousness and their neurophysiological substructure.

Consciousness undeniably retains its readiness for conditions of stimulus and surprise. It can also be assumed that the brain generates intensities by repeating bio-electrical stimuli in rapid fashion. Yet these are recorded by consciousness not as a sequence but as intensities, and they somehow have to be interpreted—albeit without falling back on neuronal operations.[81] It can then be asked: where do interpretation, naming, and the ability to distinguish affect come from?

The fact that consciousness replaces a sequence through a unity requiring special qualification assures it autopoietic autonomy in relationship to the brain. At the same time, the fact that this can only happen belatedly (it often, of course, lasts just fractions of a second, such as the famous moment of shock in traffic) tells us that consciousness can only operate belatedly, exposed as it is to "eigenstates" [cf. eigenvalues in chapter 1] that have already occurred and now have to be observed. The same is true when consciousness has learned to count on unexpected irritations, such as being frightened in the dark or approaching strangers with caution. In all such instances, there is a basis or receptivity for assistance in producing meaning, something able to take on very different forms depending on what one might call a "life-world." Typically (especially in the history of society), this requires actualizations in cultic forms that constrain the perceptions of their participants.

In any case, the basis of perception for religious experience is rather amorphous and unspecified, even with respect to religion. To be able to observe its own experiences as religious, consciousness is dependent on externalizations. It has to activate its own perceptions or be able to remember how to define eigenstates by means of other-reference. Here myths can be of service, those listened to when they are narrated (assuming the stories are well known). As narrators and as listeners, our bodies and consciousnesses are part of a complete orchestral staging, so to speak, where our consciousness finds itself involved "rhapsodically."[82] Similar functions are fulfilled by specially prepared objects, places, times, and stagings. These can be marked as holy and, when myths are being narrated, they can enter into a relationship of mutual reinforcement—while also bridging over the distinctions between various media of perception.[83] When such stagings are ritualized, semantic contents are condensed, thereby helping consciousness through perception—but not thinking (!)—to give form to an internal indeterminacy.

These very general remarks still leave open what it is that leads the corresponding experiences to be associated with religion. My thesis is that this association cannot be achieved through a certain regulation of language but only through the binary coding of religion in the schema of immanence and transcendence. On the one hand, this schema has room for the everyday, in which perception recognizes something familiar. On the other, it has meaning for what is unfamiliar within the familiar. It can mark a boundary, thereby indicating that something else is important. Consciousness may find itself fascinated by what is sacred, by what is terror- and awe-inspiring—and stop thinking about anything else. But that is only possible when social communication is reproducing the distinction as a distinction.

We are therefore able to observe that the religious system's coding at the same time serves to couple religion and consciousness structurally. Since each domain carries out very different operations, it does not matter whether consciousness is really experiencing such things in a state of shock or whether it does so in prayer and devotion, or whether it is just pretending. This applies precisely to persons such as preachers, who direct and motivate such involvement. Communication protects itself—if necessary by having a strict form—against the all too many irritations of consciousness. Yet it is exactly the condition for consciousness being able to support itself in externalizations and not having to constantly worry (or suspect) that it is a self-constructed reality, something that only exists if we believe in it. It may thus be fatal if theology teaches us that religion is a question of faith and attempts from that position to convince us.

3

The Function of Religion

I

We have become accustomed to indicating modern society's differentiation with the principle of functional specification. This approach was the basis for both Durkheim's concept of a societal division of labor and Talcott Parsons's analytical decomposition of the "concept/system of action." Even problems of religion in modern society have been discussed in this light.[1] The sole alternative of a class society (still under discussion for a time) is no longer plausible, based as it was on a model of factory organization with a capacity for exploitation. The extent of acceptance for the differentiation thesis, however, should not delude us into thinking that all the essential, central questions have therefore been answered. In particular, it has still never been satisfactorily explained how the differentiation of societal structure—as assumed in the nineteenth century—directly impacted individual behavior according to variables such as consensus/dissent, cooperation/conflict, and problems of anomie (and their consequences for illicit behavior), as well as an increasing dependence on interacting with unfamiliar people who might show one little consideration.[2] If one abandons this premise of a relatively direct connection between macro- and micro-sociological phenomena (or perhaps even that distinction), directly resorting to religion also appears less convincing as a way of addressing problems in life ultimately caused by society.

At this point, we cannot pause to review ideas of differentiation in the nineteenth century in detail. The following discussion limits itself to *system* differentiations, especially the ways modern society distinguishes between function systems. The thesis that functional differentiation is dominant does not of course contradict the existence of other forms of differentiation. Nor can it be denied that there has been progress in dismantling older viewpoints on differentiation (or "de-differentiation"). The thesis that functional differentiation is primary means only that how or where other forms of differentiation (or "de-differentiation") occur is ultimately dependent on society's differentiation into function systems. The only critical question then is: what is actually understood as the function-specific orientation of a subsystem of society? That question has to be settled before we can turn to the more specific one of in what sense religion fulfills a specific function (that is otherwise not relevant anywhere). Then we must also ask whether that is a sufficient basis for distinguishing a particular function system for religion in modern society (if not at an earlier point).

To start with, one has to agree on how the term "function" is being used. This concept is abstracted not only from mathematical applications but also teleological and/or empirical-causal ones. In cases of abstraction, function remains a problem of reference that can assume multiple solutions. Since function would otherwise not be a problem, one can also define it as a unity of the difference between a problem and several functionally equivalent solutions to the problem, regardless of whether one or several solutions are already known. The solution to the problem can consist in fulfilling a purpose or also in concretizing mathematical equations (= variation conditionings) or in finding an answer to a "what" or "how" question. What one strives to gain from functionalization is not a solution to the problem itself. (For it can be solved; indeed, the issue is usually a problem that has been solved already.) Its benefit is instead to indicate *numerous* functionally equivalent solutions, establishing alternativity or functional equivalence. Practically speaking, functionalization can (but does not have to) result in the possibility of substitution. It may also serve as a stimulus to search for other possibilities. And taking a look at the additional possibilities is what makes the question of religion's function so controversial.

Just these few thoughts lead us to two important conclusions. From a functionalistic perspective, everything that can be integrated becomes *contingent*, and everything is exposed to comparison with other options. The abstracting of the problem of reference regulates the range of this modalization, the extent to which (what can still be described as) a functionally equivalent solution to the same problem can vary. An abstraction that is too strong can be counterproductive. One might instead try "reducing the complexity." The second conclusion is that the functional referent becomes recognizable as *resolving a paradox*, specifically the paradox of the sameness (here, the functional equivalence) of what varies. Thus, contingency (i.e., giving up necessity and impossibility = sacrificing stabilities of essence) is apparently the price one has to pay for paradoxization/de-paradoxization. Whoever enters into such a world has to be able to rely on his own operations. He foregoes the certainties that in the past had been presented by the idea of nature.[3]

In the general framework of a theory of observation, there is a basic condition that also applies here: the problem of reference has to be distinguishable, and thus (at least) capable of being lifted out of the unmarked state of the world. The productivity of this technique increases in proportion to its limitations. Only if we ask precise enough questions shall we get answers that are tangibly equivalent. How can something that is far away be known more accurately? Either by going there or by looking at it with a telescope.[4] Yet when this advantage is sought and gained, the distinction in the form of the reference problem invariably becomes clear: one could also be dealing with very different problems.

We have at least figured out that functions are always constructions of an observer. This conclusion brings us to the question: who is the observer when one is asking about religion's function? Whose interest is being regulated by the range of the intended comparison? Which problem of reference is being distinguished, and by whom? Who will dare to take on the paradox, and which distinctions will be activated to resolve it? The question of the function is therefore only a form of the question of the observer and his possibilities for processing contingency and resolving the paradox. And to restate it more strongly: Who is the observer if it is a question of religion's function? Is it the religious system itself, or is science the external observer?

II

As far as coding goes, we had assumed that the guiding distinction of immanence and transcendence (in whatever time-adjusted semantic formulation) is processed in the religious system itself. It helps the system to distinguish religious operations (its *own* operations) from others. It serves as a form of constructing contingency, and as a form that can serve as a starting situation for resolving paradoxes—all this for the religious system itself. For the contingency formula of function, the opposite applies. This formula serves to open up functionally equivalent solutions to a problem. It generates alternatives, thus serving to break apart the established religious forms. Even on a concrete level, it is difficult to accept opening up to alternatives. To be sure, one can ask: If wine and bread are not available, why not malt beer and bananas? Yet it would first have to be determined which problem is being solved here, since one might otherwise lose sight of all limitations. This problem is being posed all the more whenever the question of religion's function is abstracted so that functional equivalents (such as narcotics) become visible and cannot be adapted to the religious system itself (or only in very specific settings such as in Native American mushroom sects).

To be able to make the most out the contingency formula of the function question, one has to be able to take the position of an external observer. One can then adhere to the distinction of manifest and latent functions. *Manifest* here means accessible to the observed system itself; *latent* means inaccessible to the system.[5] Although the question of latent functions glosses over the self-understanding of the system being studied, it is associated with the limits of every functionalistic formulation of the question. It does not explain why something is the way it is (and not different). It is also incapable of justifying any faith, instead exposing all assumptions to comparison.[6] That does not change when we distinguish between manifest and latent functions. Evidently, this is also a distinction made by an observer, a distinction on the level of observing observers—and thus a distinguishing that must ask itself what (latent?) interest motivates distinction in just this way and not some other. We should not rule out the possibility of this distinction. But in the following, the insight will suffice (as a starting point) that, in the case of the religious system, we are dealing with a system observing itself. In addition, our question about its function cannot easily be copied onto that system.

Another preliminary decision concerns the question of whether one should be talking about a single function or several functions of religion. In sociology, it is customary to put together entire lists of functions when discussing function systems such as the law, the economy, politics, the family, and religion. This can be done since the distinction schema of problem/solution can be applied in a large variety of ways. One can thus see it as a function of religion to provide comfort, to soothe fears, to answer questions of meaning plausibly, and to generate community by ritual activities or activities confirming faith. All that and more. Nonetheless, the unity of religion is then reduced to the unity of such a list. The large variety of functional equivalents breaks apart anything that could still be considered religion's core function. And the question of whether the unity of the list is a religious unity therefore ought to be answered this way: the function of religion is to manufacture the unity of the list of religious functions. Or at this point, one does without specifying a super-function and focuses instead on religious "meaning."

Finally (and especially): to assume a multiplicity of functions would collide with the notion that modern society directs its forms of differentiation at specific functions. For that is to assume that a function's unity (however it is subdivided) conforms to the system's unity. If there were multiple religious functions that could not be pursued back to a basic function, it would be hard to know what made this conglomeration recognizable as *religion*. Although there are different religions within the system of religion, their differentiation follows more the principle of segmentation than the principle of functional differentiation. I shall therefore make use of the external observer's distance to ask what *the* basic function of religion is.

Based on that assumption, one has only limited possibilities from which to choose. Hardly anyone today accepts Durkheim's thesis that religion's function is to generate solidarity and integrate morality.[7] On the contrary, religion is one of the highest-ranking sources of conflict, and not only in modern society. Perhaps the thesis holds for tribal societies that repress conflict. Yet if that were the case, the very specifying of a function, along with the intensification of religious experience and communication typical of it, would sabotage religion's integrative function. Even René Girard's account—in which religion regulates a mimetic conflict by means of prohibitions and sacrifices (on which rejection can focus)—neglects correlatives in social structure.[8] Girard particularly neglects the effects of stratification as an institution that interrupts the comparability of life situations and needs while also producing indifference. A need for sacrifices, which God requires and ultimately carries out in exemplary fashion on *himself*, can easily be documented. But as an indication of religion's function, such things actually only suggest that God ordains distinctions without which nothing can be legitimated, signified, or observed. And that is even more striking when God demands *innocent* victims: Isaac, Iphigenia, and finally his own son. It should not be a simple consequence of guilt, a simple execution of the law.

The keyword "distinction" brings us back to our starting reflections on meaning and the observation of forms. In the medium of meaning, there is no "nature" and no "essence." And there are no boundaries that cannot be crossed (for otherwise they would have no meaning as boundaries, as indications of something else). Instead, there are only horizons that move along with every movement. And meaning can only be defined self-referentially in recursive connections that refer to other things, and always to the unmarked state of the world, thus passing into instability. Identities materialize by the repetition of operations. At the same time, they are the structure by which repetition recognizes itself as repetition. In short, meaning is "autopoietically" constituted by systems that can only recognize their own boundaries in the process of constituting meaning by providing *themselves* with inward and outward referents, their *own* distinction of self- and other-reference. Each observing operation draws a distinction and is distinguished by performing the distinguishing. It is thereby observable to other observations, however, in which the same thing applies. There is always another side being included that has to be designated as incapable of connection. Even if one accepts the idea that observations can provide themselves with "intentionality" (to Husserl, a necessary condition, without which consciousness would be unable to process itself), the other side of intention—that is, the distinction of intention, its intentionality—still remains undefined.

Religion always seems to be present whenever these guidelines become a problem, when one is unable to remain in the dark about why everything is not the way one would like it to be.[9] This is what the individual cannot figure out through self-reflection, since it contradicts his self-awareness. The reason has to be given to him, along with the presentation of the problem through communication. (To Hegel, this would mean through the concept of the concept.)

Ontological metaphysics had treated the ability of propositions to be true as presupposing a defined being (and not only the clarity and distinctiveness of ideas) ever since Aristotle's description.[10] Based on its form, this led to the necessity of an external guideline. And even Husserl (though bracketing out the question of being) had still accepted that every indeterminacy posited as a horizon could be traced back to the *"determinability of a fixed predetermined style."* And, in fact, how else could one move from one operation to the next if one were unable to determine it completing the transition? At the same time, though, even what had been determined returns to indeterminacy again: "in the inverse direction, what is clear, of course, passes into unclarity, the represented into the unrepresented, etc. *In this manner, to be imperfect* in infinitum *is part of the essence that cannot be sublated, of the correlation between thing and thing-perception.*"[11]

We might suspect things are this way because this description is also based on the distinction between self-reference (thing-perception, *noēsis*) and other-reference (thing, *noēma*). This distinction has been introduced as a transcendental fact, the result of consciousness analyzing itself. George Spencer-Brown's calculus of forms approaches the same problem differently. He begins with a directive: "Draw a distinction." This directive can be understood as a condition making possible the autopoiesis of producing meaning.[12] There is nothing in being or in nature, however, compelling us to follow the directive. Every operation is contingent in the twofold sense of "being possible in a different way" and "dependent on following this directive." There is no necessity involved, but there is a sanction:[13] nothing will happen if the directive is not followed. Autopoiesis either does not begin or will not continue. The directive is just as severe as the autopoiesis of producing systems: either it happens or it doesn't. There is no third, no "weaker" possibility.

What ought to occur to us is that the directive has the same severity as a code, the same binary structure, the same exclusion of third possibilities. Coding is apparently one "version" of a problem that one can call either indeterminability, self-referential recursivity, or unobservability of the world (or of observing in the world). Or, to use a formulation closer to religion: it is a problem of the "void." That code—and (for now) every code—appears to be a form that reformulates the problem of form. It gives a different, more serviceable form to the twofold problem and internal asymmetry of the signifying distinction (observation). At the same time, the built-in contingency and the possibility of paradoxizing/resolving paradoxes survive by applying the code to itself. And likewise, the severity of the starting signal of autopoiesis applies: if it's not going to happen, it won't. But the code simultaneously gives the problem of form a more specific formulation and thus a formulation to which transjunctional operations can be exposed (i.e., accepted or rejected).[14] One could thus speak of a "formulation" [*Fassung*] of the problem of form, perhaps even of a "frame" in Erving Goffman's sense.[15]

The advantage we gain in relation to the initial problem (which we could also call the "function" of coding), is found in the specification of operations that are capable of connection with the positive value of the code. The yes/no code of language only lets us speak (or possibly write), money only lets us pay, truth only lets us produce cognitive structures, and so forth. But the advantage we gain has to be worked out by the code's distinction, by those transjunctional operations that in turn must result from the "unmarked state" of the world.[16] In this respect, therefore, the various codes of the various function systems are functionally equivalent. They each produce their own contingencies, their own paradoxes, their own programs or additional supplements. They serve as guiding distinctions for the recursive reproduction of special (social) function systems and thereby differentiate society into respective system/environment relations that maintain their own boundaries.

This analysis opens up some wide-ranging perspectives. It interprets the theorem of "functional differentiation," of a possible description for modern society. It says that all function systems have a direct relationship to society. That would also apply to the religious system—no differently than to others. One could paraphrase this by saying that modern society can be characterized by the primacy of functional differentiation. And that would harmonize with a description of modern society as a secularized society where religion is clearly present (and perhaps even with an intensity or with demands absent from older societal formations—or perhaps only linked to asceticism, that "taking leave" of society). Yet in such a society, *religion is no longer a necessary mediating instance producing a relationship of all societal activities to a total meaning.* The old thesis that religion serves societal integration can thus hardly be seen as valid. Instead, the opposite could be true (at least for mainstream forms of religion): religion itself is dependent on a high degree of societal integration.[17] All function systems find in their own functioning the meaning of their contribution to the autopoiesis of society. They do not need religion *for that.* They develop their own resolutions to their own formal paradoxes, and they can adjust themselves to their own temporal contingencies, which no longer have to be synchronized throughout society. If a religious production of meaning is nonetheless conveyed along with it, it has the appearance of inflating meaning, which is unnecessary and technically not very helpful.[18] The questionable and disputed notion of "secularization" can then be defined through functional differentiation.[19]

If we want to provide a function for religion that can also be sustained in a society of this format, we have to say more precisely what the specifics are of religion's special coding. Or, put differently, just what is it about (recognizably religious) connecting operations that, when they are linked in a recursive, sequential network, differentiate a system that is (itself) recognizable as religion? The distinction of the two code values as immanence and transcendence provides some decisive clues that now require a more precise elaboration.[20]

The ambition of religious coding appears to move in the direction of juxtaposing every distinction that can be used in observation (recognition, imagination, action, etc.) with its countervalue of transcendence. Thus, formulas are used such as "everything is ultimately nothingness" or "everything ultimately has to be accepted as God's will." But the code itself is in fact a distinction. If this is where the problem of reference of the religious function is found, it would resolve the paradox of the unity of the code. One would have to say that religious meaning refers to the unity of the difference between immanence and transcendence. Approximating the theology of Nicholas of Cusa, one would have to accept: (1) that God himself is not subject to any distinctions, because he does not need any; (2) that God does not distinguish between himself and the world, as a result taking the burden of sin upon himself; and (3) that he does not produce any self-referential relationship to himself, because to do so, he would have to distinguish between self- and other-reference. Whether that could be a theology suitable for the quotidian or if people would be served better by [the concept of] nirvana is an open question. Nonetheless, it is remarkable that the paradox still appears of a unity of what is valued differently by the code, and that *it is resolved through the negative value of the code, through the reflective value, and through transcendence.* It is remarkable because other codes use their positive value for this last possible operation. They say that it is good to distinguish between good and bad, and that it is a logical or methodological truth that one has to distinguish between the values *true* and *untrue,* and so forth.

There has to be a latent connection between the reentry of the distinction between immanence and transcendence into the immanent (that is, the sacred) and the notion of an entirely undifferentiated transcendence that absorbs every distinction (even that of immanence and transcendence). This notion is the acceptance of a shapeless, formless ultimate meaning that cannot be signified adequately as a "person" or as "nothingness." If this were accurate, the code would be "bistable," even in the resolution of its paradox, and the societal evolution of religion could be seen as shifting its focus from one possibility to the other, thus desacralizing religion.

These considerations are already concerned with the reach of a semantic *structure* of the religious. At this point, the question of religion's *function* can be addressed. Depending on how one prefers to formulate the initial problem of the indeterminability of all self-referentially operating applications of meaning, religion is not only related to this problem but in particular offers solutions to it. Religion guarantees the determinability of all meaning against the accompanying experience of constantly referring to the indeterminable. In older societies, the irreversibility of the past could be used in this way, allowing religion to be comprehended as memory.[21] This situation, however, changes if theological reflection is involved. It allows paradoxes to enter into communication precisely because a unity (which could not be formulated differently) can then be symbolized. Such reflection inserts *ciphers* [Chiffren] into the process of transforming the indeterminable into the determinable, such as the assumption of a "will" or a divine decision. The result is that human beings have to take a position on it.[22]

A theology that shifts from memory to will at this point replaces certainty with uncertainty. However, it offers the certainty that everything that happens, that is done with conviction, is subject to a transcendental secondary valuation, making possible the self-acceptance of actions and experiences. Formulations of this kind can be varied in multiple ways and brought closer to the propositional possibilities of certain historical religions. Yet that does not need to happen at this time. For the moment, it suffices to show there is a possibility of religion being able to maintain itself as irreducible in the context of transjunctional operations, in the context of society's functional differentiation.

The form in which this problem of open self-reference becomes relevant for communication in the medium of meaning depends on the structures of the societal system [*Gesellschaftssystem*], on societal evolution. When there is increasing structural complexity, when decisions and decision dependencies (e.g., of a political type)[23] are increasingly visible, and when newly discovered communication technologies (particularly printing and books) are beginning to be influential, there is an expansion in the openness of referential horizons that have to be considered in communication. Writing presupposes meaning, a unity of actuality and virtuality. But it also enables an immense expansion of a co-functioning virtuality, even if it is based on an anchoring always experienced as present. Assumptions on the essence of things, or their nature, or immutable ideas lose their plausibility as protecting against the intrusions of other possibilities. Religion becomes correspondingly more difficult and more reflective. As in other functional realms of society, structures have to be extended in view of their functions. Yet at the same time, they have to be applicable in both more specific and more universal ways. If these things succeed, a differentiation of religion directed toward its function can occur. It is capable of satisfying greater demands in assuring meaning, even in a "secularized" societal context—and even if only in the form of a church-organized activity of decisions and interpretations or in those pluralistically tolerated oddities recognizable as religion. For whenever too much seems to be expected, things still work out somehow.

III

In these reflections on the function of religion, analysis of the medium of meaning has at this point broken down. Nothing preoccupied with meaning can exclude the ability to be negated. And more fundamentally: whoever is observing has to use a distinction and should not at the same time assume the sameness of the distinguished. The affirmation/negation distinction (the being/non-being of ontological metaphysics) is merely one case where this notion is applied. Hence, every claim that meaning can be freed of distinction (a meaning that could not be negated, for instance) amounts to a paradox. A meaning is being asserted that cannot exist in the medium of meaning. That medium serves only to enable formations of form (meaning *distinctions*) in which the medium/form distinction in turn conforms to its own laws. Even this distinction is a self-containing form that can only be understood paradoxically.

This result can be confirmed by a second approach to the problem. Here the historical frame of reference has to be restricted a great deal more than when we were analyzing the coding of the religious system. By the second half of the nineteenth century, a semantic problem had been formulated where reference is made to what a subject thinks is meaningful. This approach assumes that the universal medium of meaning, which no one can elude, is structured by the meaningful/meaningless distinction. It is still possible to cross the inner boundary of this distinction, meaning to think or say that something is "meaningless." But then there is the problem of who is using this distinction and who is defining the categories by which the world is being divided into meaningful and meaningless. One is confronted once again with the problem of the observer.

The classical answer—that the observer is the subject—is only satisfying if one ascribes some kind of transcendental similarity to all subjects. But it is hardly possible to do so if one thinks of the subject as a human individual. Not even a residue [*Restmenge*] ("remainder" [*Rest*] being a fashionable notion at present) can be perceived by which the same thing is meaningful to all people. Theories have reacted to these doubts about pure subjectivity by shifting the common ground to the mechanism of how meaningful meaning is produced. It cannot simply be autobiography or some freely chosen self-thematization. Rather, according to this thesis, what is meaningful as meaning is formed in social situations of a certain kind.

René Girard's theory of mimetic conflict has already been mentioned several times.[24] Something has meaning if others are also striving for it. In a finite world, this results in a paradoxical conflict with what one is imitating. Religion offers a solution in designating a sacrifice that can be agreed upon—in a way that ultimately cannot be outbid: the sacrificial death of God and the associated mythology of a redemptive resurrection.

Pierre Bourdieu sees the social transmission of the search for meaning in a need to make distinctions that is social but manifested in objects.[25] Art, education, linguistic capacity, and other signals of status are meaningful, and their meaning is to achieve distinction vis-à-vis others. In the process, an order in the form of birth order is copied once again, and the appearance is reproduced that society is somehow hierarchically ordered. Just as in Girard's sacrificial choice, this operation only works when the distinctions are understood, and there is agreement on how to interpret their signals, as opposed to the superficial meaning initially attached to things.

In comparing these very different theories, it is particularly striking that the analysis moves in the direction of a need for redemption that is not included in the theory itself. Instead, it functions as a type of "supplement" (in Derrida's sense) that examines factually (but latently) what the theory wants to say. In the case of Girard, this problem culminates in a Christian-religious solution, however unacceptable the theory might be to theologians. In the case of Bourdieu, redemption would proceed via a social critique of a kind customary in sociology. In both cases, the need for redemption and the path it takes remain latent because the theory itself cannot decide on professing a religion or envisioning a completely different society. The way out lies in a performative self-contradiction that must ultimately end with the meaningful/meaningless distinction being deconstructed.

We might condense this argument by noting that those everyday or scientific theories that speak of meaningful and meaningless meaning have to assume that the meaningful/meaningless distinction itself is meaningful—and also have to apply it to themselves. Doing so, however, leads to an inexorable infinite regress of justifications. Or if one gives up that approach (and thereby all justifications), one is led to the paradoxical figure of the reentry of a distinction into itself. Or one returns to the idea that subjects create meaning, which only results in multiplying the problem a billion times without any perceptible order. Once again one finds oneself (while using linguistic forms that, for some sociologists and theologians, could be more plausible than those of coding) confronted by the problem of which distinctions can be introduced into the universal, non-negatable medium of meaning. These then generate additional distinctions through the in-between form of the unity of the distinguished, something that can only be formulated paradoxically. And at this point, one finds oneself once again looking for the function of religion, which evidently claims to be able to formulate this.

Paradoxes—and this has to be emphasized time and again—are not barriers to communication. On the contrary, they can be formulated. They even have a high level of expressive content. They express something astounding because they make us wonder. Older societies in particular have a tendency to signify totality by an internal antithesis: heaven and earth, the largest and smallest, everywhere and nowhere, urban and rural—all the way to court and country. The conjunction "and" prohibits taking this for a logical error or (as in the paradoxes of rhetorical literature) as a joke. And how is one supposed to express differently an encompassing "allness" that leaves out nothing and has no boundaries?

Of course, the question poses itself of what can be done with such paradoxes. It is not a problem to be solved by means of logic. Nor is it a problem whose solution could be calculated. For the problem/solution distinction would be sublated in that case, and both the problem and its solution would disappear. Instead, within the idea of "resolving" the paradox (including the paradox resolved as a tautology), there is a moment that is creative and produces information. A decision is necessary here, as religions have repeatedly emphasized, and decisions can only be made (to articulate this paradoxically) about what is in principle undecidable.[26]

We can even put it this way: paradoxes are the only form in which knowledge is given *unconditionally*. They take the place of the transcendental subject whom Kant and his successors expected to have direct access to a knowledge that is unconditional, a priori valid, and insightful in and of itself. However, even after relinquishing this figure, the unconditional/conditional distinction remains. But one has to resolve this paradox, replace it by a distinction, to be able to introduce conditionings that regulate the conditions under which one side and not the other can be used, in which truth (and not untruth) is valid, for instance. When one foregoes the transcendental subject, the idea also falls away that a priori valid knowledge is a higher-level knowledge that can substantiate other knowledge. On the contrary, one will have to assume that knowledge that is useful (i.e., capable of connection) is always conditioned knowledge,[27] and that the gain in knowledge is found in the construction of complexly conditioned systems—and hence in paradox resolutions that have to be paid for with contingency.

That conclusion does not by any means exclude questions about typical structures in which paradox resolutions gain relatively stable forms which are historically preserved and which then guide further communication as eigenvalues of the religious system. No religious semantics looking for plausibility in this context of paradox resolution can claim exclusive validity. That is precisely why (though it is not a compelling requirement) it can claim authority on the level of communication and attempt to impose exclusivity.[28] Yet above all, in light of our starting problem, there are semantic inventions that are more or less convincing. Thus, the dogma of the creation of the world by God can be assigned various paradoxes, thereby achieving a peculiar stability of meaning. On the one hand, it clarifies the problem of the unity of multiplicity. God is a unity that does not rule out multiplicity, but rather produces it or lets it emanate. At the same time, a temporal problem emerges, a problem of the beginning. When interpreted, it can be addressed as creation. Reexamined from the human situation, it must inevitably be asked: what came before the beginning? The idea that God created the world fills up this empty space: before the beginning of the world, there was God, and he is also that observer capable of distinguishing before and after the beginning of the world. That in turn calls for accepting him as a self-observer (and not simply as an emanative essence) and limiting theology by this postulate. One can then go a step further and say that time itself (as *tempus*) only emerged with creation. The before/after problem can thus be converted (as in St. Augustine) to a problem of levels à la *aeternitas/tempus*. At the same time, one can understand that the worldless eternity of God persists during worldly time. And, if nothing else, the dogma of the creation has the practical communicative advantage that it can be narrated and can take the listener or reader from one thing to the next, making it possible to experience and implement the paradoxical starting distinction as a transition. One can alternatively imagine a world without beginning or end (though that assumes that one already knows what the alternative is being directed *against*.) But then one has the resulting problem of having to mark beginnings and endings within this world—such as the beginning of the human race.

Referring to the problem of paradox and its resolution can clarify the evolutionary success story of certain ideas (as opposed to others). But not all questions can be clarified by a single idea. When there is an interest in consistency, as in the wake of written determinations, there can also be derivative paradoxes or even a long-winded (but form-seeking) dialogue between assertions and critiques of religion. In the case of Christianity, a religion of faith with a highly developed dogmatics, one sees particularly well how the strategies of resolution—and those theological disputes associated with them—are differentiated depending on the dimension of meaning into which the problem of evidence has been transmitted.

We distinguish social, temporal, and factual dimensions of meaning.[29] In the *social* dimension, the confirmation of faith is sought and found in the *encounter* with God. The dogma of a god become flesh makes it possible to retain the transcendence/immanence distinction, but leaves us with the problem of how one can infer God from the encounter with Jesus.[30] This problem can be explicated by distinguishing Father and Son, but only by way of a (difficult to repress) paradox that the father is hence his own son and the son his own father. The transcendent God is to be thought of as indistinguishable but also, in the form of Christ, as distinguishable. As God the Creator, he is independent of his creatures, although his love can only be thought of as making him dependent upon his creatures. In the *temporal dimension*, a supplemental problem is the thesis of revelation's *historical uniqueness*, of the distinction between time and history, along with the possibility of marking privileged (and unrepeatable) points of time. This is the case even if God is supposed to be thought of as being both omnipresent and at all moments simultaneous. Finally, in the *factual dimension* of meaning, the problem is shifted back onto a necessary linkage of *unity* and *complexity*, God and world, religion and cosmology. Commonly, this linkage is not presented as a structural paradox (a unity of the complex) but as an explanatory paradox. The logic of the explanation requires a component that explains itself. (Otherwise, there would be infinite regress.) The miracle of a nicely ordered world can only be explained—and the resilience of its continued existence only perceived—by reference to a superior creator who is based in himself. The resulting problem is that other explanatory hypotheses can appear, particularly evolutionary theory (since the nineteenth century). And if nothing else, this solution of the factual problem of order makes it seem uncertain how God for purposes of encounters can be thought of as personalized.

This entire framework of a religious positing of the world is highly plausible—especially since it separates dimensions of meaning and mirrors them in one another. (An encounter requires historical uniqueness, and uniqueness requires a framing cosmology.)[31] However, under the societally given conditions of written culture, a demand for consistency emerges. It is dealt with in the Talmudic context by enabling *oral* interpretation and religiously legitimized *dissent*. In a Christian context, though, the demand for consistency leads persistently to consolidations, conflicts about dogma, and finally schisms. The starting paradox, concealed by its supplements, returns to the system and is no longer recognizable.

A dogmatic determining of the premises of "correct" religious faith enables—in fact, forces—a distinction to be made between believers and nonbelievers. The paradox on which it is based drifts into this distinction. One can now ask what "the same" is in believers' and nonbelievers' attitudes toward religion. This may suggest a general concept of the religious and encourage criticism of the religious content of how forms are established. Christian churches and sects have reacted to this distinction with missionary efforts, and when those possibilities appear to be exhausted, with reflections on the "crisis of the Church." All the same, it is difficult to understand in religious terms why the "correct" faith is not being accepted. The problem can really only be displaced into a future that is still undetermined, and in which the Lord will reveal himself. Besides, orthodoxy's burden of displacing paradox (into the relationship of believers with nonbelievers) endangers those religions that take such a path. For they have to sense increasingly that there are no longer nonreligious reasons to profess a religion these days.

All these considerations suggest that religion is concerned with problems of meaning as problems of resolving paradoxes. Once a religious system in society is functionally differentiated, this is the problem of reference. To be sure, paradoxes can be generated in the most diverse manner: as a rhetorical form of joking, as a way to demolish logical systems, as a symbolic form of expressing ineffability, as an argument for differentiating levels, as an argument for or against certain types of metaphysics, or as a mystification of decisions (and of the decision-maker!). And all binary codes can be "re-paradoxized" when one asks about their unity. Hence, one cannot expect that all semantic material referring to paradox will be allocated or even systematized in terms of religion. In modified form, this would only be a new version of the (older) thesis that society ultimately has religious foundations. The formula that "problems of meaning are problems of paradox resolution" has to be understood more tightly and precisely. Seen in terms of systems theory, we are talking about how the operative closing of (psychic or social) systems is made possible, as these operate in the medium of meaning and are thus dependent on self- or other-referential observation. *Operatively* closed systems are systems that are open in their *manner of observation*. They establish their self-reference by inevitably distinguishing themselves from something else. Meaning is the medium that makes possible this way of developing forms, the development of forms by distinction. If problems then ensue, they assume (for the system's mode of observation) forms that have congealed as religion, as a semantics that can be handed down.

IV

Religion is not simply the solution of a problem that concerns logic, but that it cannot deal with. Paradoxes do not exist in advance of all observable activity. They are produced on occasion—and then resolved again. The medium of meaning provides this possibility. It cannot annihilate the possibility, since the medium itself is based on a distinction whose unity one can ask about. Religion is the paradigmatic way to carry out paradoxization/de-paradoxization whenever such an occasion offers itself. In no way is religion responsible for meaning per se. Were that the case, the result would be a thorough impoverishment of the world, robbing religion of its universalistic claim to have specific foundations in observable forms. Yet religion is responsible for the problem of constituting meaning, for providing meaning with a new foundation whenever a detour is taken via paradox.

This thesis should now be illustrated using the example of the adulteress described in the Gospel of John (8:1–11). One has to assume that the Mosaic law of stoning all adulteresses had lost credibility at this point but could not be amended because it is religiously grounded. The Pharisees and the Scribes confront Jesus with this problem. Jesus bends down and writes (a new law that the others cannot read?).[32] He then declares the new law that will prompt others to move away. "Whoever among you is without sin, let him cast the first stone." And even this is written in invisible script. But why does it read "among you" and not "among us"? Jesus himself, if he had wanted to implement the new law and have it recognized as an addition to the Mosaic one, would have had to throw the first stone himself. The new law in the Mosaic context is not applied as a modification but as a break with the old law. Or it is providing a self-exemption for the lawgiver, with the help of a constitutive asymmetry. Yet precisely that, this first rupture, this first distinction, cannot be communicated. Consequently, the document becomes unreadable. And the paradox of the process can only be recognized in being reported on by a second document, the Holy Scripture. But then one already has to believe, within the complete narrative context of the Holy Scripture, that this report is evidence of God's impact in this world.

Reformulated in Spencer-Brown's terminology, this first distinction implies and conceals an "unwritten cross."[33] For every distinction that in-

stalls itself as a form with two sides, in order to enable discriminating significations on the one side (but not the other), creates at the same time a
beyond, an additional unmarked space, from which the first distinction is
introduced—even if it is the distinction of marked/unmarked.

What we see now is that the first distinction is in no way a matter of
the distant past. It is not like a coincidence that sets an evolution in motion and thus loses its meaning because it is replaced by history. Rather,
every meaning can provide an occasion for invoking the paradox and replacing it by one or other distinction (here, the distinction between being
with sin or without sin). The paradox is made invisible by generating criteria. And in the Christian context, sin is the central notion of cosmology,
referring to the first distinction of prohibition and transgression.

V

Here commentary is called for on the range of our analyses of religion's function—in other words, the system reference. Normally, if religion
is at all interpreted functionally, it is traced back to deep-seated human
needs. I do not think this is a productive point of departure. One reason
is that such needs cannot easily be determined independently of religious
suggestions. Another reason, however, is that the needs ascribed to "humanity" vary from person to person and are not at all present in many (or
even *most*) people. It is often said that when people are in distress, they
turn to religion. But even that is in no way always the case. Moreover, it
is a feeble argument if one is trying to determine the function of religion.

If we are empirically serious about individuals, anthropological generalizations get us into trouble. It was not for nothing that Kant found it
necessary to distinguish between transcendental and empirical arguments.
It is thus best not to resort to anthropological arguments concerning religion's function. This is obviously not to dispute the actual incidence of
deep religious commitments, experiences, and motivations. But when this
is asserted as fact, it ought to be specified who (name and address!) is involved. But then it would hardly be worth it to concentrate religious research on such exempla—unless we see in them a relevance that is social
and mediated by communication.

We are thus taking also the system reference "society" as a basis for
determining religion's function. Whatever religion may mean in the con-

sciousness or body of individuals, all that counts for society is what happens
in the recursive network of communication reproducing communication.
In the matter under discussion, we are constantly dealing with religious
communication. The previous mapped problem of meaning is being raised
with particular acuity here. Organic systems are alive, and consciousness
systems can hold onto the perceptions they are able to process to the greatest possible extent. This provides them with direct evidence of the world—
at least as a framework for resolving doubts. Consciousness can also operate
very erratically, latching on here, latching on there. It has a great tolerance
for inconsistency, because its own identity is sufficiently guaranteed by its
own perceptible body (and its performance of externalization). All that
is different in the case of communication. Communication cannot perceive, and for that reason alone it is dependent on a high level of coherence among contexts of meaning. In addition, if communication is to be
continued, more than one consciousness must continue participating in it.
This progression can be transmitted by consensus or interested disagree-
ment, but it assumes sufficient understanding all the same. And understanding is only "local," only achieved when the specific relevant context is
strongly restricted. The progression of communication to communication
still has to remain plausible—or it must be bridged with marked changes
of topics or partners. As a result, the tolerance for inconsistencies in a communication system is much lower than that of an individual consciousness
system. And that applies again in a reinforced manner when dealing with
written communication. Quite dramatic evidence for this is found in the
Middle Ages, in the difficulty of keeping the extravagancies of written theology under control (i.e., by means of law, representation, organization).
Its well-known consequence was schism, differentiating confessions and
church systems.

And problems of closure become all the more relevant—whether it is
closing a communication system in society by restricting the meanings that
can be determined *for it*, or by shifting its coding (as in the case of morality) or by establishing indifference through all kinds of "assurances." There
are both social-structural and semantic means available for accomplish-
ing this. Society makes use both of system differentiation (the repetition
of the system/environment differentiation in society) and of condensing
and confirming recyclable meaning (meaning worth *preserving*). But each
of these solutions, social-structural or semantic, produces new forms, new

restrictions, new boundaries—as well as new vistas on the other side of the form. Whatever has been excluded is always co-present [*appräsentiert*]. What is unusual or operatively not capable of connection is communicated along with it. And one cannot be sure if the communication is not somehow, at some time, crossing boundaries.

To provide forms for communication that are still possible in *this* context is a matter for religion at the level of society.[34] As has been known for a long time in the sociology of religion, this can take place in ways that are either "religioid" or "religious."[35] For this special function, however, one can again apply the universal modes of assuring the capacity for connection—one can form subsystems, and condense/confirm meaning—and now under religious auspices, so to speak. In the process, nothing is changed: it is exclusively communication that's at work here. There is no other mode of operation available to society. And the referential problem of specifically religious communication still remains a problem of society. In contrast to older variants of "system functionalism," it can be perceived that the function of a function system does not lie in the function system itself but in the comprehensive social system of the society. Self-preservation, status maintenance, boundary maintenance (or whatever the formula might be)—these are existential predicates, not reference points for functions. As the concept of autopoiesis clarifies, a system is only operative if it can continue its operations. And if not, there is no structure available to convey its functions. Besides, its individual function systems could not be distinguished from each other with a concept like status maintenance. It would then be valid for all of them, and assuming a functional differentiation would not make any sense. One therefore has to assume that the continuation of societal autopoiesis, the reproduction of communication by communication, brings up different problems depending on the level of historical evolution. As a result, there are multiple stimuli for functional differentiation. In addition, the corresponding function is simultaneously the same formula by which the subsystem (whenever it gets around to functional differentiation) refers to the complete system, thus realizing its impact on society.

In the system reference "society" and its capacity for distinction, one can additionally say that religion under modern conditions has to satisfy the double criteria of universality and specificity. Universality implies that religious problems can appear in every communication, even in the context of specifically organizational operations or those assigned to the function systems of economy, science, law, politics, and so on. Conversely, in the same way, religion naturally costs money, has to abide by the law, can become politically unpleasant, and so forth. The operative closing specific to function systems or organizations does not rule out that every system will perceive a universal competence for its own function within the whole of society. That is precisely why the corresponding operations have to be recognizable and classifiable (with sufficient specificity) so that it does not becomes simply coincidental what happens where and how systems burden themselves reciprocally (= become integrated).

Finally, one has to make it clear that restricting the functional analysis to the system reference "society" is in no way to deny that physically or psychically created conditions impact religious communication. There is a long tradition of this applying to conditions that can be interpreted as "possession" and that can be traced back to the influence of higher powers. But it also applies when this (oral) culture is supplanted by writing,[36] making it possible for written communication (meaning communication by absent parties for other absent ones) to confuse communication through compelling linguistic formulas or religiously intended innovations. In other words, there are structural combinations between consciousness and communication that channel mutual irritations. These, in the circularity of mutual effects, can release trends that reinforce deviation in societal communication without at some point making use of particles of consciousness in the communication system.

We are getting ahead of ourselves, however, anticipating later analyses. It is only important for now to register that restricting the referential problem of functional analysis to social communication has a particular advantage. It makes it comprehensible how religion might respond to physical states and conscious experiences of individuals, although (indeed, precisely *because*) religion is exclusively determined by its own structures and operations, and although it can in no way make use of other "materials."

VI

The subject of religion's function finally requires us to take a position on the thesis that religion has suffered a "loss of function" in modern society. To elaborate: religion has retreated from many domains where it used to satisfy functions such as being the final guarantor of the validity of norms, or justifying political authority, or backing military violence, forms of conquest, and missionizing. In addition, religion no longer cooperates in substantiating knowledge. If it explains anything, then it explains something that has already been (or cannot be) explained. This thesis of the loss of function is hardly advocated by anyone today.[37] This is associated with a pervasive critique of the idea of secularization.[38] However, that still leaves open the question of why the idea does not apply, notwithstanding so much supporting historical evidence.

The thesis that religion has lost its function assumes that religion has relinquished some of the many functions that it fulfills. Yet if religion were to have only one function (as has been posited above), one could not speak of functional loss—unless one accepted that religion today is only some functionless evolutionary survival. What that means therefore has to be formulated more distinctly, as an idea, revealing how the thesis can be brought into accord with a description of modern society as a functionally differentiated system.

Functional differentiation is based on functional specialization. It creates *better chances* for specific functions on the condition that different systems can be demarcated. One might accordingly expect that every function will *benefit* whenever it *limits* itself and foregoes intervening in the functional domains of others. (Thus, the differentiation of an economic system based on monetary transactions depends on the fact that one cannot buy everything with money—for instance, redemption of the soul; that would immobilize the formation of capital too significantly.)[39] Such a representation of history certainly may not assume that there is a constant conceptuality onto which such changes could be recorded ("more of this one, less of that"). Rather, the structural reconstruction of society in the direction of functional differentiation also changes the semantics with which the society describes functions and other things. The same presumably goes for the meaning of "religion," making comparisons across time more difficult, forcing them to resort to the abstract terminology of second-order observation. The thesis of religion's "functional loss" no longer appears to be true or false, but rather too imprecise.

We have to count on the possibility that the chances for religion increase provided it retreats from many other functional domains, doing without "social control" and legitimation of political power. That does not at all have to be defined in the way major religions describe themselves, in the sense of modern devotion, or a continuous religious definition of life practice, or a communication-ready internalization of faith and doubts in faith. An increase in religion's chances does not generally have to imply a reinforced inclusion of individuals in leading a life determined by religion. What is much more likely is that the difference of inclusion and exclusion becomes greater and that *both* sides of this distinction, the religious life and the religiously indifferent one, are *socially accepted and endowed with communicative ability.*

These circumstances could also explain how the manifestation of religious phenomena in the past few decades has become more varied and undeniably more colorful. There are, moreover, new developments of the most diverse kinds: an intensification of major religions such as Islam, the broad interest of intellectuals in esotericism and spirituality, an international diffusion of (formerly) region-bound religious forms such as Zen Buddhism or meditation techniques, a congress of shamans in Europe, religious chanting on the beach at (a run-down) Coney Island. In many of these forms, there is a stronger inclusion of the body, of gesture, of unconscious monotony, the suggesting away of limits to consciousness—as if attempting on this level to correct the one-sidedness of modern developments in civilization.

We cannot in any way understand the intensification of religion under such conditions as an increase in a certain program's ability to assert itself. The facts clearly speak against it. Obviously, the disciplining that comes from religion also lapses when it withdraws from other functional domains. It becomes possible to shape things more freely. This leads to the circumstance that dogmatically preconceived ways of recognizing religion, such as the criterion of believing in God, are no longer adequate and that the classical sociological distinction between sacred and religious (made by Durkheim and by Simmel) falls apart. It probably will be all the more important to adhere to criteria of recognition such as code and function and (if necessary) to tailor these ideas to the problem of religion's self-observation as religion, and to that of the religious system's demarcation. Otherwise, every other inexplicable curiosity could figure as religion.

The Contingency Formula "God"

I

If everything determined in the medium of meaning is accompanied by endless referential surpluses, how is communication even possible? How can it have any hope of a successful outcome, whether in the form of consensus or of dissent? Negotiating meaning is thus the initial problem we face with respect to the function of religion. Since no other medium is available, however, we need meaning both to exclude and to connect to meaning. This might be said to ruin the concept of "meaning," but it nonetheless very precisely indicates the problem, which calls for contingency formulas.

The paradox involved—that connection can only be implemented by exclusion—can be transmitted in multiple forms. We had also asked how it is possible to transfer indeterminability into determinability, to transfer infinite burdens of information into finite ones. This (already functional) problem can be rendered more precisely by substituting the "how" for a "who or what." I shall call this specification, which sees a narrower version of the problem as its solution, a *contingency formula*.

From a functional perspective and described externally, one can re-resolve/re-dismantle the unity of such a formula. The paradoxical formulation that the problem appears as its solution, that the different is the same, has already been adopted for this. The distinction defining the concept of function thus disappears. In the internal domain of the system that is shifted by coding to contingency and reflexivity, the contingency formula vreplaces the reference to function. That is where the system's self-descriptions find their grounding. Although the system is a *difference* and, seen as an operation, is the *reproduction of this difference*, it can be made accessible to itself as a *unity*. It can produce a relationship to its own hypostatization, yet only such that the paradoxes of reentry and of coding are replaced by an identity that is held onto afterwards. An external observer can see how that works—and that it cannot work differently. Because the observer has no responsibility for how the system operates, he may still ask how such contingency formulas function. With the greater freedom of a second-order observer, he can tap into a comparative perspective not applicable in the compared systems. Yet it is only appropriate for him to account for the difference in perspectives, bearing in mind that the system-internal observations are at the mercy of the system-internal contingency formula, like a blind spot without which observations and self-observations in the (observed) system would not be possible. If the second-order observer imagines a correctible error here, a defect in consciousness, or an ideology, then he would be making an error himself. He would himself be using a distinction (such as truth/ideology) that impedes commensurate access to the object.

Contingency formulas are found in all function systems that are opened by their codes to contingency, reflection, and to paradoxical/ tautological possibilities of self-observation. They are distinguished depending on which of their operational types needs to have a capacity for connection. Thus, in the economic system, the contingency formula *shortage* is used for making sure that the economy can count on an operationally independent constancy of sums (although that is not accurate, either for goods or work or money).[1] The artificiality of the principle is apparent in the difficulty of implementing effective monitoring of the money supply. Its indispensability is revealed in the rule that no one can spend his money more than once. A corresponding principle of "common good" is to be found in politics,[2] or at least that was true in the medieval and early modern traditions, which assumed that people could still distinguish between public and private interests (according to their nature). Since this principle is less and less evident, "legitimacy" is the only thing that can still be specified as a political contingency formula, in that it refers to continuously acceptable values. These nonetheless leave open the question of how value conflicts will be decided.[3] It therefore becomes a matter of legitimized opportunism (though saying that would expose the meaning formula *legitimacy* as a paradox). In the educational system, the contingency formula has to provide *learning objectives*, whether in the form of an educational canon tied to content, or in the form of learning to learn.[4] In the process, it must be ruled out or go unsaid that other things are also learned at school, such as getting used to dullness or how in life it is more important to be deceitful than diligent. Operations of science depend on the truth code functioning restrictively, meaning that refuting an assumption of knowledge consolidates truth's chances. Yet the contrary experience that an increase in knowledge is tantamount to an (overproportional) increase in new uncertainties [*Nichtwissen*] is also abundantly available.[5] In the legal system, something analogous is achieved with the contingency formula *justice*, which prescribes the consistency of decisions with the double directive to treat like cases alike and different ones differently. These provide the observational formula of like/unlike that makes it meaningful to look for comparative standpoints in the legal system, while leaving open how these can be found.[6]

These examples make it clear (and clearer than a terminological definition could) what a contingency formula does and how it works. Its aim is to suppress other possibilities also given. The other side of this form may be reproduced as accompanying knowledge, but it can no longer claim that it records the system's meaning. Official communication is oriented along the guidelines of contingency formulas, thereby operating on the secure side of intended acceptance. Since the nineteenth century, the concept of value has been used to signal the consensual capacity of preferences. But we also know that professional knowledge cannot make do with that alone. Rather, completion occasionally imposes itself by transgressing boundaries, by glancing at the other side. In a normal situation, there may be little promise of success, since we can only operate in systems within the framework of contingency formulas. Communication itself favors assumptions in which one has to be involved if one wants to get around to anything. But none of these answers makes the slightest claim to satisfying the questions. With concepts of value, only what is wished for is beyond question—fewer shortages, more justice, and so on. But such formulations already open up horizons that these concepts themselves can no longer integrate.

II

The major religions have, it might be pointed out, experimented with contingency formulas for religion, without achieving a unanimous result. The most successful attempts, those of Buddhism and the monotheistic religions, appear to be founded on a common element: a redemptive outlook. They hold out the prospect of access to transcendence as a corrective for suffering from distinctions. They also hold out the prospect of sublating every distinction into something beyond all distinctions. That is the form in which the difference of immanence and transcendence is presented. The programs that become necessary appear as conditions of redemption. That in turn requires that one builds a temporal perspective into religion. The temporalization of the problem is associated with a devaluation of the world as it is found here and now, a devaluation of the *hic mundus* [this world] and thus the exploitability of chances for plausibility that are already given in the social-structural (situative, role-based, institutional) differentiation of religiously defined communication.

This much can be assumed as a common starting point, and that is a good deal. It suffices for providing an image of how the contingency formula "God" works. In the following, I shall limit my analysis to this contingency formula, even though (and because) it is probably easier to find access to Buddhism from constructivist starting positions.[7] At this point, we shall also not be dealing with polytheistic religions, in the case of which it is too tempting to define gods by their difference from other gods and to rule out questions going beyond that. In addition, their specifications were based too much on what they provided for certain formations of society (providing clues for differentiation, whether for genealogies of nobility, or for roles and competencies not yet differentiated into particular function systems).

A characteristic of religions formulated with reference to God is that they are also familiar with other holy figures that populate the religious cosmos and release the high god himself from unreasonable demands of definition: lesser gods, angels, spirits, saints, ancestors who live on spiritually, and so forth. At the same time, they serve as mediators and intervening instances when one does not dare (or see a way) to contact God directly. (Obviously, this reflects the social structures of an aristocratic society under the rule of a king.) The special position of the high god is thus distinguished by reason of his alone realizing the complete characteristics of transcendence, in particular, the characteristic of limitlessness, of ubiquity, and of universal presence even in the domain of immanence; he alone realizes the unity of the difference of transcendence and immanence. Only the high god can serve as the concluding formula of the religious cosmos. Yet that is precisely why it is difficult to know how to behave toward him. The problem of the contingency formula is therefore conveyed as a need for supplements, auxiliary institutions, and finally professional assistance. Supplements, though, are always (as is known from Derrida's analyses) moments of essence (that need supplementing). They are indications of a concealed paradox.

Contingency can best be grasped in personal behavior, because, in referring to a person, one assumes that the person might also behave differently. That, however, leads to the difficulty of thinking the highest transcendence as a person who would have other possible ways to behave—and who excludes them. More than all other religions, then, strong monotheistic religions are striking in the boldness with which they specify a contingency formula. Hence, they are also striking in the demands they make on individual religious faith. And they are just as striking in the burden of their dogmatic apparatuses (weighed down by the need to secure plausibility), in the strict way they distinguish between the faithful and nonbelievers, and (lastly) in their dependence on organization. All this is anchored in (and presupposes) the transferring of all transcendence ("there is no transcendence beyond transcendence") into an existential proposition. Transcendence exists as a person, it *is* the *one* God. And whoever does not believe in him is excluded. The "other side" of this *semantic* boldness is its correlative in the *social structure*: the possibility of being "excommunicated" and the (more or less) grave social consequences that ensue.

As long as gods were honored as house gods in ancestor veneration, it was not difficult to understand them as (invisible) persons and hence as observers of the living. If, however, the reference to those formerly alive breaks down, special reasons are needed to continue the idea of being observed by (invisible) persons and assigning it ultimately to a universal God. Personalizing ideas about God would have been a difficult, virtually counterintuitive process, especially if the idea of a transcendent power was supposed to be maintained and extended simultaneously.[8] The main risk of this semantics, the way it endangers itself, probably consist in compelling us to think of the good and bad effects—the attractive and repulsive (essential) traits of the holy—as the *intention* of a person. The Greeks had helped themselves out with terms such as "immortal" and "ageless." In this framework, they assigned their gods freedoms to decide, preferences, and dispositions to conflict. In the process, personality remained bound to a majority of gods, each of whom in their sphere of action personalized themselves (as it were). But there was too much contingency there for making greater demands of religion. The case that a single, transcendent, all-responsible God could ultimately be thought of as a person (albeit one without a name) must have corresponded to a need that was not apparent at first glance. It is presupposed that there was such a need in a social-structural development at the same time that activated social differentiations and individualizations, and that was only able to comprehend unity through the idea of an observer. For *personality* is nothing but a cipher for observing and being observed.

Yet why does God have to be given the quality of an observer? Why can he not simply exist? The best answer to this question comes from reflecting that a listing of all things that exist (P1, P2, . . . Pn) would never lead to a notion of God. Rather, it would always result in assuming that there are *additional* things. And this would also apply if one assumes (along with Deleuze) that each listing produces two series, one that moves forward and another backward—and that their unity can only be understood as a paradox.[9] God must then exist on another level, in another qualifying situation, and the notion of the observer provides at least one possible interpretation of this position. For it does not exclude—in fact, it virtually demands—that predicates like *existence* and *thing* (in the sense of *res*) also apply for an observer.

If the observer is understood not only as a form of indication that distinguishes (and that, in the case of God, distinguishes everyone and everything in its individuality) but also as a person, then it can also be made plausible for the observer to set conditions of liking/dislike. These then lead in the context of society to a difference of inclusion and exclusion that spreads across all other distinctions. Norms are always in part conditioned by what they exclude. And to the degree that they are formulated more generally, they can ultimately only be recognized by their exclusionary effects. None of that can be changed by "justification." By the form that god-based religions choose for their differentiation, they must (from a sociological standpoint) be dependent upon *socio-structural conditions*. They give weight to exclusion and, in the Middle Ages (for instance), they might even have forced an emperor to his knees. Conditions for inclusion/exclusion, however, are subject to a deep social transition,[10] and they can thus endanger the embedding (of the "outbedding") of such religions. They do so without the possibility of being intercepted on the semantic level by exchanging divine attributes (for instance) or giving up "father" symbolism (which nowadays seems somewhat anachronistic). The question thus becomes whether god-based religions today have to rely on the coincidence of individual belief decisions or on the persistence of an irrefutable error, and whether their semantics (themselves) have deeper motivations and social affinities, moving in the same direction as the function of religion. If one pursues this question from a sociological (i.e., religion-external) perspective of observation, one can examine more precisely how the contingency formula "God" actually functions (and it "functions" not in the sense of a trivial machine, certainly, but in solving the referential problem of religion: the transformation of the indeterminable into the determinable).

III

I shall not concern myself here with "proofs of God's existence." By means of such proofs, people try to deny God the contingency more customary of worldly things. This is done precisely because the world, seen from God's position, is contingent. Yet nowadays, hardly anyone still disputes that these proofs have a circular structure that must be interrupted (or made asymmetrical) one way or another, perhaps most clearly by the dogma of God's self-revelation.[11] Concluding from the beauty and well-orderedness of the world that it has an intelligent cause means offsetting any awkwardness as an error. We could also assume the contingency of all meaningful world descriptions, thus turning the argument around. In that case, God's existence is not proven by the contingency of the world; rather, the contingency of the world is proven by God's existence. In each case, the circularity is resolved into an asymmetrical relation of God and the world, which cannot be treated as reversible. And precisely that is the structure enabling us to acquire more information and that we designate as a contingency formula.

We can thus assume that an asymmetry is involved, and that the process must be hidden. The really important question is how to determine the specifics of the form making this operation possible. The notion of an asymmetry between God and world is already helpful because it prevents the development of monotheism from stagnating into a sterile idea of perfection. An absolutely perfect God is a God who cannot add anything to himself. But can such a God make a difference?[12] This problem can be metaphysically resolved, following Plato, by a theology of emanation.[13] "The concept of Self-Sufficing Perfection, by a bold logical inversion, was—without losing any of its original implications—converted into the concept of Self-Transcending Fecundity."[14] This alternative can be elaborated with a semantics of abundance, outflow, and giving. Yet it does not make it either necessary or comprehensible to think of God as a person.

The Christian tradition combined the assumption of an observer God with an ontological metaphysics, with a description of the world assuming the distinction of being/non-being—and ordering all other distinctions according to that one. If this world is understood as divinely created, it contains a normative moment. It is understood as a requirement of order. What *is* should not be what it is *not*. Hence, a human being is not an animal, a man is not a woman, and a Christian is not a pagan. Whenever there are breakthroughs within these ontological exclusions, they are understood as "miracles" and are then fed back into religion. The world of being is divinely created by God and what contradicts its organization also confirms something: that it is created by an all-powerful God whose power is not lost into the world but is maintained as a possibility of also deciding differently. In this way, metaphysics and religion corroborate each other, doing so in the form of a circle that closes the thought system.

The starting situations that have led to this special development need not be addressed here. A polytheistic cosmos was able to apply the person-form as a distinguishing principle. For the Hebraic tradition, the ability to make covenants had been important and also presupposed a divine personality. There is a rich, controversial literature on the relationship of tribal societies to notions of a high god and on the analogies and formal parallels to political rule. For the problem here of the contingency formula "God," what matters is not the semantic genealogy of this evolutionary form—"pre-adaptive advances" naturally have to be assumed—but rather the function of constructing transcendence as a person. What might be meant by "person" cannot be determined by an analogy between God and humanity—neither in one direction as anthropomorphism nor in the other in which God creates humanity "in His image." These kinds of interpretations are available, based on analogies of content that do not appear (at least nowadays) to have any apparent plausible basis. This schema of analogies, which is (as always) charged with differences, is replaced with the hypothesis referred to above: God is defined as a person because that establishes him as an *observer*. The form of asymmetry one is asking about is thus the form of the operation of observing.

What we have been asking about is contained in the idea of observing. The operation of observing is an asymmetrical (i.e., irreversible) operation that takes place exclusively *in* the observer but implies *for him* a distinction between observer and observed. It consists of a distinguishing indication, in which the *applied* distinction is not identical with the implication that the observer distinguishes *himself* from the observed. In other words, he has to distinguish *himself* in order to be able to make distinctions. This can be seen, in the case of God, as a reason why he creates the world.

Additionally, the idea of observing is so general that when applied to humanity it includes experience and action, cognitive and willed activity. The (internally experienced) distinction between experience and action depends, as Gotthard Günther has shown, on the distinction of other- and self-reference and thereby (indirectly) on the distinction of environment and system.[15] In the case of experience, the system counters the experience of external determination with internal binarizations—such as the schema of true/untrue or the schema of liking/disliking. By contrast, in the case of action, the system produces a difference that is found in the environment—such as the difference of the achieved purpose in contrast to what otherwise would obtain. Yet since one cannot assume that God distinguishes between other- and self-reference, the distinction as derived will not be appropriate for him. It does not rule out understanding God as an observer. In reference to God, however, the idea of observation does not need the distinction of intellect/will. The related controversies of the Middle Ages are now only of historical interest. The unity of observation as intellect and will tells us primarily that divine will is not bound to insights previously gained through knowledge. We do not need to argue, as in those medieval controversies, that omniscience prevails over omnipotence of the will (or vice versa). They are identical.[16]

In particular, there is a special status of this observer God that is correlated with the transcendence value of religion's code. God does not need a "blind spot." He can realize every distinguishing schema simultaneously as a difference and a unity of the distinguished. That includes the distinction between being distinguished and not being distinguished. And since this applies to each (and all) of his observations, his manner of observation—if one wished to try and observe it—can only be regarded as paradoxical. We shall return to this issue later on. For now, let us merely note that observing the transcendental observer proceeds precisely by contrast to all world-immanent observation, thus supplementing it by what it is missing. The God/human difference lies in the question of whether the unity of the operation of observing can observe itself in the operation (transcendence) or not (immanence). It could also be said that the transcendent person is self-transparent, and the immanent person is not. To that extent, the contingency formula "God," understood as an observer, is aligned with the necessity of coding religion and with religion's special way of reflecting contingency.

If God is seen as distinct from the "world" (which is unavoidable if he is said to *observe it*), the world can be differentiated from God, and this distinction determines them. Yet at the same time, if one assumes that this observer God has complete knowledge of the world, he cannot disturb its order, since possible disturbances (miracles, for instance) are always foreseen in God's mode of observing things. God and the world are in a relationship of harmony—a particularly important idea in the natural philosophy of the Renaissance. On the other hand, the distinction between God and the world is still meaningful. It enables (as is often pointed out) a desacralization of nature. As nature, the world is assigned for human use.[17] The God/world distinction further makes it possible to devalue the world in the sense of *hic mundus*, thereby societally differentiating religious concerns from subjective preoccupations with money, power, status, or one's sex life. This then leads relatively easily to calls for an anti-worldly religious (monk-like) lifestyle. And, finally, if it suffices to define the world by its difference from God, one can leave all other characteristics wide open, accepting uncertainty, hypotheticals, and so forth.[18] Even if modern, polycontextual society should require the world to be conveyed as an unmarked state, and thus as unobservable, religion might still maintain that it could itself distinguish the world, specifically from God.

All this is formulated so abstractly that neither a cosmology nor a morality is required. For human beings, it seems obvious to refer God's observation to humans (or primarily to them) and to be pleased with the illusion that nature has been established for humanity's sake. And (some say) toilets would not be able to flush without divine assistance. But the dogma of omniscience and omnipotence goes far beyond that, becoming explicitly visible for example in the doctrine of the *creatio continua*: divine observation is a condition for preserving the world from moment to moment in all its details.

Even as logos, as word or as text, the observing God is beyond all distinctions, especially all temporal distinctions. That is what guarantees the presence of being, independently of the merely momentary concurrence of all topical [i.e., individual] human experience, for ontological metaphysics. It also underwrites a life after death, that most far-reaching of theological generalizations. It is the basis for all moral conditionings of human lifestyle, condensing them into a unity (without having to rely on principles, moral laws, or the like). Time is thereby understood as a duration, and an immortality of the soul is deduced from the unthinkability of a beginning (without a "before") and an end (without an "after").[19] Derrida's critique of the metaphysics of presence and its logocentrism is still indebted to this idea; in fact, it cannot be formulated on its own but only as a rejection of the idea.[20]

Despite existing independently of distinction, God must therefore be transferred to the good, beautiful, and existentially stronger side whenever humans make distinctions. Obviously, this is not only true of such distinctions as being/nonbeing, existence/appearance, good/bad but also of more remote considerations concerning God's image in art.[21] If one wished to proceed in the other direction, using the negative side of the distinction as a symbol for the distinction, one would come close to a symbolism of death, negating all distinctions. This reflection shows that the (interest-laden) figure of life after death integrates two logical impossibilities in a single paradox, indicating the unity of every distinction either from its negative or positive side—that is, either as death or God.

One does not have to rely on employing an ontological mode of observation, observation with the help of distinguishing being from nonbeing. For doing that would only lead back to the question: who is the observer observing with this very schema of distinction, dividing up the world in precisely this way and not another? And what is *his* blind spot? Perhaps the impossibility of comprehending time? In any case, God observes without being dependent on the distinction of being and nonbeing, and as a result, there is no "excluded third possibility" for him—and thus no logic, either. Only thus can God be thought of as the creator—further abstracted here to "observer"—of being out of nonbeing, as Nicholas of Cusa holds.[22] To theologians who still think ontologically, the asymmetry of God and world gives way to the possibility of thinking of God as total meaning, as perfection of being, as *ens universalissimum*. This asymmetry has to be replaced by (an utterly faded, formal) notion of the unity of difference, for example, one based on formulations for difference such as *ens finitum/infinitum* or *ens creatum/increatum*.[23] The theory of (operative) observation is substituted here for this ontological weak point, which can only be filled by an empty formula.

In place of determining the minimal components of distinctions and how they predetermine interpretations of the world, a more exciting question emerges: How can the observer God be observed? Whoever can observe God as an observer (and not simply as a holy, untouchable object) obtains a final guarantee of meaning with regard to an infallible constructor. This constructor created the world, sees what happens, and will not change his construction—even though he could. As is reported, he found "it was good." And that is underscored by many dogmas. He bound himself to a covenant. He sees humanity as the crown of creation. And he loves us.

Yet as soon as one accepts that God observes *everything* ("nothing escapes him") and that he therefore *has to distinguish himself from everything*, he cannot be observed in (or with) the world. One cannot determine by worldly means whether God exists or not. Proofs of God's existence come to contradict what they set out to demonstrate. One must therefore repeat the question: *how* can a human being observe the observer God? Or, put more sociologically, how does one deal with differences of opinion that can be anticipated when observations of the unobservable are made? With this question about the possibilities of second-order observation, one comes across solutions that, on the one hand, make use of privileged positions and, on the other, reflect their own imperfection—setting up a rich semantic field for theological discussion.

That man is ignorant of some things—an untaught unknowing, as it were—even religions that are not self-reflective concede.[24] Such a situation is then resolved through an ambivalence of attraction and repulsion, seeking and avoiding, and asking and fearing. This state of affairs can be differentiated according to opportunities or situations, or it can be dealt with by having God transcendentally loved and immanently feared. Furthermore, there is that solution enshrined in myth where persons are punished for their arrogance and for claiming they know better than others what God actually wants. Such is the fate of the angel who is punished by falling (from heaven) and who cannot regret having fallen, since his ultimate goal was to observe God. And there is the solution of paradox, confused speech, silence, of "I know it because I don't know it," of speculative fusion ("God's eye is my eye")—the mystical solution of Nicolas of Cusa.

Theologians are only rarely insightful enough to interpret the fate of the fallen angel as a paradox of love rather than a divinely conceded freedom to do evil (an interpretation that should require explanation).[25] For that angel who loves God the most cannot be satisfied with limiting himself to discovering this paradox. Nor can he shrug his shoulders and declare: "Ultimately, He must know; it is not my affair."[26] Satan's love becomes an existential paradox, an expulsion due to love. The issue is not freedom for the devil; rather, his activism of seduction is something theologians invented to build their moral code into creation (at the expense of their theology). But such an invention is not really so inspired.[27] If it were to address the cognitive problem directly, a theology that reflected on the observation of observing could more readily make the transition from the impossibility of consciousness to a consciousness of impossibility.[28] Yet who is going to see the advantage in that?

Regardless of how deeply they might reflect, theologians find themselves, as professional observers of God and/or interpreters of his texts, subjected to questions and expected to provide answers. They have to communicate within the religion system, imparting what they know, which more or less compels them to make a fatal reinterpretation of the contingency formula as a selection criterion: "Yes to this, no to that—that is how God wants it." There is no third way [*tertium non datur*]. But in contrast to the devil—who does not himself partake of the fruit forbidden in the Bible (!)—how can one avoid the arrogance of knowing better?

One of the possibilities [two more follow below] is to appeal to divine self-revelation. Because it is so central, revelation is one of the most difficult concepts in religious studies. It has also been theologically controversial up to the present day. While we have no desire to intervene in the internal theological discussions, a distinction should be made here: revelation is not only about mantics, divination, interpretation of signs, or formal analogies between the visible and the invisible. It is therefore not about getting an answer (no matter how that answer is encoded) to questions posed to God based on some important situation or another (such as "Should I marry this person?" or "Should we go to war?"). Divination is and always has been observing the lines of a surface in the hope of being able to discover something deep and concealed.[29] Even if it is accepted that the gods make decisions each day about human destinies, the problem remains of how (and by means of what omens) we can figure out those decisions. The thought of God's self-revelation breaks off there—which is the source of its evolutionary achievement and historical volatility. A special idea of revelation is therefore only meaningful if it includes a divine initiative and an autological moment. That rules out posing the question of truth (in a scientific sense).[30] In terms of form, the revelation reveals itself, meaning that there is no other cognitive access to it besides assuming that the revelation is a revelation. In terms of content, the issue is the relationship of observing (noted above), of establishing a possibility of observing the observer God. And in terms of history, the revelation changes history so that it no longer suffices to understand religion as memory. Something has commenced that is new in history.[31]

The troubles start specifically whenever one thinks about divine self-revelation, with its well-measured instructions on observation, as *communication*. In particular, the trouble is caused by the distinction between information and utterance [*Mitteilung*]. It does not make much sense to ask why revelation, as information, is being communicated. If the issue is religious truth, there are no additional reasons or motives needed for it to be communicated. Moreover, if revelation is communication, the continuous relationship of observing also has to be understood as an event, a transitory happening that cannot be replicated. That leads then to the paradox of substantiating presence by means of absence, for which the form of text presents itself. That in turn assumes the revelation has been completed textually and historically. It would be difficult to cope with if God (with all his possibilities) were always announcing new things, if he were commenting on the ecological state of society, or if he suddenly judged sexual behavior differently than one thought. (The visionary phenomena of the Late

Middle Ages were in any case not treated as instruments for proclaiming dogmas, whatever might be seen as their cause and distinguishing effect.) The dogmatics of revelation, as in the doctrine of the Sinaitic revelation, are always legends developed after the fact. They respond to a historically given need for legitimation in already established religions.[32] In the Jewish Talmud, a way out of this dilemma was developed using the written/oral distinction to guide revelation (according to God's will) in *both* ways: the text is given in *writing* for *oral* (and thus revisable and open) interpretations. As such, it is a particularly impressive form of a resolved paradox.[33]

A second possibility is to include the first observer of God's observing, the devil, and then to distinguish oneself from him either by demonization and/or defamation, or by reconstructing the relationship of God and devil with the moral coding of good/evil. Regardless of what one doesn't know to say about God, one can issue warnings about the devil's seductions and denounce all those vices that would lead sinners into his realm. In that case, one is using negative communication, which is easier from the standpoint of communicative technique or rhetoric. One likewise has fewer problems identifying bad taste—even when what is good taste cannot be defined.

The third (and probably most demanding) possibility is a mystical solution: the gazes coincide and are collapsed. No criteria are needed here. Being seen can be seen directly. All distinctions in existence are sublated, even if only for the moment. *Such* certainty cannot be distinguished and therefore cannot be surpassed. But it cannot therefore be communicated. Getting into *communicatio* with God (and here the old idea of producing commonality is appropriate) impacts communication between human beings. One can discuss this as one does other matters. Yet this experience cannot be conveyed to anyone who has not had this experience (and does anyone really know if he has?). One might go a step further and claim there can only be mysticism if religious experience is transferred to the level of second-order observation, and if the issue of distinguishing criteria is problematized, and if ways are sought to avoid the issue as something unsuitable. When embedded in culture like this, mysticism derives its powers of persuasion from the temporary character of all other answers, both dogmatic and professional—all of which are clearly inadequate. But that does not mean that mysticism would be able to replace dogmatics in communication about religion.

In short, the complicated structure of second-order observation is important for elaborating the contingency formula "God." On the one hand, that formula unifies the code of immanence/transcendence, absorbing contingency in this capacity. On the other hand, it is a selection criterion, an almost complete formula for religious programmatics and indicating what is right and wrong in the relationship of immanence to transcendence. None of that could be achieved by object propositions, by indicating attributes of the thing called "God." The doctrine of attributes could only specify things that are unobservable. In addition, it isn't necessary to construe God himself as an observer until there is actually a context of second-order observation. One doesn't have to know *what* he is. Rather, one has to know how he renders judgment—in order to adapt one's life to his love.

IV

If we now return to the operation of communication that reproduces society and religion within society, then the contingency formula "God" is revealed as something that closes itself off from communication. It dismisses any attempt to be analyzed. Its "holiness" consists in refusing all access to its mystery, in punishing every scrutinizing or differentiating communication by recognizing that what one sought was not what one found. Yet communication is the only form in which society is capable of realizing itself. There is no other possibility for realizing meaning in society. When it is necessary, then, one has to communicate incommunicability.

To explain this state of affairs, there are a variety of major ideas that depend for their plausibility on the framing conditions of society. We can distinguish three forms (that overlap a great deal), correlating roughly to the transition from tribal (or segmentary) to stratified societies and from them to a functionally differentiated one. Three models—"mystery," "paradox," and "external (functional) analysis"—present themselves.

In early notions about sacred objects, techniques, and relationships, the communication problem was solved by the figure of a mystery equipped with sanctions. It's an idea that can apply to sacred matters of all kinds. These matters are treated as external givens and their limited accessibility is part of their essence. If one foolishly tries to penetrate mysteries, break taboos, or say too much, one has to count on there being supernatural sanctions. One had to accept that numinous powers were interested in their own sacrosanctity. The problem was thus *externalized*. In communication, one can only request that such conditions be adhered to, and *this* is underwritten by a type of collective liability. The punishment not only applied to the perpetrator but also to his kin. The sacred powers were not really geared toward individual guilt. If they operated according to moral criteria at all, they did so rather imprecisely. Society was left to take precautions so that nothing will happen, and to discipline or expel its members appropriately.

Such a notion clearly becomes problematic when monotheistic religions emerge that assume a high god or even a single god whose expectations are oriented toward morality. We have already discussed the problems with coding that become apparent in such frameworks.[34] Here, the concern is that such a god can no longer keep his identity, or how he judges people, a mystery. In such circumstances, mystery was still an acceptable thesis, but it had to be modified. God's will was now seen as unfathomable. Although he makes laws and reveals himself, he also burdened human beings to such a degree with sin that they ultimately did not know if they were satisfying his demands or whether they would be granted the mercy necessary to make up for their deficits.

The core point of incommunicability now takes on the form of a paradox. Final insights can only be communicated as paradoxes. These are specially tailored for second-order observers, that is, those who attempt to observe God's observing, particularly the devil and theologians. For *curiositas* remained prohibited in religious matters and was handled the old way, as a prohibition on intruding into mysteries [deemed sacred]. It was still regarded in the seventeenth century as "pride and wantonness of Knowledge, because it looketh after *high things* that are above us and after *hidden things* that are denied us."[35] But attempting to penetrate the mystery was now no longer punished with thunder and lightning, with poor harvests and illness—but with the banality of the formulations that emerge for it. Mysteries are sought to no avail, or (if a starker assessment is wished for) they are "a source of error."[36] God is now clearly attuned to human individuality. He punishes people by rendering their efforts useless. And, as a loving God, he makes them learn. And in the specific religious practices of the seventeenth century, it was indirectly suggested (and understood by theologians) that man could only find salvation in himself and not in curiosity about things that cannot (or should not) be known.[37]

In this phase of development, the impact of writing (and later, of printing) was clearly evident. Writing becomes a reprieve for the "obscenity of questioning."[38] And yet, texts answered questions that had not even been asked. When questions and answers could not be coordinated, the starting situation for communicative prohibitions and controls was now different. And it was probably not a coincidence that the rhetoric of paradox also experienced its highpoint with the late Renaissance introduction of printing. Texts can treat author and reader as absent, thereby choosing a representation in the form of paradox that leaves what can be said about it to the person participating in the communication.

Paradoxical communication—whether oral (as in Buddhism) or written (as in reports of mystical experiences)—claims its own kind of authenticity (indeed *rationality*) by destroying communications that can be continued by saying "yes" or a "no" to what is communicated. In this form, it documents something "beyond yes and no."[39] It puts its own honesty on display, for whenever one communicates true knowledge, one could always be making a mistake or even end up in a lie. Paradoxical communication is in this respect invincible, and it symbolizes the highest form of knowledge since it does not expose itself to refutation but represents itself as unconditional knowledge. Nonetheless, it is a mode of communication conveyed by faith assumptions that are themselves open to refutation. If it is acceptable to society, one arrives at a point in which the forms *mystery* and *paradox* are just as effective as before, but only for those who believe something here is closing itself off from communication.

Society reacted to these conditions by permitting ways of dealing with religion that did not have to be believed, that really *could not* be believed. This began with *legal* regulation of state religions and prohibitions on religion, then extends to the open, legal establishment of religious freedom.[40] Once placed in the hands of the law, there could be regulation of what could be said or what could be punished as blasphemy or as violating other people's religious feelings. Leibniz's solution to the problem of theodicy is developed in a similar fashion: God is restricted to a remainder function. He produces worlds by assuring the compossibility of this best of all possible worlds and by excluding whatever is incompatible with it.[41] Yet such an approach did not work for long. With Kant and Hegel's newly formulated dialectics, it became another issue to be addressed as part of the world: the problem of unstable antitheses.

Starting in the second half of the eighteenth century, there was a new way of discussing religious topics, and it qualifies as *scientific*. Viewed from the outside, religion appears to be culture, and it can thus be compared historically and regionally.[42] Theology itself was historicized—taking part in the same process.[43] In the empirical research on religion that emerged later, the status in society of faith in God could be analyzed either statistically or functionally. Such an external description usually dealt more with externally obtained data, such as the results of polling research or a content analysis of texts.[44] In principle, however, nothing stands in the way of doing what has just been engaged in: treating questions of dogma (all the way to their most subtle esoteric constructions) as constructions with respect to their function and the historical and societal conditions of their plausibility. A scientist, for example, could arrive at an understanding that it is no longer advisable to speak about God in the form of paradoxical observation because it might weaken the willingness to believe.[45]

When functional differentiation had been accepted, the mystery or paradox of God could be resolved in a polycontextural manner. It was assigned to different communicative contexts depending on the system to which communication seeks to relate. There was a great deal of nonreligious communication on religion that can be treated as irrelevant in the framework of the religion system. The operative closing of function systems and the universalization of their specific functional competence made possible a great diversity of combinations in intensity and indifference. Only when the social-structural "logic" of this arrangement is understood can continuity and discontinuity be seen in relation to the forms with which earlier societies had exposed the contingency formula "God" to communication—while at the same time protecting it against communication.

V

With the institution of a single personal God, a problem already touched on many times took on dramatic significance: the relationship of religion to morality. When religions are compared, this kind of overlap in religion and morality is seen to be more the exception than the rule.[46] In the animistic religions of tribal cultures, it is almost out of the question for numinous powers to involve themselves in the moral affairs of humanity.[47] Rather, what has to be regulated normatively in society has to be protected against magic, against single-case interventions from the outside. *Structural* interrelations between religion and social life are not mediated by moral directives [*Gebote*] but by the schema of pure/impure, to name but one example.[48] That way, contingencies can be reduced. In addition, external threats emanating from magical powers are a reason to react internally by moralizing the directives for handling such contact.[49] Whoever angers the powers in the other world not only endangers himself but society in general. Yet that indicates the precise lack of morality, which should mean the same thing in both the transcendent and immanent realms. Polytheistic societies also avoid too close an association between religion and morality. The gods and goddesses with their capabilities and interests represent only differences of standpoint. If there is a higher god at all (as is typical in the African religious sphere), it becomes difficult to assign him moral preferences. In this respect, his essence remains ambivalent.[50] Nonetheless, toward the end of the development under discussion, in the eighteenth century, one encountered a God who was largely inactive. He could not let his moral preferences be known but had ordered the world with his invisible hand so well that it could run on its own. Morality, in this case, became a societal institution which (if nothing else) also evaluated religions with respect to their civilizing qualities.[51] The transcendence of the religious code represented by a personal God, who at the same time is seen as epitomizing the good, is therefore a special constellation faced with related problems that have to be avoided by a supplemental semantics.

There are a number of (nearly) compelling reasons to burden the one God, the observer God, with morality. If he already observes and sees everything but also wants all that he sees, then how could he behave neutrally in a matter as important as morality? The God of the Hebrews, unique as a universal god, learned this lesson in a paradigmatic way,[52] and one may suppose that the idea of a god having a covenant with his people supported such a development. If the observers of God are imagining an observer God who himself can be observed (at least in part), then it is hard to avoid infecting this God with morality. And that means that there is a problem of how the codings of immanent/transcendent and good/bad relate to each other.

Yet in the beginning and well into modernity, morality implied only that God had arranged for order and dependability in the realm of free human activity. Despite this freedom, there was no sphere of natural creation incapable of being ordered. Seen thus, it is self-evident that establishing moral order among human beings—and thus morality itself—is good and not bad. By using its positive quality, the difference of good and bad is attributed quite naïvely to creation. And using this kind of natural moral awareness, one could extrapolate back to what God preferred to see.[53]

It isn't surprising that the necessity of distinction has a moral valuation in the case of older societies. What might be surprising, though, is the perverse idea of priests that God would enjoy being repeatedly confronted with the moral defects of his creation in the form of confessions.[54] If confession is then enforced organizationally and intended to have a socializing effect, doesn't theology have to take on itself in order to make it comprehensible that permission to sin comes from God?

The resolution of this figure did not begin until the seventeenth century. On the one hand, the history of sin was seen as a success story, triggered by the *felix culpa* of the Fall,[55] and man might now see himself as capable of moral improvement. On the other hand, God fell into a trap set by himself: if he established the world according to moral criteria, then wasn't the world morally optimal? There could be no *moral* reason to create a world that is *morally defective*. God was acting on moral necessity. And if his knowledge were thought to be defective, he could be recalculated out of the world. We thus arrive at Leibniz's "theology."[56]

There was another problem as well: the old religious symbols had to go without authoritative interpretation and explicit reference. In practicing public communication, both "papists" and "enthusiastic" Puritans could make themselves suspect.[57] Consequently, it could no longer be safely assumed that observing God directly or institutionally would help one figure out what he expects. Or there is the question on internal enlightenment posed by Hobbes, Locke, and Leibniz: how can one distinguish between divine inspiration and the devil's insinuations *without* engaging one's own (human) reason? It was thereby suggested that the natural capacity for moral and aesthetic feelings should be valued more. It was also assumed that one might rely on this capacity because God had given us such inclinations. But it should be enough to observe humanity on the path of civilized progress; as a result, the eighteenth century developed a semantics of civilization and culture that spoke to this issue.

The issue was no longer that man was observing how God observes him. Nor was the issue "theological"—even if religion was not being questioned as a core certainty or as a social institution or accomplishment of "culture." If reason (reflection) had to be entered into the equation, then it really meant that human beings had to be assumed to function as non-trivial machines.[58] And only then was it deemed worthwhile to observe their observing, since one could no longer manage only with divine knowledge, principles, and laws.

In the eighteenth century, the unity of religion and morality fell apart completely as the result of the Enlightenment and with the knowledge that a historical and regional majority of "cultures" had their own particular religions. Morality was reformulated on an anthropological basis, using the concept of moral sentiments in particular. At least in "educated strata," it became morally unbearable to despise someone, such as a Jew or Muslim, because they had a different religion. But in so doing, one struck the criteria from the hands of one's own God, who would like to see himself being worshipped.

These considerations all lead to the question: what are the effects of such changes on societal communication? One would need an elaborate sociological theory of moral communication to see the problems involved.[59] A few keywords will have to suffice for the time being. Moral communication regulates the division of respect [*Achtung*] and disdain [*Mißachtung*] toward [both] those present and those absent. This distinction of present/absent already causes problems, since respect is more readily shown for those present, and disdain more often for those who are not. This problem and the similar one of a certain temporal consistency are solved by conditioning the "deserving" of respect and disdain. As a consequence, moral communication can refer back to itself recursively. These conditions (or rules) can assume a normative form but can also determine the criteria by which accomplishments earn recognition (accomplishments that cannot be demanded "beyond the call of duty"). The problem of morality then lies in the invariance and certainty of such programs. On the same level of generalization, a universal moral code of good/bad is formed (or, if internal attitudes are included, a code of good/evil). Yet that code does not create the necessary certainty since it actually reflects contingency, leaving open which modes of conduct relate to which moral values. It seems to be this uncertainty that has triggered demands for a transcendent guarantee of moral criteria.[60] What appears and is practiced as morality is a supplement of its coding, and the need for reasonable explanations is another supplement.

The attempt to solve the problem of moral rules by externalization, however, returns the problem to the source. It brings us to the question of why God has created or permitted the difference of good and bad, and why he does not use the possibilities available to him to help the good triumph instead of the bad. Only in the modern era do people speak of "theodicy," but it is a problem as old as identifying God with morality.[61] One can imagine the most diverse solutions. An opponent of God might be projected into a transcendent realm, creating an ambivalent situation until the final victory of the good. Or the observability of the observer God could be acknowledged then restricted. God lets himself be observed only to a limited extent (in giving humanity its freedom, for instance).[62] In these cases, significant temporary conditions are tolerable because one presumes there is immortality. Hence, the final victory of good or (in the other case) the Last Judgment will bring clarity to these conditions, albeit in the manner already proclaimed (but nonetheless surprising to stubborn moralists). Whoever had relied too greatly on morality will think he has been deceived, and an indirect path via sin will prove necessary for achieving redemption.[63] Yet redemption can only be achieved using the dialectic of moral values applied beforehand. It is only necessary to take this zigzag path to it because the problem of theodicy had already been raised.

Further solutions come into view when one dares to reconstruct how divine calculations are made. For a solution in which only the good achieve happiness also has disadvantages that God would clearly wish to avoid. In such cases, those deemed good could not at all know if they are good for the sake of what is good or for the sake of the happiness associated with it.[64] In order to avoid such calculations, the distinctions of good/bad and happiness/sorrow have to be uncoupled. Although some good people have to be asked to suffer, they are at least able to know that their suffering is observed and approved of by God. They may then cling all the more to their goodness instead of its consequences. Here as elsewhere, theodicy also means having more variety within a more reliable order.

Another difficulty is when the moral rules not only have to be confirmed religiously but (precisely for that reason) when the binary code of morality also has to be copied into religion. If one wagers on a solution that makes use of temporality, then two final repositories have to be available: These are heaven and hell, the realm of God and that of the devil. Such logic is difficult to dispense with, no matter how hard people have been working at it since the eighteenth-century Enlightenment.[65] For how should a God be imagined who himself is "the good," who has made a clear moral choice, but who seems not to have made any provisions for whether our actions are good or bad?

While the questions dealt with up to now have received in-depth theological attention, a different problem has been perceived, mainly by external observers. The identification of morality with religion and the re-identification of religion with morality have infected religion as well with the "polemogenous" structure of moral communication.[66] For morality is easy to argue about, particularly when the criteria for respect and disdain are not fully insulated from their relationship to social structures. More-over, there are always friends and enemies, dependents and those more highly placed, as well as ways to anticipate the effects of communication. To further moralize questions of faith is to throw holy oil on the fire. The effect, especially in the domain of religions that link religious and moral codes, is that millions of people have been killed. The paradox of coding has thus found a fully practical way of resolving itself: one tortures and murders in the name of the "good God" because other ways of persuading people have failed, and that is the only way the difference of respect and disdain can ultimately be sanctioned. For it is no longer acceptable to say that such things do not matter.

These troubles got worse in the Middle Ages owing to the legal and organizational powers of the Catholic Church, and once again in early mo-dernity with the wars of religion, which were in part politically motivated. It got so bad that society developed immune responses, with assistance from the law. But in particular, the form of societal differentiation was al-tered and along with it, the context in which religion and morality were utilized. In the transition to a primarily functional differentiation, the reli-gious positing of the world lost its significance for the whole society (which does not, however, permit us to draw conclusions about the intensity of re-ligious communication). In addition, it became clear that morality was no longer appropriate as a form of societal integration. With stratified societies using either religion or morality to express unity, despite differences in hier-archy,[67] something else ultimately became clear: under a regime of func-tional differentiation, none of the codes of function systems could identify their positive/negative values with those of morality.[68] Moral communica-tion was certainly reproduced on a massive scale and looked for its themes in the domain of function systems.[69] Yet only the code of morality could still be applied universally, owing to its formalism and strict bivalence.

In contrast, moral programs are hardly able to achieve consensus any more. Unlike positive law, and influenced as they are by the mass media, they are not provided with normal guarantees that they will be implemented. As a result, societal integration has to be left up to the reciprocal limitations on the movements of function systems. Even (academic) ethics has lost control over morality. Instead of getting involved in problems and consequences of moral communication, it accepts the function of preparing legal regulations discursively. At this point, one might say, morality is something that is only relevant in everyday communication (including press and television) and really only in the most pathological cases.

What has been just as dramatic are the changes in the domain of communications that use the mode of second-order observation. In the meantime, all function systems have switched to this mode:[70] science with help of publication, the economy through its market orientation, politics via public opinion, and family or other close relationships on the basis of personal intimacy. Teachers are required to observe how they are being observed by children, yet no one expects them for that reason to think of themselves as gods. Jurists find their rules of positive law in decisions that make perceptible how law observes itself in a given situation. Hence, it is no longer striking that religion too makes use of this mode of second-order observation with the help of its professional experts. Here the contingency formula "God" serves as a functional equivalent for what elsewhere is realized by the marketplace or public opinion, by a look from one's sexual partner, or by the notion that children can be trained—that is, by the reflexive processing of the system using system-specific observations of system-specific observations. If one can still speak of a discourse common to all of society, then it is up to the intellectuals—who deal with such matters according to the (pleasantly unpleasant) formula of critique—to describe how other intellectuals describe what it is they describe.

In retrospect, it appears as if religions with an observer God might have prepared this shift from all-important, broad-based communication to the mode of second-order observation. To some extent, "God" has been used to try out and rehearse what was later supposed to become a universal social way of dealing with greater complexity. And if relevant function-specific forms can be found for this state of affairs (market prices and media themes, children and rules for representation in scientific publications or grounds for legal decisions), then it is no longer necessary to unify the totality of meaning in a religious-moral cosmology. This problem may recur in the future, but religion seeks to have a ready-made answer for it wherever it becomes virulent due to internal or external maladjustments of the societal system.

VI

The observer God had offered a security of orientation that was nearly unequalled. If that idea of him is given up, "orientation" becomes a problem (and a buzzword too). For he had homogenized existence, making it appear to be a continuum of rationality. He had guaranteed that everything that exists could be known (if not always by human beings). Not knowing was thus an anthropological (if not humanistic) idea; it was not a metaphysical one. In other words, we did not have to count on non-knowledge [*Nichtwissen*] being a condition for the possibility of knowledge or on efforts to know being able to result in still more ignorance. The limits on attaining knowledge were marked by the stop signs of mystery and prohibitions on curiosity.

Further, the observer God had provided distinctions (or in any case those which are most important) with a preferential side, a side on which actual existence, perfection, or nature could be found. And that had made it possible to see this side as crucial to the meaning of the distinction itself. One could consequently see man as a basis for the man/woman distinction. The city (or the political) became a basis for the *polis/oikos* distinction. The oral/written distinction replaced writing as a merely technical externalization. The soul (undying)/body (dying) distinction privileged eternal life. The concept/metaphor distinction assumed that the distinction itself was conceptual. The good was a basis for the good/bad distinction; the true for the true/untrue distinction; being for the being/nonbeing distinction. Everywhere in "old European" thought, one finds this structure of a hierarchized opposition, of a hierarchy that outdid itself. Logic had closed itself off with this (logically unreliable) double application of the preferred side as the meaning of the distinction itself—until Gödel came on the scene. In this kind of resolved paradox, the world could be read as something God wanted.

The philosophy of deconstruction takes aim at this decisive point of onto-theological metaphysics. It is the metaphysics (if it truly is one) of the regrounding upon difference; it is the metaphysics of spirit that can no longer exclude what it is not, the metaphysics of paradox. "The motif of homogeneity, the theological motif *par excellence* is what must be destroyed."[71] Even this "must" can clearly be deconstructed again. (That is always part of reflecting on it.) It becomes set on the question of how it would be if it were not so. It repeats (though from a greater distance) the "writing" of theology. This should not be understood as a denunciation—or only in the sense that the denunciation is repeating (albeit in the sense of *différance*) what it is denouncing. The denunciation lives "de-reconstructively" from what it is rejecting.

Do we thus know a great deal more when we know this? What we gain certainly does not consist in a type of knowing better which—knowing *being* to be on one's side—can be easily deconstructed. But what we gain is a larger structural abundance of forms available for observation, and thereby an expansion of the possibilities for communication.

Besides this type of hierarchy, which makes use of asymmetrical oppositions, there is the more renowned hierarchy of essences that resolves the observer paradox by distinguishing between levels. God also created angels between himself and man, giving them a different form of cognitive access to the world. Angels are capable of perceiving ideas. In their minds, there is a different world, an ideal one, a purely spiritual one that man can use to measure defects in his own state of knowledge.[72] In turn, this differentiation of levels is capable of accounting for the asymmetry in oppositions that, on their good side, direct our gaze upward.

Today, all these things are supposed to have come to an end: history, humanity, metaphysics, art, the book, and God. But perhaps we need only learn the difference it makes when we describe something this way.

The Differentiation of Religious Communication

I

There can never have been a state of society in which every communication was religious communication. In such circumstances, religious communication would not have been distinguishable; it would moreover have been impossible to signify it as religious. If there is religious communication, there always has to be nonreligious communication as well. Regardless of its societal conditions and its semantic forms, religion is always a form with two sides: an internal side on which religious communication is, so to speak, "present to itself," reproducing religious communication, and an external side on which (when this form is chosen) there are different possibilities of communication.

This distinction introduces the subject of this chapter. The issue is once again *how* religious communication distinguishes itself and how the forms of this distinction can be developed to the extent that a self-reproducing, operatively closed system emerges for religious communication. We are presuming that an actualization of the code value for transcendence was always involved (though it understandably lacked this very late theological interpretation at first). But for now, that still does not tell us a great deal. And it can only acquire more precise forms in the context of its circular relationship with the differentiation of religious communication.

Probably the least demanding—and (therefore) perhaps the oldest—form of distinguishing religious communication—ought to have been provided by its *topics* (or themes). One has religious communication when uncanny powers of the hereafter or sacred things are spoken of, and when actions are recognizably being taken in their name. One also has it when individuals report on their own religious experiences and in doing so make use of their "in-dividual" authenticity. If the identity of reference and also its iterability are guaranteed, religious communication can occur fully without rules and without predetermined reasons or purposes. The societal system [*Gesellschaftssystem*] can respond to coincidental irritations with religion inasmuch as communication can make itself understood with religious references. In cybernetic terms, this would be called an unregulated system. There is thus no feedback mechanism that determines in advance what kind of input triggers religious communication. No damage is done if opportunities for religious communication are not utilized. Omissions cannot even be identified as such. But for the sake of thematic fit (at least), this type of response cannot take place within the communication system in completely coincidental fashion. And it may be that tendencies develop for giving a religious interpretation to certain occurrences and not others.

If one is translating from communications-theoretical ideas to systems-theoretical ones, being fascinated by topics means being fascinated by other-reference. That in turn is consistent with a psychic state in which the psychic systems involved are chiefly defined by perception. That is, they are also defined by externalizations, like thematic communications that are defined by external irritations. In psychic systems, sacred powers can be imagined in the form of copies of perceptible facts—such as spirits of ancestors, or as animals or powers of nature. And that is precisely the basis for their uncanniness and their internal paradoxicality: one does not (normally) see what one could and cannot protect oneself against it the usual way.

If these ideas about the original primacy of the external are correct, any further evolution has to be understood as an increase in internalization. Here, too, one may think of communicative self-references in the societal system as "co-evolving" with increasing access demanded from psychic systems.

One can assume an initial impetus where places and times are defined for communicating about sacred matters. There are sites, especially booths and then temples, in the proximity of which people need to prepare themselves for holiness; otherwise, they risk engaging in sinful, socially restricted behavior. In addition, a temporal order may direct the movement between sacred and profane spaces. People go to church on *Sundays*—and only if to be *especially* reminded *on this day* that God, as a *universal* observer, is present on *all* days. The *actualization* of more intensive religious behavior documents a *possibility* that is *always* relevant. This form of differentiation is called "situational differentiation" in the following discussion, with "situation" meaning the world observed from a position in time and space.

Such situational differentiation obviously requires some form of communicative validation and (at least some) reflexivity, that is, communication *about* communication. It has to distinguish situations and be able to make them accessible from other situations. That is something obvious in the course of a normal day: after work, one eats dinner. If, however, a religious definition of the situation should be identified that passes through the direct logic of what can be experienced, definitions of religious connection will have to be developed including situations with different meanings of their own—such as impurification/purification or sinning/confessing. Doing so already demands a semantics that religion can "adjudicate," with which it can evaluate itself and other matters.

It is only when times and places are set up as situations for repeated religious use that strict rituals can be developed whose form verifies the exclusion (and thus the presence) of other possibilities.[1] These are celebrated in the framework of sects that in turn focus one's attention. Seen from the perspective of their function, they enable a more or less thoughtless improvement of prospects. Recursive mechanisms are now also possible and may activate a ritual on variable or established grounds. These contrast with reactive magical practices of purification, healing, or pacification, as in the case of uncontrolled triggering events.

Rituals have to be conceived of as forms of communication staged in relation to perception. They cannot be understood as an object of consensus or even agreement, because that would introduce to the institution a possibility of dissent or even revoking consensus. Social cohesion and the regulation of process come about through objects that one observes in order to know how distant something is, what there is to something, and what one has to do or expect.[2] Bodily presence is needed: people see and are seen, and people see that they are seen; that, to a great extent, is what constitutes communication. The necessary bodily presence expands the communicative possibilities. That is precisely how the body acts as a medium for constructing forms and for expressing and visualizing restrictions, all the way to realizing something correctly (when there is no alternative).[3] While in a trance, dancing or celebrating a ritual, one's observations are focused by special types of bodies. That makes it unnecessary to imagine the event as an application of rules. As Friederike Hassauer has shown, in medieval pilgrimages the movement of bodies was still more important than self-scrutiny in reaching a consensus with oneself or others.[4] Although communication is practiced and strictly supervised, it takes place with a minimum of difference between utterance and information. One only communicates the meaning of the behavior, and because that behavior is highly amplified, problems of interpretation become unnecessary for a time. Unlike in the case of the chorus in Greek tragedy, the production of meaning may not be the object of an added commentary, because that would reveal the contingency of the play.

Yet at the same time, communication is implicitly taking place about the intention of the ritual and about the world.[5] The beginning of the societal system's self-definition—of times, places, and manners—did not at all suggest that external references might have less significance. Communication that was self-referential, directed toward its own correctness, did not of course deny that it was taking place in the world and in society. It had to remain accessible and able to be resolved again. But with rituals, the need emerged for reformulating other-reference. One might then assume—as taught by the "myth and ritual" school[6]—that ritualization stimulated the development of myth as a semantic construction parallel to a boundary that must be (ritually) performed as a "liminal phenomenon."[7] It was a guideline for differences that can then be used in narratives in order to contrast present time and the reason for the ritual with something else. Differences were celebrated such as chaos/cosmos, birth/death, abundance/lack, immortal/mortal, innocence/sin, soul/body, ungendered (androgynous)/gendered, Titans/gods. Put very concretely, these were processes of shifting shapes. The other-reference was thus elaborated by using distinctions, and it became more significant when self-referential religious communications were in need of meaning. It thus enabled limited forms of freedom. Although these distinctions were necessarily predefined and not at one's disposal, what happened or was appropriate in individual cases also depended on human behavior. And, as a result, time became relevant. Time, which in itself proceeds evenly, in analog fashion, became digitalized and thus reportable. This was the origin of narrative form, in which difference can appear as unity, thus allowing paradoxes to be resolved. At the same time, in mythological narrative, it was important that times and places of the narration were often predetermined and, in particular, that neither plot nor sociality could be eliminated from the narrative context. This made it easier to formulate analogies and transmit the wisdom of myths in situations of daily life.

Myths narrate what is already known. That is their way of reproducing the unfamiliar within the familiar. What they reproduce is solidarity, not information. That is why myths always only refer to *past* events with the idea of interpreting them for the *present*. The *future* is not considered. If (as in some rare cases) we find eschatologies that go beyond a representation of life after death, the future is presented in reversed images whose fantastic character fascinates us. Here the future becomes the time when the unfamiliar will overwhelm the familiar.

Familiarity with the myth is not part of the narrative itself. It does not appear in the story but is presupposed instead. Self-referential indications are therefore operative. Yet they were not articulated or made into a subject of communication (which, after all, can always be negated). Only near the end of the (here Greek) culture of myths was the poet expected to produce something that was remarkable, surprising, or formally new. And now, the one called upon to provide it was no longer labeled a seer, but a maker.[8]

The combination of ritual and myth guided one's capacity to recognize deviance and thus how normative expectations were assigned. One can only deviate from strictly regulated ritual. In such cases, deviations can be easily recognized as errors. Myth was only narrated, and since the narrative took place orally, it was comprehended by being experienced, by being believed. The narrator could embellish and invent things as long as he stayed within a recognizable structure. Yet what was narrated did not remain fixed, without divergence.[9] Only the self-referential (not the *other*-referential) side of a total religious complex could be normatively fixed, because it would not make sense to standardize environmental circumstances that could not be influenced. The forms likewise differed in which contingencies were permitted. Myth allowed them to appear at the narrative's linking points (or transitions). In ritual, they were visible as errors and eliminated if possible. In other cases, they were understood and treated as omens or signs of misfortune.

Parallel to this development, the need emerged for social assistance in order to absorb the difficulties that increasingly arose. To the extent that transcendence became an issue and paradoxical or ambivalent formulations imposed themselves, the need for interventions became acute. These could be worked into the religious cosmos using the model of patron/client relations and could thus take the form of intervening saints.[10] A functional equivalent could be seen in differentiating appropriate roles that might offer interventions not dependent on ancestor worship.[11] In conducting an analysis based on evolutionary theory, transitional forms also became interesting, making it possible to become used to the unusual. For the threats (or interventions) of sacred powers that occasionally surfaced, occasional skills might have sufficed to mobilize members of the tribe who had stronger nerves or the ability to recognize definitions of the situation because of their age or their memory of similar past cases. Prescribed knowledge was deployed to absorb uncertainty, and in such cases it was enough to maintain that one thing or another would help. Greater demands resulted as rituals and myths were developed. Redundancy and variety then had to be guaranteed on both sides of this distinction. In addition to (or because of) those opportune competencies, appropriate roles were established. Along with the expectations associated with those roles, succession became a problem—a kind of official consciousness—whenever the bearer of the roles failed or died. The religion system reacted to such an increase in complexity with a two-fold level of differentiation, finding support precisely in such doubling, that is, in the distinction of role and person and the distinction of this special role (or roles) and other behavior.

Role differentiations could result solely from situations. They did not have to immediately make reference to their access to transcendence. Sects that work with trance states (as found nowadays in Central and South America, for instance) opened up the role of a "medium" who (in principle) was "possessed" by spirits for all participants, even when it still required that selections be made. There were therefore no fixed role asymmetries in terms of accessing transcendence. That were also presumably why there was no clear distinction drawn between black and white magic. In other cases, by contrast, a cultic sequence could only proceed in an orderly way if priests contributed their specific skills (such as providing sacraments). And these were skills that not everyone had or could use. Fixed role asymmetries suggested a need to guarantee an overall order in social status, whether in the stratification of a society or in church officialdom in particular. Sects working with trance states were less limited in this respect, and it may not be a coincidence that they are found today primarily in racially and socially oppressed strata.

An organization of roles made it possible to be flexible and firm at the same time, shaping an emergent level of religious activity. The ability to deal with religious problems could be permanently ensured, and such an organization might be differentiated by hierarchy or by division of labor. If resources sufficed, a priesthood emerged that also controlled access to these roles and that could possibly come to terms with social stratification by regulating access.

From the perspective of the societal system, all this was a way to organize self-reference. But what self-reference was able to say now became ambiguous. The issue continued to be the self-observation of communication, that is, communication about communication. But the differentiated organizing of roles in the priesthood could also develop its own interests, whether in purity, orthodoxy, or in resources. At that point, it became possible for religion itself to be conveyed into a social-structural mode of system differentiation. There were then not only holy objects or rituals and myths that had to be reproduced competently. Rather, there was also a religion system emerging that integrated several nonreligious activities and resources, and that also had to communicate about them. There were matters of buildings and administration, of subordinate personnel, and of relationships that were external to the religion system but nonetheless still occurred within society. The system was now based on a double systematization on the level of operations and semantics. It thus achieved a state of "double closure."[12] On the one hand, the operations were determined in view of the current state of the system and of their capacity to connect with the system. On the other, their orientation derived from a construction of the world aligned with the system. There transitions were carefully monitored, and inconsistencies were avoided (if possible) or depicted as merely ostensible contradictions. Above all, opposites—such as birth and death, luck and misfortune, sunrise and sunset, friends and enemies—were no longer experienced as contradictions but *incorporated into* the cosmology. One might say that the rejection of contradictions had to be handed back to logic so that things and events could be set free.

It was not mistaken to assume that religion's other-references had to be adapted at this stage of its development. There was, for instance, the doctrine of gifts that trigger the soul's redemption and, in association with it, the uncoupling of ideas about life after death from the circumstances of death (death in battle, death in bed, etc.) or conditions of class. The highly appealing notion of life after death could in any case be identified as the generalization appropriate to these new differentiations.[13] It accommodated the needs of clients, facilitated the acquisition of resources, and served orthodoxy as a general notion under which several moral states could be included. In addition, an interpretation that could be passed on was required by the difference that now opens up between priests and laypeople. Initially, it seemed like a good idea to return to the old topos of secret knowledge. Then one fells back on a special competence for dealing with holy texts or on greater effectiveness in communicating with the relevant temple god. Or one might take recourse to the higher merits associated with distinctive types of lifestyle. Asceticism could thus legitimate wealth. And if nowhere else, wisdom had to be reflected in the lifestyle of a sage, as long as independent (empirical) controls on knowledge remained impossible. But most of all, people now needed a "soul" to which guilt and fate could be attributed, before and after death. And punishment could then largely be reinterpreted as guilt feelings,[14] and what wasn't ascribed to the soul could be left to the law.

What is especially striking is how the notion of a *covenant*, of God's contract with his people, became acceptable at this stage of religion's development.[15] It replaced and (to a significant extent) devalued the quasi-objects that had guided the social event of rituals and that now led to new versions of the religious sect. Its meaning was now "synagogic"* and could be found in confirming the *covenant*, in public readings, and in the interpretive appropriation of the text. The covenant is given and accepted. Along with it, the problem of loyalty to the covenant emerged, transforming all the impurities and ritual errors that previously had to be balanced out by parallel compensatory behavior.

Shifts in the semantic relationship between self- and other-reference now reflected system-internal problems more intensely. If formulated very generally, it might be said that the system's own differences and distinctions

---

* In ancient Greek, *sunagōgē* means "meeting" or "assembly," deriving from *sunagein*, "to bring together" (*sun-* "together" + *agein* "bring, lead").—Trans.

now prompted the development of organizations and dogmas. The degree of freedom thus provided gave rise to the well-known differences among the religions of the major civilizations, which to this very day have prevented a uniform religious semantics from developing. Part of the self-specification of every religion is also demarcating itself from other religions—something done by the various religions with a very different intensity in their respective rules of exclusion.

II

To distinguish between the differentiation of themes, situations, roles, and systems presupposes that we have criteria of distinction. Themes, situations, and roles can be kept separate from one another by means of relatively simple distinctions, just like those made between objects. Each object can be described after being distinguished from all the others and from the unmarked state of the world. Disturbances can be countered by redefining the situation. Just which consistency problems emerge depends on the daily rhythm of the lifestyle. Time is needed, for example, in getting from one place to another. Not until a written culture was developed did the demands for consistency increase within the semantics that were preserved. That can be responded to with system differentiations (not to speak of other possibilities). These interrupt the burden of consistency by making system/environment distinctions. Indeed, system differentiations are themselves distinguished from all other forms of differentiation, due to the fact that observer positions are concurrently differentiated and something else is seen as environment from the standpoint of each system.

In contrast to all other forms of differentiation, we can only talk about system differentiation if the system draws boundaries between itself and the environment, in this way reproducing itself. Independent of some observers' ability to assess connections (between rituals and myths, or between religious roles), the formation of a system assumes (if one accepts this theoretical provision)[16] that the system decides through self-observation which operations reproduce it and which do not, that is, what belongs to the system and what doesn't. Clearly, there can also be external observers who work with other distinctions and caesuras. Regardless of how one approaches the system idea in this case, there are "autopoietic" systems that produce everything in the network of their own operations that counts as a system operation and that is treated as capable of connection within the system. From there it follows that these systems work under the condition of operative closure. They detach themselves from a direct external definition of their eigenstates and only get involved in structural couplings that channel those disturbances (and exclude others) that are treated as irritations in the system and thus reworked into manageable information.

Ancestor veneration plays a special role in religious tradition. Having developed independently in a range of societies, it was found in Mesopotamia as well as in China. The basic experience of one's own parents or grandparents dying motivated the question of what became of them, and this question acquired a typically religious coloring, because one could not be certain whether these ancestors survived or influenced their families as good and helpful spirits or evil ones. Sects guaranteed and reproduced memory (although extensive private genealogies did this as well) even if the lives of those departed were gradually forgotten. A genealogy thus served both as a taxonomic scheme and a reference point in rituals of ancestor worship. In differentiating ancestor veneration and recognizing its forms in institutions, societies were able to account for basic segmentary differentiation into family households even long after political structures and major religions or moral notions (fixed in textual form) had developed. The differentiation of religion was both enabled and inhibited in this fashion. One still could not speak of a system of religion that encompassed *all* religious communications and *these* alone. Ancestor worship was still too strongly tied to living in family households or even larger systems of relatives (clans) and therefore had an impetus to be reproduced.

Yet major religions, which can examine what does (and does not) make sense in their frameworks, are autopoietic systems. They reproduce themselves by means of their own operations. To do so, they need the distinction between self- and other-reference. What helped here was when a textual foundation served as a canon, as an orthodoxy with a limited learning capacity. However, these texts formulated a description of the world, thus enabling the reproduction of the *difference* between self- and other-reference. The world was religiously interpreted, but suffusing it with religious meaning was based on communicative operations capable of connecting within the system itself. Statements about something *else* could then be verified with their *own* resources. Consequently, these textual devices had be presumed to be binding, to be *religio*. Their self-interpretation had to find a limit in their holiness, since it would otherwise be *internally* permissible for descriptions to be modified continually *from the outside* (politically, for example).

When religion had achieved this form of differentiation, it was offering a world description that (from its view) is *complete*. That made it difficult (if not impossible) to recognize the differentiation of religion from within society and react *to it* communicatively, especially if everyone (more or less) shared its premises of faith. Society accepted religion's positing of the world [*Weltsetzung*]. Only (or precisely) in this world, then, was there freedom for nonreligious communication. For not every day is the Sabbath. But precisely this temporal distillate of religion established a difference, which as *difference* or *form* had religious connotations. Holy time and other times were times in the same world, the (religious) unity of which was accentuated by such a two-sided form.

The religion system is thus closed in terms of operations. But it is not closed in its meaning. It offers society observational schemata that make use of distinctions. On the one side of these distinctions, religion appears once more—as special time, a sect or a priestly profession—and it does so (typically) in all three dimensions (temporal, factual, and social). In this complicated architecture, based on religion's reentry into a religiously defined world, the operative basis of the religion system is made visible. At the same time it is invisible, such that the distinction of religion is based on religion itself. The sect, priesthood, or whatever, can then be subjected to communication (possibly even critical communication). The religious positing of the world is not thereby placed in question, for it is not subject to negotiation as long as there are no other constructions of worlds (for instance, natural-scientific ones).

An operatively closed system can neither begin nor end with its own operations. To do so, it would have to be capable of crossing its own boundaries with its own operations. It can produce a description of beginning and end, even of the world's beginning and end. But this can only happen between the beginning and end of the world, only by means of the operations of an autopoietic system that is already operative.[17] That is precisely why in Milton's *Paradise Lost* the archangel Raphael has to explain the meaning of world history from beginning to end to Adam (who cannot know it), presuming that God at least observes before the beginning and after the end what he allows to happen. Time is available as a horizon of stories that nonetheless have to take place in time.

This self-sufficient structure of a reentry of time into time is not recognizable as a paradox at the level of description. It presents only an occasion for discussing the world's spatial and temporal finitude or infinity. Such discussions, however, bypass the problem by using this (rather) objectivistic-sounding distinction. An external description of this description is not freed from the question of how the beginning of an autopoietic system of "religion" is to be imagined, how it might be "scientifically" reconstructed. It seems reasonable to look at operative closure as an evolutionary accomplishment that can be achieved "equifinally," that is, achieved from different starting situations as long as sufficient preconditions are fulfilled. We shall return to this issue when thinking about the evolution of religion, but for now we still have to complete our analysis of religion's differentiation from another vantage point.

III

Linguistic communication can respond to any linguistic communication with a "yes" or "no," with acceptance or rejection. The previous communication will (or will not) become a premise of further selections. *Both* cases can result in the breaking off of ongoing communication. In the case of consensus, it is because there is nothing left to say; in the case of dissent, because further communication seems pointless. But further communication is also possible in *both* cases: in the case of consensus, because now there is a basis for more risky, demanding and structuring communication; in the case of dissent, because now there is a reason to argue or debate peacefully but powerfully. The yes/no bifurcation thus does not mean the same thing as continuing or breaking off communication. By contrast, the linguistic code guarantees that communication can be sustained in all cases, regardless of the external influences (motives) pushing the process toward the yes- or no-track.

In distinction to positions today best represented by Jürgen Habermas,[18] I do not assume that there is an immanent telos of communication that normatively prescribes a search for agreement. Accordingly, I renounce the concept of rationality as normative. And this renunciation clears the way to presenting another problem: precisely the continuously renewed yes/no bifurcation—that binary code of language—guarantees the autopoiesis of the communication system "society." It can operate on the yes-track or the no-track, or it can break off whenever other, more attractive communication possibilities come into view. But that raises a question that will concern us in what follows: How can sufficient acceptance of communication be guaranteed if the meaning offered is becoming more and more selective, more and more unlikely? Or if what is demanded continues to increase, or society becomes more complex?

This was especially the case when writing was introduced and disseminated: communications became possible that avoided the controls imposed by interaction among people who are present to one another. Writing enabled communication among people not present to one another. In that case, people were freer to decide whether they wanted to use the meaning of what they read, whether they believed it or not, and whether they wanted to follow it as a norm or directive. What they did depended on completely different constellations, opportunities, and supervisions. The temporal extension of optional possibilities would already guarantee that rejection—or simply inconsistent communication—became more likely. Intrinsically a neutral communication technology similarly subject to a yes/no code, writing still favored the "no."

In addition, writing allowed people to avoid the compulsions that characterize face-to-face interaction, as well as its constraints on their time or the pressures of being seen together. It gave the participant in communication more freedom to choose times and moods for reading and then to break off and restart the communication, in the process gaining a more personal relationship to it.[19] Precisely the era of mass media was characterized by an intense personalization of participation in communication. That was the only way it became possible for participation in (religious and other) communication to become a very personal experience.

Significant social discoveries are particularly relevant to this problem. And it is not surprising that the further development of certain evolutionary accomplishments follows the introduction of fully phonetic universal writing, specifically of the alphabet. One can hardly speak of a causal relationship here, but rather of a fit that permits society to be realized at a higher level of complexity.

Crucial social contrivances such as politically directed state power and coined money[20]—but also the pursuit of truth through dialogues and literature[21]—raised ancient Greece to a level of complexity that was preserved in society's institutional memory. In spite of all the setbacks, it has never been forgotten. In addition, it is almost no coincidental that this took place under conditions that kept religion from intervening in adaptations of semantics or structure. At the same time, the structural differentiation thus initiated did not have to turn against religion or pursue a program of secularization. It was able to accept religion, in the shape of sects whose expansion was inwardly directed, as a phase of structural differentiation in society.

This development can be reconstructed with the help of a universal theory of symbolically generalized communication media.[22] The function of these media refers to the problem of when the acceptance of communication becomes improbable. That indeed is their common starting point, and even the solutions they offer reveal points of agreement. There are always special conditionings at work that displace the motivating situation (and "motivating situation" is not intended psychologically here but as a functioning premise of communication). One deploys threatening methods (power) or evidentiary methods (truth). Or one convinces others by a combinatorics of forms understandable to the senses (art), by agreeing to highly individual expectations of another person (love), or by means of a wild card (money) that can be reused. An artificial connection between conditioning and motivating is produced: it is compatible with higher contingencies, but at the same time has to be differentiated structurally. It understands only sub-aspects of social coexistence and, as a result, tends toward those corresponding differentiations in the system. The complete consequences of this development are not visible until modern society undergoes a shift toward functional differentiation.

Even religion must have been affected by this same problem of when acceptance becomes improbable. The general cultural shift to the new communication technology of writing was already calling for changes to be made in statements of faith, such as in the idea of an absent being who is always present, of a God who observes everything. But these statements were in the beginning still able to presuppose that in the realm of human communication, religious communication was taking place orally.[23]

At this point, ongoing divine communication with human beings had to be prevented or restricted to a fixed textual corpus. For otherwise it could have readily resulted in a piling up of the most diverse protocols about God's communications. The outcome would have been either technologically contingent high unemployment among priests[24] or retraining them to rationalize and harmonize diverging reports.[25] The ability to test and reflect individually on impositions of faith (going hand in hand with increased mastery of writing) became a problem only when books become more widely available. On the Protestant side, this led to stronger externalizations, meaning faith in writing ("if it were not written down, one would not believe it") and the need for church organization. But it also led to a stronger internalization of faith as a personal experience or as conviction in the individual's profession of faith.

There are some indications that a special, symbolically generalized communication medium called "faith" developed under pressure from this general and typical problem constellation, at least in the domain of Christianity. The conditions of correct faith were formulated in articles of faith (and thus in written form). Forms of communicative confirmation were found (the church in the spiritual sense of a "community of faith"), and the old culture of ritual was refunctionalized into a type of symbiotic mechanism, into forms of being together physically—even to the point of being with the deceased god who was physically present. All this had parallels in other symbolically generalized communication media, yet the differences are also striking. Other media were differentiated by examining whether experience or action should be motivated as improbable selections, and these media were correspondingly specialized (for example, with truth on the one, power on the other side).[26] Religion could not follow this principle of distinction, since it assumed that all life was observed by God. It would be difficult for it to accept that one could achieve redemption simply by acting based on any attitude or, inversely, by experiencing something with no relevant correlate in action. Religion also could not order the professional structure of the distinction between priesthood and laity according to the idea that "the one acts, the other experiences." This would contradict the notion of a community of faith. In other words, religion was dependent on closer proximity to the unity of a human being for whom experiencing and acting always stand in a reciprocal relation that cannot be disentangled. The one-sidedness and artificiality of attributing selections—as either externally impressed (experience) or internally motivated (action)—had the further effect of releasing one or the other side of this distinction. Yet that was precisely not consistent with what was demanded by religious faith. The question was still largely open of just how religion came to terms with the fact that it becomes increasingly easy to reject it. In other words, in which forms were (still reliable) couplings of conditioning and motivation possible if society was becoming more complex and if local communities of inclusion (based on interaction) were losing their significance for an individual's lifestyle?

One kind of functional equivalent could be discovered in a semantic complex that problematized the relationship between the one eternal God and the numerous souls surviving beyond their physical lives.[27] The construct of the soul and the resulting distinction of body and soul served religion as an anchoring point in the world, as a possibility of engaging one's interest in survival. They were also components of a distinctive medium that made it possible to imagine a loose coupling of souls and their destinies. The unity of this medium was guaranteed by the configuration of sin that generated the problem of whether God would ultimately save an individual's soul or abandon it to eternal damnation.[28] It is a medium to the extent that the relationship of God and souls permits a large number of combinations, even if only two (but at least *two*!) final values—redemption or damnation—were possible. Sin was understood both as analog and digital, that is, as both a permanent condition (*habitus*) of physical life in this world and as an action in the present, a type of guilt. God's participation was guaranteed by ruling out self-gratification (which incidentally was ruled out in all symbolically generalized communication media) or, as in this case, self-redemption. One could attempt to lead a life free of sin, doing good works. But it would be fully counterproductive to assess the situation and end up counting on redemption; that would be a diversion, a trick of the devil (so to speak) who had set traps for us along the path to heaven. Mercy was indispensable for being rewarded with salvation, precisely in the case of sins one regretted, and not only for individually chosen paths to it. Nonetheless, each redemption of souls had (or preserved) a unique individual form, with God knowing and judging each individual *individually*.

This sophisticated constellation appeared to fulfill all the presuppositions of a religious medium. The love of an omniscient God offered a medial substrate, frequently leading to specifically articulated forms. The motivational force of these conditionings cannot easily be disputed, in the course of a few centuries at least. Furthermore, the way it worked was highly plausible and well-established—with the notions of a single God who sees everything and of a human soul that survives physical death. Yet, seen another way, there were clearly certain historical conditions at work, certain ways of administering this medium that were institutional, legalistically structured, or ecclesiastical. Along with that, the opportunities were relatively favorable for moral consensus on the criteria programming the code of redemption versus damnation. All this was called into question with the Reformation, as well as by state appropriation of ecclesiastical jurisdiction and effects of the spread of the printing press. It is thus doubtful whether such a religious medium was an evolutionary achievement that would be capable of outlasting the circumstances of its emergence and success in that historical context.

We might suppose that a functional equivalent for this omission of a symbolically generalized communication medium can be found in the structural differentiation of the system, in a difference of inclusion/exclusion that (when necessary) can be supported by a relevant organization. The degree to which the Catholic Church in the Middle Ages took on the form of an organizationally and legally well-constructed *universitas* supports this hypothesis. So too does the fact that heresies could now be countered only by making exclusions or, after printing was introduced, by making further structural differentiations within Christianity.

In any event, the situation was more complex than such easy contrasts might reveal. Other functional domains of society also tend toward differentiation once symbolically generalized communication media develop and become effective. This is how the money economy, which was quickly expanding in the Middle Ages, invalidated the old differentiation of domestic economy and civil society: by means of an economic system that could not be controlled either politically, religiously, or by stratification. Across today's world, this type of economy is busily ruining the traditional family ones based on agriculture or craft. And as far as official power is concerned, an analogous situation obtains in the modern territorial state. In such cases, the technical possibilities of a special motivation for specific problem constellations evidently resulted in the later differentiation of the system. In the case of religion, this process could have taken the opposite path. People might at first have relied on inclusion/exclusion and—only when mobility increased with religion-internal divisions—seen a need to make greater efforts to acquire system-internal methods of convincing others. Clear evidence for this can be found in Luther's translation of the Bible, in the religious duties of the (male) head of household, and in the enormous school network of the Jesuit order—all developments which would have been quite unusual in the Middle Ages. Only now, with the rise of Protestantism, did it become apparent how much popular beliefs still deviated from the ideas of the Church.

Because of its special position (particularly in the early modern era), it became impossible for religion to participate in many of the semantic innovations shaping the conceptual world of modernity. In early modernity, for instance, the term "interest" began a career directed toward a combination of specification and universalization, ruling out (despite Kant's "interest of reason") any aggregation of *the* interest *of* people into a unified final objective. As a result, all attempts failed at comprehending redemptive interests as interests, or at privileging them over secular interests. An observer of the observer might suppose that God might then (and immediately) change the way he implemented his mercy, thereby derailing such a strategic, calculated rationality. Religion thus stood outside all attempts to calculate and restrict another person using his specific interests (assuming that interaction and stratification would fail). The necessary combination of specification and universalization, and its institutionalization in autopoietic function systems, could not be transferred to religious faith.

That would imply that everything depended even more on the mechanism of inclusion (versus exclusion) functioning with sufficiently strong motivation. Here, however, religion stands in its own way whenever describing itself with reference to human needs. Each person can all too readily confirm that he does not have these needs: neither a fear of death nor a (vain) desire for comfort in case of sorrow. Nor does he does need to be provided with meaning or an increased altruistic motivation. The question then becomes: If there is no self-supporting communication medium for religion that structures communication in all its particulars, how can the "framing" of motivation be left entirely to the system's boundaries (especially under social preconditions that favor the eroding of all separations and that invite the continuous crossing of boundaries)?

On account of these specially burdens, religion finds itself today in a society whose structures have been reoriented for functional differentiation. In this situation, it does not pose a problem that religion (now) finds itself as one functional system among many. It can keep up with the others concerning operative closure, binary coding, and functional specification. Such an idiom of describing religion from the outside is clearly inadequate and cannot be used for its self-description. But that holds true in the case of the other function systems as well. We are thus compelled to ask: Can religion still—the same way it did before—make use of its system boundaries, the distinction between inclusion and exclusion, as its mechanism of motivation?

We shall come back to this at a later point. For now, it is sufficient to note that this question is not fully answered by referring to the evolutionary trend toward differentiation [*Ausdifferenzierung*].

IV

The differentiation of religious communication begins with thematic distinctions and ends with a self-manufactured distinction of a system that is anchored in religious communication. At least in retrospect, it can be described as a historical process. That is not saying anything other than that a kind of Guttmann scaling might be applicable. Later phases of the process assume earlier ones; the process could not run in the opposite direction unless it were to destroy its results and start again with no guarantee of the same outcome.

If one assumes a processual idea of this kind, one is using a descriptive formula that pays attention to temporal difference. That formula can then be integrated with relevant descriptions from the history of society. Yet there is little scientific benefit from that. The idea of process may be suitable as a framing idea for narratives, yet all attempts have failed to determine precisely how such a process is structured. This is true for descriptions that find the process to be regulated by a natural law, thus having the same results in the case of the same starting conditions, *ceteris paribus* [other things being equal]. It is also true for phase models that rely on being able to date structural breaks in the transition from one phase to the next (even if it is done with considerable leeway and imprecision). And it is true for neo-dialectical theories of development in the wake of Hegel, Marx, or even Adorno. Each of these cases assume that contradictions are unstable and that transitions (in lieu of empirically determinable causes) are thereby forced into a different organization of reality, whether spiritual or material. The sequence of these theories reveals a significant refinement in construction. But distinctions are always being assumed—distinctions that structure the process itself or even pursue it reflectively, as in the case of dialectics. If one were to do without such distinctions, one would be unable to use the category of process, having nothing left to explain the unity of the process from the inside.

It is only with the rise of evolutionary theory in the Darwinistic or post-Darwinistic sense that the conditions for an alternative can be discerned. The evolution of the religion system will be treated in a later chapter. At this point, however, some evolution-theoretical questions should have become clearer inasmuch as the differentiation of subsystems of society results from evolution, specifically the evolution of the societal system itself. The differentiation of a subsystem, after all, is the evolution of a difference, a form with two sides. One of them is the inside, where the subsystem produces its own complexity and relinquishes itself to its own dynamics. And then there is the outside, what remains of society when this happens.[29] Differentiation, in any case, is a result of prior societal evolution and the occasion for further evolution. And when seen from the perspective of the societal system, it is a matter of chance whether independent evolutions begin in certain operational fields (such as those with a religious production of meaning) and whether their results have to be tolerated (or can be used) elsewhere—for the religious legitimation of political rule, for example.[30]

However, what is to be understood by "evolution"? Even evolutionary theory is often treated as a processual theory, but that misunderstanding can be easily acknowledged.[31] While evolutionary theory distinguishes variation, selection, and restabilization, it also assumes stability (the state of being restabilized) with the idea of variation. In addition, it builds this distinction into a systems theory, presupposing that a distinction to a system's environment can only be distinguished with a system. Furthermore, it should be assumed that the distinction of these evolutionary functions (and not only the particular initial conditions of specific changes) is itself a result of evolution. It can thus be explained how evolution accelerates itself in constructing more complex fields of application for differentiating the evolutionary functions of variation, selection, and restabilization.

Understood as a series of events, this distinction might be construed as a process, although from a logical standpoint, it is a circular one. The task of theory is to clarify unplanned structural changes, and thereby the "morphogenetic" construction of complex systems (or with Darwin, the diversification of species). In the process, it makes unnecessary one of the familiar proofs of God's existence—that because creation is so complex and well-ordered, there is a creator—which is what makes it so offensive theologically.

This very general form of (evolution-theoretical) distinguishing leaves us with the question of how these different functions are fulfilled (and thus how their realization can be thought of as evolutionary "mechanisms") and how their separation can be interpreted. This is the point at which the sociological and biological applications part ways.

My thesis in this case is that variation applies to operations, selection applies to structures, and restabilization applies to the relationship of system and environment. This explains as well the necessary circularity of evolutionary theory, since operations, structures, and systems cannot arise independently of one another. The separation of evolutionary functions should be understood as an absence of systemic coordination in the sense that variation has not already determined what is being selected (positively or negatively). Nor does (positive or negative) selection establish whether (and how) the system will preserve its boundaries to the environment in the case of changed structures or repressed changes—or whether (and how) it takes an expansive or a restrictive and (seen long-term) possibly destructive course. The classical term for this built-in uncertainty is "chance" [*Zufall*]. And one outcome of this arrangement is unpredictability.

What is clear is that operations of social systems are always communications, and thus occurrences that lack duration. Hence, one can only speak about variation if the communications strike one as unexpected. In normal cases (indeed, almost always) one attributes this to the situation, and it is thus inconsequential. In fact, there is the additional possibility of reacting with a "yes" or "no" in the communication itself, without it leading to a structural change. The system protects itself almost completely against chance variations, the causes of which it cannot control.

But it may be the case that such variations allow structural patterns to be recognized that deviate from what one is used to. Then (and only then) can one pose the question of a positive or negative selection. That way, specific topics can be subjected to a religious interpretation—or lose that interpretation whenever better explanations are communicated. The results can be confounding and can only be remedied if one deviates from one's habits. Or chance coincidences can turn out so convincingly that one attempts to repeat them in rituals. Virtuosity in dealing with sacred subjects may be a reason not to leave matters to chance any more. Instead, if the expert is no longer available, a successor can be found and a new role thus defined. The differentiation of roles can lead to problems in regulating access to succession and in defining official duties that both predecessor and successor must fulfill in the same way. That makes it possible to see how individuals differ in the way they act in their official roles.

From this, it can be presumed that there is a relationship between a separation of variation and selection as establishing evolution (on the one hand) and an increased reinforcing of a form consciousness (on the other). It is thus understandable that from very different initial constellations magical formulas and rituals develop "equifinally," making conformity and deviation distinguishable (and, in some sense, evolution-tested). That then enables specifically religious observations that can be distinguished from other fields of meaning. In other words, one does not need to assume specific situations of need (Malinowski) or specific functions (Radcliffe-Brown) in order to explain the emergence of forms. However, additional working assumptions are needed if one wishes to explain how forms remain stable and enrich themselves (by repeated use) with meaning, interpretations, or legends. Classical evolutionary theory would have argued on the basis of natural selection here and would not have distinguished between selection and stabilization.[32] It probably is more correct to assume that structural determinations can lead to internal as well as external maladaptations[33] that later on might turn into stability problems. For (unplanned) systems resulting from evolution are always characterized by a high degree of "error friendliness" and "robustness" or "loose coupling." Otherwise, the functions of selection and restabilization could not be separated at all.

The differentiation of a religious world of forms may start and continue moving by means of (a type of) self-motivation. But it also always makes reference to an already existing societal differentiation and its ecological substrate. If that differentiation only refers to people's age and gender, problems in the transition and thus the "processing" of this distinction will seek to take on a religious form. How is a child made into a man or woman? If there is already the formation of families and thus segmentary differentiation, it may be important when making a plausible choice of religious form whether segmentary unities are defined primarily by family relation or primarily by territorially-bound social existence. Depending on the circumstances involved, one will either be persuaded more by ancestor veneration or more by a system of local gods promising protection and fertility. The option chosen will be co-determined in each case by the necessity of avoiding conflict and by the exogamy associated with segmentation.

On the one hand, one can presume that variations will occur to a massive extent at the level of everyday communication and that these will still be communicatively reportable for a short duration through a kind of short-term memory (case or situational memory). On the other hand, positive selections are only likely if they are capable of connection in the framework of an existing social differentiation. Now that doesn't always have to be the case. Precisely the religion system also develops ideas with a self-created plausibility—such as the idea of the miracle. And it also allows the successful breaking of taboos that so often distinguishes religious heroes or founders of new religions.

Neither preexisting fundamental human needs nor social functions are therefore useful starting points for evolutionary explanations. Such theories have been developed with reference to primitive social systems and underestimate the enormous morphogenetic potential in the autopoietic operation of communication. This applies especially if one wants to explain the transition to major civilizations and modern society in terms of evolutionary theory (and what other option is there?). The significance of needs or functions is not being disputed, but they are relevant with respect to problems of evolutionary restabilization, that is, the external or internal connective capacity of new developments and the tolerability of their resulting burdens (such as overwork, shortages, slavery, and so forth, as consequences of higher economic development). A functional shift typically takes place in the transitional phases of evolution. Those functions that initially favored a positive selection of new structures (such as the formation of families, writing, coined money, and contracts as grounds for the emergence of obligations) do not need to conform to those that crystallize later on.

In this way, however, a break can be made away from classic "causalistic" explanations. If autopoiesis is saying that systems reproduce themselves with the help of those operations that had produced them, then the burden of explanation falls back on evolutionary theory. For within systems theory, the question of the takeoff, of what triggers the start, cannot be answered. But evolutionary theory also begs the question: it explains evolution by differences that themselves result from evolution. The question of the origin ultimately reaches its vanishing point in the assumption of a "big bang," of an initial difference. Yet perhaps one can do without any such mythological narrative if one restricts oneself to describing structural innovations in the model of evolutionary theory. For the problem of a break—whether at the beginning or at some time in the middle—is always a paradoxical one. It specifically poses the question of the unity of the difference of before and after. Religion has found ways to resolve this paradox, whether by narrating myths or by observing the observer God who is always already present (as the presupposed unity) in all differences. Science will not be able to resolve it any better—only differently.

V

After these evolution-theoretical analyses, we shall now return to structural problems in the differentiation of the religion system. These can become relevant in different ways. On the one hand, a rather developed major religion will have problems "in its own camp." Those problems may specifically involve popular religion, "superstition," a magical religiosity (persistently surviving but also emerging) or an indifference that is content with a minimal knowledge of faith. On the other hand, the religion system is also confronted with its self-produced external boundary, on whose other side something different is occurring.

On the "internal" boundary of the system, an unremitting, profoundly hopeless struggle has to be waged, especially on the part of "studied" knowledge (that is, knowledge acquired with much time and effort). In practical situations, that kind of knowledge has no further resonance when it is contrasted with divinatory knowledge, ritual knowledge (such as that of the Brahmins), or medical knowledge of healing—all forms of knowledge that are constantly being called on. Where there are formal rules of attribution, as in Christianity, the degree to which religion penetrates daily experience and action is thoroughly overestimated. This was true for Europe well into modernity despite the introduction of the confession (which follows its own casuistry and doctrine of sin). In recent times, religion's lack of success can ultimately be explained as "secularization." This circumstance applies even more to the regions of Latin America colonized by Catholics, where syncretic sects of the most diverse kind attract the religious interest of the people, where the association to Catholicism (for instance) is only achieved via the Virgin Mary. The cartographic perspective also contributes to the overestimation of religious unity. It is as if all Chinese had heard of Confucius or Buddha and clan-specific ancestor worship would only have played a subordinate role. It wasn't until there was modern social-scientific research that the realities of religion were observed more accurately.

In comparison to this "internal" boundary of the religion system, the external boundaries of the relationships to other function systems seem to receive less attention. The first striking thing is that traditional religious semantics worked to a considerable extent by deriving its plausibility from nonreligious sources, something that succeeded into the modern era. The major examples refer to the family and/or clan structure as well as to political rule. In both instances, one can point out limits to functional differentiation in traditional societies. These limits are based on using semantic coupling on each side. As long as this can be assumed, religion can maintain a significant distance (if not outright rejection) in relation to other domains of social existence, such as an unrestricted (and politically always dangerous) pursuit of profit in a monetary economy or in the case of love relationships without the firm support of kin.

If family clans are held together by ancestor worship, as is very pronounced in China, they enable multifunctional units of relatives to be formed. To an enormous extent, these provide a guarantee for the economy, for the mediation of political contacts, for education (including the selection of those whose careers will be supported), and for upholding the laws (without a need for use of the courts by individual legal subjects). The considerable resistances to modernity observable in modern China, in comparison to Japan, may be related to these circumstances.[34] On the other hand, these ties can relieve the religion system of religiosity. Compared to the faith religions of the West, it can limit itself to cosmological and moral questions. In many cases, ancestor worship also help to solve problems of religious orientation "domestically," thereby "domesticating" (one might say) the intimidating aspects of otherworldly powers.

Similar symbioses can be observed in the relationship between religion and politics. The conceptual terminology of rulers is adopted by religion and supports a hierarchization of religious powers who, as a consequence, do not act as arbitrarily as they would without rulers. Whenever there is a king, it makes sense for religion to imitate political terminology.[35] On the other hand, this same pattern served to legitimize political power until far into modernity, when it was replaced by the seventeenth-century construction of social contracts. Until the French Revolution, the sacred body of the monarch served as an identification point for politics and religion, and in the Revolution it was only supplanted (and not without a struggle) by the general will (*volonté générale*), that is, by decision-making. Even the early modern state's postulate of sovereignty (including legal sovereignty) reassured itself (more or less) by presuming that everything takes place under God's supervision and within the limits of his divine law—at least until the civil liberties of the bourgeoisie were developed to the point where they could adopt this function of restricting power.

The breaking down of these symbioses is linked to the successful prioritization of the functional differentiation of society. Nowadays, religion's relationships to the other function systems are so different and the challenges to religion so intense—by the simple fact of the autonomy of other function systems—that the problems can no longer be resolved using semantic equivalencies. We shall now discuss the current predominant problematic by means of two examples: the relationship of the religion system to the science system and to the art system.

The generally (and sociologically) predominant conception is that religion is shaped by the impact of secularization, precisely in its relationship to the sciences, and that religion tries to preserve itself against that impact under more difficult conditions. Empirical studies clearly show that scientists as well as intellectuals are generally less religious than the average person.[36] Yet such findings, based on surveys of individuals' attitudes, say little about how (and whether) the religion system is affected by the scientific view of the world. It may truly be that science, more than religion, has to keep its distance and defend its own constructive interests.[37] Leading Church circles no longer felt confronted by grievous issues. Rather, science presented them with tasks for resolution and clarification based on mutual respect. In the realm of the sciences, there was an accommodating tendency toward a constructivist epistemology.[38] Clearly, peace has been made under conditions of a fully realized functional differentiation, and neither side claims anymore that it is (better) able to fulfill the other's tasks. They instead encounter each other on the system-neutral terrain of ethics in order to discuss what is permitted and prohibited. Here the scientist sees that he does not get far by appealing to "truth" because the problem is precisely the harm caused by it. And the theologian in such instances avoids appealing to his knowledge of the criteria that God would base a decision on.

The question persists of whether this mutual respect between religion and natural science can be transferred to the social sciences—and especially to sociology when it examines religion. Something similar can only be achieved if system references are provided and a distinction is then drawn between an external (sociological) and an internal (for example, theological) description of religion. Yet both descriptions involve the same object, for otherwise the distinction of external/internal does not make sense. Sociology can react to this circumstance (with significant theoretical burdens and unsettled logical problems) by structuring its theory as the theory of a system describing itself. It can afford to assign the system a function that cannot show up in its self-description (or can only do so paradoxically). It remains to be seen what theology would say if sociology were to functionalize the most holy figures and indispensable aspects of faith. The problem will not present itself as an alternative between acceptance and rejection. Rather, the religion system will gain the opportunity to observe its own relationships, as though observing them from the outside.

The relationship of religion to the art system that is gradually becoming detached is quite comparable, even if one has to account for differences in operations, coding, functions, and in the history of differentiation. Even if there was no notion of the unity and autonomy of all the fine arts until the eighteenth century, art had already broken away from religion's aegis by the fifteenth century (if not a century earlier). Images are no longer primarily devotional ones; nor are they learning or memory aids for the illiterate.[39] And literacy is no longer restricted to clerics. As a result, controversies about texts, such as those involving rhetoric and poetics, are no longer internal religious controversies per se. Yet most of all, the rediscovery of ancient art and poetry in the Renaissance implied that there had been perfection *in this world* once before. It also implied that the recovery of the corresponding skills was a goal clearly distinguished from religious veneration and the symbolization of transcendent references, *without that having to imply criticism or even rejection of religion.* The *antiqui/moderni* debate,[40] already initiated in the Middle Ages, clearly cannot be understood as referring to religion. To the extent that it involved discussion of criteria, it resulted in a special awareness of skills involving literature, painting, technology, and so forth. Soon after book printing was introduced, a critical literature emerged, commencing in Italy and difficult to assess today. It was based on both ancient texts and prominent contemporaries (Ariosto, Tasso, Michelangelo, Raphael, etc.) Merely by adopting the title *Le vite de'più eccellenti pittori, scultori, et architetti italiani* [The Lives of the Most

Excellent Italian Painters, Sculptors, and Architects], Vasari still slightly called to mind the types of texts that had at one time concerned themselves with the lives of the saints.*

When focusing on a special topic—the treatment of what is astonishing, miraculous, or inspiring of *admiratio* and *stupor*—one can also find discussions of art and literature gradually releasing themselves from religious connotations and liabilities of acknowledgment. The thematics here (borrowed from the poetics of Aristotle) shifts to the relationship of imitation and astonishment, of redundancy and surprising variation.[41] And it ultimately shifts what one expects as *meraviglia* from thematic eccentricities to the artistic performance itself. When he calls the *bello poetico* "vero nuovo e maraviglioso dilettevole," someone like [the critic Lodovico Antonio] Muratori is thinking chiefly of the artist's achievement.[42]**

In light of this, one finds in Protestant purism and in the Counter-Reformation after the Council of Trent a critique of artistic permissiveness, especially with respect to those arts of music and painting thought to seduce the senses. At the same time, however, these are no longer internal-religious or theological controversies (such as whether to make an image of God or to respect his prohibition on making images). Instead, the dispute is now about relationships between the religion system and art system. And it can be resolved by reserving an especially sterile domain for sacred art, through a baroque style respecting decorum or an expressive mannerism directed toward religious ends, while the self-reflection of the art system and its history of style take diverging paths.

To sum up, these examples show us that for a long time religion was indebted to societal differentiation for the special efforts it undertook. At the same time, however, religion was able to formulate a description of the world that was binding for society and that in turn was only differentiated—parallel to a stratification—into more dogmatic and more magical-popular variants. When modernity got under way, function systems emerged side by side that could completely respect religion but followed their own dynamic. Religion could offer little resistance to this change in societal evolution. It tightened up its own organizational and dogmatic methods, "helping itself"

* Giorgio Vasari (1511–1574) was an Italian painter and architect famous for his biographies of Italian artists, as in the aforementioned work of 1550.—Trans.

** Muratori calls the *bello poetico*—"the beautiful poetic"—something "truly new and marvelously delightful."—Trans.

(one might say) by outsourcing and rejecting communicative domains that interfere too greatly with it. In the end, precisely because it tried to provide the utmost relevance and something beyond the everyday, religion could only be one function among others.

VI

The differentiation of the religion system leads to an operative closure and an autopoietic reproduction of that system. There is no other way to assure that religious communication recognizes itself as such in a network of religious communications. Being detached from the societal environment can result in internal structural uncertainty, along with a surplus of communicative possibilities. That in turn forces the system to organize itself. Self-organization, however, is only possible if the system has sufficient "microdiversity" at its disposal.[43] In the legal system, for instance, there have to be a sufficient number of different types of legal controversies. In the economic system, there have to be a sufficient number of different transactions. In the religion system, one can assume that sufficiently different occasions have to appear on the level of religious communication. Participation in religion becomes personalized—not least because holy texts are printed and approved for private reading. A highly standardized practice of piety that restricted itself to regular churchgoing, for example, would not fulfill this requirement and would in a sense dry up the religion system. It would transform itself into an authoritative regulative system that (to a great extent) would be susceptible to a loss of authority and/or a reduction in interest and motivation.

On the level of institutions, organizations, and texts, the differentiation of a function system for religion can be described very well. There are a sufficient number of specific practices and readings that can be qualified as clearly religious. The religion system has differentiated itself by its own operations and can thus be recognized through this. Doubts can be more or less remedied in communication, and those differences of opinion that remain can be handled in different ways, depending on which system is involved.

In concluding, however, we have to point out that this picture needs to be modified in at least one point. There are religious movements that are also political movements (and, conversely, political movements with religious foundations and an intensity that is religiously conditioned). We might think of the Islamic movement that led to the fall of the Shah's regime in Iran. Or the Polish trade union movement *Solidarnoáć*, which burst the boundaries of the unions' political mandate, not least by laying claim to religious resources. Or the many civil rights movements in the United States, especially those that work for the rights of people who are discriminated against racially. As these examples show, there are societal systems that cannot clearly be attributed to one or another function system. They refer to religion, for instance, in their motives and their communication. Yet their objectives are primarily political.

The explanation for such mixed forms should likely be sought in the specifically modern form of the social movement. As a type of social system, it already has the status of an exception. For social movements are neither interaction systems nor organizational systems, and they are certainly not function systems of modern society. They are catalyzed by using the form of protest—with demands that they cannot and do not want to fulfill themselves. In this type of opposition, which nonetheless demands activity from its opponents, religious roots can be combined with political objectives. It is certain that there are also purely secular movements and especially participants who get involved for a multiplicity of nonreligious reasons (perhaps for self-fulfillment?). At this point, we are interested only in the *possibility* of merging religion and politics in spite of an existing and visible differentiation of function systems.

In the form of the protest, social movements give themselves permission to ignore the self-descriptions of function systems and the logic of functional differentiation. They can therefore merge religion and politics in the framework of their own communication. But protest, like every form, has another side. If what is demanded has to be carried out, whether by the victorious movement or those whom it addresses, differentiations will almost inevitably emerge again. These can then connect up with the functional differentiation of the social system. Otherwise, regional anomalies (such as in Iran) will emerge that have trouble connecting to a functionally differentiated world society.

Religious Organizations

I

In all function systems of modern society, organized social systems play an important, indispensable role. It would be surprising if this were different in the case of religion. Yet it is difficult to imagine that organized decision processes operate in the form of religious actions, that decisions constraining an organization are made in the form of a common prayer or are merely accompanied by a request for divine inspiration. Archives are not sacred objects even in church administrations, and majority decisions have to be made and implemented even when individual participants believe those decisions deviate from God's declared will.[1]

The Old European tradition, the implications of which reach far into modernity, did not distinguish clearly between society and organization. The organizational conception of the present did not even emerge as something separate from the general semantics of order and organism until the nineteenth century.[2] Society itself was understood (in very different conceptual variants) as a natural order of human living together, the result of a social contract motivated by nature. That tradition can be summed up in a term such as "corporation." In the process, it also becomes clear that this terminology distinguishes what it signifies from families or family households. People are born naturally into these, and they define everyone's place in the differentiated order of society.

Organization mediates between the production of religious meaning, resulting in myths or dogmas, and the daily practice of specifically religious behavior. It thereby takes the place (even when organizing sects) that sects had occupied in the ancient world—whether ancestors in families were being worshipped or rituals were being institutionalized socially. The direct reference of sects to concepts of faith is mediated today by organization, and up to that point there were neither problems of belonging nor decisions for or against it.

Since the Middle Ages, corporative society as understood legally by the term *universitas* has developed into a diversity that was confusing at first. Besides the civil society (*societas civilis*) determined by political rule, there was also a church based on its own law. There were also cities, monasteries, orders, universities, guilds, and similar associations, even corporative entities [*Standschaften*]. The motivations for differentiation were in part those of internal order and special discipline, in part those of political representation in the town and the surrounding territory. As "church," but also as holy orders and monasteries, the religion system takes part in this special corporative regulation. Indeed, in defending itself against the theocratic tendencies of imperial rule, the Church elaborates for itself the (much copied) theory of *universitas*.[3] It does so by judicializing its system-internal problems to a great extent, and by having its own jurisdiction, its own textual systematics, and (most of all) a clearly elaborated hierarchical structure guaranteeing its ability to decide on faith and Church policy. Yet at the same time, the religious significance of the Church as a community of faith is preserved, providing indispensable sacred support to what can almost be described as organization.

But there were no regulations here for joining or withdrawing that could function as a motivational basis for selective membership. Christian baptism was not thought of as a decision to join but as a sacrament, the completion of which transformed one's natural state of sin and conferred the prospect of redemption. In lieu of a system boundary that could be crossed by joining or resigning, making all internal decisions of the system (including recognition of the authority to issue directives) dependent on this, there was an *uncertainty of salvation produced in the system itself*; it was the premise by which the justified and the damned could be distinguished. No one could then be "dismissed" [*entlassen*], but one's prospects for redemption could be taken away by means of excommunication. And moral programs and prayer rituals could be provided to reduce uncertainty, replacing it with an (always precarious) expectation of redemption or damnation. On the level of roles, the system defined itself in the continuation of a very ancient tradition by differentiating between the status of priests and laypeople (following the exclusion of pagans). This distinction also made use of sacred productions of meaning, and it differentiated ways of life and claims regarding the intensity of religious concern. The analogy to the prevailing differentiation of nobility and commoners was certainly no coincidence. At the same time, it also supplied the necessary personnel resources for filling Church offices, even though priesthood and holding of office were separate in conceptual and personnel terms (even long after the Council of Trent). The result was a large number of clerics who could not be disciplined officially (or organizationally), but who had nonetheless been ordained.

Seen from the perspective of evolutionary theory, one can recognize foreshadowings of something that could possibly be conceived of as an organization and then developed by exploiting the possibilities of this system form. There was an increased use of organization after the sixteenth-century religious schisms, after differential awareness was disseminated by book printing, and after an awareness of confessions was systematized and all attempts to fix religious differences territorially had failed (following the early modern formation of states). Organization had to make decisions for all cases and, like a central bank, could not avoid keeping an eye on the external value of its own currency. The salient issues were how faith appealed to individually mobile parishioners and how self- and other-selection operated in the recruiting of new members. Still, the idea of a faith community clashed with the idea of a member organization that would align its requirements with such motivations.[4] If necessary, such an organization had to compensate by providing a zone "of indifference."[5] It could arrange this by specifying rules or directives and could adapt it to changing conditions. The problem was typically sidestepped by keeping the requirements of formal membership extremely limited, practically restricted to those (already) registered. The circle of membership thus constituted differentiated the official Church, based on self-selection by more strongly motivated and committed members, who volunteered more than others.

The distinction between religion and Church appears at first glance sufficient to preserve terminologically how a society, even in its function system, provides organizations for religion but also cannot be reduced to an organization. The term "institution" [*Anstalt*], first developed for legal purposes, might then be interpreted as an organization. The special power relationship of this public institution could be interpreted as a membership role: by joining, one submitted to it, and by withdrawing, one resisted it. Although the theological doctrines of the Church, its ecclesiology, might stand in the way of this, couldn't it be reinterpreted as a cultural self-description, as a "corporate culture" for this particular type of organization—at least from the perspective of a second-order observer? And in terms of labor law, it could be termed an "ideological enterprise" [*Tendenzbetrieb*] with special rules for giving notice that would apply whenever there were marked deviations from the required faith.

We should still note that organizations of the "church" type have not been formed by all religions, but actually only by the Christian ones. Other religions are satisfied with schools or assemblies for textual exegesis (e.g., synagogues), or have temples or monasteries to which it is not expected that all believers will be recruited. More than the term "church" might allow, one would have to pay attention to the multiplicity of shapes in which organizations appear within the religion system of world society. On the whole, however, a theory of organization has to be elaborated that gets beyond the oversimplification of concepts such as "corporation," "institution," and "bureaucracy." Only then will one be able to evaluate why a religion system that seeks to preserve its functional differentiation might need organization.

II

Like society and its function systems, organizations are also autopoietic systems that operate on their own. They can only form themselves within a society, thereby realizing society, because even their mode of operation is nothing but communication. Organizations presuppose as their environment the differentiation of society, language, and the fulfillment of all kinds of functions. If (and as long as) this is assured, they form and reproduce their own boundaries, their own interruptions in the continuum of societal communication. And they do so specifically by distinguishing between members and nonmembers. That makes it possible for organizations to make special demands on the conduct of their members (to the extent they have succeeded in making such membership attractive). Yet autopoietic systems can only be formed on this basis when the communications attributable to members can be recursively networked so that one operation connects to another and a system thus becomes differentiated within self-established boundaries. It is not enough then for individuals, roles, or conduct to be classified by membership—just as there are limits to what a shoemaker does as a shoemaker. Put differently, at stake are not only professions or other similarities based on specific obligations or ways of thinking. Rather, in organized social systems, the communication of one member is always a premise for the behavior of others,[6] and in such a way that granting those premises produces a decision behavior, which recursively makes clear that the granting of the premises was itself a decision. This applies, too, when recruiting and releasing, admitting and dismissing members. These are conceived of as decisions to submit to or free oneself from the special conditions of the system's decision processes. Organizations are autopoietic systems formed in society. Their autopoiesis is based in the self-guaranteeing capacity of decision processes to be continued, in which affiliation with an organization, and thereby the responsibility of making decisions, is recognizable in members' roles.[7]

A self-guaranteeing autopoiesis of decisions is at work, then, and not only in the case of explicitly provided rules or programs, but also (and above all) through the pure fact of decisions having been communicated and thus not having to be elaborated again. As "decision premises," decisions have ambiguous effects: they are both enabling and restrictive. The system is constantly pulsing between expanding and restricting possibilities for making further decisions. And this is precisely how the system assures its continuing autopoiesis, through an organizationally typical medium for decision possibilities. Every further decision creates a break in the system, reducing complexity and enabling additional decisions on that basis.

If they were to be worked out, these points of departure would lead to a completely different organizational theory than the classic one based primarily on Weber's bureaucratic theory. This distinction is also not grasped by older comparisons of mechanical and organic models of organization. Organization is not an instrument of power [*Herrschaft*] deemed to be independent. And it is not a social system guaranteeing the realization of specific goals for society.[8] Nor is it a machine designed as a mechanism. Yet organization is also not a system the way an organism is, ordering living parts in relationship to a whole. The key point is that it reproduces a difference between system and environment that is independent and not determinable from the outside. This organizational system has the capacity—even vis-à-vis a largely unknown, surprising, and turbulent environment—of being able to continue its own mode of reproduction, of producing decisions by decisions, while either maintaining or varying the structures necessary for it (self-organization).

In the present context, we are only interested in this theory's consequences for understanding the relationship between society's function systems (here especially the religion system) and the organizations formed within them. If one starts from the (Weberian) bureaucratic model, one ought to presume a hierarchical structure, the top of which would (independently) see to it that the apparatus realized its societal function. Even using this theory's usual paradigm of state organization, such a model can no longer be rendered plausible. And in the case of religion, there is simply no way to see how *its* function could be fulfilled by a ruling authority or the implementation of an apparatus. There have to be other possibilities for doing more (theoretical) justice to its realities and for understanding the relationship between functional differentiation and organizational formation as what it is: a mutually enhancing relationship of operational contingency and self-dynamics at both the societal and organizational levels.

To clarify this relationship, we shall again need to use the concepts *of inclusion and exclusion.*[9] It is a relationship that involves structural coupling between psychic and social systems. There is inclusion whenever a specific relevance of the environment's organic and psychic systems is acknowledged in the social system in the form of "individuals" [*Personen*].[10] Hence, we speak of exclusion whenever a system assumes it can afford to be indifferent, ruthless, and rejecting toward (societally constituted) persons. In other words, the inclusion/exclusion schema indicates a form whose inside is inclusion and whose outside is exclusion. Or again, put differently, the marking of inclusion leaves behind an unmarked space that can be indicated as an exclusionary domain to the extent that it deals with individuals.

In a modern functionally differentiated society, there is neither a central instance nor an institution like the family household of the ancient world, where inclusions and exclusions could be regulated while attending to differences in rank. Instead, the issue is left for function systems to deal with. Semantically speaking, it is expressed by principles such as freedom and equality (whereby criticism of these principles as ideologies of "bourgeois society," even without an adequate analysis, correctly indicates that positively accentuated inclusions also always have an exclusionary side).[11] At the level of society's function systems, there are no functionally meaningful exclusionary interests (unless they refer to bodily or psychic incapacities). If the difference between inclusion and exclusion is supposed to be applied as a form, organizations will have to be formed (based on the rules of membership constituting them) that can apply this difference and do so legitimately, including some individuals as members and excluding all others. And this happens typically within the inclusionary domain of the function systems, specifically among economically powerfully individuals who are able to pay or work, or among individuals with access to law constituted by their general legal capacity. And this transpires just as often within the context of a presupposed interest in religion.

The relationship of function systems and organization systems can likewise be understood as complementary. The more function systems open themselves for inclusion under freedom and equality (but also because they have no cause to restrict access), the more they have to arrange for secondary possibilities of exclusion within the system as constituted. This is precisely what happens when organizations are established that can justify specific criteria for inclusion/exclusion using specific requirements. All special requirements therefore lead to breaks within function systems, not only by simply characterizing individuals according to system-relevant characteristics—such as free/enslaved, rich/poor, knowledgeable/ignorant, more or less committed to their faith—but also in the peculiarly modern mode of forming an organization that, for the most part, can make itself independent of those personal characteristics. Instead, the organization relies on the formal rule of membership, which reacts to selection criteria that are mobile and internal to it. Not every believer is allowed to speak from the pulpit, yet being relieved of one's office is not the same as excommunication and even official excommunication in this day and age would not immediately silence one's religiosity.

There are many reasons to reintroduce the (previously assumed) difference of inclusion/exclusion into the inclusionary domain of function systems and thus also into the religion system (a "reentry" in Spencer-Brown's sense). One such reason is that interruptions of interdependence are necessary in the system when a faith is imagined to be mutual. In particular, however, organization is necessary for providing collectives with communicative capacity. Organizations are the only social systems that can give binding explanations in their own name and that are able to commit themselves outwardly because they are able to commit their members to accept system decisions that are outwardly effective. To the extent that (socially given and) unvarying framing conditions of religion disintegrate and religious communication is released and thus overwhelmed, there is also an increased need for structure, a demand for self-modification—that is, for the communication of decisions. This can already be observed in the medieval Church, with its emphasis on law and a corporative structure, and even more after an entire society is no longer prepared to follow the universalistic pretentions of certain forms of faith. These reflections could be expanded upon. But then one would quickly enter into realms where different world religions tend toward very different organizational solutions, or where they do not follow the trend toward organizational problem solving, instead persisting in the old forms, such as mutual relationships between temples (priests) or monasteries (monks) and faithful followers. Rather, one will want to know what the costs are of an intensive usage of organizations in the religion system and whether these impede possibilities that other religions still have.

III

Organizations tend to have idiosyncratic ways of "absorbing uncertainty" (a term proposed by Herbert Simon).[12] Thanks to their continuing transformation of decisions into premises for further decisions, they can build certainties into a world that is extremely uncertain (and whose unity is elusive). At the same time, organizations only have to verify these constructions by internally processing irritations. They can therefore maintain and specify a self- and global-description of society. In the special case of religion, they even can do so by crossing into transcendence without losing their ability to make statements. Yet how can these abilities be deployed subject to the conditions of modern society, in which every societal and world description is exposed to comparison with other possibilities?

Organizations almost inevitably give form to hierarchical structures, because vertical integration enables them to operate under conditions of uncertainty. That is to say, hierarchies minimize the costs of confrontations with uncertainty.[13] When uncertainty is transformed into certainty, there are good, strong reasons for sticking with it. Why should one open up Pandora's Box each time there are minor irritations? This may apply particularly when there is greater background uncertainty, such as in the case of the religion system when one secretly has to admit that the background world [*Hinterwelt*] of the sacred is unfamiliar, and many deny that it even exists. Or when one succeeds in replacing the uncertainty in matters of our own conviction with enemies who can be identified and fought against. Clearly, one does not want to relinquish the stability thus produced—precisely when our own decision processes (at least in stretches) are capable of being identified and remembered, or precisely when they can be read as sequences of cause and effect (or of reason and implication), or precisely when they serve to maintain distinctions.[14] This conclusion may apply to all social systems, revealing itself in being linked to their respective histories. But it applies particularly for organizations, inasmuch as their history is preserved as a history of explicit distinguishing and indicating. All of the foregoing applies to a considerable extent to modern religious organizations. Even— and especially—in a world that mainly pursues other offers of meaning, these can preserve themselves by means of self-produced certainties of faith, which are available as texts and can be reinterpreted on demand.

This peculiarity of organizations to conserve distinctions to a certain extent replaces different kinds of arrangements for conserving distinctions. These arrangements include rituals (with correct implementation and with distinctions of time and place that can only be made observable locally) and myths (those narrative units of a sequence of distinctions that only become plausible in their particulars by fitting into the narrative at an appropriate place). These kinds of conventional forms are complemented, reformed, interpreted and re-illuminated by another type of text: a religious dogmatics. There are still narratives, but now parables or short stories mediate between religiously interpreted viewpoints and life experiences—precisely what religiously inspired writers are aiming at.[15] This further assumes that there are canonizations of the correct doctrine; their maintenance depends on the teachers themselves and (if available) on organized processes of deciding in the midst of doubt.

These considerations give rise to a sociological hypothesis: there is a connection between organizational forms as well as between the religion system's degree of organization and the religion's degree of dogmatization. Dogmatics can be used in such organizations for making distinctions—

whether for recognizing the correct faith and excluding heresies, or for testing one's faith, or—in the form of articles and pre-formulated confessions of faith—for establishing the conditions of membership in religious organizations. At the same time, decisions have to be made that appear contingent and therefore have to be legitimized within an organization. When interpretive variants and consistency problems of a higher order have been manifested, an incentive emerges for developing reflective figures[16] while at the same time a need is produced for organizational regulation of controversial questions. Such regulation takes place by majority decisions of a differentiated commission, as in Rabbinic doctrine, or by an authority of the highest instance, as in Catholicism. There is an awareness that reflective figures, on account of their self-justifications, are highly problematic in religions. And that is exactly why there are purely organizational solutions to the problem, forms of absorbing uncertainty that continue to be recognizable as such no matter how they are then "canonized."

IV

The formation of religious organizations in the form of a separate priesthood would already have been necessary at an early point in history. For resources had to be acquired, religious services had to be regulated and communication had to be enabled vis-à-vis political (and other) powers. Yet—in a completely different, much more problematic sense—organization was also used to make (visible!) decisions about questions of faith. In a world of increasing contingencies, of widespread literacy, of rapid change and greater self-dynamics of highly varied function systems, such a path now seemed unavoidable—if only because new issues were always cropping up, and coordinated positions were expected of "religion." (To what extent, then, was religion accepting of new technologies and modern freedoms in sexual behavior? Was AIDS to be interpreted as a divine punishment? Were indigenous dance groups to be admitted to the Church as collectives or only as individuals, simply because they think they are disciples of the Virgin Mary and therefore Catholics?) For such matters, organizations have techniques of deciding and a form of member obligation that at first appears to demonstrate itself. Yet at the same time, the limits on this form of absorbing uncertainty become clear. On the one hand, such limits are apparent—and people are used to this—in the persistence of opposing minorities who conform only unwillingly (if at all) or who firmly strive to become the majority. If it is a question not only of proceeding strategically in this world but also of faith, it is virtually impossible to silence minorities or at least commit them to being discreet. They do not become martyrs but nowadays access the media of mass communication to voice their concerns—and with no pangs of conscience.

In terms of internal organization, this dissent may be seen as endangering the organization's unity and hence the unity of the faith defined by it. The organization then recommends (to itself) that it maneuver tactically and, if necessary, exercise power. When there are such conflicts, the organization maintains its ability to transform uncertainty (about the true faith) into certainty (about the conflict diagnosed). And it may be able to endure this situation because it still falls completely within typical organizational behavior. But it may be that organizations so focused on themselves become blind to a completely different problematic, that of societal inclusion.

Difficulties remain even if one accepts that questions of dogma can in all cases be decided, and left to be decided, by an organization. It thus seems advisable to use caution in exercising this option. For it is always implicitly acknowledged in the form of a decision that the decision could also have been made differently. Decisions therefore undermine claims to truth—something they also do when a decision is issued as an interpretation of texts that themselves are not based in a decision. In addition to this option for using organizations, there are also many more deformations typical of organizations, such as the (in)famous ends/means displacements.[17] Religion may be first and foremost about redemption or salvation of the soul. But for organizations, objectives such as these are difficult to operationalize. How can one determine whether the objectives have been achieved—and why they were achieved? As a result, religious organizations typically make do by transforming means into substitute ends. One pastor may be more successful than another in persuading people to attend worship services. And after membership has become an individual decision, a steady (or increasing) supply of members might be attributed to the success of the organization.[18]

All that said, the contrast between an organization's own logic and what society requires of its function systems turns out to be especially significant in the case of the religion system. There is a dearth of institutions—such as markets in the economic system—that mediate between different organizations or between organizations and societal expectations of meaning. It is not surprising, then, that the organizational petrifications of the religion system (and that does not only mean its administrative activity) always also serve as an impulse for new religious movements. Those movements, at least at the start, hope they can escape this fate.

V

As a function system in society, religion has no reason to deny inclusion, thus refusing inclinations to religion (in whatever form) the opportunity of social communication. By contrast, organizational systems deal with inclusion/exclusion in a completely different fashion, deciding to permit membership according to relevant criteria. Exclusion is the normal case for them, against which they form their special requirements. They therefore have the tendency or habit—indeed, they are faced with the necessity—of *drawing boundaries inside of* their function system. Doing so is likely inevitable even when the religion system forms its own organizations. Not everything that identifies itself as religion can be welcomed by such systems if (otherwise) each feature of their requirements (which of course can be moderated but not abandoned) would be endangered.

At the outset, the only consequence of this potential conflict is that there is organized and unorganized religion. For sociological diagnosis, one also has to sever the concept of religion from the self-descriptions of religious organizations,[19] although this does not necessarily mean that religion would be able to distinguish between transcendence and immanence without distinct credal ideas. But are these distinctions useful and satisfactory in the present-day social context?

There is at least one additional matter to consider. Among the function systems of modern society, there is little positive coordination.[20] Instead, a "loose coupling" obtains that is not pre-structured by society and that conforms to the very different internal dynamic of function systems. Integration (as a mutual limitation on systems' degrees of freedom) comes about by way of mutual problem burdens, when problems are externalized that cannot be solved in their own functional domain. The inclusion of individuals is likewise regulated through careers. The other, dark side of this arrangement is that it results in massive exclusions.[21] Large parts of the world population find themselves almost entirely excluded from all function systems. They have no jobs, no money, no identity cards, no rights, no training, inadequate medical care, and often hardly any schooling. As a result, they also have no access to work or to the economy, and no hope of receiving justice from the police or in the courts. These exclusions reinforce one another. And, at a certain threshold point, all remaining time and energy are taken up with bodily survival. The strict couplings of negative integration appear to correspond to the loose couplings of positive integration.

In our present age, these are still problems at the periphery of the centers of modernity, to be addressed by additional foreign aid or credit, or by combating corruption and inflation. That is what a functionally differentiated society would prescribe for itself, but those prescriptions can only function to the extent that its media and means of inclusion are available. Yet it may as well be that another—and rather demographic—difference will superimpose itself over the difference of function systems, that is, the difference of inclusion and exclusion. That again may be a stable condition, in which unrest and uncontrollable violence may be expected, but no more "revolutions." And that would be the shape of a modernity grown old, beyond which we can no longer recognize a more distant future, for we cannot imagine what things would be like without functional differentiation.

The harshness of negative integration (even if its boundaries are diffuse) results when there is mutual reinforcement of completely unscheduled, functionless exclusions from function systems. One exclusion is followed by another, not with a compelling logic in each case but with a fatality that only few can avoid—with (or without) assistance from others. Yet there are also function systems that would not necessarily have to participate in this downward spiral, but that could retain inclusions even when other systems have participated in exclusion. This inclusionary possibility applies to the family to the extent that it is still present in such domains. Above all, it may apply to religion.

Organized religion will in this case encounter problems involving charity, social work, or "love activism." Nothing can be said against such efforts, and this definition of the situation may be confirmed in the event of success. The regional cloisterings of different Christian orders might constitute the basis for countermeasures against both the human and natural ills of civilization. But that would only be included in the religion system if it succeeded in activating the function and code of religion, that is (putting it in traditional terms), in producing a church in the sense of a community of faith. And that is where the organization appears to stand in the way of its own success, since it always already knows—having always already decided—*which* faith that would have to be. Official voices in Catholicism proclaim that their Church must always be concerned with the political and economic conditions of life and must (if necessary) intervene when it finds conditions that exclude those who believe in the message of salvation, redemption through Jesus Christ, and so forth. But why this approach? Why aren't there different paths to the world beyond this one? Why are there sacraments instead of the production of trance states? Why are there temporally deferred hopes of redemption but no magic that is helpful in the present? Why are there confessions of sin and not rituals in which black and white magic are indistinguishable—and do not have to be distinguished?

These kinds of questions follow upon any observation of religiosity that is formed spontaneously under the described conditions (and all the questions asked above refer to present-day syncretic Afro-indigenous sects). If there are possibilities of observing religiosity as it expands and develops, one can identify possibilities of religious inclusion (if one is theoretically prepared to observe them) that also seem to be compatible with exclusion. One also sees that such religiosity cannot and will not be permitted by the organization. However, society will allow it.

VI

At present, religious organizations like other organizations use reform to help themselves out. Reforms are ways to plan changes, as only can be found in organizations. They distinguish themselves from religious or social movements or otherwise observable structural changes by tending toward decisions that have to be made and implemented within organizations. They can refer to the formal organization, as in struggles between centralization and decentralization or between monocracy and group principle. They can, however, also refer to the system's programs, to those factual criteria that articulate the difference between correct and incorrect applications of the code. They always assume a distinction between decision premises and operational communication of decisions, such as between the implementation of baptism and the determination of the conditions under which such implementation is recognized (and acknowledged) as baptism. Organizations further assume that the system is capable of making decisions on both levels: on the basal one of implementing decisions and on the other of deciding decision premises. What is being assumed is a type of "double closure" at the base and the coordinating levels—double closure in the sense that the system is autonomous on both levels and determines itself by its own operations.[22]

Put more simply: reforms treat questions of faith as a matter of decision. Since the organization operates in a closed manner, it clearly does not mean that decisions can be made about society itself or about one of its function systems. An organization can only reform itself. It can only decide how communication will take place within itself, that is, how decisions can interpret or initiate other decisions. And even that is an overstatement, after all of our experience with reforms within organizations of the economic system, the political system, the educational system, and so on. For the most part, reforms exhaust themselves, accentuating on a verbally elevated plane something that is remembered or forgotten in the system and that (in both cases) might give rise to further reforms.[23] An "implementation" in the sense of their original intentions almost never takes place, and when it does, the original intentions become adjusted to realities so that, after some time, one can no longer distinguish between the conditions before and after a reform. Often it may be relatively unproblematic to redescribe the current practice in the rhetoric of reform without allowing it to be unsettled by the reformers' objectives. That can then be a reason why the reform is seen as a success if it continues to be represented verbally, and why shortcomings that persist can motivate the organization to initiate new reforms.

All of that can be modified if one is only thinking about very narrow segments of the formal organization, such as the admission of women to priestly office. It may be that an organization is forced into making reforms under pressure from its environment and adjusts its self-descriptions accordingly. In typical cases, however, the coupling of decision premises and base-level deciding is so loose that intentions of making changes either come to nothing or activate unobservable changes beyond their intended effects. Reforms are practically never evaluated. In the best case, they implement an official version of things but hardly ever the projected outcomes. This might even be true where objects are regulated in a relatively demanding way, such as in a business or government accounting office,[24] or in the moral casuistry of a Catholic's confession. One shouldn't even try to monitor whether women, when admitted to the pulpit, really preach differently.

Precisely when reforms exhaust themselves in motivating other reforms and this verbal dynamic of change becomes a habit, the distinction between reformers and anti-reformers loses a great deal of its importance. The key structural transformation takes place on the level of a society's religion system and cannot be copied adequately into organizations. It takes the form of evolution, not of planning. Its effects are unforeseeable (but effective), yet on the level of organized or organizational planning, its effective intentions are at best be taken up in a fragmentary manner. None of that speaks against reforms. On the contrary, reforms can be better evaluated if one makes realistic judgments on their level, acknowledging their function as lightning rods and noting that when reformative reflective loops are built into the system, a function is fulfilled, even if such reforms do not change much of what gets done.

Attitudes toward reforms shape the professional self-understanding of the leaders in organizations. Since elites these days not only work (unlike in the past) but also work specifically in organizations, the usual tendency of organizations to initiate reforms forces people at the same time to take a position on the reform. Regardless of their consequences, decisions can always be made in organizations, and they have to be made in many cases, because even a negative decision (such as "no women!") is still a decision. As a result, the participants always have to have a relevant option, something that was already clear in the fifteenth-century dispute between having a papal church or a conciliar one. This can be seen as an occasion for constantly regenerating articulated differences in opinion, resulting in identity problems of a biographical sort. For these individuals typically live longer than the reforms, whether or not they are approved for implementation. To outside observers, this may leave the impression that there is always controversy within a church establishment. But it can also be regarded as an occasion (that repeatedly comes up) for reflecting on preliminary questions and objectives of reform. Helmut Schelsky once asked in a highly respected article: "Can continuous reflection be institutionalized?"[25] The answer to that question has to wait until the concept of "institution" is clarified. In any event, it can be observed that professionals (theologians but also educators, jurists, and newfangled CEOs) are driven to reflect, not by philosophy, but by an addiction to reform within their organizations. And that may have fringe benefits for determining the place of religion in today's society, advantages that do not accrue to unorganized religions.

VII

Organizations are established as practical helping institutions. One does not wish to leave certain accomplishments to chance or ad hoc motivation but ensure that they take place reliably. If this founding intention is taken as a basis for describing organizations, then they appear to be a relatively unproblematic means to an end. The only problems are expenses and unintended side effects. A very different picture emerges when organizations are understood as autopoietic systems that reproduce decisions from decisions. In this way, characteristics are highlighted, such as operative closure (based on the operation of deciding) and self-produced uncertainty. Each decision observes other decisions and reproduces the need for further decisions. Decision premises too now have to be seen as results of decisions, at least as results of their ongoing acceptance and reimpregnation in other new decisions. Seen thus, organizations appear to be systems for reproducing self-produced uncertainty, which has to be processed by decisions that are always new (but have the same effect). If nothing else, this approach explains the typically hierarchical structure of organizations, because vertical integration is the most important means of converting uncertainty into certainty.

When organizations live from self-produced uncertainty, from a future yet to be determined, it remains questionable to what extent religion as a function system of society can depend upon systems of this kind. It is clear that religion will help itself by canonizing decision premises so as to deprive certain matters of being decided. Yet whether this is compatible with the operative logic of organizations is an open question. The autopoiesis of the organization will force it to register even these types of prohibition as decisions. But the possibility of changing such decisions cannot be ruled out. An organization may decide not to make use of such a possibility, but if it cannot be excluded as a possibility, everything else becomes merely a question of opportunity. Based on the autopoiesis of making decisions, no organization can exclude its own operational possibilities. Every attempt at making such exclusions serves to point out this possibility. Hence, the Fall of Man takes place when God goes to enjoy the cool evening air in the back part of Eden, giving up ground to the serpent.

These considerations lead to the issue of whether religion and organization are fundamentally incompatible. Such a question does not have to lead to a religious catastrophe but may result in a situation that is commonly signified as crisis. When the organization sees a decision in everything it accepts and reproduces, that has to lead to a deconstruction in matters of faith. In this matter, it doesn't make any difference whether such decisions are "infallible" or not. The problem consists in there being decisions that could be made differently, or not at all in the first place. Decisions are experienced as contingent, as already indicated in the concept itself, in the directives the concept makes for observation. And that is precisely the basis for the future of an organization, which can only become present in the form of possible future decisions. But religion wants to be able to rely on what it already is.

The Evolution of Religion

I

The evolution of a particular religion system cannot be equated with universal societal [*gesamtgesellschaftlich*] evolution. Nor does this evolution take place exactly like other function systems of society that differentiate and then evolve according to their own dynamics. It is not the same as universal societal evolution, because whenever religion is recognizable as a distinct phenomenon, there are always other kinds of meaning and communication in society leading us to assume a comprehensive social evolution.[1] For example, it is not possible to trace the evolution of writing exclusively and in all cases back to religion, even though divination plays a significant role in addition to the problems of managing budgets or maintaining records of services offered. On the other hand, religious evolution also deviates from that of other function systems. It begins a great deal earlier, for the first time creating a system that can be described as differentiated within society.[2] Moreover, it does not coincide with the need for a (particularly) symbolically generalized communicative medium and its differentiation. By contrast, one could say that differentiation of the economic system assumes the introduction of money, and that differentiation of a political system assumes the establishment of positions for the exercise of power. What is likewise missing is the reason that typically launches the development of particular symbolically generalized communication media: that certain, very specific communications become more and more unlikely to accept. This does not exclude any relation to the evolution of other function systems. It is well known that the impulses given the Jewish religion by its prophets assumed the existence of rule by kings, just as the splitting off of Buddhism (from Hinduism) presupposed an existing caste system. This is comparable to the way that the invention of coined money launched the transition to *tyrannis* and other political developments in ancient Greek city-states. Or the way that the late medieval formation of courts, especially in Italy, resulted in the differentiation of a particular art system no longer bound up with crafts, guilds, or monasteries.[3] That does not at all exclude the theoretical generalization of these evolutions. One could not speak of "evolution," of "differentiation," or of "system," if there were not general theoretical foundations for them. But the particularities of religious evolution deserve special attention. It is indisputable that there were close involvements between societal and specifically religious evolution in early times. It's hard to avoid the impression that earlier societies were differently—and more intensively—defined by religion than society today. Regardless of its special situation (or precisely because of it), the question of how religious evolution made itself possible deserves independent elaboration. Here, too, one has to study how religion fulfilled specific evolutionary mechanisms of variation, selection and restabilization, and above all, how it could separate them.

One might think that Weber's sociology of religion would provide a useful foundation on such questions. However, that is not the case—or only to a very limited extent. Of course, Weber's clearly historical mode of inquiry is still momentous for everything undertaken in this field. It was also significant in highlighting the evolutionary unlikelihood of an explicitly ascetic, world-negating religiosity directed toward transcendent objectives of salvation. These all take the form of differentiating and rationalizing *specifically religious* attitudes, along with forms of "lifestyle" [*Lebensführung*]. This unlikelihood is not only grounded in psychology but also in earlier forms of religious practice. All these are issues that nowadays could be treated with more terminological rigor in an evolutionary-theoretical framework. But Weber was primarily interested in explaining the conditions of the economic system's evolution toward modern "capitalism"—a different system reference. In clarifying this, Weber (bound as he was to the methodological ideas of his time) thought he needed a causal motivating factor and believed he had found it in religion (while appropriately acknowledging other causalities). The particular force of the religious motives supposed to have brought about this transformation explained itself to Weber precisely in their unlikelihood. However one may assess it,[4] Weber's thesis (elaborated in a vast number of comparative studies) does not make reference to evolutionary theory.[5] Although the central problem of this theory—the becoming probable of what is improbable—is also Weber's problem, the evolutionary theory that responds to this problem is structured differently. It does not rely on particularly strong causes, only then to get lost in endless problems of attributing causality. Instead, it relies on "chance"—particularly on a coincidental (not system-guided) cooperation of variation and selection, on a random readiness of helpful circumstances that can be utilized until the newly developed form produces its own needs, motivations, semantics, and stabilities.

In this special sense, the following considerations have been developed according to evolutionary theory. Yet Weber aficionados will find that he has not been neglected.

II

Based on a matter that came up earlier, the general notion of evolution serving as our basis here has already been introduced.[6] Every treatment of morphogenetic questions in evolutionary theory has to pay particular attention to how forms of variation and forms of selection are separated. That is the special hallmark of evolutionary theories today—and not, for instance, periodizations concerned with progress. In addition, the linking of variation and selection has to be treated as a coincidence; there is no other way to speak of "separation." On the one hand, then, determination by causal laws is thus negated; on the other hand (and more extensively), every systemic integration of both these requirements of evolution is specifically negated. From this complicated theoretical construction, it can also be observed that whenever one speaks of "coincidence" (in the sense of systemic noncoordination), chances are that the environment will influence the systems despite their operative closure. The system exposes itself to coincidences that it can ignore or, after they have transpired, exploit as opportunities. To recap: a system that is evolving can convert the lack of coordination between variation and selection into environmental sensitivity. It delivers itself up to environmental influences by not providing any rules for selection out of the "variety pool" of variations. Consequently, it can also—and this is decisive—use temporary environmental conditions to construct a structure that it could not have established on its own.

In the special case of religious evolution, one can assume that there are permanent initiators of variation situated in the difference of familiar/ unfamiliar or later in that of "this world/other world." The "other side" of this distinction can (and must) be accounted for without the customary this-worldly empirical limitations. Here, no limits are set on fantasy initially—*unless they are being drawn in this world using the "reentry" of the distinction into itself.* Because for religion as well, the entire experience of reality has to be produced by the resistance of system operations against system operations, by communication's resistance against communication. There is no information that comes from outside. The system has to discipline itself.

For early periods of religious evolution, one had to count on institutions that enabled variations largely without implications and (especially) without remembering them. This was true for practices of communicative secrecy and for constructing taboos. It was also true of relatively pragmatic dealings with holy things by those who had access to them and claimed to know them. In its communicative representation (toward the outside), religious activity appeared to be fixed in form, that is, "stereotyped" (according to Weber's terminology), both in the magical and ritual domains. This was the only way the communication of meaning could be understood. At the same time, this fixing of forms was an indispensable condition for understanding the reference to religion in communication, without there being a need for an elaborate, expert-driven pre-understanding of what religion "means." But this fixing also had the latent function of preventing deviations from *being remembered* as innovations that had proven themselves. In that era, no practiced distinctions were made between variation and selection, even if the ancestors' bones preserved in the men's house were replaced from time to time,[7] and even if the signs for the necessary deployment of magical or divinatory powers had to be provided in a way that met the requirements.[8] In a state of partially no assumptions, religion could be established, develop recursivity, and discover its own autopoiesis.

Magic is attractive and easy to imagine, specifically because it is really only a parallel construction to natural outcomes and technologies, a parallel construction displaced into the other world. It can be preserved redundantly so as to guarantee success or as an attempt to reverse a fate that is nonetheless being manifested. It is a variant acquired in a copying procedure, which has its own explanations for success and failure. It is thus really not a recipe for certain success that could be given up immediately if it failed. Magic can also be used to explain events (which indeed have already occurred!) that are unusual and affect individuals. Further, what is remarkable about it is its close connection with all kinds of life problems and its inherent stability—and hence, its evolutionary dissemination and insensitivity. Even modernity has not been able to extinguish faith in magic, especially since one does not at all have to ask or decide whether one believes in it or not.[9] It confirms the presence of a different world, but it runs so close to everyday experience that consistency problems do not appear in the relationship between that other world and this one. Instead, the problems are located in the relationships between situations—if, say, someone was healthy before and then became ill. Religious and everyday practical connotations can be distinguished quite well. If the smoke of the sacrificial flame does not rise, this may be a bad sign, but if someone has forgotten to bring a lighter, they'd better go get one.

Clearly, questions of religion are never ever decided according to "reasonable agreement." And religion never ever evolves by a process of "finding consensus." Instead, social coordination takes place with the help of objects or "quasi-objects."[10] Evolution can make use of the object track and substitute other quasi-objects, which are better suited for more complex situations. In this sense, from trance states come prophets, and metaphysics will ultimately offer a distinction between visible and invisible things to be able to place the world completely within the world. In this sense, sacrifices and rituals are stage-managed as complex unities and thereby objectified. People may disagree about the necessity and opportunity of these practices but not about the way they are realized per se.[11]

Even the early periods of religious evolution—familiar with adaptive variation but not with a real separation of mechanisms for variation and selection—already assume a social differentiation. That boundary enables a separation and combining of strict binding and pragmatic utilization. It is necessary to start with this difference to answer the question of when and how religion passes over from a simple repetition in always different forms to the selection of rather improbable forms. As a consequence, the system of religious communication has to be restabilized.

As is so often the case, here too one finds that boundaries are creative structures because they reveal a difference and conceal its unity. The system can grow and develop new forms alongside the difference between competent and incompetent handling of sacred power. It can grow wild at this point, can switch from situational to professional roles with heritability or with specific demands for suitability; it can accumulate abilities, skill, and so on; and it can develop authority and responsibility for problematic situations. Distinct roles emerge for magicians, shamans, and priests. From the standpoint of those who are now laypeople—helpless but not guiltless—two boundaries coincide with or reinforce each other: the social difference on the line of competence/incompetence and the difference between the everyday world and uncanny powers from beyond.

Within such a *"hier-archy"* [literally, "sacred rule"] of experts, self-blocking may have taken place, making difficult to handle daily needs too generously—or to let that happen without remembering it. These were problems of mutual observation. A drastic change only took place when writing was introduced to prevent forgetting (no matter how beneficial the latter might have been).[12] Writing's invention had an ambivalent, if not paradoxical, effect. Certainly it was meant to preserve structure and to be used repeatedly, and it was equipped with unmistakably religious valuations of memory. At the same time, it destroyed the (previously) effective mechanism of stabilization, of not being able to recognize and hand down deviations. Writing seems to have been invented in order to make visible possible deviations, especially in household-like ("economic") and legal domains, and it did so prior to any coordination of text and language.[13] However, as soon as it was made linguistic and (ultimately) phonetic in the multilingual realms of the Near East, a new kind of difference emerged, going beyond the registrational aims of writing: the difference between oral and written *communication*.[14]

If meaning is understood as the unity of actuality and virtuality, then writing might be understood as a vast expansion of the realm of virtuality. One must not and cannot do without actuality, but the actuality of writing and reading was relieved of the social pressures of interaction, letting communication (along with consciousness) focus completely on the virtual aspects of experiencing meaning. What emerged were new and more abstract constraints on order, for not every idea could apparently be included in the world. Precisely when something was imagined as possible, it had to satisfy special conditions of plausibility, of possibly becoming real.

If the two (evolutionary) advances coincided—the differentiation of the competence for treating sacred affairs and the expansion of writing—significant outcomes could be expected. One result of evolution altered the conditions of further evolutions. As competence was established, there was a narrowing in the circle of those for whom the mastery of writing was possible and meaningful. It is therefore plausible that, in its beginnings, knowing how to write was treated in many cases as secret knowledge.[15] That must have made it easier to absorb the consequences of "literalization." Yet that is even more of a grounds for accepting that a new phase of evolution was introduced when knowledge was written down. In addition—and precisely after book printing was introduced—the religious significance of writing was reemphasized. Writing was said to be suited exactly for making the occult science of religion visible, yet without touching on its mystery.[16] And it gave the individual an opportunity to experience his participation in communication as his own behavior and to divert side effects from it in constructing his own personality.[17]

Nonetheless, it has to be admitted that not all the major religions depended on writing for their emergence and transmission. In particular, the religion of the Brahmins and Buddhism were exceptions to this rule, which can perhaps explain their tendency toward increasing ritualization. Even the relatively late availability of writing did not change this much. Despite that, there can be no doubt that writing, when it impedes on religion, has significant consequences. This can be substantiated in many particulars. For instance, divinatory knowledge gathered in a purely casuistic manner is ground down into a knowledge of method that is coded in binary fashion according to favorable/unfavorable signs. Another example is when the awareness of contingency is expanded because of the comparisons now possible. It is also demonstrated in the expansion of temporal horizons (that then have to be filled by genealogies),[18] and in the possibility of making present an "origin" that is past but still having effects. And if nothing else, there is the expansion of possibilities for symbolizing what is absent. Yet not only humans write but also the gods. They did so to keep accounts. Initially in Mesopotamia, they determined fate by council order.[19] In the Christian realm, their accounting took the form of a catalogue of sins that was available at the Last Judgment and could be used as the basis for decisions. Divine bookkeeping itself developed from a belief in fate to a justice based on works. Greater regard was given for the human freedom to make decisions, since there is an incorruptible memory available in heaven, a photograph (as it were) of real events in this world.[20] Although magic could not be extinguished as a popular belief, and although a rigid bookkeeping also contradicted faith in the efficacy of prayer, an alternative to representing meaning could therefore be drawn into the religion system, at least permitting other religions' faith in magic to be dismissed as an abomination.

In this complex framework (which cannot be exhausted in this chapter), the question of the repercussions of evolution on evolution constitutes a special problem that has rarely been addressed. Writing broke with the pre-existing self-stabilization of variation by repressing deviations and changes due to forgetting. It inserted a new process between variation and restabilization, the selection of a variation—positive or negative—from the standpoint of a structural change. After all, texts make recognizable—and that is why one has them—a distinction between conforming and deviating proposals of meaning.

Although it had only just emerged at this point, writing appeared to wholly dominate religion. It became the most important means of domesticating the world of the gods. The gods of Mesopotamia, as noted already, determined fate in writing and thus made it legible. Clearly, these determinations were rendered in secret signs that only a few people could read. Divination, a type of religious life-counseling, became an issue for a literate elite. *By contrast*, the religion of the prophets developed by reverting to older traditions of oral cultures as well as to dreams, visions and trance states. Here the deity became active, inspiring the prophets in ad hoc fashion; he provided directives and warnings while proclaiming his own will.[21]

At this point, too, God proved to be a power based on will and an observer, an intervening divinity who had to be treated as a person. Politics and religion could be separated. Since phonetic writings now could be used, this development can immediately be recaptured through texts. Reports about communicative events witnessed by prophets were made in writing. These reports, which had to make the unbelievable believable, also included the reactions of those in attendance. They were then embellished into narratives. Of course, religion then had to always protect itself against new interventions, which in turn called for writing. Prophets accepted the dictates of their god or they made dictates themselves. In the case of Sinai, the text was ultimately written by God himself. But it was still the idea of a god who communicates in an inspirational manner and who accompanies human life as an observer ready to intervene.

It is not until there was writing that a concept of tradition became possible that could be used in creating dogmas and thus destroying information. It was then handled as a preference for what had already been handed down. To the extent that things worked this way, the selection would now guarantee stability. It was treated as holy knowledge worthy of preservation—but not by necessity and not in all cases. When confronted with current needs, the texts were short and vague (in the eighteenth century, the term "sublime" was used admiringly). These writings demanded and enabled interpretation. And once again, guided by our reflections on evolutionary theory, one might assume that chance would have an impact at the breaking points of the evolutionary mechanisms for variation, selection, and restabilization. This means that what ephemeral circumstances might make particularly illuminating in the moment could plausibly be represented in communication.[22]

Proceeding from this assumption, we can understand one of the most stable solutions of this problem to have been found for a typical religion of the book: to be precise, the theory of Torah interpretation elaborated (relatively late) in the Talmud. That doctrine assumed a text that existed in written form, a text that served God as a basis for creating the world. Yet because Yahweh was the God of the past and the future, the text existed in order to be passed down orally and in writing. One had to stick to that text, but it was capable of being interpreted. Oral interpretation was an instrument for adapting to a future that was still uncertain. It took place through majority decisions of rabbis, and their rights extended so far that they were even able to deviate from a divine opinion stated clearly at the time of the decision, as documented in the renowned case of the "Oven of Achnai."[23] In this form, a reflection is found that is built into the scriptural tradition on the disadvantages of writing. It is admittedly different from Plato's polemic against writing, a reflection that *on the basis of a fixed text* remains explicitly open to a future for *selections that presently cannot presently be defined.* In particular, it may have been this way of dealing with writing that made possible the religious and legal survival of Judaism after the destruction of the Second Temple, when it lacked the security of political self-rule. (Or it may also be that this approach to writing was developed precisely for *this* problem on account of its historical emergence).

By contrast, in the sphere of the Christian religion and similarly in Islam, writing has mainly been cause for theological speculation, the emergence of inconsistencies, and religious schisms. One might also consider whether the lack of a political state for ensuring religion and the law was decisive in the evolution of Judaism.

Writing may have acted as a trigger, but it does not explain what then emerged as major religions. Their emergence, like the development of autopoietic systems per se, was an abrupt switch to a different principle of stability. In the precise systems-theoretical sense, this meant a religious catastrophe. Ancient sacred structures were thus supplanted—for instance, in erecting new buildings on holy sites.[24] And extravagant new demands were consequently made. Myths of suddenness [*Plötzlichkeitsmythen*] emerged concerning awakening and conversion. People were this way obliged to make a choice, even coerced into doing so, but without the option of choosing what religion calls the wrong path—leading an "unholy" life. A clear-cut distinction thus emerged between "internal" and "external" that, at least in some major religions, demarcated its own medium of "faith." Through the elaboration of figures and myths, a self-development of considerable complexity could take place. Provided it would succeed, that is.

III

One of the most important circumstances to have influenced the evolution of religion is the relationship between religion and morality. It might not have become a problem if religion had never made a pretense to being universalistic or related to the world. With the emergence of the major religions, however, the question arose of why there was morally good and bad—indeed, even evil—behavior in the world. The "Fall of Man," the staging of humanity's specific contribution to creation, had introduced the code of morality into the world, and its consequences could no longer be avoided. People saw themselves prompted to make moral judgments and, worse yet, they were themselves morally judged.

The myth of the Fall of Man sanctioned a variety of interpretations. One could view the introduction of morality as the devil's work and accordingly view hell as the site of its implementation, where physical tortures were substituted for spiritual ones.[25] But that would not answer the question of why God permitted the Fall to occur, thereby exposing the sinner to morality as a type of just punishment. Both codes, that of religion and that of morality, make universalistic pretenses in developed societies. The problem that emerged was regulating their relationship to each other.

This is a conflict that cannot be solved either logically or cognitively. A decision has to be made from which side to approach the world. Yet that does not eradicate the problem from the world; rather, it returns in a form dependent on the primary distinction. Even if it is granted primacy, religion still has to position itself according to the fact that both good and bad behavior are possible, indeed (one could almost say) *permitted.*

This problem had considerable influence not only in the evolution of religious notions but also in that of religious institutions, which cannot escape constant provocation by "the world." If their faith was to be accepted or believed, they would have to guarantee it themselves and be drawn into worldly affairs. At first, they may have faced a constant barrage of micro-events, but dogmatic positions and institutional customs could be developed through selection and restabilization, building up expectations that would now have to be fulfilled. Whatever its semantic and institutional imprint, no religion would easily be able to avoid dealing with morally coded affairs of the world. It could not simply sit around and hold out its hands for alms. This problem was framed by the fundamental separation of religious and political roles in many societies of the old world. Yet that was not enough to fully solve the problem, in terms of preventing it from reoccurring.

From the perspective of evolutionary theory, then, one can accept that the mere emergence of behaviors judged good or bad was able to pressure religion into making selections. That did not mean that religion had to adopt a society's moral standards. Yet the question remained of how religion could develop and preserve its own standards for such occasions. It might concur with them by distinguishing between paradise and hell as differing forms of life after death. In the process, however, it created for itself problems of theological consistency that could lead to controversy—such as the relationship of such distinctions to the dogmatics of original sin or the question of whether eternal punishments in hell were compatible with the compassion [*misericordia*] attributed to God.

Compared to the structural problems involved in the interpenetration of religion and morality, these may have been "easier" problems, better left to theologians to debate. Yet the development of an internal Church jurisdiction in the Middle Ages and its elimination by territorial states in early modernity show that evolution also developed solutions that later turned out to be dead ends. Structural evolutionary advances might prove themselves for a time but then later lead to crises, making it necessary to give them up. In general, the increasing individualization of morality since the Middle Ages (specifically, the increasing reference to the internal attitudes of individuals) appeared to define the terrain on which possible solutions were to be negotiated. And this comes about because the individuality of individuals was required on the basis of evolution in the social structure.

IV

If at this point there was "tradition," and variation and selection thus had to be separated, what opportunities and dangers remained for further evolution?

From the perspective of evolutionary theory, "major religions" (however vague the term may be and however broad its zone of difficult attributions) are defined by the fact *that their selection mechanism is oriented toward stability.* They do not distinguish systematically between selection and restabilization but try to orient their mode of selection (for both negative and positive selection) toward existing dogmas. According to the major religious faiths, these can only be clarified but not changed. That is how we shall define the term "dogmatics."

This can be recognized in efforts to synthesize religious forms that had originally developed with a view to a multiplicity of situations. In such a context, the world of gods was ordered by hierarchy, family, or another structure—de-randomized, one might say. At the same time, a concern for consistency meant a more focused demarcation had to be made toward the outside with respect to nonreligious realms of meaning. Outside of religion, there could be no religious meaning, thus resulting in the well-known problems religions have of acknowledging each other as well as their attempts to identify gods by various names. Religion then found stability in itself and precisely in the difference that separated religious meaning from other kinds. With reference to Egyptian religion, Jan Assmann maintains that there is a transition from implicit to explicit theology and, within that context, that history is theologized.[26]

Such a reorientation revealed a trend of shifting from a primacy of other-reference to one of self-reference. Yet as religion, both of these refer to becoming acquainted with the familiar/unfamiliar distinction, that is, to this precise reentry. In this new way, religion became a system that reproduced itself, its own boundaries, and its own history. It continually reactualized its own recursions. In short, it became an autopoietic system. Religious semantics were completely reformulated, becoming a doctrine that could be fixed in writing—a dogmatics. Dogmatization could also occur in polytheistic contexts if, as in the case of ancient Greece, they were closely interwoven with genealogies of nobility and therefore preserved (with a considerable loss of plausibility and amplified by a number of mystical sects). But the semantics of major religions reached their most convincing form when symbolizing their own unity—whether in the person of a single god, in a religious principle, or in a specifically religious duality.

It has often been commented that the religions of the book—and only these—have brought about a distinctive monotheism. Only in these cases does the god documented in the text become a world deity, who has established the world as it is found. We have already touched on the construction of an observer god. Everything was created through him, and nothing eludes him. For all the daily relevance of the "this-worldly" life, this construction made it possible for everything that exists to have a religious second meaning. And religion attempted to make the individual acknowledge that these meanings are the ones that actually count. Both Jansenists and Jesuits can be found propagating this attitude, with all their energy, at the same time when the fear of hell is declining and greed is on the rise.

Part of this concept is a less noticed parallel construction: the invention of the soul. This would have originated in the liminal experience of death, the observed dying of others. Here, too, there is a boundary that triggers semantic growths. It produces the figure of life after death as a reentry and needs an identical substrate for doing so, that of the soul. Since no one can really imagine the end of his own consciousness, the soul is a highly plausible construction, and one finds it not only in the strictly text-oriented religions of the book but pretty much everywhere else—be it in the form of ancestor worship, in a shadow realm of the dead, in the "grand tour" of reincarnation, or in the form of modern spiritism. In the framework of monotheism, the extreme disengaging of these two boundary concepts of God and soul provides latitude for a dogmatic shaping (with room to expand), for a type of medium that is still open to the formation of shaping forms.[27]

Humans were then no longer simply at the mercy of their fate, which religion could at least justify at a later point, even if it could not influence it by powerful magic. Rather, man was himself seen as a participant who co-determined the form of his relationship to God—whether by his works or by hoping for a mercy strengthened by the correct faith. Yet, in this open context, the key question would now become how there came to be forms in the medium, and how a strict coupling of redemptive certainties emerged in the face of the loose coupling of possibilities. The problem of redemptive certainty would become a polarizing problem, and precisely because none of the variants of religion could create final certainties, already on the grounds of the established God/soul semantics. In any case, if God was at all a just god, he would permit the possibility of doing things wrong. But that only increases and does not remedy uncertainty in the question of criteria. A clear indicator for this increased uncertainty was the appearance of paradoxical formulas: the more external the sign (*verbum solum habemus*), the more internal the certainty. The greater the level of anxiety and fear, the stronger the conviction of having been chosen.[28] In the end, there could be no institutional solution, no sacramental solution, no solution through the gentle pressure of Jesuit life-counseling, and no solution through putative demonstrations of probability. And of course, there would be no solution through nonsolution, by acknowledging the unrecognizability of God's dispositions toward redemption.

In these circumstances, Luther's emphatic stress on "writing" was a more nostalgic concept. In the writing handed down, one finds arguments, examples, and a continuous polemic on sin—an abundance of material for sermons. But there were also warnings that the matter is not so simple and that the Day of Judgment would be full of surprises—both for sinners and the righteous. The final words spoken on the cross also indicate how religion could set aside its own information. Even if they were written down, they could be forgotten or merely not mentioned. But the God/soul semantics dissolved the medium of religious faith to such an extent that the texts did not offer any greater certainty of form. At best, they supplemented what could be followed *instead* (if need be).

And in the end, the world was also no longer a sufficient text to guarantee for oneself God's love. He might in fact have had good intentions, but how was one to know that? God does not let himself be observed in nature; he remains invisible by choice.[29] Nature itself got lost in the space of endless inquiry. "For my free exercise of religion," asked Jean Paul, with clear naïveté, "is it really necessary to have so many stars and parts of the world (and their islands) that never interest me—as well as previous centuries, bugs, mosses, and the *entire* plant and animal kingdom?"[30] Ultimately, "world" was only that most extreme horizon that retreated into inaccessibility with every step, every signification of something defined by it, because another question could always be posed of what the thing defined is distinguishing itself from.

How should this finding be interpreted? It is difficult to follow Weber here, converting the finding into a rejection of the world or the ascetic rationality implied by it. As most, it would be a variant of a much more general problem. From the standpoint of evolutionary theory, however, one could recognize that the (previously valid) relationship between selection and restabilization was disappearing. Both the cosmology of ontological metaphysics along with its concept of nature (including self-norming)—as well as the specifically religious (here biblical) textual tradition—had assumed that the world (in its God-given facticity) contained recognizable criteria of correct selection. On that basis, people might endure (or indeed expand) variation, having always thought that they could make selections with a view to stability while readapting innovations (above all, as a return to what was older and better). That idea was consistent with a stratified society that, despite all kinds of turmoil, could not give up the notion of a natural correctness, of an order of fixed places or an ability to distinguish between perfection and corruption.

Yet changes set in with the transition from stratification to functional differentiation—and on the broadest of fronts. Everywhere, selection criteria had to relinquish the prospect of stability. This applied (for instance) in the economic realm as the criterion of profit emerged. In the political realm, too, there were reasons of state [*Staatsräson*] that were bound by time and could not become morally fixed; and later there was a concept of "popular sovereignty," compatible with all modifications. In the realm of intimate relationships, there was passionate and then romantic love. In the undecidability problem posed by redemptive certainty, religion faced a (precisely) analogous problem. For religion confronted a societal situation in which the evolutionary functions of variation, selection, and restabilization were completely uncoupled and could no longer (in their connection) be pre-formed as a system. Evolution was thus a completely coincidental event. That didn't at all mean that just anything could happen or that one had to be prepared for all possibilities; in modernity, chance was precisely a reason for an orderly processing of information. Nor did it mean that religion could no longer fulfill its function (for the same would then be true of the economy, politics, intimacy, etc.) And it really didn't mean that individuals were now going to have to live without psychological stability or a soul (whatever that might be). What it did likely mean was that each time *absolute criteria* were asserted, the effects were now *socially discriminatory*: there were those who "believed" and others who did not.

The problem of criteria became a theme everywhere in the eighteenth century: in the economy, it was highlighted in the contingency of market successes; in politics, in the figure of a sovereign state arranging its "international" relations on its own; in science, in the inability to substantiate inductive conclusions (Hume); and in love, to the extent that it only depended on being requited. In art, the principle of imitation was relinquished, relating criteria now to taste. With respect to works of art, taste and the capacity for judgment were no longer expected of philosophers, but only the technical competence to construct theories (of aesthetics, etc.). Giving up criteria like these could hardly be demanded of religion, which instead took refuge in higher-level notions of pluralism and tolerance.

But the comprehensive solution now offered by the societal system was found in the invention of "culture." People were no longer having arguments; they were making comparisons. We shall return to this issue below.

V

At the end of a long evolution of its own, the communication of religion became a problem, specifically for religion itself. This was at least the case if the forms of major religions were supposed to be maintained, thus if evolution were still making selections based on a predetermined, stable dogmatics. For in a situation of strongly accelerated societal transformation, the outcome would have to be a relatively slow evolution in the religion system itself. A careful modification of dogmas would result, while their core—against which acceptances and rejections could be tested—would be preserved.

Using "deconstructionist" terminology, one might also say that religious communication is increasingly implicated in "performative contradictions": if claiming something, it first of all has to claim it. The constative sides of its communication—the utterance "this is the way it is"—are unsettled and even discredited by the utterance itself. If the utterance is in writing, one could almost say it is already false, for one can immediately ask when and by whom it was written. Then as now, narrative moments ("myth" in the sense of "plot") and internal consistency controls may have had a plausibilizing effect. But as with Gödel, Escher, and Bach,[31] it is always possible to figure out the point at which the unsolved problem of consistency becomes noticeable. In order to be able to believe, one always already has to want to believe.

Some major religions are involved in such difficulties with their own communication—and not only with being accepted—more than others, depending on the extent to which their hardening is dogmatic and organizational. These difficulties cannot in any way be assessed as signaling the "end of religion." But they force concepts to be abstracted so that religion can then be described adequately.

This argument can be expanded on. Religion also (and particularly) distinguishes itself under modern conditions from other function systems of society in a clear manner. It fulfills a particular function and is oriented toward a code of its own not used by any other function system of society. Religion recognizes itself as religion whenever it refers to everything that can be experienced immanently as transcendence—regardless of how such a directive is semantically realized. We are forced to see that there is a function system for religion operating worldwide in our modern world society, a system that defines itself as religion through a distinction from other function systems. To that extent, the situation is no different from the political system with its multitude of states, or the economic system with its multitude of markets. Even the system of religion finds itself segmentally differentiated into a multitude of religions. These have to account for the necessity that faith choices have to be specified, which inevitably leads to diversification. Varying traditions can be taken into consideration, particularly in the case of the major religions, where it is assumed that one already knows what is being talked about when one is talking about religion. But new formations can also be imagined that react to various social situations—and to various reasons for resisting what modern society suggests as lifestyles. The key point is that the world system of religion does not block or suppress such internal differentiations by means of dogma or organization. On the contrary, these very differentiations are made possible by the interpretive deficiencies in the coding. From the Catholic Church to voodoo sects, from the spiritists' belief in incarnation to Zen Buddhism—it is (all) still religion. And it is this way not because of some holy central mystery or because their articles of faith are translatable into each other. It is rather because all religious forms in society distinguish themselves as religion from function systems with other objectives—but also from everyday communication that is nonreligious. In fact, they *distinguish themselves* regardless of whether the environment adopts the distinction or not. The constitutive principle is not unity but difference. In the overall context of world society, religion's variety (and thus opportunity for evolution) appears far greater today than could be foreseen in the nineteenth century. New beginnings are found, appearing virtually without precedent, in sects that no longer seek any kind of connection with modern modes of persuasion. There are more magicians than priests.[32] One finds charlatans, miracle workers, and low-priced providers of all kinds who immediately turn the code of religion into an option. One finds fundamentalisms that cling to selected elements of tradition while renouncing claims to universality. One finds appearances of intellectualization within professional theology that attempt to maintain a flexibility of formal options. In many respects, there is more reflection on communicating than on presenting certainties of belief. Modern theologians love "conversations."

Viewed superficially, this high degree of diversity, diffusion, and variability in appearances seems to speak against assuming a "system." But that is deceiving since that is precisely how the religion system fulfills the evolutionary function of restabilization under modern conditions. However the selection of innovations may come to be, and however different the religions entering the religion system, the population of religious communications nonetheless forms a societally autonomous realm. It articulates the circumstance that religion still exists. Under such conditions, it is difficult to foresee further evolution within the religion system (apart from the fact that there are no starting points for organizational or dogmatic centralizations). But what evolutionary theory tells us is that evolution does not lead to predictable results anyway.

VI

The discussion up to this point has been oriented toward the monotheistic religions of the West. We also, however, need to look at a completely different religious structure, that of the Indian (Hinduistic, Buddhistic) doctrine of rebirth in an infinite cycle of life and death. Here, too, there is no recourse to individual memories, and it differs from the Brazilian spiritists' attempts to reactivate experiences, situations, and ways of reacting from a previous life in order to explain our obsessions and blockages at present (so that we might gain some psychological distance from them). One's previous life cannot be remembered, thus providing a type of security for a religious interpretation. The theory is framed by the idea that death is only the transition to a different life. The liberated figure is reincarnated and has to attempt life again under different conditions.

Furthermore, it is assumed that there is a cosmic hierarchy of better and worse situations. People can be reborn as kings or as street cleaners, or even as animals. The relevant situation depends on one's present conduct, especially one's moral life. Here a fixed doctrine of better and worse places applies, as well as the assumption that one's present lifestyle is being judged morally.

One might suspect that the objective of this doctrine is to improve the moral level of a society. And that may be the case. Yet if members of this society were to see through this "function," it would no longer be effective. Seen from the perspective of evolutionary advances, another question becomes interesting. How could a construct as improbable as rebirth have entered the world and have had such success as religion?

In answering this question, we have to return to the starting situation, in which there was a hierarchical society and a correspondingly hierarchized cosmology. There is no reason to doubt that this was the situation in which people had to conduct their lives if they wanted to avoid the path of exclusion. At the same time, however, society was so complex that free spaces emerged for individuality and for observing it—spaces that somehow had to be occupied. In such a situation, arguments for combining hierarchization and individualization were persuasive. The concept of a rebirth guided by individual merit was a response to this need. The success of this concept can thus be explained as the result of a historical situation, and the religious (and not political) treatment of such problems explains the long-term restabilization of the solution found. This solution cannot be offset by its usefulness for the individual.

We are thus able at a glance to understand variation, selection, and restabilization. In ancient societies, people had already experimented with notions of a life after death, subject, for instance, to the manner in which someone died. The variation did not have to invent something new or completely unfamiliar. Nonetheless, the systematization and universalization of these notions only emerged thanks to the doctrine of rebirth. And a restabilization took place when religion could apply that idea in solving its own problems, such as giving meaning to the divergence of individualization and hierarchization, a meaning that matches other assumptions of religion.

VII

The emergence of *world religions* surely must count among the most important results of religious evolution to date. The term does not refer to religions that have a more or less worked out cosmology, something that is ultimately a concept of the world, which is the more typical case. Rather, world religions are religions that offer their faiths to all people with no ethnic, national, or territorial restrictions. That is not at all self-evident, from the perspective of religious history. It does not apply to the Jewish religion or to Japanese Shintoism. If something was to aspire to be a world religion, it had to do without ethnic, national, or regional supports. Those would have to be abstracted, meaning that the historical origin of one's own religion was often forgotten or touched up. Every person who was recognizably human was to be addressed, and one saw immediately that much would be abstracted that might have been near and dear to the individual.

If a religious option is supposed to be formulated as a world religion, it is something that has specific consequences for the contents of faith. But these consequences were at first rather negative. Familial, ethnic or otherwise social-structural traits had to be abstracted since access to religion might depend on them. And even the gods had to be deregionalized. They were not to distinguish themselves by preferring certain places or certain human groups. The most effective formulation was likely that affairs of religion always depend "on faith alone." The plausibility of a faith arises from the experience of faith itself. Yet if this sounds too tautological, too arbitrary, or too much related to individuals, it might be suggested that such an experience is a unique act of divine mercy. Or one can assume along with Buddhism that the foundations of the world of phenomena and thus of individual faith are a "void," to which all distinctions are admitted. But it is a void that is still accessible to reflection, and thus to anyone who strives to reach it.

World religions are an important—perhaps the most important— contribution to differentiating a religion system. They more or less anticipate a world society, at the same time cutting off possibilities (and thus plausibilities as well) for justification, which might arise from nonreligious sources. As a sociologist might well assume, this inevitably leads to an intensification of demands on faith, and thus to a tightening of the difference between inclusion and exclusion, between the orthodox and heretics (or those who do not believe at all). Religion vibrates (as it were) with its own claims and with the necessity of replacing external supports of a group or regional type, reversions to the familiar.

It will be asked why such an effort is necessary at all. The answer can only be that it is one of the forms in which the differentiation of the religion system becomes accessible to religion itself.

Secularization

I

It is difficult to deny sociology's identification with secularization. Ever since the time of Auguste Comte, secularization has been a part of its thematics, and one in which it includes itself.[1] Sociology does not proceed from axioms of faith, even (in fact, especially) when the issue is religion. To preserve its scientific credentials, it maintains a "methodological atheism." In comparison with religion, sociology's self-description can thus accommodate secularization only to the extent that it makes no theological commitment. Yet that still does not tell us whether secularization is a meaningful subject for research or—unlike in Comte's day—something self-evident needing no commentary.

The thesis of religion's demise—of its loss in social significance and in individual motivation—was taken as an established truth in the nineteenth and early twentieth century. It was a premise of more progressive and more conservative social theories (both sides of the ideological spectrum) and thus not really an object of controversy.[2] The notion of secularization referred to the societal system and was supposed to serve as a kind of explanation, an alternative description. Today, the concept is hardly used anymore in scientific writing. It is not deemed viable.[3] It brings together too many heterogeneous traditions in a single term. Among sociologists of religion today, it is regarded as an established fact that one can speak of "de-churchification" or "de-institutionalization" or even of a movement away from organized access to religious behavior[4]—but not of a loss in the significance of the religious as such.[5] The secularization thesis with its predetermined direction is therefore replaced by the much more open (but highly vague) question of religious transformation in our times. This approach makes possible theory-free empirical research, which at least until now has not taken on a clear, interpretable outline.

Even the history of the concept provides little in the way of useful guidance. It mirrors constellations far too conditioned by the situation of their emergence. "Saeculum" used to designate the state of a world marked by sin and sorrow and in need of redemption. A "secular depravity" was how Jean Paul described the particularly distinct rupturing of all forms of the most sacred in his lifetime.[6] One form of "secularization" [*Sakularisation*] was the expropriation of massive accumulations of idle Church property and the suspension of Church privileges and sovereignty rights. Another type of "secularization" [*Säkularisierung*], especially in Catholic countries, involved a program of political ideology for dismantling religious influences on society, education, science, and self-defined individual lifestyles—a program of anti-clerical "positivism" often associated with Comte's theory of universal history. We can also understand secularization as projected goals, according to which structure and difference are introduced into an unknown future. When discussing secularization in the twentieth century, even after Comteanism was itself treated as an ideology, one could still point to an increasing popular indifference to religious questions, a decline in church attendance and in formal church membership. These are facts. Yet while there are still empirical studies of the topic, these now employ a multidimensional concept only unified by the relations under investigation.[7]

Although the notion of secularization in this form appears to have some objective-descriptive content, designating particular facts, it is predominantly a historical concept that gets filled with different contents in different time periods. As a historical term, however, it enters nowadays the maelstrom of philosophy of history where it loses any distinctive—even epochal—reference. While secularization had once indicated "enlightenment" [*Aufklärung*], it now enters into that term's dialectical self-negation. While it had once been "modern," its figures are now freed up for all kinds of postmodern combinations. While it had once been "European," one is no longer surprised about the many religious revivals of non-European provenance. While it had once been "empirical," religious and moral themes have become so significant in school curricula,[8] it is as if *they* prepare schoolchildren for a civilized life in modern society. Finally, no one studies any more whether modern society is secularized but only why anyone would make that claim.[9] And this too is counterfactual (so to speak), in face of the indisputable fact that secularization in no way excludes religious activities and experiences.[10]

For all these (good) reasons, one cannot get rid of the concept of secularization without proposing a replacement for it. Few would deny that serious changes were being openly implemented around 1800. Hence, with the French Revolution, intolerance migrated from religion into politics.[11] And the function of religious symbolism was taken over, or at least conveyed, by aesthetics.[12] At least for the Romantic period, secularization could be understood as a "displacement," a shift of religiously influenced expectations into extrareligious—or worldly—realms.[13] If there were no concept for such radical changes, it would produce a vacuum, a gap in theory. And no other candidate has arisen to take its place. The problem can be illustrated with the help of observation theory and the concept of form. If wishing to observe religion, we have to be able to indicate (and thus distinguish) it. The form of religion that instructs observation and makes it distinguishable is a form with two sides. The one side is religion, which distinguishes itself. But what is the other side?

One could make do with the knowledge that the other side is everything else, everything that cannot be indicated when religion is being designated. The other side is then assumed to be the unmarked state of the world. That assumption would satisfy minimal demands, but it still leaves (at least) two questions unanswered. First, is there a narrower domain on the other side that could be made indicatable—specifically, for sociologists, that of nonreligious societal communication? And second, how does religion itself see its other side? As the rest of the world, for which it would like to have its own signification, or as nonreligious societal communication? For religion apparently can only gain determinacy in its self-description if it can say more precisely what it is including or excluding.

Using the concept of secularization, an answer can be provided to both questions, without having to make statements of meaning or descriptions of a condition. The description of the other side of religion's societal form is involved, the description of its environment within society. Hence, it does not involve worldly objects of some kind or another. We would not want to speak of a secularization of the moon if it were being denied divine qualities. And a description by a certain observer is involved—specifically, religion—or more precisely, a description *of* the description of the social environment by this observer and no other.[14] Other observers may thus describe the same facts differently, such as in a scientific experiment in a laboratory. And, in such cases, observers would never get the idea that they should not pray for the experiment to succeed—or that doing so, if it were effective, would violate the conditions of the experiment (*ceteris paribus*, the complete inclusion of the relevant variables, and so on). A system operating in the environment of the religion system is *itself* not determined by the fact that it performs and observes *its own* operations in the environment of religion. As a result, "[t]here is a difference between sleeping late on Sunday and refusing the sacraments, between having a snack and desecrating the fast of Yom Kippur."[15]

A concept of secularization thus understood fulfills the requirements of scientific limitationality. This means that it excludes something. At the same time, it is formulated relative to the observer. That means it includes the fact (as something implicated in the concept of secularization) that there can be other observers for whom the secularized nature of their observing is latent, serving as a blind spot that makes it possible for them to see what they see in the first place. This statement in turn can only be made if one formulates it on the level of a third-order observation. That means observing the observer who, with the help of this secularization concept, observes what another observer cannot when observing nonreligious patterns of observation.

In considering these issues, one runs up against logical difficulties that are nearly unresolvable or, in any case, exceed the limitations of bivalent logic.[16] At the same time, though, these difficulties reconstruct the historical relativity of the category of secularization, even if structurally rich logics are not (yet) available. For only modern society requires and enables these kinds of complex descriptions. Older societies were able to content themselves with observing sacred objects or observing the observer God—assuming this God (in extreme cases) to be all-observing, an observer outside the world. As a consequence, it made no difference for observations *in* the world whether these were being observed by *Him*, and there was a complete reversion to the assumption of a fully secularized world, one *in which* observers were free to define themselves as (not) religious. Only when the world was prepared for this theologically did observers appear who still saw and described this as well. Further, they were also able to reflect on the fact that they were themselves observing (with religious or nonreligious intentions) that observers were using the pattern of secularization to make comprehensible the possibilities of observing the world.

As we understand it, secularization is a concept tailored to a poly-contexturally observable world in which the contextures of observers are no longer identical (or flawed) from the standpoint of existence or of God. Secularization is therefore a concept that belongs to a society whose structures suggest polycontextural observation—and which thus demands prior decisions about acceptance or rejection (itself a second-order contexture). This demand is not applicable in every single instance. But it has to be at least considered if one wants to exhaust the possibilities of such a society and comply with its reality.

Understood in this way, the secularization concept does not lead those who nonetheless draw on it to hypothesize that religion has lost its relevance in modern society.[17] Instead, it calls attention to how religion reacts to the assumption of a secularized society, the kinds of semantic forms and arrangements used to include or exclude members. Secularization is observed as a provocation to religion, and that is why religion responds to this provocation in several ways—with forms that may be incompatible, culturally acceptable, or perhaps even "strange." We shall return to this point in chapter 9, on the religion system's self-description.

II

After these introductory considerations, it is easy to see that—and how—secularization has to be associated with functional differentiation as a modern form of differentiating the societal system. In the history of the terms *saeculum* and "secularization," this association can only be understood in broad (yet sufficient) outlines. It is striking, for instance, that some of the points of departure in the medieval world for the eigenrationality of central domains of life, especially for money and (sexually based) love, were presented in religion as symptoms of vice in "this world." They put pressure on religion—more than it might sustain—to rely upon asceticism and poverty. Forms of "secularization"—such as expropriating Church properties and eliminating clerical rights and privileges (presiding over marriages, for instance)—were only consistent in having shifted resources into systems that needed them to continue functioning. Secularization ultimately registers how God's hand becomes invisible and how "le monde va de lui-même" [the world goes on by itself].* It also compels a deep breach between the functional demands of societal systems and an individual's religious scruples, hopes, and hardships. Functionally speaking, it makes little sense to refer to religion—either economically, politically, and scientifically, or in the family, socialization, education, or medicine. This is the case even when religion's (now outdated) forms are given a type of state assistance in the form of legal protections, tax advantages, or school-based activities. In addition, people still readily make use of certain religious services, such as family rites of passage. But somehow the sum of all these marginal parts does not provide an adequate sense of how significant religion is in modern society, because each of these descriptions is based on the system reference of *other* function systems and *not that of religion*.

Only if one analyzes carefully the form of differentiation oriented toward functions is it possible to get beyond these loose associations taken from the history of ideas. But that is a task exceeding the scope of what can be addressed here. We shall have to make do, then, with a few roughly sketched suggestions.

Function systems are systems that operate self-referentially. They are characterized by autopoietically closing their operations while basing themselves on their function and their code and while accounting for other cognitive or normative viewpoints only on the level of their programs (which are alterable, not those which are decisive for their identity). In some instances—and this can be seen this in the case of the religion system—such an order can develop in an evolutionary manner. If this occurs, such function systems initially maintain themselves by the primary mode of societal differentiation: functionaries of the Church, even its saints, are drawn from elite circles.[18] Without that backing, religion would presumably return to a state of mere magical and ritual operations, one that does not permit itself to be determined exclusively by its own operations and structures.

Similarly, premodern religion correlates with a differentiation of center and periphery. In fact, it contributed significantly to the emergence of

* This maxim is attributed to Jean Claude Marie Vincent de Gournay (1712–1759), a French economist and one of the creators of the *laissez faire, laissez passer* economic philosophy.—Trans.

this form of societal differentiation by differentiating religious centers. To be sure, the major religions may assume the equality of all their adherents, that each is born with a soul and dies with one, so that all of them are guaranteed this life and an afterlife.[19] But statements (and confirmations) of faith may differ substantially along the distinction between center and periphery, and this difference itself forms a structural coupling between religion and the rest of society, without in this function becoming a subject of religious belief.

These formations change to the extent that more and more function systems in society are differentiated as autonomous, operatively closed systems. Such an evolution undermines the primacy of traditional forms of differentiation. Function systems become less reliant on structural couplings with stratification and with center/periphery differences. The population is no longer classified primarily according to differences in rank, thereby distributed by a fixed "status." Instead, every function system regulates inclusion and distribution of opportunities for itself. Individuals increasingly have to get along without a social status guaranteed by birth. Yet since they can read and write, they are available for more complex conditions of inclusion. Society replaces its principle of stability in the form of a structural and semantic "catastrophe." In other words, it alters its form of differentiation, that form in which it brings together unity and diversity.

Semantically, this catastrophe reveals itself especially in the dissolution of all cosmic correlates. The function-oriented form of internal differentiation distinguishes itself quite plainly from all structures that might be projected into an environment. Consequently, society can no longer understand itself as a system that is supported by the world. Stratification was able to be cosmologized as a difference between above and below, or as a "chain of being," and the center/periphery differentiation likewise as a distinction between midpoint and margin. Despite that, it is no longer possible to project a division into the world corresponding to these functions. The representational schema of "dividing up" the world into categories, species, or types is losing its hold. Accordingly, the above/below schema is replaced (at first only in regard to humans) by an inside/outside one. The world loses its character of a surroundings (*periechon*) and is marked by a difference of system and environment, in which environment is what is different (or unknown) from the standpoint of every system, something for which no common essential traits can be discerned.

Ultimately, this leads to a cognitive constructivism. For only the system can make distinctions and only the system can therefore make observations, whereas the environment is merely the way it is. Since it is well known that there were no distinctions made in paradise before the Fall (although the reports, formulated in our observer language, repeatedly contradict that), one can assume the environment is nothing but the lost paradise, the *natura lapsa*. Only once the prohibition is transgressed is it possible to make moral (i.e., distinguishing) observations. In this way, paradise becomes the environment one cannot return to, because the system can only preserve its own distinguishing practice as an operatively closed system.

Among the most important and (for the topic of secularization) serious implications of functional differentiation is that almost all structures and operations can now be traced back to decisions. Looking back ideologically, even the market economy was treated as if it had been introduced by decision (and could therefore be introduced in circumstances where it had not been realized up to that point). But what is attributed to decisions cannot be traced back well (or only very artificially and implausibly) to a religious world order. According to a very conventional view of things, the attribution would end with the decision that had set in motion a distinctive course, a new turn in history. If one asks what was behind it, one winds up with ideologies or unconscious motives, with semantic figures explicitly developed to correct attributions to a decision. Even though there is enough evidence in the Bible (and ultimately in the myth of the Fall) that God involved humanity in creation, accounting for that theologically would mean having to rewrite salvation history.

But this issue can be set aside for now. In any case, this differentiation of function systems, which are operatively closed and exclude themselves from their environment, would be registered in modern society—in expectations of progress, in future horizons of uncertain content, and in categories of loss. Yet this occurred without a structural description having to be successful in the process of transition. The religion system (as well as all those who try to observe how *it* observes things) reacted to this differentiation by describing society and its world as "secularized." Symptoms and indications could be found for this description, not particulars but rather the image offered by society's religion. The "secularization" description was supported by the fact that no convincing answer was provided by the other self-descriptions of the societal system—either as a "capitalistic" society, as operating on science and technology, as a "risk society," as an "information society," or finally (in purely temporal terms) as a "modern" or "postmodern" society. A religious "world view" thus became impossible, particularly since *the other* descriptions of the world and society were *also not* convincing, either.

III

Among the most widespread definitions of the concept of secularization is that it had become a matter of individual decision whether people had religious commitments at all, and if so, to which religion. Religion, it was said, had thus become a private affair, nothing more than the object of a person's private sense of well-being.[20] Religion became à la carte.[21] But that only generated more problems. "Private" is an unwieldy description, since the opposing concept, "public," is also accurate in describing most religious exercises. Whereas "privacy" was a category of *exclusion* in the old world (*privatus = inordinatus* [irregular]; *privatio = negatio in subiecto* [or deprivation]), privacy and individuality merged in the transition to modernity. As a result, the concept tended in the direction of social importance (for the consumer, the voter, the subject of critical judgment, and so on), in the direction of *inclusion*. But the individuality of a person or a decision was also (historically speaking) a very imprecise definition. With respect to the intensity of devotion, it has always already played a role, and the limit case of continuing abstinence cannot easily be distinguished from a decision to be irreligious. The problem is presumably that those individuals whom society offers the option of deciding for or against religion are the very ones who do not make a decision.

In the Protestant movement especially, the individual increased in status as (magical-sacred) differences were undermined in the lifestyles of monks, priests, and laity. But this could not be referred to as secularization. The same might be said for the "modern" notion of religious devotion (François de Sales). Or for Herbert of Cherbury's deism, a type of meta-confessional religiosity that was supposed to enable *everyone* to connect his specific practice directly to the will of God. In any event, individualization should be examined from a more precise theoretical and historical perspective.

For now, let us remain on the level of a social semantics favoring "individual," "individuality," and "individualism."[22] These orienting terms had provided a kind of security in the period of transition from stratified to functional differentiation. With "individuals," a new kind of microdiversity would be identified that had to be presupposed in the transition to self-organizing function systems.[23] Even if all social classifications—of nobility and common people, places and nations, churches and sects, patron/client relations and (particularly) households—began to fluctuate, this process could at the same time be carried out by reverting back to the individuality of individuals. It is a process that was also able to be given a foundation of sorts untouched by societal change. This semantics of individuality had to be freed of all social labelings and limit itself (initially) to a few basic anthropological facts: these include not only cognitive abilities and passions but also an endogenous restlessness that exposed human relationships to turmoil.[24] Such assumptions about human nature were reduced once more in the eighteenth century. If one were to begin with the (by then) highly developed "biographical" awareness and milieu-dependent formation of individuals and then subtracted them (as it were) as an explanation for diversity, the only *universal* propositions about *human beings* that remain would be natural attributes of freedom and equality. These openly contradicted the state of civil societies at that time (and probably all times) and were therefore revalued as "human rights." This point divided the ways the world was viewed by modern individualism and religion so that no resolution is in sight for today's conflict between religious fundamentalism and its human rights counterpart. Not every individual is concerned about the salvation of his soul, and personal redemption is not a human right, anyway. And yet, those looking for a religion might be turned off when it is offered as a menu from which they cannot make selections.

The principle of human equality allowed for differences in religious confession, but leveled them out as differences to be individually selected.[25] The principle that all people are free reduced those ties [*Bindungen*], which were once formed and acknowledged as *religio*, to something external and (in the end) indifferent. They appeared to be constraints for which there may have once been (more or less) good reasons and legitimacy. From the side of religion, this development may be denounced as a collective ideology of individualism,[26] or (and here the embarrassment may become clearer) a religious meaning might be assigned to human rights as an afterthought. However, the problem lies deeper, in the restructuring of options for representing such ties. Since in modernity one is always (simultaneously) observing *how* ties are being observed, it inevitably has to be admitted that every determination is a contingent one and is therefore itself in need of legitimation. Consequently, even the tricks of legitimation appear to be contingent. The only "innocent" ties now were those that an individual had freely decided upon. Ties were becoming "commitments."

If the decision on a religious affiliation has to be represented, however, this could be substantiated biographically, if need be, but not as resulting from human nature. People had long mistrusted the old conclusion that human nature led to certain religious convictions. According to Shaftesbury, people's thinking about natural religion was inconsistent.[27] In a critical time, wrote Jean Paul, they were finding themselves "suspended between the desire to believe and the incapacity to do so."[28] Yet that only leads to the conclusion that a state establishment of religion by means of law is necessary for producing consistency. Such a situation would still be tolerable, following Shaftsbury, if the actual social disciplining of humanity were transferred to a morality it perceived as natural. Yet if that did not convince people on a religious level—and was it ever able to do so?—we are left with the natural inconsistency of human religious dispositions. If individual experience is then raised to the status of a final grounds for religious convictions, the consequence is letting the individual choose his religion (if he chooses one at all). And once that notion has been accepted, it is only a small step until one understands that social inconsistency—that is, thinking differently from others—can become a strong motivator of religious convictions.

In more recent literature, it is often said that (religious) *experience* is what counts. The experience is held to be incommunicable. It can only be referenced but others cannot be granted access to it. Hence, linguistic usage confirms modern individualism, as well as the unbridgeable difference between psychological experience and social communication.

Thinking about this from a societal standpoint rather than a psychological one helps clarify matters, especially with regard to individualization. It can be assumed that presuppositions of faith (existential assumptions, myths, and the meaning and effectiveness of ritual) apply to communication in older societies, if only because others also assume them to be true.[29] This changed fundamentally once communication always had to make certain which religious propositions were believed and by whom.

One way out of this might have been to avoid the subject—if only to save time. But that of course did not lead back to a religious "life world" accepted by everyone.

In the transitional period of the seventeenth century, there was plentiful evidence of a "no longer/not yet" situation. Religious faith, as well as a moral way of life, was still thought to be possible—possible, in fact, only in one correct way. However, it was also considered incommunicable. The "world" consisted of appearances, images, and manipulated signs, and no trust could be had in the courts, the priesthood, or in one's social status. "See, hear, and be silent" thus became Baltasar Gracián's watchword.[30] And if communication in the world could not be avoided, one would have to learn to operate in that world of appearances, always assuming that what was manifested was completely untrue.[31] Unity was still presupposed, but could only be achieved in a reverse procedure. Nonfaith presupposes faith, and only by reflecting on this could one be an individual and save oneself as such.

As a result of this bifurcating of the cultural religious option and personal religious decisions, there is currently widespread incoherence in individual opinions that qualify as religious.[32] Those who consistently follow Church orthodoxy and do so on the basis of authority are just as much a minority as those who consistently hold atheistic views or reject religion. Most people accept a few components of religious belief and not others. Perhaps they affirm the existence of God but not the dogma of the Immaculate Conception. They might accept a number of esoteric ideas but not astrology, healing by faith but not redemption by mercy alone, individual survival after death—perhaps even with biographical details of incarnations (spiritism)—but without rule-flouting miracles. Or they accept these and similar components of faith in different combinations. Doing so does not require support in communal life forms that would include every aspect of life. What it instead requires are selective social bases such as spiritist meetings or self-discovery seminars, newsletters or fellowship groups with similar preferences. Here one might refer to weak institutionalization, as the sociologist Loredana Sciolla does.[33] In any case, society does not leave the individual unsupported, but releases him from constraints of coherence, leaving him the option of modifying elements of his faith or letting them fade in importance.

It has to feel like a relief whenever someone finds himself in the situation of (legitimately) believing in something that others do *not*. The authenticity of faith persists and demonstrates itself by means of differences.[34] The paradox is resolved in social differentiation. After the individual assignment of religious decisions has gained acceptance, with each individual becoming accountable to (and needing motives for) himself and others, the only serious question left is that of social support and approval. Social like-mindedness can no longer simply be taken for granted, and the opinions of others can no longer be intuited arbitrarily. Instead, a visible and identifiable formation of community has to be introduced where one's faith is socially sanctioned, *even when others believe different things or do not believe at all.*[35] Like-mindedness is an exception in modern society, a surprising and gratifying experience that can lead the individual to join a group where he might count on repeating this experience. There are fundamentalisms of the most diverse kind, revivalisms, remystifications, renewals of faith in sacred stagings, and so forth. And each of these, in their attentive intensity, might be said to oppose secularization, while at the same time being conditioned by it.[36] They are based less in the historical sources that they fundamentalize and more on modern conditions that offer them the opportunity for opposition. As a result, they develop a paradoxical relationship to modern individualism, since they assume individual attention to religion (in contrast to a natural form of life) yet do not permit one to live in accordance with one's own ideas. In the form of religious fundamentalisms, modern individualism is turning against itself, and that is why its communication has to insist on radicality, on the plausibility of the implausible.

By way of elucidation, we once again ought to make it clear that states of consciousness are not at issue, but rather *communication*. States of consciousness, whether in reference to experience or action, are always individual and extremely unstable. That can never change, not even through an in-depth transformation of social structures. What can change is the extent to which states of consciousness can—or even must—be communicated as individual, that is, as unique or as different. To the extent that this is true (and only then), motives are needed with which one can hopefully find agreement. (For whenever individualization is mandatory, it does not at all mean that everything is permitted; one only has to recall the spectacular conversions of some Romantic artists.) Hence, communication of individually attributable experiences and decisions in a realm as important as religion always implies new formations of acceptance and rejection (which are now likely more explicit). Only that can explain how there are now divisions in a previously unified framework of religious faith, and how there are some sects that become eccentric, having found that it made them stronger to have counted on being rejected at first.

One of the most important effects of such individualization can be observed when individuals turn toward or away from religious groupings. The enlarging of one's spectrum increasing the chances of encountering one or another religious idea and feeling attracted or repulsed by it (depending on one's life situation). "Seek, and ye shall find," it is said. Yet what used to be called "conversion" is also undergoing "liquidation" (in a manner of speaking).[37] It is no longer an overwhelming event as in the case of Saul/Paul, something entering from the outside and permeating one's entire way of life. It is also no longer a kind of transcendental brainwashing but an individual decision to get involved in something. It is often a process that develops in phases. At first, someone (who is not fully convinced) tries out new conditions of social contact. Then that person—as an individual and self-observer—is drawn into a commitment. In terms of content (and in accordance with old models of religion), people are not infrequently seeking to be redeemed from society—something requiring the social support of like-minded communication. This phase can be followed by another one of self-limiting habit formation and lowered expectations, in which other religious options may appear attractive. In that mode, conversion is no longer a change in one's status but instead closer to the model of a (fortunate or unfortunate) career, as is typical nowadays when relationships of the individual to society are being organized.

Against this backdrop (including the mobility of entry and exit) what we have been discussing are the after-effects of releasing individualism on the authority structures and faith dogmas of religion systems, according to the pattern of "exit, voice, and loyalty" (to take but one example).[38] The trend toward self-defined individuality, authenticity, and disclosing one's opinion encompasses not only the laity but also (and more ominously) the priests themselves. One can retain one's membership in a church, attempting to participate but also making (more or less) frequent objections, such as "this makes no sense to me." Nonetheless, authority lives from being rarely forced to give explanations, and dogmatic questions (if one has to decide on how to interpret them) easily lead to verbal disagreements. When religious decisions are individualized, it affects not only the quantity of members but also what is (internally) self-evident to them. People possess their *own* individual souls, which only they—and ultimately God—manage. In whatever way religion itself may have contributed to its beginnings, modern individualism approaches it from the outside and disrupts it. The semantics of individuality was always a form of structural critique.

IV

For the phenomenon described by the word "secularization," the new communicative technologies of distribution were definitely important as well. First, there was book printing, then newspapers, and finally everything that today falls under the heading of "mass media." To be sure, everyone able to read the Bible could also read other texts, and print distribution was determined by the marketplace, not religion. In a much more radical sense, however, these new distribution technologies profoundly changed society's understanding of reality, altering in particular the relationship of image and text to reality.[39] The old idea that image and text themselves attested to reality lost currency. Even "Holy Scripture" was no longer considered an authentic explication of reality but only a testimony to faith, one to be accepted or rejected (as the case may be). The question that ought to be posed is: what combined these (more or less) arbitrary extracts, which impressed or irritated individuals in their daily lives, into an imagined unity—into something they presupposed because others also extrapolated their experiences from it?

Perhaps the most important effects of secularization are found in the dimension of time, specifically as a new way of understanding synchronism [*Gleichzeitigkeit*]. At least since the advent of newspapers, synchronism was defined by the new point in time [*Zeitpunkt des Neuen*]. It was thereby limited to the present (and then possibly extended to past or future presents). It was no longer possible to think of past and present as synchronous—as in the origin of a family or holy revelation being synchronous with what is called for at the moment. There a breach opened up—already in the Renaissance, but irreversibly with the rise of newspapers—between the (currently relevant) present and the past. The past distanced itself more and more from the present. If it were to remain relevant, the past needed to be brought up to date forcefully, as in the form of communion, which was supposed to be not only a memory but also a presence to be identified with symbolically.

In the process, this new synchronous present affected how one's experience was socially confirmed in the experiences of others. For synchronism now signified a mutual inability to observe and influence one another. From the fragments accessible to an individual when reading or watching a television show, he had to extrapolate what others were experiencing and what conclusions they were deriving from it. One could assume that they were receiving the same news, but what kind of world it led them to construct was still not clear. That gap was filled by imagination.[40] It was assumed that the mass media were representing "the reality" that each individual only got in fragments (though these fragments were capable of being amplified). Without doubt, this imagined world still contained religion; one had heard about it and seen impressive, colorful performances of it. Nevertheless, the imagination itself no longer accepted the form of religion. It had accepted the form of a secular world, and it was the only form in which one assumed that others concurrently experienced something confirmed by one's own imagination.

By this era, a huge number of completely different events were capable of taking place synchronously. Indeed, they had to happen synchronously because nothing was now capable of taking place in the future or in the past. Synchronism, however, entailed incoherence, since time would have been needed for observation—and even more for causal influence. But how might this world of incoherent synchronism be understood as a unity? Probably not religiously. Rather one might (at best) imagine temporally stable recognition and causal effects as something somehow "inserted" into the world. Yet this had its costs: the opportunity for error and the possibility of causal failures or unexpected side effects. If need be, religion could be regarded as a consolation for people who had good intentions.

V

A theoretical interpretation was needed if such changes—which could be understood well in descriptions and substantiated as empirically convincing—were to be related to fundamental changes in modern society and thus "explained." A fitting starting point for this can be found in Talcott Parsons's treatment of the problem.[41] Although he also refers to privatization, what he means by it are changes in the social regulation of inclusion, changes that have evolutionary effects on other variables of the general action system. In this sense, secularization is a *specific* expression of a *general* phenomenon, of an evolution directed toward distinguishing more strongly between adaptive upgrading, differentiation, inclusion, and value generalization. One important consequence is that religions—in the process of adapting to increasing differentiation and inclusion rules— have to generalize more intensely the symbolic structures with which they (nonetheless) want to preserve unity and pattern maintenance.[42]

There is also the notion of a "secularization of theology."[43] Parsons here is thinking particularly of the complex often referred to as "civil religion."[44] Going beyond Parsons, one could point to the post-Reformation strengthening of the organizational factor as a kind of adaptive upgrading of the religion system. Secularization then does not entail a loss of religion's function or significance, but perhaps a (temporarily?) poor adaptation to the conditions of modern society.

We want to follow up on this here, interpreting the concept of inclusion more narrowly, only with reference to societal systems. Inclusion takes place when persons (as attribution formulas for psychological systems) are considered as participants (actors, addresses, etc.) in the communication of societal systems. With the help of this concept, it can be visualized how the inclusion rules of a society change with its forms of differentiation. While older societies attributed a fixed place to individuals using a differentiation of households according to status or an urban/rural distinction, inclusion in modern society has been left to function systems—and there is no longer an overall formula for the relationship between them.[45] As a result, it would be fundamentally flawed to imagine the Middle Ages as an epoch of particularly intense piety. Religious inclusion at that time primarily used programs that were corporative, legal, ceremonial and (in the context of the confession) moral-casuistic. The site guaranteeing one's way of life was not religion but the household, or possibly—as a replacement or an extension of it—a corporative body such as a monastery, university, or guild. It was only in the wake of the shift to functional differentiation that the family household declined as an influential structure for inclusion/exclusion, and it was only at that point that function systems were able to develop their own inclusion/exclusion rules, to be aligned with their eigenvalues. What someone "is" was then defined according to: what he possessed or earned, the rights he had acquired, his schooling, and his reputation in politics, science, art, mass media. It was also defined (in the same sense) by his religious confession. At most, the concept of career was now appropriate (in a sense that was comprehensive and applicable to all function systems) as a total formula for societal inclusion. This structure, correlating with functional differentiation, permitted individual decisions to become more important. And it preferred youth to old age, providing a framework for possible self-definitions of the individual while largely leaving open how this could be realized—or, alternatively, endured—on a psychological level.

Moreover, if seen from the vantage point of the individual's life story and "time budget," it appeared that religion could not always be brought up to date, but only on occasion. In the fifteenth century, it was already observed (and conceded) that masses held at the royal court had to be scheduled according to the prince's (extremely full) appointment calendar. And by the eighteenth century, it was entirely clear that an individual's day could not continually be burdened with religion: "It is uncommon in the course of life that it is always given the respect it is due, or that one does not send it away as unwelcome, or that one does not treat it like people one has to see sometimes but whom it is bothersome to always have to see."[46]

At the same time, it is preordained that function systems will affect the total outcome in very different ways when inclusion rules are "delegated" to individual function systems and realized in the form of careers and schedules. One can practically not exist without money, and even less without legal protections. And everyone, unless fully unsuited, is sent to school and then forced to answer what they accomplished there. Sick people have to be cared for, and the chronically ill (a rather different type of case) have to be chronically cared for. But no one is compelled to take part in art, nor really in politics (except passively via the mass media). Tourism is not at all necessary; even if many enjoy it, they don't all have to participate in it. Nor does one have to take part in religion. Certainly this applies only from the standpoint of the individual, without indicating anything about the societal relevance or necessity of these function systems. That said, forms of inclusion are an extremely important variable in every function system, and much is dependent—as it is for individuals—on whether they participate (or not).

In addition to this issue, there are also interdependencies between the inclusions. These emerge from how inclusions are realized, for example, in the form of organizations. Whoever doesn't have an identity card cannot get a job. And whoever has to live on the street cannot register his children for school (as I was once told in Bombay). Without schooling, one barely has a chance of practicing a reputable career,[47] or obtaining a better job. Without income, one barely has access to healthy nourishment, and no energy for regular work. Illiterates, for instance, barely have the opportunity to exercise their right to vote. To be sure, no one is fundamentally excluded from function systems (whereas all organizations, even in function systems, rely on selecting members, i.e., on exclusion). Yet the aforementioned negative interdependencies completely exclude individuals (more or less effectively) from participation in all function systems. In fact, a large part of the population is excluded, as can be observed in the Third World and U.S. slums. All that's left to the individual is his own body and concern for its survival—not to mention hunger, violence, and sexuality.

In society's domain of inclusion, one finds significant levels of freedom in the combination of costs and benefits, in the exploitation (or nonexploitation) of opportunities, and—along with all that—in the realization and intensification of individual differences. Here, individuals have to rely on knowing others (more than acknowledged in official accounts of society). Society is loosely integrated, as a consequence. It is thereby cushioned against blows that can only be reproduced from coincidence to coincidence insofar as they do not affect structural variables in the systems. In the domain of exclusion, by contrast, society is strictly integrated. Each deficit reinforces another one; the circulation of disadvantages continues—and is inescapable (unless, admittedly, one is in the Mafia). In its domain of exclusion, society is nonetheless well protected. When something takes place there, nothing has (actually) taken place. And once more, criminal vocations and their rigid organization—crimes being the condition for membership—are a significant (and perhaps the only) exception.

Classical theory of societal integration (such as Durkheim's) must therefore be turned on its head. Strong integration is always negative integration and for that reason ominous. Positive integration can only be established loosely, thus providing greater opportunities for socially acceptable individuality. Neither morality nor religion are decisive variables in this context. Instead, one will have to assume realistically that the ruling morality adapts to inclusion/exclusion relations (when life, violence, and sexuality are under consideration), or that this morality incorporates a "social" component so it does not have to accept the full rigidity of the difference prefigured in the societal structure.

And what about religion?

The question is highly complex, and this rough sketch has served only to prepare us for it.

These days religion, too, practices system-specific inclusion/exclusion, doing so independently of memberships registered by organizations. (Or even without membership, one still has access to religious communication in various ways.) Nonetheless, what is remarkable is that there are so few interdependencies with the inclusion/exclusion regulations of other function systems. Being excluded from religion does not, as in the Middle Ages, exclude one from society. On the other hand, religion can blithely ignore any near exclusion from other function systems, such as not having money, an education, an identity card or a chance of being taken seriously by the police or a judge. That doesn't necessarily mean that those exclusions provide special opportunities for inclusion with respect to religion. This would have to be clarified empirically, as would the question of the extent to which religions are capable of adapting to the social-structural difference of inclusions and exclusions.

If one also restricts oneself to the finding (empirically easier to verify) that religion is independent of inclusions/exclusions originating in other systems, it raises important questions for religion in modern society. The issue can hardly be recognized anymore as one of "secularization." Although the inadequate integration of religion—both in inclusionary and exclusionary realms—results from the differentiation of other function systems, it does not somehow entail a disadvantage or even a loss of function for religion. Rather, the issue is whether and how religion can take advantage of the ensuing opportunities (a question already posed in the treatment of religious organizations above).[48]

At first glance, one might get the impression that religion is well-prepared for such possibilities, at least in the realm of Christianity, which has a long tradition of caring for the poor. In the domain of social benefits, there are commitments that are adapted to the welfare state and developmental aid policy, intended to fill in the gaps (as it were). Religious organizations are certainly in a position to concentrate funding and motivation on social assistance.[49] It used to be taught that God is closer to the poor than the rich, but that patronizing theology has lost its basis in social stratification. Even assuming that those with financial clout (and above all, the multinational banks) are still concerned about spiritual salvation, a return to a gift- and donor-based economy [*Schenkungs- und Stiftungsökonomie*], as in the Middle Ages, cannot be expected—and certainly not recommended. At any rate, it would not lead to an economically rational (or reproductive) use of funds. *Ressentiments*, whether pro-Marxist or of the anti-liberal kind encountered in theological circles today, are not particularly helpful in confronting economic-political conditions that are insufficiently understood. They reveal instead just how poorly adjusted theology is.[50] Such resentments pretty clearly demonstrate the secularization of theology itself, but do not constitute some kind of religious solution for an increasingly unbearable situation.[51]

Church policy and dogma have adapted only up to a point. In Latin America, the Catholic Church appears to be opening itself cautiously to more popular variants of religion—with Rome's blessing. And notwithstanding that it avoids making recommendations of an economic or political nature, the Church evidently sees a need to be active wherever social conditions are such that faith in God and Christ can no longer be expected or accepted. Ultimately, the trouble is that one's fate is evidently far more arbitrary than one used to think. Decisions are thus experienced as contingent, as depending on: interest rates and loans, legal regulations and their enforceability, the high cost and risk of advanced technologies, as well as the rapid increase and decrease in the popularity of social movements. But contingencies of this kind depend on conditions that are not susceptible to decision-making, and religion is almost inevitably forced to adopt a conventionally critical stance with regard to this state of affairs, while unable to suggest anything better.

VI

It has been argued that modern society has not yet found "its religion," a religion appropriate for it, and is thus in a state of experimentation—with sophisticated refinements, theological bombshells (such the claim that God is dead), an *aggiornamento* as regards dogma [i.e., the "updating" of Catholic dogma by Vatican II in the 1960s], and prescriptions of "geriatric medicine" for its organizations. Or society is experimenting with a literalist fundamentalism or with pluralistic options, from which each can choose what suits him. Or with additional legitimations of a scientific kind in a New Age style. Or with neurophysiological research that examines meditation and mescaline, whirling dervish dances, and Mexican mushroom sects as variants of psychoanalytic therapies. Or with rapidly changing (but always oppositional) styles of expression such as "Flower Power" or concern about the fate of future generations or those already dying of hunger. Secularization could then be understood as a cleaning-up project, clearing the terrain so that religious forms adapted to the times can then be developed.[52]

The future of theism might be seen as an important question from the perspective of religion's history. Does one need an observer God as a representative of transcendence, a God who looked at everything one does and experiences, who always willed everything that happens, and who could not forget but only forgive? Or do nontheistic religions of love have options for finding certain commitments "unconditionally mean-ingful" without having to rely on the success and legitimation criteria of other function systems? In both cases, breaking with tradition would be imaginable, but both would only be recognizable as religion (according to the theory advocated here) if they claim a point of difference that—as transcendence—is contrasted with everything that happens immanently. Hence, it can never be just a matter of affirming certain aims.

Typically, sociological observers react by weakening the demands they make on the concept of religion.[53] Religion needs to be imagined as an object that expands it own boundaries. In the process, however, one has to ask whether there is ultimately such a thing as an indispensable es-sential criterion for religion. Especially in the sociology of religion, sci-entific research has not unable to agree on such a criterion.[54] Within its specific domain, modern (avant-garde) art has been a paradigmatic site for experimenting with this question, by eliminating all sense-perceptible differences (including textual differences in the case of Borges) between individual artworks as well as between artworks and other things. *Using the artwork itself*, it poses the question of how art distinguishes itself in the first place.[55] It certainly does not suffice to answer by indicating the definitional *intention* of the artist, since that only leads sociologists to ask the further question of what defines that intention and who is identifying it. In the case of religion, we have to exclude similarly "subjectivistic" an-swers. We thus replace a psychological answer with a sociological one, yet it likewise remains formal. Religion is what can be observed as religion— on the level of a second-order observation. Whoever observes something in religious certainty (and at the risk of sounding repetitive, "observe" here means to experience or act) does so at the second-order level if he knows that his observing is being observed. It doesn't have to mean that he must look for and find agreement, but that his observation is qualified as religious. Or, formulated more carefully, the primary observer must be able to observe his being observed as something religious, regardless of what other observers may really be experiencing. That excludes other commitments that are clearly attributed to another category (such as stamp collecting) as well as those that can only be observed apparently as individual quirks or idiosyncrasies.

The topic "secularization," in its classical construction, thus disappears. One aspect of religion points toward modern society: the determination of what is religious is left to the recursive network of the religion system's self-observation. Yet this situation applies equally to all other function systems (such as art, mentioned just above). One can go a step further and theorize that binary coding is necessary in order to reflect any operation as contingent in a system-internal context of observation. One can also argue that a function has to be fulfilled, since otherwise the likelihood of operations being reproduced is lowered in the context of a functionally differentiated societal system (or, one might perhaps say, it can only be guaranteed by organization). In that way, limiting guidelines are clearly formulated for a sociological (and thus, religion-external) description of the religion system. For reasons related to the science system [*Wissenschaftssystem*], no one can or should rule out these guidelines being supplemented or replaced. In any event, they exclude science from having to commit to a definition of a "true" religion's essence. Doing so would inevitably mean that science is biased in intervening in something which, according to its own theory (inasmuch as *that* theory is scientifically sustainable), is an autonomous, structurally determined autopoietic system.

VII

If the concept of "secularization" as a definable compact term thus disappears, the issue remains of whether and how one still might make statements about the conditions of practicing and observing religion in modern society. The problem, however, is not therefore the "modernization" of religious thinking, its possible accommodation to a scientific worldview, or of a theology that merely understands religious forms as "symbolic." That approach is contradicted by too many practices and forms that are specifically active as religion. Yet one can observe that a new concept of "culture" emerged in the second half of the eighteenth century and was rapidly extended to all artifacts and texts created by humans. Until then, culture had been understood as the care of something, such as *agricultura* or *cultura animi*. At that point, culture became an independent phenomenal realm distinguished from "nature" and developing according to its own requirements, if not logics.[56]

Along with this concept of culture, (European) society of the eighteenth century was reacting to an immense expansion (and filling in) of its spatial and temporal horizons. Within larger ranges, more varieties were registered. As a result, old historical ruptures—such as between Greeks and barbarians, Christians and pagans, the civilized and the wild—lost their ability to order phenomena. Taking their place were regional and historical comparisons. Initially these were still Eurocentric and present-oriented, but in the course of the nineteenth century they were supplemented by concepts from the humanistic and cultural sciences. Comparisons require comparative viewpoints, which in turn have to be located in culture, so that the syndrome of "culture" is based on itself. On the one hand, culture was observed without spatial or temporal restrictions. It was seen as a universal human phenomenon, to Talcott Parsons, as a component of the concept of action. On the other hand, however, the fact that observation took on this form at all was a decidedly modern and (at the start) specifically European phenomenon. As such, it ought to be explained using the history of society and ultimately sociology. The modernity of this "culture" syndrome ultimately consisted in the emergence of a very specific universalism that still included what is most strange and distant, what is most unsettling and incomprehensible, to the degree that these could be made "interesting"—that is, represented comparatively.

A doubling of all phenomena takes place as a result of this universalization of comparative interests, and precisely that is what is meant by culture. Culture is a redescription of those descriptions that inform daily life. Nature, too, is included in culture (especially in aesthetics) if one postulates that it is an experiential nature that clings to culturally given (and thus culturally different) viewpoints. Since there has been culture, distinctions have had to be made between first- and second-order observation. In first-order observation, one looks to how objects are used and what they appear as. Examples also include the positive or negative meanings of regulations, as well as the holiness of sacred objects and actions. None of this is denied or treated with hostility by culture.[57] Only now, the meaning of these objects is duplicated and copied onto a level of second-order observation. At this point everything that was treated as natural and necessary appears artificial and contingent. One then has to "co-observe" [*mitbeobachten*] an observer if one wants to understand (and cultural assets do not at all have to be "understood" until that point) why and for whom something is the way it is. Within modern culture, additional problems are the result of this doubling. These are treated using terms of reproach such as "relativism," "historicism," "positivism," and "decisionism." On the other hand, these problems lead to a troublesome cult of immediacy, authenticity, and identity—that in turn cannot resolve their own promises because they too are only cultural concepts. Using Matei Călinescu's felicitous terminology, one can also say that a cultural symptomology emerges that deals with every cultural item as a symptom for something else, thereby always suspecting the presence of interests, repressed motives, and latent functions.[58]

Here we are only interested in what it means for religion once it is observed in society as a partial domain of culture.[59] The greatest impact is on theology, as the reflective form of the religion system. It finds itself confronted with (the most diverse) sciences of religion, while also having to account for the fact that the faith it represents is only one among many. What is quite different from the older tradition is that the idiosyncrasy of religious faith—and the distinction of one's own faith as the true faith—becomes a background topic of theological reflection. While "secularization" implies that religion is concerned with the increasingly nonreligious directions in modern society, "culture" exposes a religion to comparison with others, thus making it surrender its sovereignty in determining comparative points of view. The question is no longer what the one God responsible for everything has in mind for other peoples. Instead, the comparison is now able to refer to monotheistic vis-à-vis polytheistic religions or animistic religions without a clear concept of divinity. Or it can apply to religions that affirm the world and those that negate it, or to differences in relation to morality and to the question of life after death. Cultural comparisons can turn out differently, depending on their tacit, built-in preferences. In each case, if the comparison is meant seriously, its standpoint has to be chosen neutrally—and not tailored to one of the religions compared, since then the others might not appear to be religions at all in the actual (or central) sense of the term.

Unlike cultural phenomenologists suppose, the substantiating power of comparison as a methodology does not consist in teasing out of invariants, which can then be represented as the "essence" of the matter.[60] Instead, the more varied the phenomena under comparison, the most conspicuous their likenesses. The comparison tends to be exaggerated, thus undermining what for certain phenomena is peculiar in terms of their internal self-determination. It bases the acquisition of knowledge on surprise, on *unexpected* similarities. Hence, it can no longer really maintain that this kind of insight is equivalent to a "revelation" that makes understandable from a religious point of reference what is always already presumed.

Every religion now has to count on being treated in societal communication as contingent, that is, as matter of options. But this issue is only relatively superficial. A more precise analysis of the comparisons underlying all culture brings to light a number of much deeper incompatibilities. Every comparison assumes a comparative point of view that itself is not part of the comparison or the process of comparison (even when other comparisons can include it). Comparison therefore presupposes a "third" value, that of an unobserved observer. But this unobserved observer is no longer God, as was traditional. It is an observer more like Maxwell's demon,* who defines relevant differences and then sorts them out accordingly.

The same applies to the secondary culture of suspicious motives that is stimulated by comparisons. In order to explain differences, people since the nineteenth century have drawn on latent motives, interests, functions, and structures that are said to guide their actions unconsciously. Here as well, the power that is decisive (because it operates unnoticed) was not God but something else: the unavoidable intransparency of systems to themselves.

The traditional forms of the knowing *ratio* and the action-defining will, the highest forms of which merge in God (and cannot be exceeded in thought), now suddenly had an alternative. That alternative absorbed some of the divine attributes, primarily the inability to be seen and the in-

---

* "Maxwell's demon" is a thought experiment, first formulated in 1867 by the Scottish physicist James Clerk Maxwell, meant to interrogate the second law of thermodynamics. —Trans.

ability to be controlled. These attributes did not provide any final legitimation. (But what does that really mean?) They were the object of suspicion, critique, enlightenment, therapy, or second-order observation. For God remained the default position when all these efforts failed to control intransparency. But then it was no longer the old God, to whose mercy one could entrust one's life.

One might suspect that such cultural comparisons have a weakening effect on religion. Yet that conclusion may be premature. In the end, a decorated pot is not just less beautiful because other cultures decorate their pots differently; such comparisons may even make people pay more attention to certain characteristics and better understand the peculiarity of cultural objects. On the other hand, the characteristics with which certain religions distinguish themselves from others are not necessarily those that prop up or strengthen faith. The effects on religion of the invention of "culture" would require more detailed studies—comparable to those on the effects of writing or of the shift to functional differentiation. The outcome of such research cannot be predicted, but the problem should not be ignored when judging the significance of religion (or *religions*) in modern society. In addition, the acceptance of latent structures and functions does not at all rule out another (call it "higher") meaningful type of intransparency. But if one makes this argument, one is at the same time establishing standards for testing which religious forms could stand the test of time.

Modernity appears to enforce a mode of second-order observation extending to all function systems. Within those function systems, a state of hypercomplexity is also achieved—meaning that the function systems simultaneously elicit a variety of descriptions of their own complexity. The associated challenge to all reality constructions is at first unsettling. The Cartesian subject can no longer be called on to guarantee the facticity and security of one's own observations. Proofs of God's existence have remained, in fact, the most deficient side-product of this form of self-assurance. Here there are no more possibilities for connection, since that would only lead to the empty formula that it is ultimately up to each individual to find some certainty in religious matters. Religion's problems have to be reformulated with reference to the possibilities for communication in modern society. But if the entire culture is directed toward polycontextural descriptions and second-order observations, then there is no reason why religion could not be involved in this as well. It would obviously have to do without its ontologically based cosmologies, as well as its self-certainty in matters of morality. Yet precisely in such respects, some religions (Christianity, for instance, but also Buddhism) had always dared to cross boundaries.

Finally, we should ask about the conditions and possibilities of religious evolution in modern society. Neither the keyword "secularization" nor that of "culture" completely get at the problem. In the case of "secularization," one only thinks about the consequences of functional differentiation, which results in religion yielding control of other systems to themselves. Culture, if understood as establishing possibilities for comparisons, is telling us that restrictions have to be introduced as conditions of comparison—and does so at the level of second-order observation. The "inviolate levels" (Hofstadter) that now have to be reformulated lose their religious quality. And, in the end, evolutionary theory itself offers no option for a prognosis. It is only capable of showing how evolutionary structural changes become likely to the extent that the autopoiesis of differentiated systems is guaranteed.

It is nonetheless possible to assemble other aspects that appear to be characteristic for the (already recognizable) evolution of religion (or better, *religions*) in modern world society. A great deal of material on this can be found in discussions on fundamentalist currents, which can be increasingly (and more clearly) observed (especially) in the second half of the twentieth century. There appears to be agreement that this is the way the religion system is reacting to the "globalization" of the modern world.[61] But there are still too few theoretically informed formulations of this reaction.

One possible hypothesis would be that all function systems in the modern world, including religion, have come under vastly increased pressures of complexity. If evolution had not made available any appropriate media (one paradigm being "money"), it would have become more and more difficult to obtain "requisite variety" in systems. Such variety was always impossible, given the disparities in complexity between systems and environments. But under modern conditions, this impossibility was also *observed* in the systems themselves. The systems then had to adjust their own production of meaning. It was a fact that they could not operate in a way that was commensurate with the world, *and that they had to acknowledge this*. In the philosophy of science, constructivism (which doesn't need be radical) appeared to be the answer to this problem. In the religion system, such an adaptation was likely to be much more difficult. It could be tested by asking whether the idea of God as a "contingency formula" was religiously acceptable. But if the starting point of this analysis was appropriate, and "requisite variety" was evidently unachievable (in the sense of an adequate representation of the world in the system), then how could the religion system explain this circumstance *without coming into open conflict with its own function*?

It seems that the religion system at present is searching for an appropriate mix in the relationship between "requisite variety" and "requisite simplicity."[62] In resolving such a fundamental paradox in the relationship between system and environment, a wide variety of experimentation is currently taking place in various religions. And perhaps this is also a reason why at this time the idea of a unified world religion seems pale and unattractive. "Requisite simplicity," on the one hand, can be offered to individuals—as in meditative practice for their personal problems, or (for example, in Japan) as a way to preserve the residual forms of older divination practices, which solves problems of indeterminacy that cannot be absorbed by the group culture. It can, on the other hand, be identified as a structural characteristic of certain religions—as in the thesis that there is only one (if also threefold) God. Dogmatized religions of faith are themselves familiar with a highly individual awareness of sin that reverts to self-observation and confession. Through names for sins and their relative assessment (through quasi-grammatical rules), it can fall back on worldly issues, such as handling money or sexuality, and can thus be irritated by changes in society. One might then surmise that "requisite simplicity" itself runs the risk of becoming implausible and can only be sustained if there is sufficient group-specific backing for it. On the whole, the religion system would then have to be able to accept the differences between believers, nonbelievers, and those who believe otherwise. At the same time, precisely this distinction, this otherness, may actually strengthen faith.

VIII

In secularized society, the situation of the churches—if not religion itself—is often demonstrated in the concept of "crisis." One refers to a crisis of the churches in order to explain the seriousness of the situation. Yet it is mistaken to portray things this way. One can only say there is a crisis if change is expected in the foreseeable future—no matter whether it's for better or worse. Such a change, however, is not on the horizon. The central phenomena here are related to the situation of religion in a functionally differentiated society. What is involved are structural incompatibilities, at least whenever religion is being interpreted from the standpoint of its traditional resources. Religion and church dogmas may be engaged in this state of affairs in one way or another, by means of this or some other "script." But that doesn't mean that the "crisis" has ended. Rather, religion is (at best) attempting to do justice to its possibilities and limitations as a function system of modern society.

Describing this situation as a "crisis" is needlessly dramatic and suggests that what is at issue are decisions. Yet precisely decisions (on questions of dogmatics or church organization, for example) that are communicated as decisions are not helpful in such situations. Instead, it should be assumed that what is at stake are the possibilities of an evolutionary adaptation to new circumstances.

Evidently, the form that religion will take on in the new society, the modern one, still cannot be understood and described appropriately. This should come as no surprise, since when change is evolutionary, it can only be accessed retrospectively (in all cases, including this one). Nor should it surprise us that negative tones are prevalent in this case. In discussing theories of development, Jerome Bruner refers to the "unspoken despair in which we are now living."[63] That prognosis should not be interpreted as pessimistic. Rather, it testifies to the impossibility of seeing a future in a society undergoing radical transformation.

In closing, is the ordinary concept of secularization sufficient, as it has been used up to this point? Or does it conceal something essential instead? These are questions that can be illuminated with the comparative method, along with the Romantic concept of "displacement" used to signify changes in the dominant semantics at the end of the eighteenth century. The comparative method itself was already an indicator of secularization to the extent that it interrupted any direct relationship to the other, attributing to it an identity that (unlike religion) did not engage or involve the observer.[64] This distancing has forced on us a notion of culture that impinges on what is to be compared, leaving its various identities intact. At the same time, it places the observer in a "transcendental" status, thus removing him from the world. We could refer to Romantic "displacement" inasmuch as Romanticism relocated previously religious content into other domains, particularly aesthetic (but also individual biographical) ones. This could be seen quite distinctly in the new ways that the concept of symbol was applied. Neither "displacement" nor comparison immediately indicated a break with the religion that one simultaneously professed (and continued to profess). But the impression conveyed was that another reason was being tried out in order to see if it could be sustained.

Self-Description

I

All attempts to define the "essence" of religion "objectively" (and even phenomenologically) can be seen as having failed. Or at least they have been profoundly discouraged after long debates.[1] It is only too evident that definitions of religion are always committed to a religious viewpoint—and that these invariably represent the definer's own religion, despite the existence of others.[2] This may motivate us to pose a different type of question. Instead of asking about religion's "essence" (in the singular), one might also ask how religions describe religion. Here one can avail oneself of a universal concept that works for all religions, namely, "self-description." Not only is this approach sufficiently formal, but it can also be applied to other realms of social communication, indeed to society itself, without assuming that the self-description is either true, correct, or even appropriate. It is simply a matter of one kind of communication among others. Furthermore, it is not at all certain that religious activity (ritual, for instance) understands itself as an "applied self-description" of the system, or is even communicated in that fashion. Rather, it has to be seen as unlikely that a system's self-description will congeal into principles or dogmas that permit religious communication to recognize itself as religious. There are several different (and much more practicable) ways of distinguishing religious from nonreligious communication. But that is precisely why religion's self-thematization is a variable deserving of special attention from the perspective of sociology. So we shall ask: when does it take place? Is it perhaps precisely when the essence of religion is no longer self-evident—when it becomes only too clear that pagans have religion, too? And if it leads to doctrines of faith and dogma that propagate the right faith, then how does such a self-obligation impinge upon religious communication?

Parallel to a need for textually fixed "theological" self-descriptions, there are differentiations within the religion system itself. Starting in the twelfth or thirteenth century, well-developed representations of theological questions could be found in monastic and cathedral schools, and later university faculties. Efforts were made to be systematic and consistent, as well as to deal with impending questions of controversy. Working on texts became separate from rhetoric that was directly relevant for sermons. Nor was there assumed to be any worship or holy presence directly affecting the production of texts. Instead, texts were directed toward other texts. (Today one would speak of "intertextuality.") Priests received theological training, and the profession required formal study. In professional practice, nonetheless, other demands on communication pushed to the fore.

In any case, self-thematizations of this type did not emerge until there was an advanced level of complexity, probably not until writing had been introduced, and then only as a correlate of observing system boundaries. Inasmuch as social systems do not only operatively produce their own boundaries to the environment but also observe that this has happened and is continuing, they need an identity with whose help they can distinguish (and combine) self-reference and other-reference. The problems of identity and boundary are closely linked. For in the case of meaning systems, boundaries are not only outer membranes or skins or spatial lines but are defined with every operation—since every operation is exposed to references to meaning (both self- and other-referential) and has to assign itself to the system using this distinction. Not every operation has to be oriented toward the system's identity. Not every prayer has to say to itself, "I am an operation of the religion system." In normal cases, it is enough to have "connectionistic" self-localizations, as in the case of prayer, with the help of formulas, places, and occasions. But doubts can creep in from one moment to the next as soon as problems of demarcation and belonging appear, and especially in a secularized societal environment when religious communication is involved. (Should one pray that the bus will be on time if one is in a hurry? Or pray loudly so as to strengthen one's lungs?[3] And if one does such things and thinks they matter, what kind of faith should one admit having to others and oneself? Or what if one thinks these things would not help, inasmuch as God no longer works in the realm of special providence?)

An initial hypothesis may now be formulated. The need and occasion for the religion system's self-thematization are linked to the extent that society provides for a distinction and a separation of religious and nonreligious communication. Seen historically, this was the process I have been calling "differentiation [*Ausdifferenzierung*] of the religion system." Self-descriptions thematize boundary experiences. Religion is looking for a form of its own whenever it is also looking at what it does not mean, what it excludes, the other side of the boundary. But then: must the excluded be included? Or does it have to be qualified religiously, as in the case of "secularization," even though (or, indeed, precisely because) it is not religion?

For now, it should be emphasized that including the fact of a non-religious environment does not at all have to mean that religion sees itself as forced to give in to pressures to adapt and "liberalize." Religion can profit just as well from stressing the difference. It might do so in the form of a morally charged schematism, in which only a religious way of life (meeting specific requirements) is good and everything else is bad. Or it might do so in the form of a counterculture that formulates the eigenvalues of religious communication so that they are not in competition with (environmentally) common assessments (such as scientific review, economic wealth, or misery), but also not in agreement or concerned with them.[4] In that way, the distance from society (once it is noticed) becomes an underlying theme of religious self-descriptions, the most representative example being St. Augustine's doctrine of the two cities. In other words, religion sees itself as forced to hold out the prospect of a redemption from society. Yet that alone does not identify which of its forms meet this requirement, and the underlying theme allows various kinds of implementation. Whatever choice is then made, the fact that several options are possible and prove (or do not prove) themselves in the religion system according to internal criteria gives an indication of the system's autonomy, and the fact that its self-descriptions are its own accomplishments.

That the world is not what one expects based on a religious cosmology is an old problem for religion. Buddhism found a way out of this problem by substituting different distinctions—or a complete absence of them. With differing degrees of sophistication, theology has attempted to save God, such as by assuming a program of historical detours. Since the seventeenth century, the term "theodicy" has been employed. In doing so, however, people assumed that it was their own fault that the state of the world did not conform to the expectations deriving from a (universalizing) religious conception of the world—and that this contradiction had to be explained. In barely noticeable transitions, secular society confronted religion with a different problem. In such a society, several things became evident: other function systems did not need religion; their codes generated their own paradox unfoldings; their rules of inclusion/exclusion were not integrated with those of religion; they had their own "rejection values" (which also neutralize religion's distinctions); and there was no dominant relationship of contradiction, of choosing the wrong option (which religion would have no trouble assessing) but instead a relationship of functionally necessary indifference. As a category of bivalent logic, the concept of contradiction was in need of reevaluation, including the more recent notion of dialectics, according to which contradictions are the driving motive behind historical transformation.

Modern religion's self-description must therefore engage with new forms while in the older mode of a perceived distinction between system and environment. Simply blaming disregard of religion on nonreligious communication is no longer enough. Nonparticipation cannot be characterized very effectively as "sin." From the viewpoint of religion, such a finding is still regrettable, yet such denigration and moralizing no longer suffice for assigning the religion system's self-description to the framing conditions of modern society. Put differently, it is no longer enough to describe the system/environment relationship with a positive/negative schematism, to understand the environment as deviating from what actually (and also in God's sense) could be demanded.[5] The religion system's autonomy has only now been fully realized to the point where not even the positive/negative schematism is adequate for describing the relationship to the environment. If the system assigns its environment a negative value, it has to do this on its own, and take responsibility for it as a moment of its own self-description. Autopoietic autonomy demands the inclusion of the system's negation in the system—one finds examples of this especially in avant-garde art as well as in political utopias.

The religion system has a long tradition of distancing itself from the society surrounding it. One thinks here of [the Hebrew] prophets' criticisms of royal authority, of solitary ascetic religiosity in late antiquity, and of Buddhism's religion of renunciation. Extreme forms were found in the regulations of those orders that instructed their disciples to minimize communication or avoid it altogether, because it inevitably led to participation in society, that is, in sin.[6] In this context, sociologists stipulate a distinction between churches and sects; it is interpreted as resulting from differences of opinion on the degree to which adapting religion to society is bearable.[7] Precisely in distancing itself in this way, however, religion makes a bid for social support. Thanks to an appropriately tailored religious semantics, one can communicate against society from within society—and obtain religious approval for it. It is only a variant on this "with/without" position when religion acquiesces in social injustices, (not actually accepting them, but) promising recompense for them in the other world. Put in religious terms, one might say all these cases involve redemption from society. Although one's own sins are individually assigned with guilt, the dogma of original sin also provides an understandable reason why immorality persists. It teaches us that humans are latter-day descendants of Adam, social beings utterly unable to avoid sin. Here as well, then, what religion holds out as a prospect in its societal communication is redemption from society.

If this is the framing condition that provides an outline for the self-descriptions of the religion system, an ultimately paradoxical problem is being posed. In its specific form, it limits what is semantically possible. The religion system's self-description is not free to allow the imagination to run its course and then give the result a religious connotation. In one form or another, it has to do justice to the framing issue of redemption from society, the theme that reflects the system's differentiation into the system. And it has to do so in a way that is crafted in accordance with religion, consistent with the religion system's coding and function.

The latitude for semantic possibilities, shown in the examples above, is considerable enough to allow for very heterogeneous solutions (and thus different religions). Solutions can evolve by using exemplary, meritorious concepts that follow the model of asceticism. Or by using concepts such as sin, corruption, and distance from God that explain deviations from a norm—as normal. Time is quite typically used as well. Original sin is a permanent condition, lasting until death, yet it does not rule out the pursuit of redemption in imitation of Christ [*imitatio Christi*]. In the case of these variants, the problem was assumed to have cosmic dimensions. Religion accordingly had to design its self-description as a cosmology with reference to an order beyond the difference of order and disorder.[8] This other world is nothing more than a position of transcendence toward everything that can be observed immanently and that is thus linked to distinctions. But does this "grand style" solution to the problem have to be (or remain) the only one, against which every other has to be measured?

Were that the case, new religious movements could not be taken seriously, particularly those from the second half of the twentieth century. Nor could they be trusted to make a contribution to the religion system's self-description that could be developed further.[9] The abstract presentation of the problem, however, also enables other answers that are better suited to the structural conditions of a "secularized," functionally differentiated society, one with a high degree of individual mobility. The problem of redemption from society is evidently still relevant, and social resonance in society is evidently still necessary for it. The social resonance needed, however, is presented differently than in the past; specifically, it becomes accessible using individual decisions and is geared toward this type of entry and departure. I had already noted that one has to expect much greater individual mobility, specifically the mobility of individuals who observe themselves while also seeking out and evaluating experience.[10] Participation by the individual and the religion system thus becomes contingent. This can lead to a competition for attention, but also to a diversification of offerings and to the insulation and consolidation of partial systems in niches. These systems "smell" attractive (so to speak) yet do not depend on mass attention or the acceptance of generalizable concepts. As demonstrated by anthroposophic and "New Age" movements, cosmologies are still available, but their basis in the social structure has shifted and does not deviate from the pattern of inclusion otherwise observable. On the level of self-descriptive semantics, there is no consensus if looked at from the present situation. Yet, in retrospect, one might ask: when was it ever any different?

The question of how to sustain oneself vis-à-vis an environment with an different orientation is repressed by other reflective impulses in this situation, primarily by the distinction of continuity and discontinuity. This distinction does not really invite options that are fundamental or comprehensive, but instead ones that vacillate. In the process, one can try to agree on essentials that cannot be surrendered. However, that does not entirely close off objections. A different possibility would be to link every innovation to a "redescription" of tradition.[11] That would require discontinuity to become continuity and would limit the degree of freedom possible for variation. The same issues and concerns are still present, but now we see them differently.

II

Each self-description calls for a self-presupposing of the description itself, an undermining of the distinction between the description and the described, between the performative and constative functions of the texts being prepared. Each self-description consequently has the problem of having to distinguish itself from its object as an operation, while at the same time having to encounter itself in that object. Put in linguistic terms, the problem is that the self-description's performative activity is in tension with the constative side of the same activity. Derrida's concept of "deconstruction" is directed at this problem (besides others). The concept refers to an operation that uncovers how a text's performative operations contradict what the text itself is claiming. When applied, for instance, to Schleiermacher's famous work *Über die Religion. Reden an die Gebildeten unter ihren Verächtern* (*On Religion: Speeches to Its Cultured Despisers*), deconstruction would show that the text, when referring to issues such as religion, art, and education, is trying to convey an unmediated relation to itself—or specifically, to render that relation plausible as education. But it also shows that this text is performing this operation through rationally monitored distinctions, which in their form contradict that objective. Schleiermacher's text makes use of distinctions to insinuate how a direct (distinction-free) unity of singularity (of religious feeling) and of universality can be achieved. Were the text a document of its author's education, it would not be able convince others of religion's educational value. (Or it could do so only by defining education with the help of distinctions, making it seem inappropriate as a form of religious faith.)[12] "On Religion" derives its power to convince and communicative effect not from its arguments but from a type of conspiratorial relationship between its performative and its constative functions, between its argumentation and what it sets out to prove, between the distinctions necessary for its argumentation and its (ultimately *artistic*) self-representation as education. "Deconstruction" is not anything but a way of displaying this double game. It is neither an intervention in the text's argumentation nor a refutation of it, neither a proposal for a more appropriate interpretation nor a statement on the text's theme, on religion.[13]

If one looks within the biblical tradition for a concept that in itself is conspiratorial, and that can thus be deconstructed (if one wishes to do so), then what suggests itself is discussing the (Holy) Spirit. In evidence both from the Old Testament and the New Testament (and thus also independent of situations, times, localities, and persons), this Spirit manifests itself as a way of being moved *and* as an observation of thus being moved. This extraordinary condition of those it moves expresses itself in confused speech (speaking in tongues) *and* in the public visibility of this event. The Spirit communicates without agreeing to a distinction between information and utterance. It communicates in the form of communicative incomprehensibility, which in the form of its incomprehensibility is nonetheless understandable as its presence. Since the Spirit's appearance always presupposes a specific historical situation (that of the prophets or of Jesus's disciples), there is a context that enables understanding of the incomprehensible and that makes communication succeed, although (or because!) the situation does not fulfill the operative requirements of communication. But that context can, like every context, be decontextualized; its helpful limits can be respectively transcended. The Spirit manifests more than an interpretation of the situation. It relies, to that extent, on a conspiracy within a distinction—specifically the deconstruction of situation and world, a distinction whose deconstruction seems to matter to it. It is self-evident that this deconstruction can in turn be deconstructed—and even if only shifting it back onto the other opposition between the constative function of speech (testifying to God) and its performative function (speaking in confusion). Derrida would refer to this capacity for deferral—which simultaneously negates that there can be a stable place, a secure presence for these things—as *différance*.

From what is known today, it should not be hard to explain the appearance of the Spirit in medical, especially neurobiological, terms. One might think of trance states brought about by meditation, dancing, or drugs. A spirit thus provoked—if it is to be interpreted religiously—would still always require a ritual framework and the observability guaranteed by it. (Otherwise, it would be treated as a kind of therapy.) In this manner, the comparability of religious communication could be expanded substantially in the direction of phenomena that are likely to be found in all religions—from shamanism and dancing dervishes all the way to the monotony of common prayer, from meditation to mescaline intoxication, and so on. One could, for example, include voodoo worship, which allows every participant to be "ridden" by the spirit (an example that additionally illustrates how outsiders' descriptions diverge significantly from what insiders report).

Clearly, the shaman is always in danger of having a "bad trip" and not being able to return from it (meaning: he dies), along with everything implied by this sign of misfortune. However, the (Holy) Spirit no longer seems to be familiar with this danger or the relevant techniques for guarding against it. With this development, religion has progressed from an ambivalent to a clearly positive valuation of the other world. Prayer takes the place of participating in forms of worship that brought about trance states. A wide-ranging and religiously secured knowledge, which goes beyond one's local area, takes the place of an interest in being healed or protected.[14]

Such comparisons would be important for clarifying the fundamental structures of all religions in the world religion system—a topic we shall return to. But ultimately, they only shift the problem onto the question of which framing conditions enable an interpretation of religious communication. They may not restore the old pre-Hippocratic unity of religion and medicine but let us to see that there are very different distinctions at work on both sides of this bifurcation of religion and medicine.

There is no denying how meaningful and productive this type of scientific comparison and explanation is. Such productivity should also become apparent in the study of religion itself. Yet this approach does not precisely enough address our problem of self-description. It thus misses what in the biblical tradition was signified as Spirit—and precisely what that concealed.[15] On the one hand, comparing religions allows us to recognize that the notion of the other world has transformed itself into something good from something that was ambivalent and suffused with horror. That may have been one of the reasons why discrepancies in how life is normally lived in society now emerged more strongly. On the other hand, to understand more clearly the ensuing consequences, we have to look for a solution in religious communication itself, in the texts that it produces and—if those texts are holy or canonized—in the texts that interpret those texts.

The way in which texts, as supplements to canonized texts, insert themselves into the context of the religion system's self-description could be illustrated by numerous cases. I've chosen Michael Welker's book *Gottes Geist* (*God the Spirit*), mainly because it elaborates the public efficacy (or resonance) of the Holy Spirit, and is therefore close to my view of the problem sketched above.[16]

Welker's text does not permit any doubts about the existence or efficacy of the Holy Spirit. Having doubts is of course still possible, but these are relegated to the other side of dogma and thus left void, included without being mentioned. The text attempts to demonstrate the significance of the Holy Spirit and the figure's unity using a wide range of testimonies from Scripture. In its style, the argumentation follows the testimonies. It is addressed to those who are surprised by the Spirit's appearance and avert their eyes from it. The characteristic style of argument sticks monotonously to the proven model in sermons of concession and instruction: "something may appear to be one way, but appearances are always deceptive."[17] Everywhere, rhetorical formulations are encountered, leading us to suspect that the text needs them to prevent any looking across the boundaries at what is not mentioned. (There is no "outside the text," however, Derrida would say.) Statements confirming faith are given in the indicative mood ("that is how it is"); other-references within the religion system are introduced as "experience." Welker's account is animated by the internal unfolding of its argument for the existence and presence of the Holy Spirit. It does not, and cannot, attempt to include nonbelievers (such as through generalizing formulas that overcome the distinction between believing and not believing). The text remains concrete, text-related, and historical.

The *frame* of Welker's study, the belief/unbelief distinction, does not become a *theme* of the text—just as the frame of an image cannot be seen in the image. This exclusion of the exclusion is the basis of the wealth of possible statements that his text can open up. When read impartially, abstruse texts such as the Samson narratives (Judges 13-16) are able to be included in his text. Fundamental distinctions (good/bad, truth/lie) can also be incorporated, making it plausible that the Spirit opts for the right side *in* these distinctions, while at the same time "blowing *across*" them (so to speak).[18] Welker's temporal perspectives can be modernized (again with the figure of a time that is above temporality).[19] His text is able to demonstrate that the situationally based public efficacy of the Spirit *in* society can at the same time entail redemption *from* society. The unfolding of this paradox utilizes and interprets the topos of mercy.[20] The "powerless servant of God" is consequently not interpreted in a worldly manner, as accepting a difference between religion system and political system. Rather, the idea is interpreted intra-religiously, as a specific surprise effect with which religion refers to itself.[21] In passages where the reference to other kinds of religion virtually imposes itself (for instance, in the discussion of prophetic ecstasy), the reference to biblical texts limits the thematization, or relegates it to a footnote or bibliography.[22]

Judged against examples found in poems,[23] Welker's text is not a self-confirming one. In this sense, it is not a symbolic text that understands itself as performing the unity it intends. Instead, it points to other texts, to biblical ones. These in turn are understood as symbolic or revelatory, as texts that are what they say. One could designate this referencing as a "framing up," making use of a frame that in turn does not have to distinguish between frame and theme. In that way, there is no avoiding the problem of paradox, the problem of the identity of the unidentifiable (here, the problem of theme and frame). Rather it can be deferred, and specifically *into* the religion's holy text, where it belongs and will be believed. Welker's own analyses can then proceed discursively, making do with identifiable identities.

If Welker's case can be regarded as typical, it lets us to draw a few conclusions about self-descriptions in general and about self-descriptions of the religion system in particular. The most important perhaps is that the system's boundaries are being treated as horizons. As boundaries thematized in the system, they would be invited to be crossed; as horizons, however, they are unreachable. The position from which every additional thematization has to proceed is made clear, and it is reinforced in existential statements. The descriptions are based on the possibility of referring back to this position. Everything else is a question of the wealth of meaning that can be accessed from there. With increasing complexity, the system becomes increasingly capable of irritating and resonating. It can then also take up counternotions, such as "lying spirits" [*Lügengeister*], an emphasis on the life of the flesh, or the better-known problems of theodicy. These are problems that introduce the negation of the system into the system, but only ostensibly, as will be demonstrated in the course of the system's self-description. For the system monitors the distinctions with which this is caused.

As if it were an automatic process, a "sanctifying" [*Heiligung*] of the system's institutions and practices can result—a sanctifying of ceremonies, of interior spaces (that only admit broken light or are illuminated from within), of songs that suppress other noises, of priests breathing incense, of guaranteed repetitions. In all these cases, one remains aware that this is not "the matter itself" but its appearance, "in which" what is communicated as religion is concealed.

It would be quite mistaken to understand this self-confirmation as an imposition of norms that have to be enforced against deviant behavior. The crucial point is specifically that this self-representation can be implemented *without prohibiting its opposite*. It is enough for itself, self-sufficient, but it is based on not thematizing the framework of the thematization, thus remaining in this respect deconstructable.

III

While the Holy Spirit represents the system's unity, and while the distinction assumed by its coding is expressed in the infrequence of its appearances, it still leaves another problem unresolved. If the system can inform itself about itself only in the mode of self-observation and self-description, how can the relationship between description and the described be depicted? How can confusion be avoided—confusion in the form of an equation or identification of the described with the description? Or, if formulated in more modern fashion as a problem in linguistics: how can one avoid understanding the information the text intends to provide solely as an utterance? Or put another way: how can one avoid reducing the constative function to the performative?

It has already been noted above that in monotheistic religions, the assertion of revelation solves—which is to say, *covers up*—this problem.[24] Revelation is a divine communication that identifies itself as such. It claims to be authentic communication. Its necessity results directly from the code, specifically from the necessity that transcendence appear in immanence. In this abstract form, however, it is all too transparent that a *petitio principia** is involved. For if one can only extract from revelation itself that a revelation is involved, how should one be certain that it is a revelation, especially if there are several options available? That, after all, was precisely the issue in the crucifying of Jesus.

---

* *Petitio principii* is the fallacy of "begging the question."—Trans.

This point presents a challenge for self-descriptions of the religion system. They have to provide *parerga*, those incidentals that (as additions) are more essential to what is essential than the essence—which is not maintained without them.[25] Such displacements are frequently labeled as "parasitic" on the assumption that parasites profit from the code's binarism and the essence's undecidability. Profiting from the presence of what is absent, those deemed parasitic secretly take over control, which then exposes them to renewed parasitism. Whatever the terminology (making it plain that we are talking about a alarming state of affairs), our problem is still the unfolding of the paradox that the description does not want to be the described, because it would not otherwise be a description. Yet at the same time, without description, the described would be nothing more than the unmarked space.

This point of departure may be unsatisfactory for a logic concerned with truth. Still, for empirical historical analysis, it has the advantage of making it possible to ask about the historical conditions of plausibility and the loss of plausibility of such *parerga*, such paradox unfoldings. As far as revelation is concerned, I am assuming that the referential concepts for its *parerga* changed fundamentally in the sixteenth (and particularly) seventeenth centuries. This happened for a variety of reasons that are difficult to get a handle on: because of the effects of the Protestant Reformation and the invention of printing, because of the market economy was expanding, because the superficial world of courtly culture was criticized, because there was a new description of royal legitimacy (since the monarch was no longer a representative of other-worldly powers but a representative of the unity of confederated subjects), or particularly because a modern theater emerged that was no longer representative but fictional.

It can likely be assumed that the revelations reported by Christianity were taken as worldly facts and believed after the religion had caught on in the territories it shaped. There may have been doubters, but whoever attempted to express that doubt was executed. First-order observation could thus include the idea that all observers were observing the same things. That in turn made it possible to build up a culture that symbolized the revealed knowledge. That went together with a purely practical understanding of its implementation and with a corresponding ecclesiastical monitoring, and with (for example) a constant struggle against the extravagant theatricality of religious dramas. The symbols could have been images, buildings, rituals, but also stagings of religious plays. Yet their symbolic quality always consisted in that they *were* what they allowed to appear. The symbolic is precisely the fusing of what it has to presuppose as different; it is paradox that has taken on shape. As a symbolic representation, revelation was thus a part of the real world—and not only a matter of faith. What thus appeared as "being" contained a normative claim at the same time. It, too, was the way it was supposed to have been. According to the logic of ontological metaphysics, it was not supposed to be what it was not. And similarly, deviating opinions were also to be treated as errors and as norm violations.

The fusion of description and the described breaks down in the skeptical century following the Reformation. Once there were different rituals and each person claimed that his own were the only correct ones, such rituals became recognizable as stagings that offered no guarantee that religion as such was occurring. Now, instead of having faith, one had to ask about the sincerity of the heart.[26] The "other side" of religious communication, the world it could not reach, was displaced into individual consciousness, which alone was capable of clarifying its relationship to God. There was accordingly more emphasis on education within the family and in schools. Here, texts became helpful. They were now available in printed books, replacing those formulaic repetitions (such as the Lord's Prayer) on which a primarily oral culture depended. Symbols were now understood as a sign of something they were not on their own. They were resolved into signs, emblems, and allegories, in a general society-wide development of social semantics that even religion could not elude. Art began to elaborate its own world of self-sufficient beautiful appearances. By contrast, religious resistance to this development failed on the Protestant side as well as that of the Counter-Reformation, and religion was only left an enclave of sacred art that was no longer recognized in the art system itself. At the same time, markets in the economic system developed themselves into a system of transactions that determined the satisfaction of economic needs, not only in exceptional cases, but as a rule. Even the courtly culture representing that system's alleged pinnacle (yet now *merely* representing it) confirmed this image of a reality that the individual could only respond to reflectively. In all these cases, the individual's participation in social affairs became a problem—for himself and others.[27] In Baltasar Gracián's extreme formulations, everything offered by the world became an image, an appearance. In a sophisticated as well as religious fashion, matters might only be remedied

by accepting that everything was the opposite of what it appeared to be.[28]
Contempt for the world [*contempus mundi*] turned against religion itself.

For religion, the consequence was that faith in revelation now had to
be anchored in the individual, specifically in the form of the authenticity
of one's own faith. Yet what for Luther was still a considerable focus on internal truth vis-à-vis external seductions cannot withstand more intensive
scrutiny. Soon one saw that authenticity could not be communicated, so
communication (and thus Church) were no longer available to eliminate
doubts. The problem of a recurring contradiction between constative and
performative aspects of communication returned in a new form, as doubt
in individual sincerity. Weber's thesis does not make sense until looked at in
this context. Accordingly, people are looking for redemption not in religion
but in tangible worldly success, for which there is no lack of external, communicable signs. But that still doesn't answer the question of how religion
can respond to this circumstance in its own self-description.

Religion can regenerate itself as an organization and then wait to see
whether individuals accept it as an "option." That way, it adapts itself to
a society that it understands as having become "secularized." Likewise, religion's god turns into a God who offers his love and leaves it to humanity to decide whether to accept or reject it. Hence, revelation is saying that
people still believe in this account (at least). They do not treat this distinction as yet another of the Church's autosuggestions, as something to be
disregarded. What remains is the offer of a possibility for giving the world
and one's own life meaning, as well as the knowledge that society would be
poorer if this opportunity no longer existed.

Self-descriptions encountered new kinds of problems after the invention of a new semantics of "culture" and in the wake of a comparative
treatment of "major religions" (and finally all religions in the eighteenth
and nineteenth centuries). These were problems that could no longer be
solved by falling back on special dogmas or orthodoxies. "Dogmatics,"
"dogmatic," "dogmaticism"—each of these terms came to have negative
connotations in general societal communication. In their place, new possibilities were sought for determining religion's meaning—and these were
found in anthropology.

"Human beings," it was assumed, had a need to give their lives meaning and to achieve the certainty of leading a meaningful life, or of (at least)
overcoming the lack of meaning (or meaninglessness) of their worldly ex-

istence. Religion at this point was understood as an option that responded to this need for meaning. This response could and had to take place in forms that were historically varied and that derived their plausibility from their respective social and cultural circumstances. The formula of unity for this variation in forms was anchored in "every human's" subjective experience, and was, in this sense, externalized. It adapted itself to a world that was described as secularized, and it adjusted itself to a societal communication that could also be used and understood nonreligiously. Similarly, anthropology came to be regarded as philosophy, if not science.

It is nonetheless easy to recognize that the religious attribution of a need for meaning involves religion's self-description. The old worry about salvation and redemption can be undogmatized almost seamlessly, and is then transferred into a newly conceived worry about meaning. In that process, the "human" becomes a fiction that is does not correspond to any reality. In all periods, the tremendous diversity of individual worlds of experience was systematically overlooked, and relevant information was systematically repressed or "forgotten." The putative "human" need for meaning was already an interpretation, one that religion hoped to provide an answer for. The solution to the problem was already present in religion's wealth of forms and in discourse about "redemption" and "salvation." The problem merely needed to be invented.

What has to impress an observer schooled in systems theory is that the closing of the system's self-description is achieved via externalization. Yet this externalization is an "eigenachievement" of the system, an eigenvalue of its autopoietic operational mode. It is a cognitive construct with which the difference between system and environment is reintroduced into the system. The system "gödelizes" itself in this fashion in order to be able to convince itself of its coherence [*Geschlossenheit*]. At the same time, it becomes clear that the system's self-description (as a reflection of the system in the system) denotes a special achievement. It appears under certain societal conditions, but is not at all necessary for religious practice and is also not capable of removing doubts in faith. For no one can be convinced that his religious beliefs are sincere by someone telling him they are needed for giving his life meaning. To that extent, the communication of this option is also paradoxical and susceptible to deconstruction. The performative implementation of such a communication contradicts what it maintains constatively.

IV

This analysis began by noting that self-descriptions are occasioned by the observation of a self-produced difference between system and environment. All function systems in modern society are increasingly faced with this problem, thus guaranteeing the comparability of relevant findings and making it possible to use them in attempting to understand modern society. But having said that, one can most likely specify an individual function system's self-descriptions, here the specifics of religion's self-description.

One of the most striking findings is the preponderance of major religions that distinguish themselves from one another. Moreover, there is a vast number of religious sects, cults, and movements, many of them very recent and short-lived. If one assumes there is a communications network spanning the globe, a system of world society, it is striking that there is not a worldwide religion that is uniform in its principles. That fact need not prevent us (assuming certain foundations of systems theory) from accepting a function system for religion as a subsystem of world society. For religious communication is everywhere distinguishable from communication with a different orientation. System boundaries exist and are reproduced. The interregional mobility and disseminatory tempo of some religious forms—whether new cults and sects or forms with a long tradition (only now distributing themselves worldwide in the wake of an interest in religious mysticism and esotericism)—speak for the existence of a context in world society for the most different kinds of religion.[29] Among these are the strangest syncretisms of indigenous, African, and Christian-European provenance at the margins of Catholic South America; they call attention to migrations of forms that no religion has been able to control. Moreover, world society (and more generally, the exceptional quirks of modern life) is a favorable breeding ground, not only for countless new forms of religious communication, but also for a radicalization and revitalization (in the form of self-conscious opposition) of older religions, such as Islam.[30] Yet a standardized world religion has evidently not yet appeared—not even under the pale sign of "theism." Talcott Parsons's principle that culture reacts to a stronger structural differentiation with a stronger generalization of its symbolism of unity evidently finds its limit in this case. A semantics that performed the necessary generalization would have to renounce all ties to religious traditions, myths, and texts, and it would presumably no longer be recognizable as religion. This semantics would still be able to maintain a code of religion using the distinction of transcendence and immanence, but it could no longer respecify that code using continuously accepted programs. The reason for this limit on generalization must lie in religion itself.

Religions are already disposed toward diversification because none of them will permit itself to be refuted by external criteria. To take but one example: for Jews, the Torah is a self-referential, complete, and coherent text that does not permit any external clues of how it should be interpreted. That is all the more reason why the freedom to spiritualize meaning and engage in controversy are admissible in the interpretations themselves.[31] The Christian faith, being so strongly based on the historical uniqueness of Christ's appearance (by which it insulates itself), is immune to historical research. The results of such research might contain suggestions for interpreting dogma, but any analysis of them will end when the continuing existence of the dogma is questioned. The myths and rituals of tribal cultures (and their contemporary reproductions) are even more immune to analysis and assessment. The more the diversification of forms of faith progresses on all levels of intellectual refinement, the more the very diversity of such forms becomes an argument for rejecting external controls. Amalgamations are in no way ruled out, then. Yet once they are formed, their inventory of forms becomes closed. Even the extremely syncretic cults on the periphery of modernity decide (by themselves and using their own schema of forms) whether to absorb new figures or whether to divide and recombine the spirits they know. Only in that way can structural changes—which could be interpreted as adapting to their own expansion, or to changed conditions of suppression—be provided with religious efficacy. Another inevitable consequence of this circumstance are demarcations within the religion system. Other religions are precisely *different* religions. To a significant extent, this recalls the genetic isolation of populations in the course of biological evolution. But that is merely an instructive parallel, not a well-substantiated argument. The reason for the insulation of religions has to be sought in the peculiarity of the medium of meaning, and thus in the distinctive function of religion.

These grounds for a closure—which is not only operative but also semantic—might lie in the referential openness of all meaning, as well as in religion's specific function of transforming the indeterminable into the determinable, and of unfolding paradoxes of linguistically coded meaning (positive/negative). As formulated by Nicholas of Cusa, the world is a unity that has been transformed into diversity, contingently and for no apparent reason. And this lack of an apparent reason—that is the very basis for accepting God. At the same time, this insight has been formulated from a Christian standpoint. Abstracted into the purely logical, a paradox can be unfolded in different ways, and what is contingent [*contingenter*] would then no longer be entities in the world of being but rather forms of believing, of observation, or of description.

Forms of faith thus tend to assume the form of a dogma set against other possibilities, a direct consequence of the function of religion. Such dogmas perform the exclusion—the inclusion of excluding the unfamiliar—and thereby place themselves operatively under a repetition compulsion of having to identify and remember. They are fixed against possible doubts and doubts recognized as possible. At best, such dogmas retain their own capacity for self-refutation and have to present themselves to the outside world as unshakable.

Dogma develops according to the *principle of adapting to itself*, constituting an elaborated "selfness" [*Selbstheit*]. Christian religion knows only one Holy Spirit (although its texts are not at all clear in this respect). For functions of diversification, it created special beings such as angels or saints. Simpler religions know a range of spirits and do not take on the difficult distinction between spirits and angels. They are also entirely unable to distinguish saints (as opposed to the [demonically] possessed). The concept of dogma in the sense of an explicit determination of tradition and doctrine is only acknowledged in major religions with fixed articles of faith. However, the latent proviso about self-refutation applies in general, being directly linked to the sense of religion (*re-ligio*) and the principle of self-adaptation.

If a religious semantics evolves at all under such conditions, a diversification of types is almost unavoidable. Of course, this takes place within the societal system and finds its foothold in society, as well as a restriction of what is possible. Religions also have to remain plausible in view of given societal structures, especially when they seek to distance themselves or risk being rejected. But this "containment" is in turn an evolutionary variable, and its stabilizing and limiting effect changes in the course of the evolution of society as a whole. The familiar implications of writing and printing come to mind here, as well as the establishing and dissolving of a stratified societal order in the transition to primarily functional differentiation.

Both writing and functional differentiation relax commitments and expand the opportunities for variant forms of religion to assert themselves. Written tradition separates texts, opening them up to exegesis, to oral explication, and to their hermeneutic reproduction from other texts. The remarkable immunity of the Christian Middle Ages against highly developed Jewish and Muslim learning provides just such an example.[32] The autopoietic autonomy of the function system of religion protects it even more against the unreasonable demand that it be linked uncritically to opinions circulating in society. This situation is strengthened even if function systems emerge in the societal environment of the religion system—function systems that only reproduce themselves (recognizably) by means of eigenvalues.

Such eigenvalues may take the form of religious dogma observed and confirmed by one's faith. Although traditionally seen as authenticating a faith's creedal basis, this dogma nowadays functions more as a differentiating factor, a point of separation permitting decisions to be explained and inconsistencies to be eliminated. Dogma provides an orientation—provided that one doesn't opt for a given religion intuitively or out of "sympathy." With dogma as a differentiating factor, the policing of the boundary between orthodoxy and heresy by means of systematic theology declines in significance. This certainly doesn't imply that dogmas are losing their significance. Rather, dogmas mark certain elements of faith while at the same time rejecting what would be possible on their other side, in other religions or completely without a belief in their possibility.

The result of this analysis only seems paradoxical. Precisely because of the religious framework of globalization, one can count on an increased diversity of religion's "species." Those very factors that initiated a trend toward a societal system that is globally consistent—specifically, technologically expanded communication (writing, printing, electronics) and functional differentiation—also contribute to something else: they make religions possible that rely on different textual traditions or that are newly forming, whether in the centers or on the periphery of modern civilization. Examples include Californian "New Age" creeds; the María Lionza cult of Venezuela, with its appeal to racially and socially oppressed population segments; the Tenrikyo sect in Japan and elsewhere, recruiting from the career-oriented middle classes and teaching that every misfortune always has its bright side; esoteric circles in European university towns; and the Latin American intellectualized spiritism called "Kardecism" after [the nineteenth-century French mystic] Allan Kardec [né Hippolyte-Léon Denizard], focused on reincarnation and therapy. It cannot be expected that all of these would be able to be integrated into a single description of "the" religion system. For that (it can be safely assumed) would lead to abandoning the possibility of demarcating the religion system, thereby devaluing the religious as such.

Instead, we find a system (*one* system!) with a preponderance of nonintegrated self-descriptions. It can be assumed these have a common coding, function, and ability to be distinguished from nonreligious communication. That makes "transjunctional" operations possible, in Gotthard Günther's sense of switching from one contexture to another, from one guiding distinction to another. One other continuing characteristic is the self-validation of a faith, which can take on different forms. In the religion system, there is no centralism of self-description, such as can be found in discussions on epistemology, or legal or economic theory—discussions where different theories are in competition and that competition is ultimately carried out on scientific or "philosophical" terrain. Instead, a remarkable ability is found to adapt to different local and social-structural demands, different types of audience, and different conditions for inclusion and exclusion. The impression of diversity and liveliness in religious communication is empirically and theoretically justified. At century's end, this impression has also gained acceptance in the sociology of religion, against all the prognoses (such as Comte's) that such a quagmire of mysticism and irrationality would eventually be done away with. And the religion system's self-descriptions likewise have to comply with this state of affairs.

World religions had traditionally worked with notions like symbol or sign, or some of their semantic equivalents. Doing so assumed a difference between sign and signified. Yet the self-critical semiology that began with Saussure reformulated this distinction (*signe* is the *difference* between *signifiant* and *signifié*), in addition to deconstructing it. One referred to utilizing signs without referents (aware that this was illogical). Yet similarly, there would have to be something signified on the other side of the sign's form that was not consistent with any sign, a *signifiant* without *signifié* and therefore without *signe*. Could that be what is meant by transcendence?

To be able to speak of translations, one would still have to accept, as in the case of language, a relation of signs, a difference between the signifying and the signified. And because translations are possible, one can do without a world language. The same will have to be admitted in speaking of a world religion system.

V

The insight that the religion system has to forego a uniform self-description of the entire system or has to externalize it as anthropology does not prevent us from posing more questions. On the contrary, the vibrancy of the images compels us to look for questions that might order the richness of these appearances. And our starting point can once more be: what produces diversity?

The assumption here as in all evolution is that there is always already religion, and deviations from the given (such as distinctions!) can be grafted onto it. Even when there is a "take-off" of an autopoietic system, which is closing itself operatively and semantically, its previous condition has to be interpretable for the system as religion. Otherwise, a religious diversification of forms would not occur but something (altogether) different. And even if religion acquires its ultimate forms only on the level of reflexive self-organization, doing so assumes a comprehensive "micro-diversity" of religious communication. Given that, one can distinguish at least two different kinds of activation, a distinction that is itself a product of evolution.

New religions have cropped up, often in great numbers—as in Hellenistic antiquity or today—for as long as can be remembered, and they continue to do so. Much religious energy seems to have been channeled into these sources. New sects arise when the inclusive capacity of existing religious forms declines and the function of religion is no longer fulfilled adequately. This happened in antiquity after the secularization of poetry, especially tragedy, as the Homeric figures—defunct as deities and limited chiefly to aristocratic genealogies—were becoming obsolete. In our day, it is more the result of functional differentiation, from which religion profits in various ways. Religious communication becomes visible as a *distinctive operational mode*—and not only in certain situations but also with *enduring* system boundaries. It is thus made difficult, for example, to persecute *politically* those who deviate *religiously*—unless there is some political basis for it.[33] Functional differentiation also has innumerable *side effects* that are not appropriately processed by the function systems and are left behind, so to speak. The increasingly stark differences between included and excluded segments of the population have already been mentioned above. But even less flagrant differences can lead to questions that are not answered—or answered adequately—by the major religions. Examples are provided by career uncertainties and the shortcomings that continually materialize in the occupational integration of individuals into society.[34] New religious movements such as sects that work with trance states both minister to insiders' career problems and offer religious inclusion to social outsiders. Esoterically minded intellectuals may also resort to "consciousness expanding" techniques or drugs and a religious body of thought associated with them.

Entirely different forms of diversification emerge within the major religions, particularly as a result of the writing down of holy texts and interpretive dogma. As is typical in the case of writing, inconsistencies in the tradition can become evident or even be produced if one wishes.[35] At the same time, that increases the demands to monitor consistency and preserve the unity of a respective religion system's self-description. However, every systematization also generates a sensitivity to divisive arguments, and everything that is conceived strictly produces a different side that does not conform to this conception. The most significant example of this tension can be found in the Catholic theology of the Middle Ages and its attempts to control Church politics by organizational and legal means. The very attempt to systematize theology consistently—whether on a basis that is more cognitivistic or voluntaristic or on one that is more realistic (toward essential forms) or individualistic and nominalistic—elaborates the breaking points (such as in the understanding of the sacraments or in the area of redemptive certainty and mercy). That is what finally led to schisms in the Church. Articles of faith can be the subject of dispute as soon as they are established, and arguments are not limited to individual points if dogma is well developed with respect to conceptual foundations and connections. As soon as there are religious schisms, the consistency/inconsistency problem is duplicated in entities now revealingly termed "denominations" [*Konfessionen*]. And even more than the entirety of medieval Catholicism, the (now Reformed) denominations are obliged to systematize their rules of faith and theological doctrines in order to dissociate themselves from one another. More than ever, the self-description becomes an operational mode meant to assure the system's unity—and thus endangering it.

For understanding how diversification comes about, a key variable appears to be the development of an operational level for a self-observation (and self-description) of religion as religion. First, one finds a spontaneous genesis of deviating forms with (mostly latent) reasons for distinguishing themselves. In the process, the distinction itself is denied—just as the faith in spirits and magic cults works its way into global notions of Catholic religion.[36] There are no concerns about consistency because the development of forms does not rely on self-descriptions of religion's identity and its boundaries. Second, though, ecclesiastical policy continues to have a consistency/inconsistency problem, having (for instance) raised the issue (occasioned by the rise of "liberation theology") of whether certain Latin American Catholics would split off from the rest of the Church.

There has evidently been no "civilizational" progress in the present global religion system, as had been expected in the eighteenth century—neither toward an increasing penetration of religion with secular elements nor toward a moral or cultural ecumenism. Those were still ideas that proceeded from a uniform, influential self-description of the religion system. And they had been ideas that endeavored to divide up the entirety of religious forms from the standpoint of second-order observation into primitive and civilized, barbarian, traditional, and modern. Such ideas were thus counting on a ("postconventional," one would say today) phase of individual religious self-discovery and communication in accordance with that. Through the figure of the simultaneity of the nonsimultaneous, one sought to take into account the realities of that time. But this "historicizing" of complexity was in turn a response to the emerging polycontexturality of religious descriptions. In the context of a culture representing itself as culture, the system's unity could (now) only be described historically. However, even that is no longer possible today or all too easily exposed as "Eurocentrism."

If one instead starts with the inclusion/exclusion problem and does so with a double reference (to the societal system and the religion system), then another question suggests itself: how (if at all) can the religion system deploy its own possibilities of inclusion so that persons are included who have been excluded from other function systems? The answer cannot be provided by the traditional guidelines of self-descriptions—as they have been developed by the reflective elites of the major religions or as they have been implemented against their system's marginal phenomena (popular faith, etc.). In such instances, sociological observers are well advised to revert to a notion of religion's function that remains inaccessible to the religion system's self-description.

Whatever type of concept one wishes to use here—a ciphering [*Chiffrierung*] of the indeterminability of meaning, a contingency formula, an unfolding of the paradox of form—unity is always being dissolved into multiplicity. This can only be deemed to ensue contingently, with a small side-glance toward other possibilities. In the classical style of theology, this is a description of the perfect world wished for and observed (in its great variety) by the one and only God. A sociologist would wish to add that the religion system (without "adapting" to society) selects from this reservoir of forms those that can achieve plausibility under given societal conditions. (One such form is the religion system's tradition itself). For the sociologist, the system's self-descriptions are operations of the system that like all other operations contribute to its autopoiesis. "Dogmas" may become fixed in the process, but these inevitably remain distinctions, forms that have another side—an opposite or even an unmarked space of different possibilities. Self-descriptions, too, are subject to a plausibility test the same as all religious communication. They may or may not change, but if they become inadequate, religious communication shifts to forms of unmediated sacrality that such a test cannot discipline. In Christian theology, there are tendencies to abandon any grounding in a "philosophy of science" or excessive generalization, and thus return to the Bible.[37] That, of course, would mean assuming that it is a sacred text.

VI

In summing up, let me reiterate a general characteristic of self-descriptions. Like all descriptions, self-descriptions are also simplifications that remove from consideration everything they cannot incorporate (the other side of their form has been alluded to above). This exclusionary effect does not only occur when a dogma is making an effort to be consistent. Rather, it also arises when one works with open paradoxes or ambivalent formulas, because these rhetorical techniques are also based on certain distinctions that are being applied and sabotaged at one and the same time. This is a phenomenon that accompanies every textual formation. Self-descriptions, then, cannot only be understood as "discourses" or interpreted as texts. On account of their simplifying structure, they are sensitive to disturbances that emanate from realms of meaning that had not been accounted for.

Hence, a self-description "controls" [*steuert*] not only what it confirms but also what causes it trouble. It both consolidates the correct faith and at the same time defines what has to be rejected even if it is imposing itself. The self-description reproduces not only its texts but also what is, discreetly or openly, opposed by them.[38] It has already been noted above that what is religiously sensible has to be communicated in the medium of meaning, and in making use of meaning, it cannot avoid the insight that different, even opposing forms are also possible.[39] A contemporary example would be the way the Catholic Church handles questions of sexuality.[40] Here, too, one has to distinguish between two issues: the determination of conformity and deviation, on the one hand, and what that distinction excludes as irrelevant or as unmarked space, on the other.

When we accept that religion's self-descriptions seek distance, if not actually redemption, from the society around them, the long-term risk of all dogmatizations becomes apparent. Their schema may make reference to a society that changes its structures and thus allows what religion is distancing itself from to become obsolete. In this respect, too, the problems may be alleviated by a number of different religious options and a kind of "market orientation" in light of individuals' readiness to believe. On the one hand, the function of self-descriptions is reinforced by being utilized in internal religious quarrels concerning boundaries. On the other, a wide-ranging spectrum is produced that targets highly dissimilar aspects of modern society. It can respond to racially and socially disadvantaged classes (and not just in the form of social welfare) while also having something to say to intellectuals critical of modernity. Apparently, there are hardly any religious movements left that can still manage without elaborate self-descriptions or can be sustained entirely by piety. Even piety needs to have reasons. This necessity is ensured by the existence of a written culture and the model of the major religions. Even elementary religious operations these days are co-determined by system descriptions, more than may be assumed by comparison with older societies. And that should not be surprising once other function systems are compared—such as the significance of economic theories for the economy's attempts at self-regulation, or of management theories for organizational planning, or of "redescriptions" of earlier artworks for the creation of new ones.

Every self-description has to open itself up to logical problems that cannot be solved with classical bivalent logic (and therefore with ontological metaphysics). To the extent that description is addressed at all, a distinction is assumed between describer (subject) and described (object). At the same time, however, the reflexivity of a self-description sabotages the very distinction it is assuming. We shall have to leave it open whether structurally rich logics can ever be developed that are a match for this problem (as Gotthard Günther hoped). But the logical problems have to be resolved somehow, and if not by logic, then by imagination.

Having said all that, there is still no agreement on the significance of sociological theories in developing new self-descriptions or modifying traditional ones in the religion system. Obviously, the religion system's reflections cannot be understood as "applied sociology." Nor can they be faulted for not satisfying the requirements of sociological critique. Content-related interventions may only lead to deconstructions and to a constant transferring of problems onto other constructions. Yet religious cosmologies, theologies, or the basic assumptions of meditation practices might perhaps be able to profit from the general doctrine of forms being proposed by sociology. At least nowadays it is possible to describe more precisely what is being agreed to when self-descriptions of a system are being produced. One can still proceed nostalgically or fanatically—but no longer naïvely.

In saying this, I am still assuming—as I have throughout the present work—that the sociological theory of society treats religion and its self-descriptions as an object of research, and that it has to produce statements about that object according to scientific criteria that it can represent as "true." In relation to itself, this sociological theory characterizes religion's self-descriptions as *different*. Hence, a very different relation emerges whenever communication takes place between sociology and religion. Seen from the perspective of sociology, religion moves into the position of an *other*, participating in communication and being made vulnerable by it.[41] In agreeing to communication, listening and understanding are called for, as well as an openness to accepting or rejecting the meanings proposed. Communication is initially unsettling, and the decision to participate already generates vulnerability. Although the participant is not committed to accept the communication, he finds himself in a position that imposes that possibility. It is at least expected that he will seriously entertain the possibility. That might lead him into having to articulate the position that a rejection would proceed from—but without having considered whether the self-description of the rejecting system (here: *religion*) can endure this degree of clarification.

Notes

EDITOR'S NOTE

1. See Niklas Luhmann, *Die Gesellschaft der Gesellschaft* (Frankfurt, 1997).

2. Luhmann's *Die Gesellschaft der Gesellschaft* probably went to press around then, and doubtless he intended to focus on religion as a social system thereafter.

CHAPTER 1: RELIGION AS A FORM OF MEANING

1. For the contemporary sociological context, see *Religionssoziologie um 1900*, ed. Volkhard Krech and Hartmann Tyrell (Würzburg, 1995); for subsequent developments in the sociology of religion, see Hartmann Tyrell, "Religionssoziologie," *Geschichte und Gesellschaft* 22 (1996): 428–457.

2. As the main work, see Emile Durkheim, *Les formes élémentaires de la vie religieuse: Le système totémique en Australie*, 5th ed. (1968; German trans., Frankfurt, 1981). See also "Détermination du fait moral," in id., *Sociologie et philosophie* (Paris, 1951), 49–90 (German trans., Frankfurt, 1967).

3. See Max Weber, *Wirtschaft und Gesellschaft*, 3rd ed. (Tübingen, 1948), 1: 227.

4. For a brief overview see the chapter "Religionssoziologie," in Max Weber, *Wirtschaft und Gesellschaft*, 1: 227ff.

5. See Georg Simmel, "Zur Soziologie der Religion," *Neue Deutsche Rundschau* 9 (1898): 111–123; and Georg Simmel, *Die Religion* (Frankfurt, 1912).

6. See René Girard, *La violence et le sacré* (Paris, 1972) and *Des choses cachées depuis la fondation du monde* (Paris, 1978).

7. Here see Philipp E. Hammond, "Introduction," in *The Sacred in a Secular Age: Toward Revision in the Scientific Study of Religion*, ed. id. (Berkeley, CA, 1985), 1–6.

8. Here I follow Rudolf Ott, *Das Heilige: Über das Irrationale in der Idee des Göttlichen und sein Verhältnis zum Rationalen* (1917; 31st–35th printing, Munich, 1963). It is not unimportant that this description is presumed to apply only to those who are familiar with such experiences. Whoever does not share that assumption "is asked not to read on" (ibid., 8). Written in 1917, this may have been a covert jab at Max Weber.

9. The sociological "phenomenologists" are typical in a different way, yet they misunderstand what phenomenology in its original sense intended.

10. "He may be in the thunder, but he is not the thunder" is the formulation of John S. Mbiti in his *Concepts of God in Africa* (London, 1970), 8. In Hegel, the distinction can already be found, e.g., in the rejection of pantheism as a possible religion (as incapable of intellectual development!); see his *Vorlesungen über die Philosophie der Religion I*, in id., *Werke* (Frankfurt, 1969), 16: 89.

11. I am referring to the famous § 10 in Heidegger, *Sein und Zeit*, 6th ed. (Tübingen, 1949) 45ff.

12. See n. 8 above.

13. See Keiji Nishitani, *Was ist Religion?* trans. Dora Fischer-Barnicol (Frankfurt, 1982); trans. Jan Van Bragt as *Religion and Nothingness* (Berkeley, CA, 1982).

14. In Aristotle, this is a reference to being.

15. See the discussion of "meaning of meaning" [*sens du sens*], e.g., in Luc Ferry, *L'homme-Dieu ou le sens de la vie* (Paris, 1996) 19, explained as "the ultimate signification of all these particular significations."

16. Here reference to the construction of Gothic churches is unavoidable. If nothing else, their peculiarity consists in letting in only broken, distinguishable light and thus *making the medium of light visible*. We could understand this as symbolic of the fact that religion claims to make meaning observable and describable.

17. See, e.g., Edmund Husserl, *Erfahrung und Urteil: Untersuchungen zur Genealogie der Logik* (Hamburg, 1948), §§ 8 and 9 (26ff.).

18. Gilles Deleuze, in *Logique du sens* (Paris, 1969), trans. Mark Lester and Charles Stivale as *The Logic of Sense*, ed. Constantine V. Boundas (New York, 1990, repr., London, 2004), seems to be saying something similar when defining the paradox of meaning as the meaning of *nonsense*, thus encountering in *nonsense* the reflection of meaning as meaning: "The name saying its own sense can only be *nonsense*" (79). Yet he then adds: "Nonsense . . . as it enacts the donation of sense, is opposed to the absence of sense" (83), ultimately calling this absence of meaning "sub-sense" or "a-sense" (103).

19. See with a view to a fully differentiated literary industry, Winfried Menninghaus, *Lob des Unsinns: Über Kant, Tieck und Blaubart* (Frankfurt, 1995).

20. Hölderlin to Niethammer, February 24, 1796: "In den philosophischen Briefen will ich das Prinzip finden, das mir die *Trennungen, in denen wir denken und existieren*, erklärt . . ."; see also Bernhard Lypp, "Poetische Religion," in *Früher Idealismus und Frühromantik: Der Streit um die Grundlagen der Ästhetik (1795–1805)*, ed. Walter Jaeschke and Helmut Holzhey (Hamburg, 1990), 80–111. On the transition from cosmos-oriented writing to (Romantic) poetry oriented toward self-reference and other-reference, see also Earl R. Wasserman, *The Subtler Language: Critical Readings of Neoclassical and Romantic Poems* (Baltimore, 1959).

21. The world is thus not realized as spirit [*Geist*] as Hegel claimed, saying: "Reason is spirit when its certainty that it is all reality has been raised to truth,

and it is conscious of itself as its own world and of the world as itself" (G. W. F. Hegel, Phenomenology of Spirit [1807], trans. J. B. Baillie, chap. 6, introduction).

22. Here I shall thus avoid the formulation "knowledge" used in similar theoretical conceptions such as "tacit knowledge" (see Michael Polanyi, *The Tacit Dimension* (London, 1966), trans. as *Implizites Wissen* [Frankfurt, 1985]) or "background knowledge" (for a life-world), in Jürgen Habermas, *Faktizität und Geltung: Beiträge zur Diskurstheorie des Rechts und des demokratischen Rechtsstaats* (Frankfurt, 1992), 37ff.

23. See Fritz Heider, "Ding und Medium," *Symposion* 1 (1926): 109–157. This distinction was revived particularly through the English translation of this essay in *Psychological Issues* 1, no. 3 (1959): 1–34. See also Karl E. Weick, *The Social Psychology of Organizing* (Reading, MA, 1969), trans. as *Der Prozeß des Organisierens* (Frankfurt, 1985), esp. 163ff., 271ff.

24. On this insight, nowadays widely accepted, see Jonathan Culler, *Framing the Sign: Criticism and Its Institutions* (Oxford, 1988).

25. This formulate draws upon Eva Meyer, "Der Unterschied, der eine Umgebung schafft," in *Im Netz der Systeme*, ed. Ars Electronica (Berlin, 1990), 110–122.

26. See Alois Hahn, "Sinn und Sinnlosigkeit," in *Sinn, Kommunikation und soziale Differenzierung: Beiträge zu Luhmanns Theorie sozialer Systeme*, ed. Hans Haferkamp and Michael Schmid (Frankfurt, 1987), 155–164. See also Georg Lohmann, "Autopoiesis und die Unmöglichkeit von Sinnverlust: Ein marginaler Zugang zu Niklas Luhmanns Theorie 'Sozialer Systeme,'" ibid., 165–184.

27. I prefer the term "redescription" because it does not compel us to distinguish constantly between describing again and describing anew—a distinction that itself can be questioned.

28. See George Spencer-Brown, *Laws of Form* (1969), new ed. (New York, 1979), 76. "An observer, since he distinguishes the space he occupies, is also a mark. . . . We see now that the first distinction, the mark, and the observers are not only interchangeable, but, in their form, identical." Cf., closely following Spencer-Brown, Louis H. Kauffman, "Self-Reference and Recursive Forms," *Journal of Social and Biological Structures* 10 (1987): 53–72 (here 53): "At least one distinction is involved in the presence of self-reference. The self appears, and an indication of that self can be seen as separate from the self. Any distinction involves the self-reference of 'the one who distinguishes.' Therefore, self-reference and the idea of distinction are inseparable (hence conceptually identical)."

29. Spencer-Brown, *Laws of Form*, 56, 69ff.

30. See also Niklas Luhmann, *Erkenntnis als Konstruktion* (Bern, 1988).

31. This was the starting point of "second order cybernetics." On this, see the interview with Heinz von Foerster in *Cybernetics and Human Knowing* 4 (1997): 3–15.

32. According to Spencer-Brown's "law of crossing": "The value of a crossing made again is not the value of the crossing" (Spencer-Brown, *Laws of Form*, 2). Or,

put differently, the sides cannot specify themselves reciprocally. We cannot bring anything across, but wanting to accumulate or correct information, we have to stay on the inside of the form. The "form of cancellation" is also only valid if the other side remains indeterminable as an unmarked state.

33. Richard Harvey Brown, "Rhetoric, Textuality, and the Postmodern Turn in Sociological Theory," in *The Postmodern Turn: New Perspectives on Social Theory*, ed. Steven Seidman (Cambridge, 1994), 229–241 (here 229); see also the considerations under the heading "The Rhetorical Construction of Social Reality." Religion's ability to use this rhetorical construction of the idea of reality in order to establish its immanent/transcendent code is already suggested here.

34. On this issue, see the distinction of Cartesian doubt, which can be remedied by self-signification to confirm the thinking "I," and Nishitani, *Was ist Religion?* 55ff., on the "great doubt" in Buddhism. We should in any case not only think of Descartes here. Notions like "spirit" in Berkeley and "pour soi" in Sartre refer also to a consciousness that is co-conscious in conscious operations but is not an object to itself and not yet knowledge. See George Berkeley, *Of the Principles of Human Knowledge*, ([1710] London, 1957), 1.2, on "mind, spirit, soul, or myself": "By which words I do not denote any one of my ideas, but a thing entirely distinct from them, *wherein they exist*, or, which is the same thing, whereby they are perceived" (114). On Sartre, see his *L'être et le néant: Essai d'ontologie phénoménologique*, 30th ed. (Paris, 1950), 115ff. Even sociology of religion, from Simmel to Luckmann, has always referred to a subjective consciousness, thus presupposing a consciousness that is conscious of itself.

35. Spencer-Brown, *Laws of Form*, 3.

36. Ibid., 1.

37. See W. Ross Ashby, *An Introduction to Cybernetics* (London, 1956), 206ff., and id., "Requisite Variety and Its Implications for the Control of Complex Systems," *Cybernetica* 1, no. 2 (1958): 83–99.

38. Cf. § III above.

39. Spencer-Brown, *Laws of Form*, 64–65.

40. See here David Roberts, "Die Parodoxie der Form: Literatur und Selbstreferenz," in *Probleme der Form*, ed. Dirk Baecker (Frankfurt, 1993), 22–44.

41. Religious literature, particularly of Buddhist provenance, often reports the precise opposite: after returning from the religious experience of dissolution, the things of the world are *no longer the same as before*. Accordingly, it is precisely this logical point at which religion draws attention to its own performance.

42. According to Gudmund Hernes, "Comments," in *Social Theory for a Changing Society*, ed. Pierre Bourdieu and James S. Coleman (Boulder and New York, 1991), 125–126.

43. See "Cybernetic Ontology and Transjunctional Operations," in Gotthard Günther, *Beiträge zur Grundlegung einer operationsfähigen Dialektik* (Hamburg, 1976), 1: 249–328.

44. According to Nishitani, *Religion and Nothingness.*

45. Aristotle, *De anima*, bk. 3.

46. For a similar view but with a somewhat different specification of the components, see Deleuze, *Logic of Sense*, 22ff.

47. For more on this topic, see Niklas Luhmann, *Soziale Systeme: Grundriß einer allgemeinen Theorie* (Frankfurt, 1984).

48. On organisms, see A. Moreno, J. Fernandez, and A. Etxeberria, "Computational Darwinism as a Basis for Cognition," *Revue internationale de systémique* 6 (1992): 205–221.

49. This is Bateson's idea of information: a difference that makes a difference. See Gregory Bateson, *Steps to an Ecology of Mind: Collected Essays in Anthropology, Psychiatry, Evolution, and Epistemology* (New York, 1973), trans. as *Ökologie des Geistes: Anthropologische, psychologische, biologische und epistemologische Perspektiven* (Frankfurt, 1981), 488.

50. Here see esp. Magoroh Maruyama, "The Second Cybernetics: Deviation-Amplifying Mutual Causal Processes," *American Scientist* 51 (1963): 164–179. See also the postscript to "The Second Cybernetics," *American Scientist* 51 (1963): 250–256.

51. This does not mean that every ritual of this kind has religious connotations. According to the custom in villages in southern Italy, after the death of a spouse, the widow or widower may not leave the house for a time, during which relatives, friends, and neighbors provide for her or him in a strict order of precedence based on relational proximity. The problem is thus as it were artificially duplicated and reformulated so as to be resolvable by prescribed conduct. Or, seen differently, the death is *additionally encumbered* with obligations and restrictions on conduct, thus displacing its difference and distracting attention onto a painstakingly precise fulfillment of the requirements.

52. St. Augustine, *Confessions* 11.12ff.

53. From a formal standpoint, this implies a reentry of the distinction between life and death into itself, with all the consequences of an unresolvable indeterminacy, as can be seen in Spencer-Brown, *Laws of Form*, 56ff.

54. Here we naturally have to distinguish again among notions of meaning. By reason of its inevitable appearance of being "meaningful" [*Sinnförmigkeit*], death can be experienced and communicated as meaningful with respect to given expectations of life.

55. St. Augustine, *Confessions*, esp. 11.14, 17–20.

CHAPTER 2: CODING

1. On this issue, see Mary Douglas, *Purity and Danger: An Analysis of Concepts of Pollution and Taboo* (Harmondsworth, UK, 1970).

2. This formulation is from Georg Wilhelm Friedrich Hegel, *Verhältnis des*

Skeptizismus zur Philosophie, Darstellung seiner verschiedenen Modifikationen und Vergleichung des neuesten mit dem alten, in *Werke*, vol. 2 (Frankfurt, 1970), 213–272 (here 229). I am grateful to Karl Eberhard Schorr for this reference.

3. See Klaus Krippendorf, "Paradox and Information," in *Progress in Communication Sciences*, ed. Brenda Derwin and Melvin J. Voigt, vol. 5 (Norwood, NJ, 1984), 45–71.

4. For a case study in the field of law, see Niklas Luhmann, "The Third Question: The Creative Use of Paradoxes in Law and Legal History," *Journal of Law and Society* 15 (1988): 153–165.

5. Eric A. Havelock speaks of "preserved communication" in his *Preface to Plato* (Cambridge, MA, 1963), 134 passim. See also id., *Origins of Western Literacy* (Toronto, 1976), 49.

6. On the genealogy of a preference for paradox in Renaissance literature, see A. E. Malloch, "The Technique and Function of the Renaissance Paradox," *Studies in Philology* 53 (1956): 191–203.

7. On play (and fantasy), see Gregory Bateson, *Steps to an Ecology of Mind: Collected Essays in Anthropology, Psychiatry, Evolution, and Epistemology* (New York, 1973), trans. as *Ökologie des Geistes: Anthropologische, psychologische, biologische und epistemologische Perspektiven* (Frankfurt, 1981), 241ff.; on art, see Arthur C. Danto, *The Transfiguration of the Commonplace: A Philosophy of Art* (Cambridge, MA, 1981); on statistics and their inferences for probability, see George Spencer-Brown, *Probability and Scientific Inference* (London, 1957), 1ff. On (semiotic) markings per se, see also Jonathan Culler, *Framing the Sign: Criticism and its Institutions* (Oxford, 1988).

8. See also Erving Goffman, *Relations in Public: Microstudies of the Public Order* (Harmondsworth, UK, 1971).

9. In the sense of Michel Serres, *Genèse* (Paris, 1982), 146ff.

10. See, e.g., Fredrik Barth, *Ritual and Knowledge Among the Baktaman of New Guinea* (Oslo and New Haven, CT, 1975), a study based explicitly on communication.

11. See Jean Bottéro, *Mésopotamie: L'écriture, la raison et les dieux* (Paris, 1987), 259ff.

12. On this comparison, see Susan A. Handelman, *The Slayers of Moses: The Emergence of Rabbinic Interpretation in Modern Literary Theory* (Albany, NY, 1982).

13. See David Daube, "Dissent in Bible and Talmud," *California Law Review* 59 (1971): 784–794; Jeffrey I. Roth, "The Justification for Controversy Under Jewish Law," *California Law Review* 76 (1988): 338–387.

14. Plato *Cratylus* 436Aff.

15. "J'entend par religion des choses oubliées depuis toujours," Michel Serres writes in a simple, if inadequate, reversal (Serres, *Genèse*, 98), trans. Geneviève James and James Nielson, *Genesis* (Ann Arbor, MI, 1995), 55, as "by religion I mean the things forever forgotten."

16. On this term in linguistics, see Roman Jakobson and Morris Halle, *Fundamentals of Language* (The Hague, 1956), 5ff.; in sociology, see Shmuel N. Eisenstadt, *Tradition, Change, and Modernity* (New York, 1973), esp. 133ff. and 321ff. Conceptual precision is not to be found in this literature. It is replaced by formulations such as cultural symbols, models, cognitive maps, and categorial structures, and by distinguishing between a structural level and a level of situative action. In most cases, we are required to figure out whether the symbols of a code are being applied accurately or not. Talcott Parsons, *Societies: Evolutionary and Comparative Perspectives* (Englewood Cliffs, NJ, 1966), 20, thus regards even linguistic codes as normative structures. But this ultimately only means that it is a matter of formulating a binary schematism. I account for that here by distinguishing between *coding* and *programming*.

17. A different, conventional example would involve determining a coefficient that rules out all other numbers as inappropriate and ineffective. This too is called a "code."

18. In the sense of Gotthard Günther, "Cybernetic Ontology and Transjunctional Operations," in *Beiträge zur Grundlegung einer operationsfähigen Dialektik*, vol. 1 (Hamburg, 1976), 136–182 (here 140ff.).

19. See, above all, Gotthard Günther, "Strukturelle Minimalbedingungen einer Theorie des objektiven Geistes als Einheit der Geschichte," in *Beiträge zur Grundlegung einer operationsfähigen Dialektik*, vol. 3 (Hamburg, 1980), 136–182 (here 140ff.).

20. This has long been emphasized, even for morality. See, e.g., Sir Thomas Browne, *Religio Medici* (1643; repr. London, 1965), 71: "They that endeavour to abolish Vice destroy also Virtue; for contraries, though they destroy one another, are yet the life of one another." Note how this escalates into a paradox! In other versions, this problem of how moral codes refer to themselves is treated as a problem of theodicy, or it is seen religiously as an appearance of God in historical time.

21. Here I am interpreting the term "contexture," which emphasizes an indifference toward the outside, with the help of Spencer-Brown's definition of "distinction" as "perfect continence" (George Spencer-Brown, *Laws of Form* [1969], new ed. [New York, 1979], 1). We shall have to leave it open whether this is entirely in Günther's sense.

22. See Günther, "Cybernetic Ontology."

23. On the lines of connection between observer theory and Günther's logic, see Elena Esposito, *L'operazione di osservazione: Costruttivismo e teoria dei sistemi sociali* (Milan, 1992).

24. For the sake of clarification, it should be noted that the use of a rejection value does not interfere with the rejected distinction (because that would indeed presuppose accepting the distinction). If law rejects the moral distinction of good/bad, that does not mean that distinctions cannot be made this way. It does not even mean that law could not be subject to moral evaluation. It only means that

the pending operation does not use the distinction and instead focuses on the code of law. It is not the values of the rejected distinction that are being negated, which would only be possible by using this very distinction, but only the distinction itself. "The very choice is rejected" (Günther, "Cybernetic Ontology," 287). The reader is asked to note this, since it would otherwise constantly lead to misunderstandings, precisely in questions that are normatively controversial.

25. That according to Francisco J. Valera, "A Calculus for Self-Reference," *International Journal of General Systems* 2 (1975): 15–24.

26. See the critique of the ontological "filiation" of Aristotle and Hegel, which strives for an adequate understanding of time, in Martin Heidegger, *Sein und Zeit*, 6th ed. (Tübingen, 1949), 432–433n2.

27. This distinction of condensation/confirmation derives from George Spencer-Brown and is elegantly explained by him by a further distinction, specifically that the equation ⌐⌐_⌐ can be read from left to right (as condensation) and from right to left (as confirmation) (Spencer-Brown, *Laws of Form*, 10). Here as always, it is assumed there is an observer who can distinguish these readings and decide on this distinction. The same idea can be formulated with Wittgenstein's notion of a rule, which presupposes that it can be applied in more than one case, or with Derrida's notion of *différance*.

28. See Talcott Parsons, *The System of Modern Societies* (Englewood Cliffs, NJ, 1971), 26ff.; id., "Comparative Studies and Evolutionary Change," *Social Systems and the Evolution of Action Theory* (New York, 1977), 279–320 (esp. 307ff.).

29. See here merely the numerous collections of essays by Paul de Man, such as *Blindness and Insight: Essays in the Rhetoric of Contemporary Criticism*, 2nd ed. (London 1983), and *The Resistance to Theory* (Minneapolis, 1986).

30. See Gerdien Jonker, *The Topography of Remembrance: The Dead, Tradition and the Collective Memory in Mesopotamia* (Leiden, 1995).

31. "One is never installed in transgression. One never lives elsewhere. Transgression implies the limit is still at work" (Jacques Derrida, *Positions*, trans. Alan Bass, rev. ed. [New York: Continuum, 2004], 10).

32. This has particularly been a theme in Gotthard Günther's work; see his *Beiträge zur Grundlegung einer operationsfähigen Dialektik*, 3 vols. (Hamburg, 1976–1980).

33. Cf. § III above.

34. See, e.g., *Ways of Transcendence: Insights from Major Religions and Modern Thought*, ed. Edwin Dowdy (Bedford Park, South Australia, 1982), and Thomas Luckmann's equally generalizing definition of the function of religion as the socialization of dealing with transcendence in "Über die Funktion der Religion," in *Die religiöse Dimension der Gesellschaft*, ed. Peter Koslowski (Tübingen, 1985), 26–41.

35. This is based on Barth, *Ritual and Knowledge*. One gets the idea that the bones (like other kinds of relics) should be signified as a transformed, canonized "rubbish" in Culler's sense (Culler, *Framing the Sign*, 108ff.), following Michael

Thompson, *Rubbish Theory: The Creation and Destruction of Value* (Oxford, 1979). Thompson, for his part, applies the catastrophe theory of René Thoms to give form to such discontinuities of valuation. But elsewhere in research on the religions of tribal societies, we also find a great deal of evidence for a completely pragmatic and yet distinction-focused treatment of the sacred—provided that the mystery is retained and tabooized along with it. That of course presumes that the question of whether one has faith [*Glauben*] never gets asked—or put differently, that faith here is not the "form" of religion that defines itself from the other side, i.e., nonfaith.

36. On the cultural history of heaven, see Bernhard Lang and Colleen McDannell, *Heaven: A History* (New Haven, CT, 1988). For examples from African religions, see John S. Mbiti, *Concepts of God in Africa* (London, 1970), where one finds striking myths of creation: God is said to have first lived with humans or at least near them, but He then distanced himself from them to avoid aggravation or to punish their disobedience (171ff.).

37. See Mbiti, *Concepts of God*, 12ff.

38. On this issue, there is much ethnographic evidence. For a short summary, see, e.g., Edmund Leach, *Culture and Communication: The Logic by Which Symbols Are Connected* (Cambridge, 1976), 71ff.

39. On the evolution of religion, see chapter 7 in this volume.

40. "Reentry" in Spencer-Brown's sense (see id., *Laws of Form*, 56ff., 69ff.).

41. See Roy A. Rappaport, *Pigs for the Ancestors: Ritual in the Ecology of a New Guinea People* (New Haven, CT, 1967); id., "The Sacred in Human Evolution," *Annual Review of Ecology and Systematics* 2 (1971): 23–44; id., "Ritual, Sanctity and Cybernetics," *American Anthropologist* 73 (1971): 59–76.

42. On this, see Roy A. Rappaport, "Maladaptation in Social Systems," in *The Evolution of Social Systems*, ed. Jonathan Friedman and Michael J. Rowlands (Pittsburgh, 1978), 49–71.

43. Max Weber, *Wirtschaft und Gesellschaft*, 3rd ed. (Tübingen, 1948), 1: 227, trans. in *Economy and Society: An Outline of Interpretive Sociology* (Berkeley: University of California Press, 1978), 399.

44. "A process of abstraction, which only appears to be simple, has usually already been carried out. . . . Already crystallized is the notion that certain beings are concealed 'behind' and responsible for the activity of charismatically endowed natural objects, artifacts, animals, or persons. This is the belief in spirits." (Max Weber, *The Sociology of Religion*, trans. Ephraim Fischoff [Boston, 1993], 3). Instead of *behind*, it would be better in many cases to say *in*.

45. In Hartmann Tyrell, "Das Religiöse in Max Webers Religionssoziologie," *Saeculum* 43 (1992): 172–230 (here 194).

46. See Madeleine David, *Les dieux et le destin en Babylonie* (Paris, 1949); Jean Bottéro, *Mésopotamie: L'écriture, la raison et les dieux* (Paris, 1987), 243ff. See also chapter 5 in this volume.

47. See Louis Schneider, "The Scope of 'The Religious Factor' and the Sociology of Religion: Notes on Definition, Idolatry and Magic," *Social Research* 41 (1974): 340–361.

48. "Just as the opposition of things bestows beauty upon language, then, so is the beauty of this world enhanced by the opposition of contraries, composed, as it were, by an eloquence not of words but of things" (St. Augustine, *The City of God Against the Pagans*, trans. R. W. Dyson [Cambridge, 1998], 472).

49. See chapter 1 in this volume.

50. This is probably best understood as a counter to the tradition in Mesopotamia. The god Marduk had fifty names (why not fifty-one, then?), and names were not only verbal significations there but themselves competencies. On this, see Bottéro, *Mésopotamie*, 125–126. At the same time, giving up the identity of name and being solves the problem of whether the name is correct and whether each list of divine names is complete or incomplete.

51. This principle is retained in the much discussed (and in turn controversial) legend of the Oven of Achnai. See, e.g., Ishak England, "Majority Decision vs. Individual Truth: The Interpretation of the Oven of Achnai Aggadah," *Tradition: A Journal of Orthodox Jewish Thought* 15 (1975): 137–151.

52. This according to Shmuel Noah Eisenstadt, "Social Division of Labor, Construction of Centers and Institutional Dynamics: A Reassessment of Structural-Evolutionary Perspective," *Protosoziologie* 7 (1995): 11–22 (here 16–17).

53. Nonetheless, without being able to sustain this renunciation of any distinction in the margins of a possible theology. A case in point is that the personality and trinity of God cannot be subject to doubt. In Cusa's "On the Pursuit of Wisdom," we read that God is "before all things that differ"; for the original, see Nicolas of Cusa, *Philosophisch-Theologische Schriften*, ed. Leo Gabriel, vol. 1 (Vienna, 1964), 1–189, 56. Yet the inadequacy of human understanding (dependent on using distinctions) is being reflected on here. Moreover, we ultimately know what the Church is providing for us.

54. See Jacques Derrida, *De la Grammatologie* (Paris, 1967), trans. Gayatri Chakravorty Spivak as *Of Grammatology* (Baltimore, 1976), 141–157.

55. The same outline of the problem can be found in Kant, where freedom is understood as a *ratio essendi* of the moral law [*Sittengesetz*] and where the moral imperative is assured in its canonicity (*sit venia verbo*) as a fact of reasonable consciousness. Finally, *both* are combined together in a single idea of the subject (a notion from which philosophers are today still deriving capital).

56. On such other codes, see Niklas Luhmann, "Codierung und Programmierung. Bildung und Selektion im Erziehungssystem," *Soziologische Aufklärung* 4 (Opladen, 1987), 182–201; id., *Die Wirtschaft der Gesellschaft* (Frankfurt, 1988), 243ff. and passim; id., *Die Wissenschaft der Gesellschaft* (Frankfurt, 1990), 401ff.; id., *Das Recht der Gesellschaft* (Frankfurt, 1993), 165ff.; id., *Die Kunst der Gesellschaft* (Frankfurt, 1995), 301ff.

57. See St. Thomas Aquinas, *Summa Theologiae* IIae, q. 91, a. 2: "This participation of the eternal law in the rational creature is called the natural law."

58. See here esp. Renate Blickle, "Hausnotdurft: Ein Fundamentalrecht in der altständischen Ordnung Bayerns," in *Grund- und Freiheitsrechte von der ständischen zur spätbürgerlichen Gesellschaft*, ed. Günter Birtsch (Göttingen, 1987), 42–64.

59. For widely divergent evidence varying by region and on the axis of major/ minor civilizations, see *The Anthropology of Evil*, ed. David Parkin (Oxford, 1985).

60. See specifically Keith Thomas, *Religion and the Decline of Magic* (London, 1971); id., *Man and the Natural World* (London, 1983).

61. We shall return to this issue in chapter 4 when discussing the observer God.

62. For evidence from Africa, see Mbiti, *Concepts of God*, 17–18, 35–36, 247ff.

63. The "Ethics" of Peter Abelard is pathbreaking in this respect. For Abelard, vice (*vitium*) is defined as sin if we agree with it internally: "This consent is what we properly call 'sin,' the fault of the soul whereby it merits damnation or is held guilty before God. For what is this consent but scorn for God and affront against him?" (Peter Abelard, *Ethical Writings*, trans. Paul Vincent Spade [Indianapolis, 1995], 2–3). In and of itself, vice can be understood as a natural orientation (*habitus*), and to God, it only matters if we consent to it.

64. See St. Anselm, archbishop of Canterbury, "De casu diaboli," in *Opera omnia* (1938–, repr., Stuttgart, 1968), 1: 233–272.

65. As indicated in § IV of this chapter, it was precariously plausible to have such a circular self-legitimation of a code through its positive value.

66. For a brief overview, see Niklas Luhmann, *Die Gesellschaft der Gesellschaft* (Frankfurt, 1997), 413ff.

67. Michel Serres, *Le parasite* (Paris, 1980).

68. For more detail here, see Niklas Luhmann, "Die Paradoxie des Entscheidens," *Verwaltungsarchiv* 84 (1993): 287–310.

69. This is only another, more decision-oriented formulation for what is termed "condensation" and "confirmation" in § IV of this chapter (following Spencer-Brown, *Laws of Form*).

70. See Hegel's *Vorlesungen über die Philosophie der Religion* I, in *Werke*, vol. 16 (Frankfurt, 1969), 215 (Hegel's emphasis).

71. Bourdieu's entire oeuvre could be cited here. A short sketch, supplemented by the concept of *pieuse hypocrisie* (pious hypocrisy) and referring to jurists, can be found in Pierre Bourdieu, "Les juristes, gardiens de l'hypocrisie collective," in *Normes juridiques et régulation sociale*, ed. François Chazel and Jacques Commaille (Paris, 1991), 95–99. See also Pierre Bourdieu, *La Distinction: Critique sociale du jugement* (Paris, 1979) and *Ce que parler veut dire: L'économie des échanges sociales* (Paris, 1982).

72. Formulated based on Jacques Derrida, *Marges de la philosophie* (Paris, 1972), 76–77.

73. See, e.g., Keiji Nishitani, *Was ist Religion?* trans. Dora Fischer-Barnicol (Frankfurt, 1982), 379ff.; trans. Jan Van Bragt as *Religion and Nothingness* (Berkeley, CA, 1982), 258ff.

74. Charles Herle, *Wisdomes Tripos, or rather its inscription, Detur sapienti* (London, 1655), 49.

75. See Spencer-Brown, *Laws of Form*, 105.

76. For the utmost clarity on this, see Horst Baier, *Soziologie als Aufklärung— oder die Vertreibung der Transzendenz aus der Gesellschaft* (Constance, 1989).

77. On the relationship of semantics and social structure, see Niklas Luhmann, "Individuum, Individualität, Individualismus," in *Gesellschaftsstruktur und Semantik*, vol. 3 (Frankfurt, 1989), 149–258.

78. There is a "transcendence in self-immanence," Luc Ferry maintains, e.g., in *L'homme-Dieu ou Le sens de la vie* (Paris, 1996), trans. David Pellauer as *Man Made God: The Meaning of Life* (Chicago, 2002), 137. Theologians also touch on the possibility of such changes in disposition. "If we ask how speaking of God can be possible, then we must answer: only by speaking about ourselves," Rudolf Bultmann asserts in *Glauben und Verstehen* (Tübingen, 1960), 1: 33, quoted in Michael Hochschild, "Die Kirchenkrise und die Theologie" (Ph.D. diss., Bielefeld, 1997), 163.

79. On this tradition, see Bernhard Lang and Colleen McDannel, *Heaven: A History* (New Haven, CT, 1988).

80. In "The New and the Old in Religion," in *Social Theory for a Changing Society*, ed. Pierre Bourdieu and James S. Coleman (Boulder, CO, and New York, 1991), 167–182 (here 177), Thomas Luckmann speaks of a "sacralization of subjectivity." We should consider whether "sacralization," which in fact assumes openness to others, is the right word. In any event, the text above is not working with the distinction between sacred and profane but with that between transcendent and immanent.

81. On this, see Brian Massumi, "The Autonomy of Affect," *Cultural Critique* 31 (1995): 83–109.

82. In our culture, which tends to understand situations in which something is narrated according to the model of written texts, it is difficult to make this comprehensible. See, inter alia, Dennis Tedlok, *The Spoken Word and the Work of Interpretation* (Philadelphia, 1983).

83. For an approach from the viewpoint of externalization, see Edmund Leach, *Culture and Communication: The Logic by Which Symbols Are Connected* (London, 1976), 37ff.

CHAPTER 3: THE FUNCTION OF RELIGION

1. See Alois Hahn, "Religiöse Wurzeln des Zivilisationsprozesses," in *Kultur im Zeitalter der Sozialwissenschaften: Friedrich H. Tenbruck zum 65. Geburtstag*, ed. Hans Braun and Alois Hahn (Berlin, 1984), 229–250.

2. For an example of such exceptions, see the critique of the notion of differ-

entiation in Charles Tilly, *Big Structures, Large Processes, Huge Comparisons* (New York, 1984).

3. Specifically, this can be done by excluding the superfluous and by integrating the necessary. See St. Thomas Aquinas, *Summa Theologiae* I–IIae q. 91, a. 2: "For nature neither lacks of necessary things nor abounds in the superfluous."

4. *Here*, incidentally, as so often, seeking to do both *simultaneously* can be disastrous: think of Mister Pief falling in the pond when he tries to walk and look through his telescope at the same time in Wilhelm Busch's *Plisch und Plum* (see http://gutenberg.spiegel.de/buch/4189/27 [accessed June 16, 2012]).

5. The classic work normally cited in sociology is Robert K. Merton, *Social Theory and Social Structure*, 2nd ed. (Glencoe, IL, 1957), 60ff. The Marx-Freud genealogy is fairly obvious. Research has thus taken a tack that unavoidably restricts it to the question of ignorance. This leads among other things to a bracketing out of the problem of the foundational intransparency of all systems, as well as the problem of the blind spot in all observation.

6. As justifiably noted by Robert Spaemann, "Funktionale Religionsbegründung und Religion," in *Die religiöse Dimension der Gesellschaft*, ed. Peter Koslowski (Tübingen, 1985), 9–25.

7. For an explicit critique, see, e.g., Richard K. Fenn, "Toward a New Sociology of Religion," *Journal for the Scientific Study of Religion* 11 (1972): 16–32. On the other hand, Fenn remains indebted to the idea when he can no longer perceive this function. He thus assigns a loss of function to religion, reducing it to residual functions. For an analysis of Durkheim's thesis that is nearly functional, see also Horst Firsching, "Die Sakralisierung der Gesellschaft: Emile Durkheims Soziologie der 'Moral' und der 'Religion' in der ideenpolitischen Auseinandersetzung der Dritten Republik," in *Religionssoziologie um 1900*, ed. Volkhard Krech and Hartmann Tyrell (Würzburg, 1975), 159–193.

8. See René Girard, *La violence et le sacré* (Paris, 1972); *Des choses cachées depuis la fondation du monde* (Paris, 1978); and *Le bouc émissaire* (Paris, 1982).

9. "Religion is just man seeking to know the basis of his dependency," we are told in Hegel's *Vorlesungen über die Philosophie der Religion I*, vol. 16 (Frankfurt, 1969), 308.

10. Aristotle *Metaphysics* 4.1006a19–24.

11. Edmund Husserl, *Ideen zu einer reinen Phänomologie und phänomenologischen Philosophie* (1913; The Hague, 1950), 3: 100–101 (Husserl's emphasis).

12. On this, see Elena Esposito, *L'operazione di osservazione: Costruttivismo e teoria dei sistemi* (Milan, 1992).

13. Recall here Durkheim's linking of *sanction* and *sacré* (which also explains why Durkheim's ideas still require theoretical elucidation).

14. See chapter 2 in this volume.

15. Erving Goffman, *Frame Analysis: An Essay on the Organization of Experience* (New York, 1974).

16. One may share the view of Gotthard Günther that more than two logical values are necessary to represent such circumstances. Or we can conclude that realizing such circumstances requires time and cannot assure any determinable relationship to the (always simultaneous functioning) world. But such thoughts only raise additional questions, which then disappear into the unanswerable.

17. With reference to the situation in the former German Democratic Republic (GDR), see Detlef Pollack, "Kirche in der Organisationsgesellschaft: Zum Wandel der gesellschaftlichen Lage der evangelischen Kirchen und der politisch alternativen Gruppen in der DDR" (habilitation thesis, Bielefeld, 1993), 107ff.

18. See, e.g., the recourse to Torah at the end of a discussion on the paradox of self-amendment (the constitutional rule on changes to a constitution) in David R. Dow, "When Words Mean What We Believe They Say: The Case of Article V," *Iowa Law Review* 76 (1990): 1–66 (62–63). The point is that a paradox can be condoned—one just has to refer to the Torah.

19. For more detail, see Niklas Luhmann, *Funktion der Religion* (Frankfurt, 1977), 225ff. Discussion of secularization has long been dominated by skeptical distance, attempts to form a multidimensional idea, all the way to outright rejection of the idea as unusable. We shall return to this subject in chapter 8.

20. See here Thomas Luckmann, "Über die Funktion der Religion," in *Die religiöse Dimension der Gesellschaft*, ed. Peter Koslowski (Tübingen, 1985), 26–41. A more precise elaboration is needed than Luckmann's, which defines the function of religion simply as the socialization of dealing with (great) transcendence.

21. For the case of Mesopotamia, see Gerdien Jonker, *The Topography of Remembrance: The Dead, Tradition and Collective Memory in Mesopotamia* (Leiden, 1995), 177ff.

22. On this, for Mesopotamia, see ibid., 180–81.

23. On this, see esp. John G. Gunnell, *Political Philosophy and Time* (Middletown, CT, 1968); Hartmut Gese, "Geschichtliches Denken im Alten Orient und im Alten Testament," *Zeitschrift für Theologie und Kirche* 55 (1958): 127–145.

24. Girard, *Des choses cachées* and *Bouc émissaire*.

25. Pierre Bourdieu, *La Distinction: Critique sociale du jugement* (Paris, 1979).

26. "Only *those* questions that are in principle undecidable, *we* can decide," is what we read in Heinz von Foerster, "Ethics and Second-Order Cybernetics," *Cybernetics and Human Knowing* 1 (1992): 9–19 (14).

27. For a parallel thought in systems theory, see W. Ross Ashby, "Principles of the Self-Organizing System," in *Principles of Self-Organization*, ed. Heinz von Foerster and George W. Zopf (New York, 1962), 155–178; reprinted in *Modern System Research for the Behavioral Scientist: A Sourcebook*, ed. Walter Buckley (Chicago, 1968), 108–118.

28. We shall come back to this point in chapter 9, on the religious system's self-descriptions.

29. For a refreshing approach to what follows, see Ronald W. Hepburn, *Chris-*

tianity and Paradox: Critical Studies in Twentieth-Century Theology (New York, 1968). This analysis, however, lists the thematic categories as paradigms and limits itself to demonstrating their immanent paradoxes, without including a systematic viewpoint of classifying them according to dimensions of meaning. For that approach, see Niklas Luhmann, *Soziale Systeme: Grundriß einer allgemeinen Theorie* (Frankfurt, 1984), 111ff.

30. Hepburn, *Christianity and Paradox*, 69ff., speaks here of the paradox of a "logical construction of God" on the basis of available sense data.

31. In the Hebraic context, the text given at Mount Sinai, the Torah, is at the same time the plan of creation that already existed prior to creation. In the social context, it is the law accepted by God's people (and not an unquestioned heavenly code). And apart from that (and this too is paradoxical), this law has to be accepted precisely because the paradise of natural distinctions has become inaccessible through sin and has to be replaced by reflection, as called for by freedom.

32. A mundane interpretation would be that Jesus is trying to win time without being seen by the others. Or that he is mystifying the situation to heighten tension and so as to be able to offer his words as liberating.

33. See George Spencer-Brown, *Laws of Form* (1969), new ed. (New York, 1979).

34. Organizationally, there are other options, in particular, hierarchy and exclusion (masterfully handled by the Catholic Church), but it is predictably difficult to maintain that the result of using such organizational options is still "religion."

35. See Georg Simmel, *Die Religion* (Frankfurt, 1906); Thomas Luckmann, *The Invisible Religion* (London, 1967).

36. On this, see Heinz Schlaffer, *Poesie und Wissen: Die Entstehung des ästhetischen Bewußtseins und der philologischen Erkenntnis* (Frankfurt, 1990), 11–88.

37. See, however, Bryan Wilson, "Secularization: The Inherited Model," in *The Sacred in a Secular Age: Toward Revision in the Scientific Study of Religion*, ed. Phillip E. Hammond (Berkeley, CA, 1985), 9–20 (here 14–15).

38. See chapter 8 in this volume.

39. Clearly, it was different in a primarily agrarian economy, involving land and not liquid capital. And even back then, the administration of Church capital by Florentine banks led to considerable problems that could not be solved in a "pious" manner.

CHAPTER 4: THE CONTINGENCY FORMULA "GOD"

1. See Niklas Luhmann, *Die Wirtschaft der Gesellschaft* (Frankfurt, 1988), esp. 177ff.

2. For an early comparison of politics and religion from a similar standpoint, see Hans Kelsen, "Gott und Staat," *Logos* 11 (1923): 261–284, and as a "refutation," Wenzel Pohl, "Kelsen's Parallele: Gott und Staat: Kritische Bemerkungen eines Theologen," *Zeitschrift für öffentliches Recht* 4 (1925): 571–609.

3. See Helmut Willke, *Ironie des Staates: Grundlinien einer Staatstheorie polyzentrischer Gesellschaft* (Frankfurt, 1992), 35ff.

4. See Niklas Luhmann and Karl Eberhard Schorr, *Reflexionsprobleme im Erziehungssystem*, 2nd ed. (Frankfurt, 1983), 58ff.

5. See Niklas Luhmann, *Die Wissenschaft der Gesellschaft* (Frankfurt, 1990), 392ff.

6. See Niklas Luhmann, *Das Recht der Gesellschaft* (Frankfurt, 1993), 214ff.

7. See Francisco J.Varela and Evan Thompson, *Der Mittlere Weg der Erkenntnis: Die Beziehung von Ich und Welt in der Kognitionswissenschaft* (Bern, 1992).

8. On this, see Burkhard Gladigow, "Der Sinn der Götter: Zum kognitiven Potential der persönlichen Gottesvorstellung," in *Gottesvorstellung und Gesellschaftsentwicklung*, ed. Peter Eicher (Munich, 1979), 41–62.

9. See here Gilles Deleuze, *Logique du sens* (Paris, 1969).

10. See here Niklas Luhmann, "Inklusion und Exklusion," *Soziologische Aufklärung* 6 (Opladen, 1995): 237–264.

11. For a detailed discussion, see *L'argomento ontologico*, ed. Marco M. Olivetti (Padua, 1990).

12. The problem of standardizing and impoverishing this ultimate referent continues to exist in spite of all the richness of cosmological elaborations and moralistic casuistry, and it is reinforced by the organized use of forms. On this, see Jean-Pierre Decouchy, *L'orthodoxie religieuse: Essai de logique psycho-sociale* (Paris, 1971), esp. 57ff. See also *L'analyse du langage théologique: Le nom de Dieu*, ed. Enrico Castelli (Paris, 1969).

13. The category of emanation had the logical advantage that nothing historically new was planned. It could therefore deal with time in a "time-abstract" way, as it were—or, put differently, as though seen from the perspective of omnipresence. It did not have to count on a momentary present in which solely a difference between past and present could be observed or effectuated. That is why it also did not have to break the frame of classical binary logic. On this, see Gotthard Günther, "Logik, Zeit, Emanation und Evolution," in *Beiträge zur Grundlegung einer operationsfähigen Dialektik* (Hamburg, 1980), 3: 95–135 (with a structural-theoretically more complex idea of emanation).

14. Arthur O. Lovejoy, *The Great Chain of Being: A Study of the History of an Idea* (1936; Cambridge, MA, 1950), 49; on the problem of sterility, see 43ff.

15. See Gotthard Günther, "Cognition and Violence: A Contribution to a Cybernetic Theory of Subjectivity," in *Beiträge zur Grundlegung einer operationsfähigen Dialektik* (Hamburg, 1979), 2: 203–240. I have not modified Günther's presentation significantly here.

16. By contrast, it will lead to very deep theological doubts about our ability to perceive divine criteria if one continues to uphold the *primacy* of the power of will, the *potentia absoluta* of God (as in late medieval voluntarism) and if one also accepts (as in nominalism) that every reality is only given in the form of individu-

als and not in the form of universals. God's will is not guided by rules and his access to individuals does not allow us to draw conclusions about how he operates in other cases. In such preliminary matters, theology starts by such an admission of weaknesses in perception—an old reservation predominant in the divination practice of early Mesopotamia—and has to shift to a fundamental inability to perceive God's mode of observation. It must then be consistent and retreat from giving any advice about life, instead appealing only to the self-affirmation of faith by individuals.

17. That only *men* are being thought of is almost self-evident, yet clear evidence can also be found for the claim. See Sir Thomas Browne, *Religio Medici* (1643; repr., London, 1965), 79: "The whole World was made for man, but the twelfth part of man for woman. Man is the whole World and the Breath of God, Woman the Rib and the crooked piece of it."

18. Benjamin Nelson, in particular, has indicated the specifically religious grounds for the unreasonable demand that science limit itself to hypotheses, which science in its own interest had to contradict by appealing to the possibility of *natural* knowledge of *nature*. See Nelson, "The Quest for Certitude and the Books of Scripture, Nature, and Conscience," in *The Nature of Scientific Discovery*, ed. Owen Gingerich (Washington, DC, 1975), 335–372; id., "Copernicus and the Quest for Certitude: 'East' and 'West,'" in *Copernicus Yesterday and Today: Proceedings*, ed. Arthur Beer and K. A. Strand, Vistas in Astronomy 17 (New York, 1975), 39–46. See also the contributions in Benjamin Nelson, *Der Ursprung der Moderne: Vergleichende Studien zum Zivilisationsprozeß* (Frankfurt, 1977).

19. See, e.g., Jean Paul, "Das Kampaner Tal oder über die Unsterblichkeit der Seele," in *Jean Pauls Werke: Auswahl in zwei Bänden* (Stuttgart, 1924), 2: 170–229.

20. See, e.g., in the form of a critique of Spinoza and Hegel, Jacques Derrida, *De la Grammatologie* (Paris, 1967), trans. Gayatri Chakravorty Spivak as *Of Grammatology* (Baltimore, 1976), 71ff.

21. From the period of the Counter-Reformation, see Gregorio Comanini, "Il Figino overo del fine della pintura," in *Trattati d'arte del cinquecento*, ed. Paola Barocchi (1591; repr., Bari, 1962), 3: 239–379. The starting point is associated with Plato (*Sophist* 236) in a universalizing of the principle of imitation by an internal paradox: there are imitations of things that exist (*imitazione icastica*) and imitations of things that do not exist (*imitazione fantastica*). The image of God thus has to be brought onto the side of *imitazione icastica* even though God has no form, as the theologians assure us.

22. See, e.g., Nicolas of Cusa, "De Deo Abscondito," in id., *Philosophisch-theologische Schriften* (Vienna, 1964), 1: 299–309 (here 304), in addition to many other passages.

23. Material on the development of this problem can be found, e.g., in research on Duns Scotus. See Karl Heim, *Das Gewißheitsproblem in der systematischen Theologie bis zu Schleiermacher* (Leipzig, 1911), 181ff.

Notes to Chapter 4

24. For many instances in African religions, see John S. Mbiti, *Concepts of God in Africa* (London, 1970).

25. But there are indeed suggestions of this, above all in Sufi mysticism. An easily accessible treatment is Peter J. Awn, *Satan's Tragedy and Redemption: Iblis in Sufi Psychology* (Leiden, 1983). In the area of Christianity, there is the idea of punishment as proof of God's love, but as far as I can see, it does not refer to the devil as the most beloved angel. See, e.g., "whomever God loves, He corrects and castigates" as a way to indoctrinate princes, not to doubt their faith, in Joannes Jovianus Pontano, *De principe*, quoted in *Opera omnia* (Basel, 1556), 1: 256–283 (here 261).

26. That is what the archangel says in Mark Twain's *Letters from the Earth* (New York, 1962).

27. Banished to earth, Satan reports upward (ibid.).

28. See, e.g., Nicolas of Cusa, "De visione Dei," in id., *Philosophisch-theologische Schriften* (Vienna, 1967), 3: 93–219, with the metaphor of the image that looks at the observer from wherever he may be looking at it.

29. What follows from this is that divinatory religions cannot distinguish in the end between space and time. Religions of revelation, by comparison, can free time from spatial connotations.

30. It should only be mentioned as a precaution that this is a *modern* conclusion, which presupposes a functional differentiation of society and thus the abandonment of a consistent religious ontology.

31. This thought should not, however, compel us to accept the widespread opposition of cyclical (mythical) and linear (historical) time, which in the case of Babylon is a historical fiction and can probably only to be explained as Christian apologetics against comparisons of "Bible and Babel." For a critique, see Jonathan Z. Smith, "A Slip in Time Save Nine: Prestigious Origins Again," in *Chronotopes: The Construction of Time*, ed. John Bender and David E. Wellbery (Stanford, CA, 1991), 67–76 (69ff.).

32. See here, e.g., Peter Eicher, " 'Offenbarungsreligion': Zum sozio-kulturellen Stellenwert eines theologischen Grundkonzepts," in *Gottesvorstellung und Gesellschaftsentwicklung*, ed. Peter Eicher (Munich, 1979), 109–129.

33. Only in this way (and this was why it is done) can the revelatory text be concurrently understood as a *legal text* that is supposed to be valid *for all times* and thus open to interpretation.

34. See chapter 2, § VII, in this volume.

35. Edward Reynolds, *A Treatise of the Passions and Faculties of the Soule of Man* (1640; repr., Gainesville, FL, 1971), 462.

36. Ibid., 497ff.

37. See Thomas Wright, *The Passions of the Minde in Generall*, expanded ed. (1601; repr., Urbana, IL, 1971).

38. See Aron Ronald Bodenheimer, *Warum? Von der Obszönität des Fragens*, 2nd ed. (Stuttgart, 1985).

39. On this issue, see Henri Atlan, *A tort et à la raison: Intercritique de la science et du mythe* (Paris, 1986).

40. On the inviolability of faith in the "Doctrines of our Holy Church, as by Law Establish'd," see Anthony Ashley Cooper, earl of Shaftesbury, *Characteristicks of Men, Manners, Opinions, Times*, 2nd ed. (1714; repr., Farnborough, Hants, UK, 1968), 3: 316 passim.

41. In theoretical terms, this assumes that the problem is shifted to modal theory, that there are no longer the old schematisms of logic (true/false) and causality (cause/effect). This enabled the new science of physics to be released from its theological implications. Science may then decide whether physics is true or not and how the causes and effects fit together here independently of assumptions about the origin of the world.

42. For more detail, see chapter 8, § VII, in this volume.

43. See G. W. F. Hegel, *Vorlesungen über die Philosophie der Religion* (I and II), in *Werke*, vols. 16 and 17 (Frankfurt, 1969). On historicization as a sign of the declining significance of dogmas, see esp. pt. I in 16: 47ff.

44. This has been done with a great deal of methodological care. For (randomly selected) examples, see Godelier Vercruysse, "The Meaning of God: A Factor-Analytic Study," *Social Compass* 19 (1972): 347–364; and Mark van Aerde, "The Attitude of Adults Toward God," *Social Compass* 19 (1972): 407–413.

45. This is the conclusion in Konstantin Kolenda, "Thinking the Unthinkable: Logical Conflicts in the Traditional Concept of God," *Journal for the Scientific Study of Religion* 8 (1969): 72–78. To continue in this vein: instead of speaking paradoxically and incomprehensibly, one should instead make sure there are parking places near the church.

46. Based on George P. Murdock, *Ethnographic Atlas* (Pittsburgh, 1967), see Ralph Underhill, "Economic and Political Antecedents of Monotheism: A Cross-Cultural Study," *American Journal of Sociology* 80 (1975): 841–861. He arrives at the result that only 25 percent of societies studied are familiar with a high god interested in the morality of humans; 36 percent do not know any high god; and the remaining societies know one (active or inactive) who is not, however, concerned with human morality. The material suggests that the state of economic development makes a difference in such contexts, and it is indeed plausible that religious guarantees of morality are more necessary when a society has to cope with property distinctions, contractual relations, uncertainty about the future, etc.

47. One indicator of this is the question of whether or not social conduct in one's lifetime has an effect on one's destiny after death. These connections are not found until the rise of the major religions. On this, see Christoph von Fürer-Haimendorf, "The After-Life in Indian Tribal Belief," *Journal of the Royal Anthropological Institute* 83 (1953): 37–49; id., *Morals and Merits: A Study of Values and Social Controls in South Asia Societies* (London, 1967); Gananath Obeyesekere, "Theodicy, Sin and Salvation in a Sociology of Buddhism, *Dialectic in Practical*

Religion, ed. Edmund R. Leach (Cambridge, 1968), 7–40 (especially 14–15). See Mbiti, *Concepts of God*, 253ff., on African religions that (with few exceptions) also do not anticipate a settling of sins or fate in life in the other world, and thus expect no judgment in the hereafter, but at most difficulties in transitioning to the realm of the dead. In principle, the powers of the other world punish and reward us in this world.

48. See Fürer-Haimendorf, *Morals and Merits*, esp. 126ff.

49. Monica Wilson sees in this nonetheless an argument that relationships exist between religion and morality; id., *Religion and the Transformation of Society: A Study of Social Change in Africa* (Cambridge, 1971), 76ff.

50. See Mbiti, *Concepts of God*, 16–17, *passim*.

51. See, e.g., Michel de Certeau, "Du système religieux à l'éthique des Lumières (17e–18e s.): La formalité des pratiques," *Ricerche di storia sociale e religiosa* 1, no. 2 (1972): 31–94.

52. Plentiful evidence of a deity in early Israel who is not yet fully disciplined by ethics can be found in Johannes Hempel, *Geschichte und Geschichten im Alten Testament bis zur persischen Zeit* (Gütersloh, 1964).

53. One of the rather puzzling, but illuminating, refinements of theological history is that *this* knowledge was originally prohibited and could only be regained by sin. Clearly, God resolves this moral paradox by a positive value, humanity by a negative one. For God it is good, and for man bad, to let oneself be oriented by the difference of good and bad, since that way man ends up in opposition to himself and then has to (first) be rehumanized by a prolonged history of redemption.

54. This is more understandable if one replaces God with the reading public, like Rousseau in his *Confessions* (1.3). See also Henry Adams, who writes "that the Eternal Father himself may not feel unmixed pleasure at our thrusting under his eyes chiefly the least agreeable details of his creation" (*The Education of Henry Adams* [1907; Boston, 1918], ix).

55. See Arthur O. Lovejoy, "Milton and the Paradox of the Fortunate Fall" (1937), in *Essays in the History of Ideas* (Baltimore, 1948), 277–295, with references to older sources; see Herbert Weisinger, *Tragedy and the Paradox of the Fortunate Fall* (London, 1953); further, see several contributions in *Text und Applikation: Poetik und Hermeneutik* 9 (Munich, 1981), esp. Odo Marquard, "Felix culpa?— Bemerkungen zu einem Applikationsschicksal von Genesis 3," 53–71.

56. For a long preliminary discussion, see Sven K. Knebel, "Necessitas moralis ad optimum: Zum historischen Hintergrund der Wahl der besten aller Welten," *Studia Leibnitiana* 23 (1991): 3–24.

57. See Anthony Ashley Cooper, earl of Shaftesbury, "A Letter Concerning Enthusiasm" (1708), in *Characteristicks of Men, Manners, Opinions, Times*, 1: 3–55; Ronald A. Knox, *Enthusiasm: A Chapter in the History of Religion with Special Reference to the Seventeenth and Eighteenth Centuries* (Oxford, 1950); Susie I. Tucker, *Enthusiasm: A Study in Semantic Change* (Cambridge, 1972); John Passmore, "En-

thusiasm, Fanatism and David Hume," in *The "Science of Man" in the Scottish En-lightenment: Hume, Reid and Their Contemporaries*, ed. Peter Jones (Edinburgh, 1989), 85–107; and Robert Spaemann, " 'Fanatisch' und 'Fanatismus,'" *Archiv für Begriffsgeschichte* 15 (1970): 256–274.

58. "Non-trivial machines" is meant in the sense of Heinz von Foerster, *Wissen und Gewissen: Versuch einer Brücke* (Frankfurt, 1993), 244ff.

59. See Niklas Luhmann, "Soziologie der Moral," in *Theorientechnik und Moral*, ed. Niklas Luhmann and Stephan Pfürtner (Frankfurt, 1978), 8–116. Also see Niklas Luhmann, "The Code of the Moral," *Cardozo Law Review* 14 (1993): 995–1009; and id., "The Sociology of the Moral and Ethics," *International Sociology* 11 (1996): 27–36.

60. Only since the second half of the eighteenth century have there been pro-posals for religion-free solutions to this problem. These have not been very con-vincing—whether calling for endowing the subject with "practical reason" (Kant), or whether applying a discursive ethics that bets on future results of communica-tion set up according to rational criteria (Habermas). Both proposals are based on a comprehensible rearrangement of external to internal reference—self-reference of consciousness or of the societal system.

61. This literature of justification is endless. On the early history, see, e.g., Johann Jakob Stamm, *Das Leiden des Unschuldigen in Babylon und Israel* (Zurich, 1946); William Green, *Moira: Fate, Good and Evil in Greek Thought* (Cambridge, MA, 1944). For a comparison with a balancing of welfare from the standpoint of resymmetrization, see Georg Katkov, *Untersuchungen zur Werttheorie und Theo-dizee* (Brünn, 1937).

62. This notion stems from Tertullian and later St. Anselm of Canterbury. See Victor Naumann, "Das Problem des Bösen in Tertullians zweitem Buch gegen Marcion: Ein Beitrag zur Theodizee Tertullians," *Zeitschrift für katholische Theolo-gie* 58 (1934): 311–363, 533–551.

63. In a kind of refinement of outdoing others, it can then become the devil's goal to prevent humans from sinning because the ensuing repentance is the greater accomplishment. This is in any event the case with Islam with respect to viola-tions of ritual.

64. See Jean Pierre de Crousaz, *Traité de l'éducation des enfants* (The Hague, 1772), 2: 192ff.

65. The attempt even precedes the eighteenth century. Sir Thomas Browne, *Religio Medici*, 56ff., contends that hell is in the person feeling contrition. It is not necessary for faith itself. God does not punish (and yet Browne is plagued by concern for the state of the pagan philosophers, who had to die without faith in Christ!). Bishop Paley, over a hundred years later, dismisses talk of the torments of hell as "figurative speech," but reasons that it actually serves to evoke the torments of the lost soul (!) before they have begun. See William Paley, "Sermon XXXI: The Terrors of the Lord," in *The Works* (London, 1897), 700–702. The Jesuits also ac-

cepted that transcendence comes into play only after death but can no longer be corrected after that; they thus specialize in the practice of calculation and warning. See, e.g., Juan Eusebio Nieremberg, *La balance du temps et de l'eternité* (French trans., Le Mans, 1676). See, in particular, "Le temps est l'occasion de l'Eternité" (100ff.), which means that a lifetime is the opportunity to decide for eternity, specifically at every moment in life since one may *always* die at *any time*.

66. On the term "polemogenous," see Julien Freund, "Le droit comme motif et solution des conflits," in *Die Funktionen des Rechts: Vorträge des Weltkongresses für Rechts- und Sozialphilosophie* (Wiesbaden, 1974), 47–62; id., *Sociologie du conflit* (Paris, 1983), 22, 327ff.

67. The best known example of a society that was integrated religiously chiefly by differentiating purity from impurity is the Indian caste system; see Louis Dumont, *Homo Hierarchicus: The Caste System and Its Implications* (London, 1970). In Europe, one finds a clearly moral definition of nobility that, besides serving to emphasize the criteria of birth, also distinguishes itself from what is below. At this same time, this order is extended with other catalogues of duty [*Pflichtkatalogen*] down to the bottom, to the point of demarcating "dishonest" professions and people (with explicit associations of "impurity").

68. In the area of theory, this becomes paradigmatically clear in the thought of Adam Smith between *The Theory of Moral Sentiments* (1759) and *Wealth of Nations* (1776). The result, with regard to shoes, is that Smith trusts his ability to pay more than the morals of the shoemaker.

69. For an example, see Niklas Luhmann, "Die Ehrlichkeit der Politik und die höhere Amoralität der Politik," in *Opfer der Macht: Müssen Politiker ehrlich sein?* ed. Peter Kemper (Frankfurt, 1993), 27–41. See also id., "Politik, Demokratie, Moral," in *Normen, Ethik und Gesellschaft*, ed. Konferenz der deutschen Akademic der Wissenschaften (Mainz, 1997), 17–39.

70. See here Niklas Luhmann, *Beobachtungen der Moderne* (Opladen, 1992).

71. Jacques Derrida, *Positions* (Paris, 1972; English trans., Chicago, 1981), 64 (82?). I am citing the English translation because of the special rigorousness of the English term "must."

72. The art theory of the Renaissance refers to this distinction when understanding the principle of imitation not as merely copying what exists but as making visible ideal forms as these exist in the minds of angels. See Federico Zuccaro, *L'idea de' pittori, scultori ed architetti* (Turin, 1607), in *Scritti d'arte di Federico Zuccaro*, ed. Detlef Heikamp (Florence, 1961), 159.

CHAPTER 5: THE DIFFERENTIATION OF RELIGIOUS COMMUNICATION

1. On the transition and the establishment of a field of ritualistically limited communication, see Mary Douglas, *Natural Symbols: Explorations in Cosmology* (London, 1970).

2. On quasi-objects as functional equivalents for social contracts, see Michel Serres, *Genèse* (Paris, 1982), 146ff.

3. On the "body as social medium," see Douglas, *Natural Symbols*, 65ff. See also Roy A. Rappaport, *Ecology, Meaning, and Religion* (Richmond, CA, 1979), 126, 173ff.

4. See Friederike Hassauer, *"Santiago"—Schrift, Körper, Raum, Reise: Eine medien-theoretische Rekonstruktion* (Munich, 1993).

5. See here Anthony F. C. Wallace, *Religion: An Anthropological View* (New York, 1966), 233ff.

6. See *Myth, Ritual, and Kingship*, ed. Samuel H. Hooke (Oxford, 1958). See also Wallace, *Religion*, 106ff.

7. This is the claim of Victor W. Turner, "Myth and Symbol," in *International Encyclopedia of the Social Sciences* (Chicago, 1968), 10: 576–582.

8. No longer *aoidos* [bard] but *poiētēs* [maker].

9. That also changed in the case of the Greek tragedies, specifically as a result of writing. A binding performance version of the text was preserved in the city offices and used as a criterion of correct portrayals.

10. In African religions, there is pervasive use of the dead for this function, in which those who have passed away can reach their ancestors and they in turn can reach God. See John S. Mbiti, *Concepts of God in Africa* (London, 1970), esp. 230ff., 267ff.

11. Here as well, the spectrum of transitional forms is very broad. There is, e.g., the state of being possessed by spirits (trance) and the well-known disposition (which might be inherited) of certain people to such states. And, related to that, there is the interpretive need that results from confused statements or physical appearances and that calls for special experts all the way to the difficult questions of authentic or inauthentic stigmata, which can only be resolved in the Vatican.

12. On this term, see Heinz von Foerster, *Observing Systems* (Seaside, CA, 1981), 304ff.

13. Here I am following a suggestion by Talcott Parsons that evolution be described in terms of the variables of adaptive upgrading, differentiation, inclusion, and value generalization. See, e.g., Parsons, *The System of Modern Societies* (Englewood Cliffs, NJ, 1971), 11, 26ff.

14. See Alois Hahn, "Unendliches Ende: Höllenvorstellung in soziologischer Perspektive," in *Das Ende: Figuren einer Denkform*, ed. Karlheinz Stierle and Rainer Warning (Munich, 1996), 155–182.

15. It should clearly not be overlooked that the notion of a synallagmatic [reciprocally binding] contract, which also determines how mistakes and impossibilities are dealt with, is a legal invention of Roman civil law that emerges much later.

16. For more detail, see Niklas Luhmann, *Soziale Systeme: Grundriß einer allgemeinen Theorie* (Frankfurt, 1984).

17. See Niklas Luhmann, "Anfang und Ende: Probleme einer Unterscheidung," in *Zwischen Anfang und Ende: Fragen an die Pädagogik*, ed. Niklas Luhmann and Karl Eberhard Schorr (Frankfurt, 1990), 11–23.

18. See Jürgen Habermas, *Theorie des kommunikativen Handelns*, 2 vols. (Frankfurt, 1981).

19. See Elena Esposito, "Interaktion, Interaktivität und Personalisierung der Massenmedien," *Soziale Systeme* 1 (1995): 225–260.

20. On the mutual effects at the start of both these innovations in the form of Greek tyranny, see Peter N. Ure, *The Origin of Tyranny* (Cambridge, 1922).

21. See G. E. R. Lloyd, *Magic, Reason and Experience: Studies in the Origin and Development of Greek Science* (Cambridge, 1979) on this, and on the long symbiosis of science and magic going back to the seventeenth century.

22. See the short overview in Niklas Luhmann, "Einführende Bemerkungen zu einer Theorie symbolisch generalisierter Kommunikationsmedien," *Soziologische Aufklärung* 2 (Opladen, 1975): 170–192; on individual media, see id., *Die Politik der Gesellschaft* (Frankfurt, 2000), 18ff.; id., *Liebe als Passion: Zur Codierung von Intimität* (Frankfurt, 1982); id., *Die Wirtschaft der Gesellschaft* (Frankfurt, 1988), 230ff.; id., *Die Wissenschaft der Gesellschaft* (Frankfurt, 1990), 167ff.

23. See on this Walter J. Ong, *The Presence of the Word: Some Prolegomena for Cultural and Religious History* (New Haven, CT, 1967); id., "Communications Media and the State of Theology," *Cross Currents* 19 (1969): 462–480.

24. I am borrowing this formulation from Arthur C. Danto, *The Philosophical Disenfranchisement of Art* (New York, 1986), 55.

25. To some extent, this problem is found in the popular belief in "heavenly letters" and in the numerous visionary manifestations in the Middle Ages, the authenticity of which had to be settled by Church policy.

26. For details, see the references to the literature provided in n. 22 above.

27. For more detail, see Niklas Luhmann, "Das Medium der Religion: Eine soziologische Betrachtung über Gott und die Seelen" (MS, 1994).

28. See again Hahn, "Unendliches Ende."

29. On this point, see Niklas Luhmann, "The Paradox of System Differentiation and the Evolution of Society," in *Differentiation Theory and Social Change: Comparative and Historical Perspectives*, ed. Jeffrey C. Alexander and Paul Colomy (New York, 1990), 409–440.

30. Such a before/after depiction simplifies a great deal, of course. In the history of society, a kind of dual system is very often found with religious and political-military notables—an early case of the structural coupling of subsystems and simultaneously a form in which stratificatory or center/periphery differentiation of the societal system can be strengthened.

31. The social sciences, which are always interested in history, have in particular been misled by this misunderstanding and have never really worked with an evolutionary theory, despite all the oscillating between structuralism, functional-

ism, and evolutionism. This is a point made by Marion Blute, "Sociocultural Evolutionism: An Untried Theory," *Behavioral Science* 24 (1979): 46–59.

32. See the formulation "selective retention" in one of the most impressive attempts to convey Darwinistic theoretical designs to the social sciences, in Donald T. Campbell, "Variation and Selective Retention in Socio-Cultural Evolution," *General Systems* 14 (1969): 69–85.

33. See Roy A. Rappaport, "Maladaptation in Social Systems," in *The Evolution of Social Systems*, ed. J. Friedman and M. J. Rowlands (Pittsburgh, 1978), 49–71.

34. On changes under a communist regime that merely copy the old clan structures into work organizations, without achieving individual behavior susceptible to direct intervention by changes in the legal , economic, and the political systems, see, however, Li Hanlin, *Die Grundstrukturen der chinesischen Gesellschaft: Vom traditionellen Clansystem zur modernen Danwei-Organisation* (Opladen, 1991).

35. For comparative study in the modern period, it is useful to look at African religions, since in traditional Africa we find both the development of kingdoms and a continuation of "stateless" tribal cultures.

36. See the overview of the research in Robert Wuthnow, "Science and the Sacred," in *The Sacred in a Secular Age: Toward Revision in the Scientific Study of Religion*, ed. Phillip E. Hammond (Berkeley, CA, 1985), 187–203. Beyond that, it may be that the contrast is more distinct in the United States, with its relatively high average religiosity (whatever these statistical values are saying).

37. Wuthnow, ibid., also draws this conclusion from the fact that social scientists' distance from religion is greater than that of natural scientists, who have at their disposal a guaranteed paradigm and a highly consensual knowledge of research and who more than the social scientists can afford to be religious. And precisely sociologists like Max Weber who have conducted research on religion been careful to make it clear that they are not interested in the subject for religious reasons.

38. See, e.g., the results of a conference on evolutionary theory inspired and introduced by Cardinal Franz König, published in *Evolution und Menschenbild*, ed. Rupert J. Riedl and Franz Kreuzer (Hamburg, 1983), or along these lines, the activities of the Forum St. Stephanus in Vienna.

39. The (now) standard monograph on this is Hans Belting, *Bild und Kult: Eine Geschichte des Bildes vor dem Zeitalter der Kunst* (Munich, 1990).

40. See August Buck, "Aus der Vorgeschichte der Querelle des Anciens et des Modernes in Mittelalter und Renaissance," in *Bibliothèque de l'Humanisme et de la Renaissance* 20 (1958): 527–541; id., *Die "Querelle des anciens et des moderne" im italienischen Selbstverständnis der Renaissance und des Barocks* (Wiesbaden, 1973); Elisabeth Goessmann, *Antiqui und Moderni im Mittelalter: Eine geschichtliche Standortbestimmung* (Munich, 1974).

41. For greater detail on this, see Baxter Hathaway, *Marvels and Commonplaces: Renaissance Literary Criticism* (New York, 1968).

42. Lodovico Antonio Muratori, *Della perfetta poesia italiana* (1706; Milan, 1971), 1: 104. And when one poet has this skill *more than others*, it is no longer understood as a divine gift (1: 217f.).

43. On this, see Stéphane Ngo Mai and Alain Raybaut, "Microdiversity and Macro-order: Toward a Self-Organization Approach," *Revue internationale de systémique* 10 (1996): 223–239.

CHAPTER 6: RELIGIOUS ORGANIZATIONS

1. See Englard, "Majority Decision vs. Individual Truth" (cited in chapter 2, n. 51, above) on the story of the Oven of Achnai in the Talmud.

2. See Niklas Luhmann, "Organisation," *Historisches Wörterbuch der Philosophie*, vol. 6 (Basel, 1984), cols. 1326–1328.

3. See Brian Tierney, *Foundations of the Conciliar Theory: The Contribution of the Medieval Canonists from Gratian to the Great Schism* (Cambridge, 1955); Ernst H. Kantorowicz, *The King's Two Bodies: A Study in Medieval Political Theology* (Princeton, NJ, 1957); Pierre Michaud-Quantin, *Universitas: Expressions du mouvement communautaire dans le Moyen âge latin* (Paris, 1970); Harold J. Berman, *Law and Revolution: The Formation of the Western Legal Tradition* (Cambridge, MA, 1983), trans. as *Recht und Revolution: Die Bildung der westlichen Rechtstradition* (Frankfurt, 1991), esp. 356ff.

4. On the growth of this problem and the increase in problems of Church organization (which for sociologists suggests a comparison with other organizations), there is now a great deal of literature available. See James A. Beckford, "Religious Organizations: A Trend Report and Bibliography," *Current Sociology* 21, no. 2 (1975): 1–170, and id., "Religious Organizations," in *The Sacred in a Secular Age: Toward Revision in the Scientific Study of Religion*, ed. Phillip E. Hammond (Berkeley, CA, 1985), 125–139.

5. This according to Chester I. Barnard, *The Functions of the Executive* (Cambridge, MA, 1938; 9th printing, 1951), 167ff.

6. The term "organization" is defined here based on suggestions by Herbert Simon, who originally spoke of "behavior premises," then later of "decision premises." See Herbert A. Simon, Donald W. Smithburg, and Victor A. Thompson, *Public Administration* (New York, 1950), 57ff.; Herbert A. Simon, *Models of Man—Social and Rational: Mathematical Essays on Rational Human Behavior in a Social Setting* (New York, 1957), 201.

7. Here see also Niklas Luhmann, "Organisation," in *Mikropolitik: Rationalität, Macht und Spiele in Organisationen*, ed. Willi Küpper and Günther Ortmann (Opladen, 1988): 165–185; id., *Die Gesellschaft und ihre Organisationen, Festschrift für Renate Mayntz* (Baden-Baden, 1964), 189–201; id., *Organisation und Entscheidung* (Opladen, 1990).

8. See, e.g., Talcott Parsons, "A Sociological Approach to the Theory of Organizations," in id., *Structure and Process in Modern Sciences* (New York, 1960), 16–58.

9. For more detail, see Niklas Luhmann, "Inklusion und Exklusion," *Soziologische Aufklärung* 6 (Opladen, 1995), 237–264.

10. Rather than signifying the organic and psychological processes that continually occur in societal environments, the term "individuals" [*Personen*] is used here (in connection with the traditional concept) as a kind of identity marker that can be used in communication to indicate a (particularly) opaque environmental complexity. See also Niklas Luhmann, "Die Form 'Person,'" in *Soziale Welt* 42 (1991): 166–175; id. "Die operative Geschlossenheit psychischer und sozialer Systeme," in *Das Ende der großen Entwürfe*, ed. Hans Rudi Fischer et al. (Frankfurt, 1992), 117–132; both articles can also be found in Luhmann, *Soziologische Aufklärung* 6.

11. Moreover, Jürgen Habermas's discourse theory comes down fully on the side of traditional liberal variants here, and not on that of ideological criticism. In a moral discourse that includes everyone, free and equal access is presumed to be a procedural condition. Tragically, it is not taken into account that under actual conditions, even this has an exclusionary aspect (even if this comes down to self-exclusion by many people). This applies all the more should such discourse, however improbably, lead to a reasonable consensus, when everyone who did not consent would be excluded as irrational.

12. This [i.e., absorbing uncertainty] is also a term proposed by Simon. See James G. March and Herbert A. Simon, *Organizations* (New York, 1958), 164ff.

13. The upshot of this, nonetheless, is that using internal structure is problematic for the treatment of uncertainty. On the issue, see Brian L. Loasby, *Choice, Complexity and Ignorance: An Enquiry into Economic Theory and the Practice of Decision-making* (Cambridge, 1976), esp. 151f.

14. In the sense of Francis Heylighten, "Causality as Distinction Conversation: A Theory of Predictability, Reversibility, and Time Order," *Cybernetics and Systems* 20 (1989): 361–384.

15. For examples, see Dschalaluddin Rumi, *Die Flucht nach Hindustan und andere Geschichten aus dem Matnawi*, ed. Gisela Wendt (Amsterdam, 1989). A more comprehensive version is *The Matnawi of Jalálu'ddín Rúmi*, ed. Reynold A. Nicholson, 8 vols. (Cambridge, 1925–1940), containing an English translation and commentaries.

16. For example, there is the doctrine of a revelation that is revealing itself as revelation. See also the specifically Judaic doctrine that the Torah is revealed as a text for written and for oral transmission, even though this latter teaching, not explicitly contained in the Torah, inserts itself into it.

17. See Niklas Luhmann, *Funktionen und Folgen formaler Organisation* (Berlin, 1964), 307–308, with further references.

18. See N. J. Demerath III and V. Thiessen, "On Spitting Against the Wind:

Organizational Precariousness and American Irreligion," *American Journal of Sociology* 71 (1966): 674–687.

19. Here see chiefly Thomas Luckmann, *The Invisible Religion* (London, 1967).

20. That is precisely why control [*Steuerung*], a specially directed activity, becomes problematic in broader sociological and political-scientific discussions. See Helmut Willke, *Ironie des Staates: Grundlinien einer Staatstheorie polyzentrischer Gesellschaft* (Frankfurt, 1992).

21. In the research literature, this is often designated by concepts such as *oppression, repression, exploitation*. But such terminology is much too weak and inappropriate in light of the circumstances involved. Put differently, it gives too much hope that things could be done differently.

22. On "double closure" with reference to neurophysiological systems, see Heinz von Foerster, *Observing Systems* (Seaside, CA, 1981), 304ff.

23. See here Nils Brunsson and Johan P. Olsen, *The Reforming Organization* (London, 1993).

24. On this, see esp. ibid., 176ff.

25. See Helmut Schlesky, "Ist die Dauerreflexion institutionalisierbar?" *Zeitschrift für evangelische Ethik* 1 (1957): 153–174.

CHAPTER 7: THE EVOLUTION OF RELIGION

1. See Niklas Luhmann, *Die Gesellschaft der Gesellschaft* (Frankfurt, 1997), 413ff.

2. See also Niklas Luhmann, "Die Ausdifferenzierung der Religion," in *Gesellschaftsstruktur und Semantik*, vol. 3 (Frankfurt, 1989), 259–357.

3. See Peter N. Ure, *The Origin of Tyranny* (Cambridge, 1922); Martin Warnke, *Hofkünstler: Zur Vorgeschichte des modernen Künstlers* (Cologne, 1985); Niklas Luhmann, *Die Kunst der Gesellschaft* (Frankfurt, 1995).

4. For treatment of this topic that is detailed, instructive, and pays particular attention to the significance of "improbability," see Hartmann Tyrell, "Worum geht es in der 'Protestantischen Ethik'? Ein Versuch zum besseren Verständnis Max Webers," *Saeculum* 41 (1990): 130–177, and id., "Potenz und Depotenzierung der Religion—Religion und Rationalisierung bei Max Weber," *Saeculum* 44 (1993): 300–347.

5. This circumstance is easy to understand if we realize that in Weber's time there were no theories of social evolution available other than a Social Darwinism based on a few buzzwords.

6. See chapter 5, § IV, in this volume.

7. This example is from Fredrik Barth, *Ritual and Knowledge Among the Baktaman of New Guinea* (Oslo, 1975). Barth also shows how strongly the semantic worlds between the initiated and the remaining members of the tribe (women, children, adolescents) differ. This can be classified as a schema that enables differentiation as well as co-existence of stereotyping and adaptive pragmatism.

8. See Roy A. Rappaport, *Pigs for the Ancestors: Ritual in the Ecology of a New Guinean People* (New Haven, CT, 1967). See also id., "The Sacred in Human Evolution," *Annual Review of Ecology and Systematics* 2 (1971): 23–44.

9. This can be studied particularly well in Japan, where in many places we encounter a continuation of divinatory and magic practices, and apparently primarily where the group does not offer adequate security, but the individual knows that he has to depend on himself. People wash their money in wire baskets at a certain spring in order to assure continued business success. (And judging by the cars arriving and the content of the baskets, it is not the poorest of the poor who are using this technique.) Prior to examinations, people go to the temple in order to receive a prophecy. And all this is done apparently without experiencing any inconsistency in relation to the rest of one's knowledge of the world. As a result, the question of whether one believes in it or not is hardly understood and is not clearly answered.

10. "Quasi-objects" is meant in the sense of Michel Serres, *Genèse* (Paris, 1982), 146ff. It is obvious that the *quasi-* of such objects is not communicated religiously. Yet here also, from the perspective of a second-order observer, an opening for discovery and fantasy—and thus for variation—can be recognized. This is very effective, e.g., in the interpretation of trance states and especially in the invention of the quasi-object of the "soul," which still serves to orient religion.

11. A modern equivalent would be the way technology works. There may be doubts and different opinions about whether the lights should be turned on at dusk, but there is no need for consensus as to whether they will turn on once the switch has been flipped. By means of objectification, the requirements of consensus can be reduced and conserved but also expanded. For the objectifications built into functional contexts—whether of rituals or of technologies—make things possible that would otherwise not be possible and only in that way configure what is required for understanding.

12. The literature on the issue of religion's transformation through writing has grown immensely, but it is generally not theoretically informed. For an introductory overview, see, e.g., Jack Goody, *The Logic of Writing and the Organization of Society* (New York, 1986), trans. as *Die Logik der Schrift und die Organisation von Gesellschaft* (Frankfurt, 1990), 25ff. See also Walter J. Ong, *The Presence of the Word: Some Prolegomena for Cultural and Religious History* (New Haven, CT, 1967).

13. See Harald Haarmann, *Universalgeschichte der Schrift* (Frankfurt, 1990), 70ff. See also Alexander Marshack, *The Roots of Civilization: The Cognitive Beginnings of Man's First Art, Symbol and Notation* (London, 1972). The evolutionary preconditions for the development of writing that represents speech (however incomplete at first) seem to have arisen in Mesopotamia, where the inherited technology for making identity and deviation visible [in the shape of pictographic cuneiform script] made it possible for this to occur relatively quickly. On this, see Denise Schmandt-Besserat, "An Archaic Recording System and the Origin of

Writing," *Syro-Mesopotamian Studies* 1–2 (1977): 1–32; Jean Bottéro, "De l'aide-mémoire à l'écriture," *Mésopotamie: L'écriture, la raison et les dieux* (Paris, 1987): 89–112.

14. See Niklas Luhmann, "The Form of Writing," *Stanford Literature Review* 9 (1992): 25–42.

15. Although the details are highly disputed, it has been speculated that incised symbols discovered in the Balkans that are independent of and predate Mesopotamian writing might be a type of occult script intended for direct communication with gods; see Haarmann, *Universalgeschichte der Schrift*, 70ff.

16. This according to Jean Pierre Camus, *Les Diversitez*, vol. 1 (2nd ed., Paris, 1612), 375ff. This work contains a detailed defense for writing in comparison with the (merely) spoken word.

17. See Elena Esposito, "Interaktion, Interaktivität und Personalisierung der Massenmedien," *Soziale System* 1 (1995): 225–260.

18. Rosalind Thomas speaks of "telescoping" in *Oral Tradition and Written Record in Classical Athens* (Cambridge, 1989), 95ff., 155ff.

19. See Jean Bottéro, "Symptômes, signes, écritures en Mésopotamie ancienne," in *Divination et rationalité*, ed. Jean-Pierre Vernant et al. (Paris, 1974), 70–197 (here 157–158).

20. See here the rich material in Leo Koep, *Das himmlische Buch in Antike und Christentum: Eine religionsgeschichtliche Untersuchung zur altchristlichen Bildersprache* (Bonn, 1952).

21. On this difference and its evolutionary force, see Cristiano Grotanelli, "Profezia e scrittura nel Vicino Oriente," *La Ricerca folkloria. La scrittura: Funzioni ed ideologie* 5 (1982): 57–62.

22. In more recent research in the history of ideas, Quentin Skinner has primarily emphasized this situative, political-polemical factor in semantic evolution, which helps semantic innovations overcome the persuasive thresholds of tradition. For a summary, see Skinner, "Language and Political Change," in *Political Innovation and Conceptual Change*, ed. Terence Ball, James Farr, and Russell L. Hanson (Cambridge, 1989), 6–23. See also Henk de Berg, "Kontext und Kontingenz: Kommunikationstheoretische Überlegungen zur Literaturhistoriographie. Mit einer Fallstudie zur Goethe-Rezeption des Jungen Deutschland" (diss., Leiden, 1994).

23. See, e.g., Ishak England, "Majority Decision vs. Individual Truth: The Interpretation of the Oven of Achnai Aggadah," *Tradition: A Journal of Orthodox Jewish Thought* 15 (1975): 137–151, with many further references.

24. Early medieval Europe and Mexico (e.g., Mitla) both offer examples of this.

25. This according to Jean-Fréderic Bernard, *Eloge d'Enfer: Ouvrage critique, historique et moral*, 2 vols. (The Hague, 1759).

26. See Jan Assmann, *Ägypten: Theologie und Frömmigkeit einer frühen Hochkultur* (Stuttgart, 1984); id., *Das kulturelle Gedächtnis: Schrift, Erinnerung und politische Identität in frühen Hochkulturen* (Munich, 1992), 248ff.

27. See also chapter 5, § III, in this volume.

28. See Karl Heim, *Das Gewißheitsproblem in der systematischen Theologie bis zu Schleiermacher* (Leipzig, 1911), 220ff., esp. 249, and Paul Althaus, *Die Prinzipien der deutschen reformierten Dogmatik im Zeitalter der aristotelischen Scholastik* (Leipzig, 1914; repr. Darmstadt, 1967), 183ff.

29. See, e.g., Johann Gottlob Benjamin Pfeil, *L'homme sauvage*, trans. Louis-Sébastien Mercier (Paris, 1767). Yet the author still has hope for the future, saying: "One day, we shall know it" (119). That remains, however, a hope that is not further substantiated.

30. Jean Paul, *Clavis Fichtiana seu Leibgeberiana*, quoted in id., *Werke*, vol. 3 (Munich, 1961), 1011–1056 (here 1053).

31. The reference here is to Douglas R. Hofstadter, *Gödel, Escher, Bach: An Eternal Golden Braid* (New York, 1979).

32. This is conveyed by the title of an article in the Italian newspaper *La Repubblica on* April 23, 1994: "In Toscana ci sono più maghi che preti: L'allarme di diciotto vescovi."

CHAPTER 8: SECULARIZATION

1. See Bryan Wilson, "Secularization: The Inherited Model," in *The Sacred in a Secular Age: Toward Revision in the Scientific Study of Religion*, ed. Phillip E. Hammond (Berkeley, CA, 1985), 9–20.

2. See Thomas Luckmann, "The New and the Old Religion," in *Social Theory for a Changing Society*, ed. Pierre Bourdieu and James S. Coleman (Boulder, CO, and New York, 1991): 167–182 (here 168).

3. Overviews with references are provided by the following articles on secularization: Hermann Zabel et al., in *Wörterbuch Geschichtliche Grundbegriffe: Historisches Lexikon zur politisch-sozialen Sprache in Deutschland*, vol. 5 (Stuttgart, 1984): 789–829; Giacomo Marramao, "Säkularisierung," *Historisches Wörterbuch der Philosophie*, vol. 8 (Basel, 1992), cols. 1133–1161; id., *Cielo e terra: Genealogia della secolarizzazione* (Rome, 1994), German trans. as *Die Säkularisierung der westlichen Welt* (Frankfurt, 1996). For a treatment that sees the relevance of this topic more positively, see Hartmann Tyrell, "Religionssoziologie," *Geschichte und Gesellschaft* 22 (1996): 428–457 (444ff.).

4. And this is in accordance with even the most recent research results. See only W. Jagodzinki and Karel Dobbelaere, "Der Wandel kirchlicher Religiosität in Westeuropa," in *Religion und Kultur*, ed. J. Bergmann, Alois Hahn, and Thomas Luckmann, *Kölner Zeitschrift für Soziologie und Sozialpsychologie*, special issue 33 (Opladen, 1993): 68–91; Studien- und Planungsgruppe der EKD, *Fremde Heimat Kirche: Ansichten ihrer Mitglieder* (Hannover, 1993).

5. Luc Ferry speaks more cautiously of a "fin du théologico-culturel" in *L'homme-Dieu ou le Sens de la vie: essai* (Paris, 1996), 207.

6. Jean Paul, *Vorschule der Ästhetik*, quoted in id., *Werke*, vol. 5 (Munich, 1963), 384.

7. See, e.g., Luca Ricolfi, "Il processo di secolarizzazione nell'Italia del dopoguerra: Un profilo empirico," *Rassegna Italiana di Sociologia* 29 (1988): 37–87. For a report on older research, see Karel Dobbelaere, "Secularization: A Multi-Dimensional Concept," *Current Sociology* 29, no. 2 (1981). See also id., "Secularization Theories and Sociological Paradigms: Convergences and Divergences," *Social Compass* 31 (1984): 199–219.

8. For a worldwide comparison, see John W. Meyer, David H. Kamens, and Aaron Benavot, *School Knowledge for the Masses: World Models and National Primary Curricular Categories in the Twentieth Century* (Washington, DC, 1992), esp. 139ff.

9. For sociology, one can in particular assume that the thesis of a secularized society is a desperate attempt to retain the centrality of the religion question for the problem of societal order—but only in a negative version. See Roland Robertson, "Sociologists and Secularization," *Sociology* 5 (1971): 297–312. For a similar argument regarding the theological interest in the topic, see Trutz Rendtorff, "Zur Säkularisierungsproblematik: Über die Weiterentwicklung der Kirchensoziologie zur Religionssoziologie," *Internationales Jahrbuch für Religionssoziologie* 2 (1966): 51–72.

10. This is emphasized repeatedly, so one is not misled by the term. See, e.g., Donald E. Miller, "Religion, Social Change, and the Expansive Life Style," *Internationales Jahrbuch für Wissens- und Religionssoziologie* 9 (1975): 149–159. His thesis: not the "whether" but the "how" of religious experience is the problem.

11. This is noted, e.g., by Ludwig Tieck, *Frühe Erzählungen und Romane* (Munich, 1963), 177–178: "Der Geist der Intoleranz ist in die Politik übergegangen."

12. See Friedrich von Schelling, *Philosophie der Kunst. Vorlesung 1802/03* (1859; repr. Darmstadt, 1960).

13. On "displacement," see Dominick LaCapra, "The Temporality of Rhetoric," in *Chronotypes: The Construction of Time*, ed. John Bender and David E. Wellbery (Stanford, CA, 1991), 115–147; Peter Fuchs, *Moderne Kommunikation: Zur Theorie des operativen Displacements* (Frankfurt, 1993). Luc Ferry, *L'homme-Dieu*, trans. David Pellauer as *Man Made God: The Meaning of Life* (Chicago, 2002), 7, speaks of "the secular reworking of religion" and cites communism as an example.

14. Meaning, in other words, that religion and secularization only represent an opposition in religious contexts. One therefore does not get any closer to the issue with empirical sociological studies attempting to establish objective facts. See James E. Dittes, "Secular Religion: Dilemma of Churches and Researchers," *Review of Religious Research* 10 (1969): 65–81, and Peter G. Forster, "Secularization in the English Context: Some Conceptual and Empirical Problems," *Sociological Review* 20 (1972), 153–168.

15. See Robert M. Cover, "The Supreme Court, 1982 Term. Foreword: Nomos and Narrative," *Harvard Law Review* 57 (1983): 4–68 (here 8), which attempts to

make the Talmudic tradition productive within a secular society in interpreting the American Constitution.

16. On this, with regard to Gotthard Günther, see Elena Esposito, *L'operazione di osservazione: Costruttivismo e teoria dei sistemi sociali* (Milan, 1992).

17. See also my remarks on religion's "loss of function," in chapter 3 in this volume.

18. On European developments since the Middle Ages, see Katherine and Charles H. George, "Roman Catholic Sainthood and Social Status: A Statistical and Analytical Study," *Journal of Religion* 35 (1955): 85–98; Pierre Delooz, *Sociologie et canonizations* (The Hague, 1969).

19. To exactly what extent this also applies to people who do not belong to one's own religion can be evaluated by different criteria, e.g., according to the stipulation presented by a distinction between center and periphery. While the Christian major religions worried about the souls of the ancient philosophers who could not be saved, I know a southern Italian who is considered a "Turk" and sees himself as one, since he was not baptized and "consequently" has no soul. Yet he has a heart, as he takes pains to assure me. On this subject, from the perspective of another religious context, see also Gananath Obeyesekere, "The Great Tradition and the Little in the Perspective of Sinhalese Buddhism," *Journal of Asian Studies* 22 (1963): 139–153.

20. See here, e.g., Gibson Winter, *The Suburban Captivity of the Churches* (New York, 1962); Harvey Cox, *The Secular City* (New York, 1963).

21. This according to Ferry, *L'homme-Dieu*, 33n.

22. For more detail, see Niklas Luhmann, "Individuum, Individualität, Individualismus," in id., *Gesellschaftsstruktur und Semantik*, vol. 3 (Frankfurt 1989), 149–258.

23. On this distinction, see Stéphane Ngo Mai and Alain Raybaut, "Microdiversity and Macro-order: Toward a Self-Organization Approach," *Revue internationale de systémique* 10 (1996): 223–239.

24. For more detail here, see Niklas Luhmann, "Frühneuzeitliche Anthropologie: Theorietechnische Lösungen für ein Evolutionsproblem der Gesellschaft," in id., *Gesellschaftsstruktur und Semantik*, vol. 1 (Frankfurt 1980), 162–234.

25. § VII of the present chapter looks at this issue from the standpoint of "culture."

26. See, e.g., Alexandre Vinet, "Sur l'individualité et l'individualisme," in id., *Philosophie morale et sociale*, vol. 1 (Lausanne, 1913), 319–335; first published in *Semeur*, April 13, 1836.

27. See Anthony Ashley Cooper, earl of Shaftesbury, "An Inquiry concerning virtue or merit" (1709), in id., *Characteristicks of Men, Manners, Opinions, Times*, 2nd ed. (1714, repr. Farnborough, Hants, UK, 1968), 2: 120.

28. Jean Paul, *Levana oder Erziehungslehre I*, in id., *Sämmtliche Werke* (Berlin, 1827), 36: 51.

29. On African religious beliefs, see John S. Mbiti, *Concepts of God in Africa* (London, 1970), 218: "The individual 'believes' what other members of the corporate society 'believe', and he 'believes' because others 'believe.'"

30. Baltasar Gracián y Morales, *El Criticón* (Zaragoza, 1651–53), trans. as *Criticón oder: Über die allgemeinen Laster des Menschen* (Hamburg, 1957), 49.

31. Ibid., 51, 67, and passim.

32. On this, see Loredana Sciolla, "La natura delle credenze religiose nelle società complesse," *Rassegna Italiana di Sociologia* 36 (1995): 479–511.

33. Ibid., 507.

34. Viewed historically, this was a Romantic idea.

35. See Bryan A. Wilson, *Religion in a Secular Society: A Sociological Comment* (London, 1966), 160ff.

36. For a comparison of Islamic and American (Protestant) fundamentalism with a focus on this point, see Dieter Goetze, "Fundamentalismus, Chilianismus, Revitalisierungsbewegungen: Neue Handlungsmuster im Weltsystem?" in *Transkulturelle Kommunikation und Weltgesellschaft: Theorie und Pragmatik globaler Interaktion*, ed. Horst Reiman (Opladen, 1992), 44–59.

37. For an overview of American research, which is especially instructive, see James T. Richardson, "Studies of Conversion: Secularization or Re-enchantment," in *The Sacred in a Secular Age: Toward Revision in the Scientific Study of Religion*, ed. Philip E. Hammond (Berkeley, CA, 1985), 104–121.

38. See Albert O. Hirschman, *Exit, Voice, and Loyalty: Responses to Decline in Firms, Organizations, and States* (Cambridge, MA, 1970).

39. See *Mundus in Imagine: Bildersprache und Lebenswelten im Mittelalter: Festgabe für Klaus Schreiner* (Munich, 1996).

40. For a special case, see Benedict Anderson, *Imagined Communities: Reflections on the Origin and Spread of Nationalism* (London, 1983).

41. See esp. Talcott Parsons, "Belief, Unbelief, and Disbelief," and "Religion in Postindustrial America: The Problem of Secularization," in id., *Action Theory and the Human Condition* (New York, 1978), 233–263, 300–322.

42. There is much evidence for this effect. One of the claims of the eighteenth century could be put thus: forget all the stipulations and intricacies—and simplify! See J. J. (Dom Louis), *Le Ciel ouvert à tout l'univers* (n.p., 1782), 163: "The art of simplifying everything is that of perfecting everything."

43. See Peter Berger, "A Sociological View of the Secularization of Theology" (1967), in id., *Facing Up to Modernity: Excursions in Society, Politics, and Religion* (New York, 1977), 162–182.

44. Parsons is not following Rousseau but Robert N. Bellah, *Beyond Belief: Essays on Religion in a Post-Traditional World* (New York, 1970). Here Rousseau is seen more as precursor of the "secular religion" of Marxism. Overall, the diagnosis is directed toward a nontheistic religion of love in this world, apparently influenced by social movements of the 1960s and 1970s.

45. On this, see also Niklas Luhmann, "Inclusion and Exclusion," in *Soziologische Aufklärung* 6 (Opladen, 1995), 237–264.

46. According to Anonymous [Jacques Pernetti], *Les conseils de l'amitié*, 2nd ed. (Frankfurt, 1748), 5. In what follows, it is emphasized that this temporal fractioning of attention is not as bad as the frontal attacks by atheists.

47. An important exception is sports, especially ice hockey.

48. See chapter 6, § V, in this volume.

49. This may be the case in the context of a particular function system in society, one that is interested in remedies; see Dirk Baecker, "Soziale Hilfe als Funktionssystem der Gesellschaft," *Zeitschrift für Soziologie* 23 (1994): 93–110.

50. See *La función de la teología en el futuro de America Latina: Memorias* (Mexico City, 1991), proceedings of an international symposium at the Universidad Iberoamericana, September 24–27, 1991, especially the discussion.

51. This has been an issue at least since publication of Alexandre Koyré's *La philosophie de Jacob Boehme* (Paris, 1929; 2nd ed. 1968); see also Berger, *Facing Up to Modernity*.

52. See Kees W. Bolle, "Secularization as a Problem of History of Religions," *Comparative Studies in Society and History* 12 (1970): 242–259.

53. See, e.g., Thomas Luckmann, *The Invisible Religion* (London, 1967), which reveals an intention to hold onto certain structural commonalities of all religious phenomena—commonalities that can be described in post-transcendental/post-phenomenological perspectives). Or see Parsons, *Action Theory and the Human Condition*, in the context of explaining the necessity of semantic generalizations in evolutionary theoretical terms.

54. On this, see Detlef Pollack, "Was ist Religion: Probleme der Definition," *Zeitschrift für Religionswissenschaft* 3 (1995): 163–190.

55. Arthur C. Danto, *The Transfiguration of the Commonplace: A Philosophy of Art* (Cambridge, MA, 1981), sees in this a "philosophical" problem with which art is identifying itself.

56. For greater detail, see Niklas Luhmann, "Kultur als historischer Begriff," in id., *Gesellschaftsstruktur und Semantik*, vol. 4 (Frankfurt, 1993), 31–45; id., "Religion als Kultur," in *Das Europa der Religionen*, ed. Otto Kallscheuer (Frankfurt 1996), 291–315.

57. I leave to one side Schiller's designation of this approach as naïve (as opposed to sentimental) in his treatise on "naïve" and "sentimental" writing [*Dichtung*]. The approach was naïve, not in its own mode of observation but only in the eyes of a present-day "sentimental writer."

58. Matei Călinescu, "From the One to the Many: Pluralism in Today's Thought," in *Zeitgeist in Babylon: The Postmodernist Controversy*, ed. Ingeborg Hoesterey (Bloomington, IN, 1991): 156–174 (here 157).

59. Systematic attention to this question can be found primarily in context of Talcott Parsons's theory of the universal action system. See his later essays on re-

ligion in *Action Theory and the Human Condition* (New York, 1978), 167ff. However, the analyses only develop partial aspects of systems and remain formal in the way they assign them.

60. On methodology, see Edmund Husserl, *Erfahrung und Urteil: Untersuchungen zur Genealogie der Logik* (Hamburg, 1948).

61. Cf., e.g., Roland Robertson, "The Sacred and the World System," in *The Sacred in a Secular Age: Toward a Revision in the Scientific Study of Religion*, ed. Philipp E. Hammond (Berkeley, CA, 1985), 347–358; id., *Globalization: Social Theory and Global Culture* (London, 1992).

62. On this formulation for a specific form of dealing with paradoxes, see Andrew H. Van de Ven and Marshall Scott Poole, "Paradoxical Requirements for a Theory of Organizational Change," in *Paradox and Transformation: Toward a Theory of Change in Organization and Management*, ed. Robert E. Quinn and Kim S. Cameron (Cambridge, MA, 1988), 19–63 (esp. 30–31).

63. Jerome Bruner, *Actual Minds, Possible Worlds* (Cambridge, MA, 1986), 149.

64. "Could it be that the deeper significance of the famous 'comparative method' that became a powerful and unifying paradigm in the life sciences and social sciences has been a kind of secularization of conceptions of religious and transcendental 'otherness'?" Johannes Fabian asks in "Of Dogs Alive, Birds Dead, and Time to Tell a Story," in *Chronotypes: The Construction of Time*, ed. John Bender and David E. Wellbery (Stanford, CA, 1991), 185–204 (190).

CHAPTER 9: SELF-DESCRIPTION

1. Max Weber exemplifies this—despite or precisely because of the significance of religion in his sociology, as Hartmann Tyrell details in "Max Webers Religionssoziologie," *Saeculum* 43 (1992): 172–230. See also Detlef Pollack, "Was ist Religion: Probleme der Definition," *Zeitschrift für Religionswissenschaft* 3 (1995): 163–190.

2. The preceding chapters have avoided this problem—and thus self-description as religious—because their premise is distinction, specifically, function and coding.

3. Jean Paul asks us to consider these arguments in his "Religion als politischer Hebel," in *Jean Pauls Werke: Auswahl in zwei Bänden*, vol. 2 (Stuttgart, 1924), 56.

4. Using Gotthard Günther's terminology, one could also say that religion has at its disposal "transjunctional operations" and "rejection values" that not only emphasize the otherness of its specific commitments but also reject positive/negative distinctions of a different origin *as distinctions*; see Gotthard Günther, *Beiträge zur Grundlegung einer operationsfähigen Dialektik*, vol. 1 (Hamburg, 1976), esp. 286ff.

5. For a resolute attempt of this kind (which nonetheless fails very quickly), see Kai T. Erikson, *Wayward Puritans: A Study in the Sociology of Deviance* (New York, 1966). The system's boundaries, which simultaneously define its identity, are de-

fined by early Puritans in New England in such a way that all deviance is described as the system's environment and in the system, the elect (who watch one another closely) are among themselves.

6. On the paradox of communicating an abstention from communication and on the silent communicating of avoiding communication, see Peter Fuchs, "Die Weltflucht der Mönche: Anmerkungen zur Funktion des monastisch-aszetischen Schweigens," *Zeitschrift für Soziologie* 15 (1986): 393–405; revised and reprinted in Niklas Luhmann and Peter Fuchs, *Reden und Schweigen* (Frankfurt, 1989), 21–45.

7. That, in any event, is the standpoint from which Benton Johnson attempts to specify this (now diffuse) distinction; "On Church and Sect," *American Sociological Review* 28 (1963): 539–549.

8. A renowned depiction of this thesis is that what matters to God is *difference, antithesis, contrast* (and not merely the simple repetition of His own self-sufficient unity), because in this way human beings are granted freedom (= sin?) and the capacity to make distinctions; St. Augustine, "De ordine libri duo," in *Corpus Scriptorum Ecclesiasticorum Latinorum* 63 (1922; repr., New York, 1962).

9. This tendency to wait can in fact be observed, and not only in the case of those who defend forms of faith that have been handed down but also in the case of sociologists of religion. See, e.g., Gregory Baum, *Religion and the Rise of Scepticism* (New York, 1970), and Bryan Wilson, *The Contemporary Transformation of Religion* (New York, 1976), both of these influenced by the youth movements of the 1960s. But see also Michael Welker, *Gottes Geist: Theologie des Heiligen Geists* (Neukirchen-Vluyn, 1992), trans. John F. Hoffmeyer as *God the Spirit* (Minneapolis, 1994), which attempts to find a connection with present-day charismatic movements within spiritism.

10. See chapter 8, § III, in this volume.

11. "Redescription" in the sense of Mary Hesse's theory of metaphors; see Hesse, *Models and Analogies in Science* (Notre Dame, IN, 1966), 157ff.

12. [Friedrich Schleiermacher, *Über die Religion. Reden an die Gebildeten unter ihren Verächtern* (Berlin, 1799), trans. as *On Religion: Speeches to Its Cultured Despisers* (New York, 1955).] On this problem (without reference to "deconstruction"), see also Thomas Lehnerer, "Kunst und Bildung: zu Schliermachers Reden über die Religion," in *Früher Idealismus und Frühromantik: Der Streit um die Grundlagen der Ästhetik (1795–1805)*, ed. Walter Jaeschke and Helmut Holzhey (Hamburg 1990), 190–200, esp. 199–200.

13. See here Jonathan Culler, *On Deconstruction: Theory and Criticism after Structuralism* (Ithaca, NY, 1982).

14. See here the case study by Georg Elwert, "Changing Certainties and the Move to a Global Religion: Medical Knowledge and Islamization Among the Anii (Baseda) in the Republic of Bénin," in *The Pursuit of Certainty: Religious and Cultural Foundations*, ed. Wendy James (London, 1995), 215–233.

15. The same argument could be repeated for other religions, with respect to

religious meditation (as opposed to helpful, everyday meditative practice) in the Buddhist context or with respect to the stereotyped formalism of prayer in Islam that exposes itself to observation.

16. See Welker, *Gottes Geist*.

17. E.g., "Doch dieser Schein trügt" (ibid., 177).

18. See the treatment of "lying spirits" (ibid., 87ff.) and the distancing of religious judgment (*God's* judgment) of good and bad from the socially circulating morality of respect and misrespect (social moralism) (ibid., 49ff., 119ff.).

19. E.g., conceiving of the resurrection of the flesh as something concomitant that occurs outside of time, salvation in the sense of the inescapability of the lived sense of life (ibid., 301).

20. See ibid., 118–119.

21. See ibid., 127–128.

22. See ibid., 82n6.

23. See, e.g., the analyses of Cleanth Brooks, *The Well Wrought Urn: Studies in the Structure of Poetry* (New York, 1947). A short version is: "The poem is an instance of the doctrine which it asserts; it is both the assertion and the realization of the assertion" (17). With the conceptuality of "speech act" theory, it could also be said to be the unity of its constative and performative components.

24. See chapter 4, § III, in this volume.

25. See the interpretation of Kant's aesthetics from this very viewpoint in Jacques Derrida, *La vérité en peinture* (Paris, 1987).

26. A symptom of this fact is that now a corresponding negative term is needed: "insincerity" was added to the language in the sixteenth century.

27. On this, see esp. Jean-Christophe Agnew, *Worlds Apart: The Market and the Theater in Anglo-American Thought, 1550–1750* (Cambridge, 1986). On the futility of a polemic that resorts to the utility of poetry—either a this-worldly or other-worldly utility—see also Russell Fraser, *The War Against Poetry* (Princeton, NJ, 1970).

28. See Baltasar Gracián y Morales, *El Criticón* (Zaragoza, 1651–53), trans. as *Criticón oder: Über die allgemeinen Laster des Menschen* (Hamburg, 1957). Reflective of this situation of a generalized insecurity is the fact that the permission to publish *organizationally* required by his order was a problem for Gracián throughout his lifetime and had to be—but also could be—circumvented.

29. See Roland Robertson, "The Sacred and the World System," in *The Sacred in a Secular Age: Toward Revision in the Scientific Study of Religion*, ed. Phillip E. Hammond (Berkeley, CA, 1985), 347–358 (esp. 352–353.). Robertson even presupposes that the "globalization" of human relationships is one of the essential factors in the revitalization of religion that can be observed at present in the spread of all kinds of fundamentalisms and in the religious thematization of the human situation in modern society. See also Robert Robertson and Jo Ann Chirico, "Humanity, Globalization and Worldwide Religious Resurgence: A Theoretical Ex-

ploration," *Sociological Analysis* 46 (1985): 219–246. For a summary, see Roland Robertson, *Globalization: Social Theory and Global Culture* (London, 1992).

30. On Islam, see esp. M. Abaza and Georg Stauth, "Occidental Reason, Orientalism, Islamic Fundamentalism: A Critique," in *Globalization, Knowledge and Society, ed. Martin Albrow and Elizabeth King* (London, 1990), 209–233. See also Peter Beyer, *Religion and Globalization* (London, 1994).

31. See, e.g., José Faur, *Golden Doves and Silver Dots: Semiotics and Textuality in Rabbinic Tradition* (Bloomington, IN, 1986).

32. This can also be demonstrated inversely by how inconsequential local forms of exception were, as exemplified by the large number of schools of differing faith orientations (and the "ecumenical" efforts these motivated) to be found in the town of Otranto in the twelfth century, still apparent today in the famous mosaic of its cathedral.

33. The conclusion of an advantage for religion through functional differentiation is thus relativized if one considers that the political system has the autonomy to define which religious movements are politically dangerous. This can be shown in nationalistic and especially one-party regimes that leave it up to the party to define the only correct opinions, or concretely in the problems that Marxist-oriented regimes in Asia have with Buddhist monks. On these matters, see Donald E. Smith, *Religion and Politics in Burma* (Princeton, NJ, 1965); Milton Sacks, "Some Religious Components in Vietnamese Politics," in *Religion and Change in Contemporary Asia*, ed. Robert F. Spencer (Minneapolis, 1971), 44–66; Holmes Welch, *Buddhism Under Mao* (Cambridge, MA, 1972). See too Urmila Phadnis, *Religion and Politics in Sri Lanka* (Columbia, MO, 1976); S. J. Tambiah, *World Conqueror and World Renouncer: A Study of Buddhism and Polity in Thailand Against a Historical Background* (Cambridge, 1976); Somboon Suksamran, *Buddhism and Politics in Thailand: A Study of Socio-Political Change and Political Activism of the Thai Sangha* (Singapore, 1982).

34. Integration here (as elsewhere) is not understood as a consensus but rather as a mutual restriction on the degree of freedom in the systems involved.

35. How little this applies to Buddhism—which (though an atheistic religion) can still accommodate gods and permits itself to be popularized in several regional versions—has been the subject of numerous treatments. See Maung Htin Aung, *Folk Elements in Burmese Buddhism* (Westport, CT, 1962); Michael M. Ames, "Magical Animism and Buddhism: A Structural Analysis of the Sinhalese Religious System," in *Religion in South Asia*, ed. Edward B. Harper (Seattle, 1964), 21–52; S. J. Tambiah, *Buddhism and Spirit Cults in North-East Thailand* (Cambridge, 1970); Steven Piker, "The Problem of Consistency in Thai Religion," *Journal for the Scientific Study of Religion* 11 (1972): 211–229. That may be due to the fact that the system's self-description in this case emphasizes how all distinctions are futile, seeking its unity therein and therefore being able to live with distinctions.

36. At a feast for the Virgin Mary observed primarily by the indigenous popu-

lation in Andacollo, Chile, a high Catholic Church official sighed: "Whether they believe in God and whether they are Catholic, I don't know; that they believe in Mary is certain." His distinction, I recall, was both visible and (especially) audible: the Ave Maria played via loudspeaker from the church above the (supernaturally inspired) dance groups with their musical instruments in front of it (which distinguished themselves from one another, but not from the Church). In addition, the groups were let into the church to receive their blessing not as groups but only as individuals.

37. See only Michael Welker, *Schöpfung und Wirklichkeit* (Neukirchen-Vluyn, 1995).

38. For related theses in literary studies, see *Kommunikation und Differenz: Systemtheoretische Ansätze in der Literatur- und Kunstwissenschaft*, ed. Henk de Berg and Matthias Prangel (Opladen, 1993), and *Differenzen: Systemtheorie zwischen Dekonstruktion und Konstruktivismus*, ed. Henk de Berg and Matthias Prangel (Tübingen, 1995).

39. See chapter 1 in this volume.

40. See merely Stephan H. Pfürtner, *Kirche und Sexualität* (Reinbek, 1972)—a publication that cost its author his professorship.

41. Here see Klaus Krippendorff, "A Second-Order Cybernetics of Otherness," *Systems Research* 13 (1996): 311–328; this is a Festschrift in honor of Heinz von Foerster.

Index

Cultural Memory in the Present

Andrew Herscher, *Violence Taking Place: The Architecture of the Kosovo Conflict*

Hans-Jörg Rheinberger, *On Historicizing Epistemology: An Essay*

Jacob Taubes, *From Cult to Culture*, edited by Charlotte Fonrobert and Amir Engel

Peter Hitchcock, *The Long Space: Transnationalism and Postcolonial Form*

Lambert Wiesing, *Artificial Presence: Philosophical Studies in Image Theory*

Jacob Taubes, *Occidental Eschatology*

Freddie Rokem, *Philosophers and Thespians: Thinking Performance*

Roberto Esposito, *Communitas: The Origin and Destiny of Community*

Vilashini Cooppan, *Worlds Within: National Narratives and Global Connections in Postcolonial Writing*

Josef Früchtl, *The Impertinent Self: A Heroic History of Modernity*

Frank Ankersmit, Ewa Domanska, and Hans Kellner, eds., *Re-Figuring Hayden White*

Michael Rothberg, *Multidirectional Memory: Remembering the Holocaust in the Age of Decolonization*

Jean-François Lyotard, *Enthusiasm: The Kantian Critique of History*

Ernst van Alphen, Mieke Bal, and Carel Smith, eds., *The Rhetoric of Sincerity*

Stéphane Mosès, *The Angel of History: Rosenzweig, Benjamin, Scholem*

Pierre Hadot, *The Present Alone Is Our Happiness: Conversations with Jeannie Carlier and Arnold I. Davidson*

Alexandre Lefebvre, *The Image of the Law: Deleuze, Bergson, Spinoza*

Samira Haj, *Reconfiguring Islamic Tradition: Reform, Rationality, and Modernity*

Diane Perpich, *The Ethics of Emmanuel Levinas*

Marcel Detienne, *Comparing the Incomparable*

François Delaporte, *Anatomy of the Passions*

René Girard, *Mimesis and Theory: Essays on Literature and Criticism, 1959–2005*

Richard Baxstrom, *Houses in Motion: The Experience of Place and the Problem of Belief in Urban Malaysia*

Jennifer L. Culbert, *Dead Certainty: The Death Penalty and the Problem of Judgment*

Samantha Frost, *Lessons from a Materialist Thinker: Hobbesian Reflections on Ethics and Politics*

Regina Mara Schwartz, *Sacramental Poetics at the Dawn of Secularism: When God Left the World*

Miryam Sas, *Fault Lines: Cultural Memory and Japanese Surrealism*

Peter Schwenger, *Fantasm and Fiction: On Textual Envisioning*

Didier Maleuvre, *Museum Memories: History, Technology, Art*

Jacques Derrida, *Monolingualism of the Other; or, The Prosthesis of Origin*

Andrew Baruch Wachtel, *Making a Nation, Breaking a Nation: Literature and Cultural Politics in Yugoslavia*

Niklas Luhmann, *Love as Passion: The Codification of Intimacy*

Mieke Bal, ed., *The Practice of Cultural Analysis: Exposing Interdisciplinary Interpretation*

Jacques Derrida and Gianni Vattimo, eds., *Religion*